An Empire Divided

EARLY AMERICAN STUDIES

Series Editor

Richard S. Dunn
Director, the McNeil Center
for Early American Studies

A complete list of books in the series
is available from the publisher.

An Empire Divided

The American Revolution and the British Caribbean

Andrew Jackson O'Shaughnessy

PENN

University of Pennsylvania Press

Philadelphia

Publication of this volume was assisted by a grant from
the McNeil Center for Early American Studies

10 9 8 7 6 5 4 3 2 1

Published by
University of Pennsylvania Press
Philadelphia, Pennsylvania 19104-4011

Library of Congress Cataloging-in-Publication Data

O'Shaughnessy, Andrew Jackson.
    An empire divided : the American Revolution and the British Caribbean / Andrew
Jackson O'Shaughnessy.
      p.   cm. — (Early American studies)
    Includes bibliographical references (p.   ) and index.
    ISBN 0-8122-3558-4 (alk. paper). — ISBN 0-8122-1732-2 (pbk. : alk. paper)
      1. West Indies, British — History — 18th century.   2. United States — History — Revolution,
1775–1783 — Influence.   3. Great Britain — Relations — West Indies, British.   4. West Indies,
British — Relations — Great Britain.   I. Title.   II. Series.

F2131 .O74 2000
972.9'03 — dc21   00-022402

The West India approach bids fair entirely to reshape the study of American history.

LOWELL J. RAGATZ,
*The West Indian Approach to the
Study of American Colonial History*

Contents

Illustrations

Preface

THE THIRTEEN COLONIES in North America represented only half the colonies of British America in 1776.[1] This book is concerned with the wealthiest of the nonmainland colonies that did not rebel: Jamaica, Antigua, Barbados, Dominica, Grenada, Montserrat, Nevis, St. Kitts, St. Vincent, Tortola, and Tobago. The study of the British West Indies allows us to refine and qualify competing explanations of the American Revolution because the Caribbean colonies shared to a large degree the essential preconditions of the American Revolution but did not rebel. They shared similar political developments and a similar political ideology to North America and were closely associated with the mainland colonies by their proximity and trade. Joseph Galloway of Pennsylvania described the British West Indies as "natural appendages of North America as the Isle of Man and the Orkneys" are of Britain. The plantation system of the islands was analogous to the southern mainland colonies, especially to South Carolina. In a period when most British colonists in North America lived less than two hundred miles inland and the major cities were situated along the coast, the ocean often acted as a highway between the islands and mainland rather than a barrier. Yet when revolution came, the majority of the white island colonists did not side with their compatriots on the mainland.[2]

It may be argued that rebellion was impractical in the islands and that a comparison with the mainland colonies is therefore invalid. The British West Indies did not rebel in response to the Slave Emancipation Act of 1833 because obstacles to rebellion among the white island elites were as overwhelming then as they had been in 1776. However, there were other possible strategies of opposition, such as vigorous lobbying, pamphleteering, framing petitions, and forming associations. The planters employed such methods in opposition to the abolition of the slave trade but only after the American War. In contrast, they did not unite in even a limited campaign of opposition before the American Revolution. Unlike Bermuda, the British West Indies did not send delegates to the Continental Congress.

The study of the British West Indies is also important because they played a crucial role in the origins and the development of the American Revolution. They received special consideration from the imperial government because they were regarded as a major source of national wealth in Britain, and their importance to Britain affected colonial policy toward North America. Their passivity toward colonial reforms helped to divide colonial opposition and sent mixed signals to the imperial government, and the inactivity of their lobby in London contributed to the fatal isolation of the North American lobby. The study of the islands offers a very different perspective of the problems that faced imperial statesmen and military strategists who were responsible for some twenty-six colonies at the beginning of the American Revolution.

Furthermore, the defense of the West Indies contributed to the British defeat in the American Revolutionary War. Sir John Fortescue, in his epic history of the British army, wrote that "the part played by the West Indian islands during the American War of Independence has been so little appreciated as to demand particular attention." Piers Mackesy, in what is still the most comprehensive study of the British war for America, concluded that the "American War had been largely fought and decided in the West Indies." Barbara Tuchman's *The First Salute* (1988) refers to the first foreign salute of the American flag, which occurred in the Caribbean in 1776. The "overriding importance the West Indies held in British thinking" is a major theme of her book.[3]

Finally, the division of British America after the American Revolution had major implications for both the West Indies and the United States. The islands and mainland colonies were previously part of the same polity, which was artificially severed by the American War. Their trade was officially restricted after the war, resulting in less interaction. The exile of black American loyalists from the United States played an influential role in the spread of Afro-Christianity in the British West Indies. The division also helped the cause of abolitionists in both Britain and the United States: it more than halved the number of slaves in the British Empire; made slavery appear virtually peculiar to the South within the United States; and prevented the island and southern planters from forming a common lobby against the abolitionists. The failure of the British West Indies to join the American Revolution therefore had significance for the history of slavery in the West Indies and the United States.

* * *

My book aims to redress the omission of the British West Indies from the scholarship of the American Revolution. Historians have long acknowledged their importance for understanding the colonial history of the United States, but this perspective has not affected the treatment of the American Revolution. In the late nineteenth and early twentieth centuries, Charles McLean Andrews pioneered an approach to the early political history of the United

States that extended to the Canadian and West Indian as well as the mainland colonies of the Anglo-American Empire before 1776.[4]

Andrews inspired Frank Wesley Pitman and the imperial school of historians who were active before World War II and who were impressed by "the significance of the West Indies in the development and also in the disruption of the old British empire." Leonard W. Labaree was emphatic that "anyone who fails to include the West Indies in the political growth of the colonies cannot fully explain the development of British governmental policies towards the continental colonies and the resulting social unrest." Lowell Ragatz also argued that "the shaping of imperial policies to serve [the] sectional ends [of the West Indies] paved the way for revolution."[5]

The imperial historians were virtually eclipsed in the nationalistic and introspective climate of the cold war. However, the emphasis on the importance of the British West Indies for the study of early America has been revived among historians who have adopted an Atlantic approach in their research on British America, including Richard Dunn, Jack Greene, Richard Sheridan, John McCusker, Stanley Engerman, David Barry Gaspar, Trevor Burnard, Philip Morgan, David Hancock, Alison Games, David Shields, and Michael Mullin. This approach is now sufficiently well established to be incorporated into a new generation of college textbooks on the history of the United States.[6]

Nevertheless, the British West Indies have received scant attention in the historical literature on the American Revolution. The imperial school dealt with the subject only tangentially. Pitman ended his major work in 1763. Ragatz was exclusively concerned with economic developments in the era of the American Revolution as a prelude to his thesis about the decline of the British West Indies before 1833. It was an obvious subject for Lawrence Henry Gipson, whose magisterial fifteen-volume history *The British Empire Before the American Revolution* (1939–1970) represented the culmination of the imperial approach to American history. However, Gipson did not integrate the West Indies into his account after 1765. He made only passing reference to the failure of the island colonies to join the American Revolution.[7]

Writing in the early 1960s, Peter Marshall criticized historians for their failure to appreciate the continued importance of the British West Indies during the American Revolution. The 1976 bicentenary of the American Revolution marked a resurgence of interest in the role of the Caribbean in the American Revolution but, according to the editors of a manuscript report, "empirical historical research" was still "virtually nonexistent." Indeed, it remains true, as Roy Clayton observes, that "historians of the United States have proved reluctant to incorporate the island dimension into their analyses of the revolution."[8] It is a serious omission given that British statesmen thought in terms of an Atlantic empire of some twenty-six colonies, not thirteen. Hence, the need for this book.

While historians of the American Revolution have largely ignored the British West Indies, Caribbean historians have focused almost exclusively on the impact of the American Revolutionary War in the British West Indies after 1783. This is largely a consequence of the influence of Eric Williams's classic study, *Capitalism and Slavery* (1944). Williams, in a modification of the thesis of Lowell Ragatz, treated the American Revolution as the beginning of the uninterrupted economic decline of the plantation economy in the British West Indies. His contention, now famous, is that the economic decline of the islands was a major causal factor in the abolition of the slave trade and the abolition of slavery in the British Empire.

Selwyn H. H. Carrington championed the decline thesis in his book *The British West Indies During the American Revolution* (1988), which was "originally conceived as a study geared towards an understanding of the British West Indian economy on the eve of the debate on slavery." He "glimpses the American Revolution from the West Indies" but this was not his chief objective.[9] His focus was primarily economic. Carrington attempted to refute Seymour Drescher, who, following the publication of *Econocide: British Slavery in the Era of Abolition* (1977), had become the most influential critic of Eric Williams. Carrington was a pioneer in writing a detailed and copiously researched study of the British West Indies during the American Revolution. My book is much indebted to his work, but my focus and interpretation are very different.

*   *   *

This book is political in its focus. It is concerned with the reaction of the British West Indies to the American Revolution and aims to explain why the island colonies did not support the mainland revolt. In addition, it considers their influence on British colonial policy toward North America and their role in the events that caused the American Revolution and aims to make more explicit their importance in military affairs during the Revolutionary War. Finally, the book explores the implications of the division of British America for the West Indies.

It is worth considering why the British West Indies did not join the American Revolution. Because the islands shared many of the preconditions of the colonies that did rebel, this is a question that deserves a more nuanced treatment than it has hitherto received. The absence of scholarship has meant that historians have only speculated spasmodically on the failure of the British West Indies to support the thirteen mainland colonies. Eric Williams concluded that "but for the British Navy, it would have been impossible to prevent the British West Indies from joining the [American] Revolution." Robert W. Tucker and David C. Hendrickson also highlighted military considerations in which the "island colonies remained as dependent as ever on British protection against foreign attack and slave revolts." In contrast, K. G. Davies stressed the economic dependence of the islands on Britain as the chief obstacle to a revolt. Agnes Whitson similarly regarded economic factors as paramount but more because of the competition between "West Indians [who] thought their interests were advanced by a restriction of the continental trade to the British islands, and the northern colonies [who] wished to trade to the best market in the Caribbean, wheresoever it might be."[10]

Robert Wells cited demographic factors in which "the high proportion of slaves may have deterred thoughts of rebellion." Cyril Hamshere argued that "the large number of West Indian colonists living in England explained why the West Indies did not join the mainland colonies in their rebellion." Gordon Lewis suggested that the lack of a national consciousness, based on unifying norms and values, was the primary obstacle to rebellion. Franklin Knight similarly argued that "incipient nationalism . . . did not evolve in the sugar islands" owing to the "tenuous relationship [of white creoles] to the land" and their "cultural dependence on the Mother Country." Edward Brathwaite found that "at every step, it seems, the creatively 'creole' elements of the society were being rendered ineffective by the more reactionary 'colonial'."[11] Selwyn Carrington was largely concerned with the war years after 1775. According to Jack Greene, Carrington only "briefly addresses the old question of why the islands did not join the continent in the struggle for independence," yet he offered a more nuanced answer than previous historians. In explaining why the islands remained loyal, he stressed "in descending order of importance planter absenteeism, deeper economic and cultural links with Britain, greater strategic vulnerability, and a numerically vastly superior slave population," but Greene suggested this order of ranking be rearranged "exactly in reverse."[12] The question clearly deserves further consideration.

I begin by examining the long-term preconditions that explain the loyalty of the white colonists in the British West Indies during the American Revolution. Chapter 1 discusses the close cultural and social ties with Britain. Chapter 2 demonstrates the dependence of whites on imperial military protection against slave revolts. Chapter 3 argues that the sugar revolution, which was responsible for the social structure of the islands and which made the islands economically dependent on the protected metropolitan market, clearly differentiated the island colonies from the mainland colonies.

The next three chapters examine the short-term reasons why the islands did not rebel. The island colonies diverged significantly from their mainland counterparts in their reaction to imperial legislation between 1763 and 1774. White society in the islands remained aloof from the imperial crisis until the eve of the Revolutionary War. These chapters reveal how the islands affected British policy toward North America and how their lobby in London contributed to the isolation of the North American lobby on the eve of the Revolutionary War.

The final chapters examine the reaction of the British West Indies to the Revolutionary War. Challenging the claim that there was widespread white support for the revolutionary cause during the war, these chapters find that the financial strain of the war and the inadequacy of imperial protection were sources of grievance among whites. However, even the opponents of the war only questioned the sacrifice it inflicted rather than the legitimacy of the cause. West Indian planters and their lobby were divided about the mildest gestures of opposition toward the home government. These chapters also show how the defense of the islands influenced British military strategy and contributed to the eventual British defeat at Yorktown. Chapter 10 explores the legacy of the American Revolution in the British West Indies.

This book differs from works by earlier historians in denying that there was a latent desire for rebellion among the white colonists of the British West Indies.[13] It argues that their loyalty was due to neither the threat of military coercion nor the physical impracticality of a revolt but rather reflected the fundamental differences between the island and mainland colonies. My interpretation also conflicts with those of historians who stress the similarities between the mainland and island colonies, of whom the most notable is Jack Greene.[14] However, because the subject has received scant attention, the main contribution of this book is not as a work of revision. It offers, instead, an overview of a much neglected aspect of the American Revolution.

Prices are quoted in local currency in the islands unless otherwise stated. The term *free colored* is used to describe people of mixed race and blacks except where specifically distinguished.

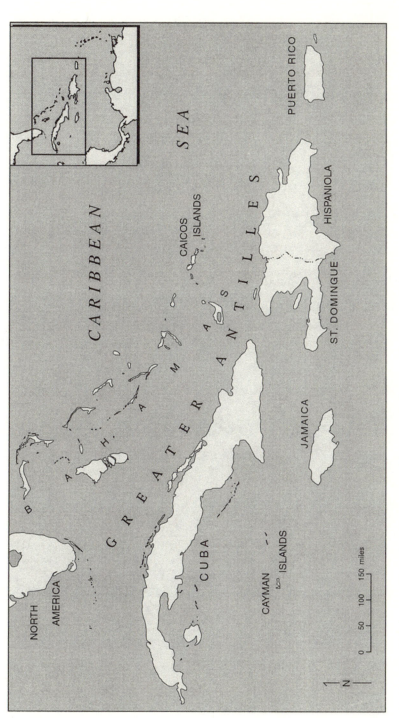

The Greater Antilles (Cartographic Laboratory, University of Wisconsin).

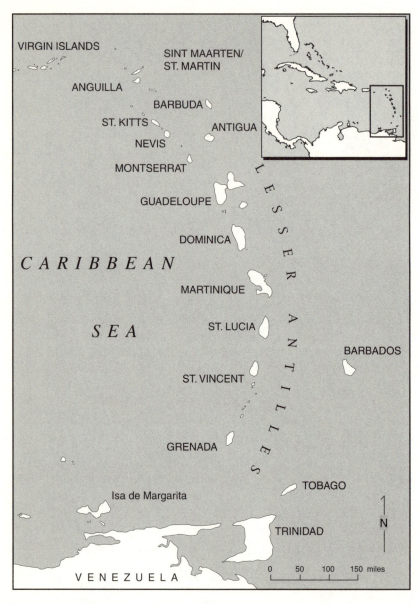

The Lesser Antilles (Eastern Caribbean) (Cartographic Laboratory, University of Wisconsin).

PART I

FOUNDATIONS OF LOYALTY

The Subjects of those islands [in the West Indies] must at all times depend upon the Parent State for protection, & for every Essential resourse. The mart of their Produce will ever be at home; & the Public credit is security for their acquired Wealth if established in our Bank or Funds. Their aim is only to get Fortunes & return to their native Land. Such is the consequence of an Empire over Islands to Britain. We have dearly experienced a contrary Effect in our Continental Colonists. Every Subject, My Lord, you ingage to Inhabit our Sugar Colonies, you acquire a valuable object to the State; every Subject that settles upon Continental America is eventually lost to the Mother-Country.
— John Drummond to Lord George Germain, secretary of state for America, March 24, 1778

I

British Sojourners

AT THE OUTSET OF the American Revolutionary War, a French visitor remarked on the differences between the island and mainland colonies of British America: "Far from settling in the islands," the white colonists regarded them "as a land of exile, never as a place where they plan to live, prosper, and die." In contrast, the Anglo-American colonists of the mainland were "permanent, born in the country and attached to it; they have no motherland save the one they live in."[1]

Writing a century earlier, a Barbadian planter spoke of this umbilical attachment in which "by a kind of magnetic force England draws all to it. . . . It is the center to which all things tend. Nothing but England can we relish or fancy." In 1760, Charles Townshend favorably contrasted West Indians to North Americans because they "never consider[ed] themselves at home" in the islands and they sent "their children to the Mother Country for education." They eventually returned to Britain "to recover their health or enjoy their fortunes" for, if they had ambition, "tis hither they come to gratify it."[2]

In 1764, following the end of the Seven Years' War, a Nevis author reflected on the transient quality of white society in the islands: "Tho' detained from their native land by mercenary Pursuits and Views of Interest, yet [they] consider their Absence from Britain as an Exile, and incessantly sigh for a return." Upon joining his regiment in Jamaica, Lord Adam Gordon commented that "the generality of its inhabitants look upon themselves there as passengers only." Bryan Edwards similarly described how "it is to Great Britain alone that our West India planters consider themselves as belonging." He added that "*even such of them as have resided in the West Indies from their birth*, look on the islands as their temporary abode only, and the fond notion of being able to go home (as they emphatically term a visit to England) year after year animates their industry and alleviates their misfortune."[3]

Colonists throughout British America spoke of Britain as their home. The expression was more meaningful in the British West Indies, however, where the white settlers were primarily a society of sojourners who aimed to return to

Britain and identified themselves culturally with Britain. I shall argue that the strength of the social and cultural ties with Britain restrained the development of a nationalistic creole consciousness among whites and was a contributory factor in the failure of the British Caribbean to support the American Revolution.

✳   ✳   ✳

Whites in the British Caribbean were creoles, if we mean simply that they made cultural adaptations to their new environment. Like European settlers elsewhere in the Americas, they possessed distinctive characteristics in their speech, diet, dress, architecture, values, and behavior that were peculiar to the Caribbean. They developed an attachment to their islands, which was reflected in the numerous prerevolutionary local histories and a literature praising the tropical landscape. They were often ambivalent about their British identity when they actually returned to the mother country.[4]

But West Indian whites were not committed to permanent settlement, and their ideal of returning home to the mother country gave white society a transient quality. They treated the islands as little more than temporary abodes to facilitate their spectacular reentry into British society. Throughout the eighteenth century, an increasing proportion of West Indian planters returned to live off the income of their plantations as absentees in Britain. The trend varied among islands, often in relation to the respective expansion and profitability of sugar production. It began in Barbados soon after the Restoration of Charles II (1660). In the last two decades of the seventeenth century, some three hundred West Indians were annually going back to Britain "with this advantage that their fathers went out poor and the children come home rich." Over one-third of Jamaican planters were absentees by 1740.[5]

In the 1730s, absenteeism was still quite rare in the Leeward Islands (Antigua, St. Kitts, Montserrat, and Nevis). Thereafter it reached chronic levels in St. Kitts, where absentees owned half the property in 1745. Absenteeism was also prevalent in the Windward Islands (Grenada, St. Vincent, Dominica, and Tobago) from the time of their acquisition by Britain in 1763. Tobago had only twenty resident planters out of a total of seventy-seven proprietors. Absentee estates in Grenada were worth upward of a million pounds of sterling in 1778.[6]

On the eve of the American Revolution, planter-historian Edward Long estimated that there were some two thousand nonresidents, annuitants, and proprietors, "who of late years" and "beyond the example of former times" had flocked from Jamaica to Britain. A visitor found St. Kitts "almost abandoned to overseers and managers, owing to the amazing fortunes that belong to Individuals, who almost all reside in England." Absentees made up 80 percent of the elite families of Antigua, and two-thirds of the planters in Jamaica were absentees by 1800.[7] Absenteeism was also common among military officers, the clergy, and patent officeholders.

These British sojourners consequently bequeathed shamefully little toward developing an infrastructure in the islands, such as schools, colleges, roads, and missions. The most enduring visible monuments to the presence of the British in the Caribbean were those commemorating the deaths of individuals who died before achieving their ambition of returning home. Some were crafted by the best English sculptors, such as Henry Cheere and John Bacon. They all shared a common feature in the complete absence of any depiction of tropical life in the West Indies. The patrons clearly wanted to be commemorated by monuments exactly like those of an English country churchyard. These decaying monuments remain English corners of a foreign land.

The transience of white West Indian society was reflected in the paucity of architectural remains. Edward Long spoke of the "make-shift" appearance of the architecture in Jamaica, and Bryan Edwards described the "meanness of their houses and apartments." There were "few of the Beauties of Architecture to be seen in Jamaica" despite the opulence of its planters. James Anthony Froude, a nineteenth-century historian, was appalled at the difference between Kingston, the largest town in the British West Indies, which "has not one fine building in it," and Havana, the Spanish capital of Cuba, which "is a city of palaces, a city of streets and plazas, of colonnades and towers, and churches and monasteries." The most impressive architectural eighteenth-century legacies were not private residences but fortresses, naval dockyards, and military barracks. "We English," Froude concluded, "have built in those islands as if we were but passing visitors, wanting only tenements to be occupied for a time."[8]

West Indian fortunes nurtured several noted writers and scholars, but they too were often sojourners. They included bibliophiles, historians, political pamphleteers, constitutional authorities, political economists, travel writers, natural historians, botanists, and agricultural commentators. There were West Indian members of the Royal Society, the Dilettante Society, and the Royal College of Physicians. The first complete oratorio in the Americas was composed and performed in Jamaica in 1775. There were also poets, landscape artists, actors, architects, and connoisseurs. Spanish Town in Jamaica had a theater, circulating libraries, a literary society, an agricultural society, and social clubs in the 1770s. West Indian literary and artistic work may indeed have "fostered local pride," but most of these authors and scholars were either visitors, temporary residents, or absentees. They also were often transients, thereby creating the popular misconception that "in literature, science and the arts, the history of the British West Indies is almost a blank."[9]

It was the ephemeral nature of white settlement that so concerned Edward Long, the most incisive of contemporary commentators. His *History of Jamaica* (1774) pleaded for greater self-sufficiency and the development of local institutions. He advocated legislative action to fund schools, a medical college, white immigration, improved military defenses, and a stronger church foundation. His emphasis on greater self-sufficiency was his most original intellectual contribution "not his political ideas *per se*" or his "constitutionalism."[10] However, even Long succumbed to the temptations of absenteeism and returned to Britain.

Only in Barbados did the British come close to developing a creole society of committed settlers in the Caribbean. This was due to the high proportion of whites, less reliance on immigration, the belief that the climate was more healthy, lower rates of absenteeism, lower sugar profits, lower rates of "miscegenation," less danger from foreign attack (owing to the windward position), and complacence about the threat of a black rebellion. Barbados contained the largest proportion of small and middling planters, numbering some four thousand resident landowners in 1765. It had a better infrastructure with the oldest assembly in the British Caribbean, the first printing press, schools in every parish, the first newspaper, and a well-supported Anglican Church.[11]

Barbados has been used as a case study to show the early development of a creole mentality in the eighteenth-century British Caribbean.[12] Even in Barbados, however, the white population was in a minority. Almost one-third of the planters were absentees like Samuel Estwick, Philip Gibbes, John Gibbons, and the Lascelles. The Barbadian elite preferred to be educated in Britain; thus Codrington College never "promised to make it unnecessary for Barbadian youths to travel to England for advanced education."[13] It closed as a school between 1775 and 1786 and was not a university or even a seminary until 1830. The yeoman class of small landholders lacked the confidence to politically challenge the planter elite until the early nineteenth century.

*   *   *

How do we explain the transience of British society in the Caribbean and the almost universal desire of whites to return home to Britain? Frank Wesley Pitman argued that the absence of religious motives among the first English settlers in the Caribbean created a transient society, which was in contrast to North America, where religion inspired ideals of a new society divorced from England. He also suggested that the settlers in the islands were drawn from "the capitalist class . . . [who] were often connected with the landed gentry, were Anglicans, and championed the social and political conceptions held by the rural aristocracy of England," in contrast to the North Americans, "who came largely from the middle and nonconformist class in England . . . [and who] had imbibed democratic and republican ideas."[14]

Pitman, in an error common among his generation, treated the history of colonial America as synonymous with the Puritan colonies of New England and ignored the more populous plantation colonies of the Chesapeake (Virginia and Maryland). There was in reality little difference in the motives and background of the early English emigrants to the Caribbean from those of the Chesapeake. The plantation colonies of the islands and the southern mainland shared a common ethos, which was materialistic, individualistic, competitive, exploitative, and comparatively secular. It was the universal aim of most settlers in all the plantation colonies to make quick fortunes and to return to a life of genteel leisure in Britain.

The peculiar transience of British society in the Caribbean can be attributed in part to demographic failure. The white population was not sustained by natural increase, unlike the mainland colonies where the white population was doubling every twenty-five years after 1700. Deaths exceeded births in the Caribbean. The migration of a little under half a million Europeans to the British Caribbean was "roughly comparable" to that of British North America before the American Revolution.[15] Yet there were fewer than fifty thousand whites in the British Caribbean, compared to two million in North America, in 1776.

The demographic failure of white society in the islands was linked to the high mortality rates: "The low life expectancy of white men in the tropics goes far to explain the large number of absentee proprietors" and the small size of the white population. Jamaica was "considered the most unhealthy [place] . . . in the world." Over one-third of white immigrants died within three years of arriving in the Caribbean. A posting in the islands consequently occasioned sudden rises in the military sick lists and even mutinies in the army in Britain. Being stationed in Jamaica became a form of punishment. The danger of sudden death was a constant topic of conversation among passengers on a voyage to the West Indies in 1775. Hector St. John de Crèvecoeur wrote of West Indians who at the age of thirty were "loaded with the infirmities of old age" and losing the "abilities of enjoying the comforts of life at a time when we northern men just begin to taste the fruits of our labour and prudence."[16] The grim prospect of a premature death was a powerful deterrent to living in the Caribbean.

Influenced by the humoral theory of medicine, European settlers feared, above all, the tropical "climate of our sugar islands," which they found "so inconvenient for an English constitution that no man will choose to live there, much less will any man choose to settle there [in the Caribbean]." They blamed the heat for causing high mortality rates, but in reality, the majority fell victim to malaria and less commonly to the more lethal yellow fever epidemics. Whites had less immunity to these diseases than did blacks.[17]

The high mortality rates of native whites were a cause of fragile family formations that also contributed to the transience of white society. Premature deaths cut short marriages, which typically lasted little more than eight years in Jamaica. The majority of children died in infancy or in childhood.[18] The size of families was consequently very small.

Even so, British immigrants continued to be a major component of white society in the Caribbean. Opportunities were good in the professions and in trades, owing to the demographic failure of the native white population, the lack of skilled white artisans, and the limited educational infrastructure within the islands. Furthermore, Jamaica and some of the Windward Islands were still frontier settlements with uncultivated land before the American Revolution.[19]

Young white immigrant males from Britain were a dominant element in the white population of Jamaica. Their presence contributed to the unbalanced sex ratios and compounded the problem of fragile family formations. There was "a whole parish [in Jamaica] without a married Man" and another parish where there was "not to be found above one married couple." Young British males who arrived as indentured servants were often more highly skilled than those of the southern mainland colonies.

The Scots were the second largest group of immigrants after the English. They made up one-third of the white population of Jamaica and were the most numerous of the British immigrants in Grenada and Tobago. Their ambition of making a fortune to return home was identical to that of the English.[20]

The transitory quality of white society was reinforced by dramatic increase of black slaves. Whites became a besieged minority in a majority black population. The displacement of white indentured servants as field laborers by slaves occurred earlier in the Caribbean than in the Chesapeake primarily because sugar plantations were more labor intensive and wealthier than tobacco farms of Maryland and Virginia. The cultivation of sugar was followed in all the islands by a massive rise in the import of black slaves from West Africa. On the eve of the American Revolution, three-quarters of the English slave trade was destined for the Caribbean. Jamaica was the largest slave society in British America after a twenty-fold increase in the number of blacks, compared to a mere doubling of the white population, between 1673 and 1774.

Blacks outnumbered whites in the British Caribbean by a ratio as high as twenty-two to one. Barbados had the lowest proportion of slaves, but they still represented 73 percent of the population, a higher percentage than that of any of the mainland colonies: only South Carolina possessed almost equal numbers of blacks and whites on the eve of the American Revolution. The 50,000 whites in the islands were a minority in relation to a black and free colored population of some 416,000.[21] The ratios were inverted in North America, where there were 2,000,000 whites and 460,000 blacks on the eve of the American Revolution.

The rise in the proportion of blacks and the frequency of slave rebellions created a garrison mentality among the whites, who became more dependent for their protection on Britain. The white population of the islands was too small to effectively police the slaves, and their vulnerability was becoming more apparent. This climate of fear was reinforced by the additional uncertainty of hurricanes, earthquakes, droughts, foreign invasion, and disease, all of which were hazards of life in the Caribbean.

The racial imbalance preoccupied whites, who tried various schemes to reverse the trend. The island assemblies attempted to mandate white immigration by requiring planters to hire whites in proportion to their slaves. These "deficiency acts" failed and became nothing more than another revenue device with planters preferring to pay higher taxes in lieu of hiring white employees. Like the Irish Parliament, the West Indian legislatures tried to impose additional taxes on the estates of absentees, but such measures were prohibited by the imperial government. In order to maintain the size of their white populations, the island colonies were unique in winning exemption from naval press gangs. Jamaica offered generous headright grants and financial inducements to white immigrants. After the mid-eighteenth century, Jamaica tried to raise the duties on the slave trade to discourage new imports.[22] These measures failed because they never tackled the fundamental causes of this racial imbalance, which was due to high mortality rates, unbalanced sex ratios, fragile family formations, and the expansion of labor-intensive sugar plantations that employed few whites.

Whites sought to remove themselves from black influence by identifying with Britain or by removing to Britain. They found difficulty in replicating British society in the Caribbean in opposition to the powerful cultural influences exerted by the black majority. Whites "by insensible degrees . . . almost acquire[d] the same habit of thinking & speaking" as the blacks and those "singularities" of the blacks "in speech or deportment, which are so apt to strike the ears and eyes of well-educated persons on . . . first introduction."

George Washington found the ladies of Barbados "very agreeable but by ill custom or wit . . . affect the Negro style." The character of Miss Prissy, a West Indian heiress living in London, was represented in Isaac Bickerstaff's *Love in the City* (1767) as tomboyish because of growing up "in the plantations" where she was among the "blackamoors."[23]

Whites were in closer contact with blacks in the Caribbean colonies than in the Chesapeake, where interactions were more limited. This was reflected in the frequency of sexual relationships between white males and women of color, which were more accepted in the islands than in the southern mainland colonies. The islands consequently possessed a significant colored population whose mixed racial ancestry often conferred privileges. The mainland colonies, on the other hand, made no such distinctions between gradations of race and treated all people of color as black. In a law of 1733, Jamaica became the only colony in British America "to give legislative countenance to the rise of mulattoes" and to enable colored people to pass as whites if they were three generations removed from black ancestors.[24]

The wealthiest planters sought to retain their racial exclusivity by leaving the "scenes which destroy their own comfort" and "injure the tempers and morals of their children." The elite educated their children in Britain in order to keep "children from the company and conversation of Negroes as much as possible." Daughters educated in England retained "very good [pale white] skins . . . and very good complexions, without the least Tinge in the world of the Country they were born in."[25] Whites feared that children raised by black domestics were susceptible to acquiring the "drawling dissonant gibberish . . . and with it no small tincture of their aukward carriage and vulgar manners." The boy who "diverts himself with the Negroes, acquires their broken Way of talking, their Manner of Behaviour, and all the Vices of these unthinking Creatures can teach." Girls who grew up "in sequestered country partes," without the "example or tuition" of other whites, dangled their arms "with the air of a Negroe-servant," lolled the day in bed, wore "two or three handkerchiefs" on their head, dressed loose without stays, and gobbled pepper pot sitting on the floor. Such girls became "conscious of . . . [their] ignorance" in later life and withdrew from society.[26]

*   *   *

The West Indian elite were able to make good their ambition of returning home to Britain because the fortunes of sugar planters in the Caribbean were greater than those of the tobacco planters in the Chesapeake: "Our Tobacco Colonies," wrote Adam Smith, "send us home no such wealthy planters as we see frequently arrive from our sugar colonies."[27] South Carolina began to produce fortunes sufficient to allow some planters to live in Britain, but their numbers were not comparable to those from the British West Indies. Furthermore, primogeniture (in which the oldest son inherited most of the estate) was more commonly practiced in the Caribbean than in North America and which concentrated wealth.

Absenteeism created a special bond with the mother country by establishing a large West Indian community in Britain, where they were nicknamed "creoles" or "pepper pots" and their lodgings "pens." West Indians dominated parts of London, Bath, and Bristol. They congregated at favorite haunts in London like the King's Arms Tavern in Cornhill, the Mitre Coffee House in Fleet Street, and the London Tavern in Bishopsgate Street. They inhabited the fashionable new developments north of Oxford Street in Marylebone, including Wimpole Street, Welbeck Street, Portman Square, Portman Street, and Montagu Square. John Baker, solicitor general of the Leeward Islands, continued friendships in England that he had forged in the West Indies. His diary reveals a great network of West Indians distributed throughout Britain like the Mannings and Akers of St. Kitts, the Skeretts and Kirwans of Antigua, the Tuites of Montserrat, and the Maynards of Nevis.[28]

West Indians possessed impressive landed estates, which adorned the British countryside. Harewood House in Yorkshire, the country seat of Edwin Lascelles of Barbados, was designed by John Carr with interiors by Robert Adam, furniture by Thomas Chippendale, stuccos by Joseph Rose, and decorations by Angelica Kauffman. Dodington Hall in Gloucester, landscaped by Capability Brown and designed by James Wyatt, was the home of Sir William Codrington of Antigua. Standlynch near Salisbury was the home of Henry Dawkins of Jamaica and was later purchased by the nation as a gift for the heirs of Lord Nelson. Fonthill Splendens, set amid a five-thousand-acre estate in Wiltshire, was the home of William Beckford of Jamaica. Lord Shelburne declared in 1778 that "there were scarcely ten miles together throughout the country where the house and estate of a rich West Indian was not to be seen."[29]

West Indians were painted by the foremost British portrait artists. Harewood House in Yorkshire contained a seventy-five-foot-long gallery to display family portraits of the Lascelles of Barbados by Sir Joshua Reynolds. In contrast, the elite in North America were painted by resident or itinerant artists of whom the most distinguished was John Singleton Copley. There was no comparable tradition of local portraiture in the British West Indies, where Copley turned down the opportunity of a visit to Barbados even though there was "but one painter" in 1766. The painter was William Johnston, who had to supplement his income as a church organist. Similarly, Philip Wicksted was

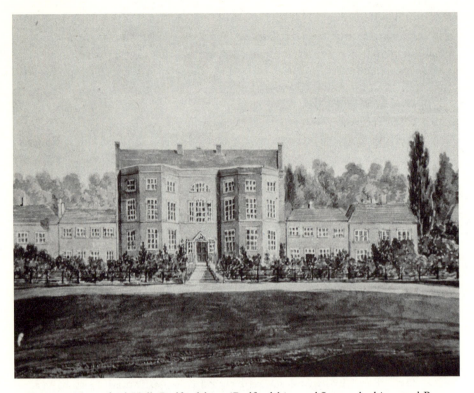

Figure 1. Tempsford Hall, Bedfordshire (Bedfordshire and Luton Archives and Records Service). West Indian absentee planters possessed impressive landed estates in Britain. Tempsford Hall was the home of Sir Gillies Payne, an absentee planter from St. Kitts who was said to be among a small minority of planters who supported the American Revolution. West Indian estates in Britain were a symbol of the close ties with the metropolis and the prosperity of the planters on the eve of the American Revolutionary War.

unable to find sufficient patronage as a portrait painter in Jamaica and turned unsuccessfully to planting.[30] West Indians preferred to be painted by the fashionable portrait artists in Britain.

Absentee West Indians were sufficiently familiar in metropolitan society to be caricatured in broadsides, newspapers, cartoons, novels, and plays. Their social pretensions were ridiculed by Tobias Smollett, who had lived in Jamaica and married a Jamaican. Samuel Foote's farce *The Patron* (1764) featured Sir Peter Pepperpot, "a West Indian of an overgrown fortune," an ingenuous and absurd character who dreams of a woman who is "sweet as sugar cane, strait as a bamboo, and [with] teeth as white as a negro's . . . a plantation of perfec-

The MIDDLE TEMPLE MACARONI

In short I am a West Indian

Cumberland.

Figure 2. Caricature of the Middle Temple Macaroni with caption "In short I am a West Indian, Cumberland" c. 1770 (Copyright © British Museum). West Indians were sufficiently familiar in metropolitan society to be caricatured in broadsides, newspapers, cartoons, novels, and plays. This cartoon alludes to Richard Cumberland's play *The West Indian* (1771).

TABLE 1   Baronetcy Creations in British America

	1660–1700	1701–1740	1741–1776	Total
Antigua	0	0	1	1
Barbados	7	0	3	10
Dominica	0	0	1	1
Grenada	0	0	0	0
Jamaica	2	1	2	5
Nevis	1	0	0	1
Montserrat	0	0	0	0
St. Kitts	0	1	0	1
St. Vincent	0	0	0	0
Total (West Indies)	10	2	7	19
Connecticut	0	0	0	0
Delaware	0	0	0	0
Georgia	0	0	1	1
Maryland	0	0	0	0
Massachusetts	0	0	1	1
New Hampshire	0	0	0	0
New Jersey	0	0	0	0
New York	0	0	0	0
North Carolina	0	0	0	0
Pennsylvania	0	0	0	0
Rhode Island	0	0	0	0
South Carolina	0	0	1	1
Virginia	0	0	0	0
Total (North America)	0	0	3	3

Note: The table excludes itinerant British colonial officials.
Source: George E. Cokayne, *The Complete Baronetage* (Exeter: William Pollard, 1900–1906), vols. 3–5.

tions." West Indian wealth and prodigality also attracted moral censure. Their ownership of slaves was beginning to attract adverse comment, like the press reference to the Jamaican lord mayor of London as "negro whipping Beckford."[31] Samuel Johnson derided the planters and the system of slavery that supported them and toasted the next slave rebellion in Jamaica.

Nevertheless, the West Indian elite successfully entered British society. West Indians were more likely than North Americans to possess minor titles like baronetcies (Table 1). Charles II created five baronetcies in Barbados alone, which was almost twice the number created among North Americans before 1776. West Indians successfully intermarried with the nobility and gentry, including the duke of Ancaster, the earl of Effingham, the earl of Buchanan, the earl of Abercorn, the earl of Home, the earl of Carlhampton, the earl of Radnor, the earl of Portmore, Lord Rivers, and Lord St. John.[32] Flattering portrayals of West Indians appeared in Sir John Hill's *Adventures of Mr. George Edwards, A Creole* (1751) and Mrs. Scott's *History of George Ellison* (1765–66). The rise of West Indians in British society defies claims of a closed elite in eighteenth-century Britain.[33]

West Indians formed the most powerful colonial lobby in London. Lord North, the prime minister during the American Revolution, "was used to say that they were the only masters he ever had."[34] After 1760, the lobby evolved from an informal group soliciting political favors into a more organized impersonal body that foreshadowed the economic interest groups that have proliferated in modern times.

The West India lobby in Britain had four major components. First, the island agents in London were the principal actors in the lobby and were in many ways the precursors of modern-day professional lobbyists. They received salaries and were sometimes individuals, unconnected with the islands and selected on the basis of their political skills. There were ten active agents representing the islands in 1774.[35] The island agents became more active, especially Stephen Fuller, who was the chief broker in orchestrating the West India interest during his thirty-year career as agent for Jamaica between 1764 and 1794. He transcended "his predecessors in office" of whom none had shown comparable "vigilance to the welfare of the colony represented, or so intelligent and perfect a comprehension of its essential interest."[36]

A second component of the West India interest in Britain were the London merchants trading with the West Indies. A formal organization called the Society of West India Merchants emerged during the 1760s. Its origins are obscure; there are no minutes for the meetings before 1769. The society, which had a chairman, a salaried secretary, and an honorary treasurer, was funded by a charge on trade. Its activities were largely confined to commercial issues, especially sugar duties and rates of freight.[37]

The Society of West India Merchants was interlinked with the City of London, numbering several aldermen among its members, including Samuel Turner, William Beckford, Richard Oliver, Barlow Trecothick, and Benjamin Hopkins. Beeston Long and Richard Neave, the chairmen of the society, were also governors of the Bank of England. The society met about once a month and attracted an average of ten merchants. The influence of the society in

Sketch for the Statue ordered to be Erected to the Memory of the late Wm Beckford Esqr by the Court of Common Council.

Figure 3. Engraving of the Monument of William Beckford at the Guildhall, London (Copyright © British Museum). William Beckford was the wealthiest and most celebrated of the absentee West Indian planters living in Britain. As lord mayor of London and a close ally of William Pitt, he personified the political power of the West India lobby. He was an outspoken champion of colonial rights in Parliament.

London was replicated in the outports, especially Bristol, where merchants engaged in the West India trade were prominent in civic offices and in the Society of Merchant Ventures.[38]

Third, there were the absentee West India planters living in Britain whose numbers cannot be precisely calculated.[39] The most prominent of these was William Beckford, who was born in Jamaica where his father was speaker of the assembly. Beckford was successively an alderman (1752), sheriff (1755–56), and twice lord mayor of London (1762–63, 1769–70), where his public banquets were said to have been the most lavish since the reign of Henry VIII. Beckford, like many absentees, was a member of the House of Commons (Shaftesbury 1747–54 and London 1754–70). He was an ally and close associate of William Pitt the Elder. Following the death of Beckford in 1770, the city of London commissioned a statue of him, which still stands in the Guildhall.

Members of Parliament with West Indian connections and interests were a fourth component of the West India lobby. The agent for Massachusetts Bay thought that "50 or 60 West India voters can turn the balance on which side they please." An anonymous correspondent of the *Gentleman's Magazine* calculated in 1766 that "there are now in Parliament upwards of forty members who are either West Indian planters themselves, descended from such, or have concerns there that entitle them to pre-eminence." An important contemporary source is that of Stephen Fuller, the agent for Jamaica, who listed forty-eight West Indian "colony" members of the House of Commons in 1781. However, calculations of the size of this parliamentary lobby vary according to the different operational definitions used to distinguish West Indian members of Parliament.[40] Nevertheless, the West India interest was a formidable lobby, causing Benjamin Franklin to complain that the "West Indies vastly outweigh us of the Northern Colonies" in Britain.[41]

* * *

There was no comparable West Indian presence in North America despite the proximity of the mainland colonies and despite the considerable ties that developed through trade. South Carolina was settled by Barbadians who introduced slaves, the plantation system, a slave code, speech patterns, and possibly architectural styles from the Caribbean.[42] Nevertheless, only a few absentees lived in North America, such as Abraham Redwood of Antigua in Newport (Rhode Island) and Isaac Royall of Antigua in Massachusetts. The Middletons, Bulls, and Colletons of South Carolina owned plantations in Barbados and Jamaica. The Sandisfords of Rhode Island and the Kingslands of New Jersey had estates in Barbados. Their numbers were negligible in com-

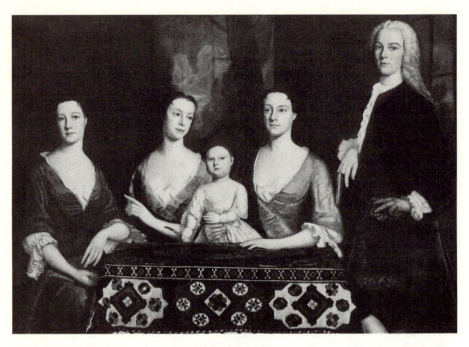

Figure 4. *Isaac Royall and Family*, Robert Feke, 1741 (courtesy of Art and Visual Materials, Special Collections Department, Harvard Law School Library). Isaac Royall was born in Antigua where his father had emigrated from Maine. He became one of the wealthiest men in Massachusetts. He was an example of the overlapping ties with the thirteen mainland colonies, especially among merchants.

parison to the absentees in Britain and they tended to be natives of North America. Some West Indians owned estates in North America, like Thomas Benson of Jamaica who owned land in Philadelphia, but many more owned estates in Britain.

North Americans were a visible presence in the islands but only a few settled as permanent residents. The Gedney Clarke family in Barbados, friends of George Washington, were from Salem, Massachusetts. Philip Livingston, one of the signatories of the Declaration of Independence, resided as a merchant in Jamaica where he married and where his oldest son settled. Benjamin Franklin sent his nephew to set up the first printing press in Antigua and several of his former associates settled in the Caribbean.[43] There was some intermarriage between prominent North Americans and West Indians: the Winthrop, Oliver, Vassal, Livingston, and Morris families in the British West Indies were related to the same families in Massachusetts and New York.

However, such examples were few in comparison to marriage alliances of West Indians and British.

Cultural ties included itinerant artists, theatrical groups, puppeteers, and rope dancers who toured both the mainland and island colonies. The Hallam family began visiting Jamaica in 1754 and later became the "first American theatrical dynasty" in North America as the American Company of Comedians. Lewis Hallam attributed his success in playing roles of blacks to having "studied their dialect and manners in the South and in Jamaica." Colleges attempted fundraising in the West Indies. Dr. John Morgan, the founder of the medical faculty associated with the College of Philadelphia (University of Pennsylvania), raised £860 in Jamaica (1772), and William Smith, the provost of the College of Philadelphia, wrote a series of articles for the *Antigua Gazette*. Networks of religious dissenters engaged in social, business, and missionary exchanges between the Caribbean and North America.[44] The majority of North Americans in the Caribbean, however, tended to be a transient community of mercantile agents, the crews of merchant ships, or visitors seeking a change of climate to improve their health. In addition, their commercial interests were shifting toward the French and Spanish Caribbean even before the American Revolution (see Chapter 3).

There were indeed important overlapping ties between the British West Indies and North America, but they were weaker than those with the mother country and tended to reinforce West Indian commitment to the integrity of the British Empire.

*   *   *

Many of the white island elite spent their formative years in schools and universities in Britain, not North America. Planters were willing to spend large sums educating their children in Britain. Most educated West Indians were sent "like a bale of dry goods, consigned to some factor, who places them at the school where he himself was bred, or any other that his inclination leads him to prefer." In Jamaica, three-quarters of the planters sent some three hundred children a year to be educated in Britain. One-third of these children never returned.[45]

Edward Long regarded the "lack of educational facilities" in Jamaica as "one of the principal impediments to its effectual settlement." There were only four schools in operation in Jamaica in 1770.[46] Codrington College in Barbados was "the only notable school in the British West Indies," but it was closed between 1775 and 1796.[47] The clergy sometimes supplemented their stipends by teaching when "the Benefices here are but of small Accomt and

TABLE 2   West Indians at Eton College, 1698–1776

	1698–1752	1753–1776
Antigua	6	36
Barbados	4	31
Dominica	0	0
Grenada	0	1
Jamaica	9	53
Montserrat	1	9
Nevis	2	1
St. Kitts	1	17
St. Vincent	0	0
Tobago	0	0
Total	23	148

Source: R. A. Austen-Leigh, *The Eton College Register, 1698–1752* (Eton, 1927); Austen-Leigh, *The Eton College Register, 1753–1790* (Eton, 1921).

indeed not sufficient to maintain the necessities of a clergyman." Bryan Edwards was taught as a youth "small Latin and less Greek" by a clergyman in Jamaica. However, Rev. Robert Robertson of Nevis found it "neither worth his or anybodys while . . . to teach school here," and Rev. James Ramsay of St. Kitts similarly gave up trying to find pupils in the 1760s.[48] There were a few schoolteachers, but they were poorly remunerated and their occupation was not respected.

Like the children of the English gentry, West Indian children initially went to private tutors and small academies in Britain. Girls went to tutors like Mrs. Este's in Queen's Street in London or seminaries, especially in fashionable Chelsea. The two daughters of Nathaniel Phillips of Jamaica lived with their aunt in London and attended a seminary for girls in Greenwich in 1772. Fanny Rutherford met many of her Edinburgh boarding school contemporaries on a visit to Antigua, where they shared "many friends to talk of, many scenes to recollect" in 1775.[49] However, planters were more likely to send their sons than their daughters to be educated in Britain.

In the early eighteenth century, West Indian boys increasingly began to attend the burgeoning public schools in Britain. Between 1698 and 1752, Eton attracted twice as many boys from the West Indies as from North America (Tables 2 and 3). During the second half of the eighteenth century, there was a sixfold increase in the number of West Indian boys attending Eton, which was displacing Westminster as the elite school in England. There was a similar

TABLE 3   North Americans at Eton College, 1698–1776

	1698–1752	*1753–1776*
Connecticut	0	0
Delaware	0	0
Georgia	0	0
Maryland	4	3
Massachusetts	0	0
New Hampshire	0	0
New Jersey	0	0
New York	1	1
North Carolina	0	0
Pennsylvania	1	0
Rhode Island	1	0
South Carolina	0	8
Virginia	4	10
Total	11	22

Source: R. A. Austen-Leigh, *The Eton College Register, 1698–1752* (Eton, 1927); Austen-Leigh, *The Eton College Register, 1753–1790* (Eton, 1921).

trend at Harrow (Table 4). Eton College library was augmented by the magnificent private collection of books and prints given by Anthony Morris Storer of Jamaica. Several portraits of West Indians, which the wealthiest boys traditionally gave to the headmaster, now hang in the lodgings of the provost of Eton.[50] By the end of the century, the duke of Clarence exclaimed that English public schools were full of the sons of West Indians.[51]

West Indians who went on to higher education attended British universities (Table 5). There were no universities in the British Caribbean, in contrast to the thirteen mainland colonies' nine colleges at the end of the colonial period and in contrast to the Spanish Caribbean, where the University of San Domingo was the oldest in the Americas. A prosopography of members of the legislature of Antigua finds that 24 percent of members of the assembly and 31 percent of the council attended university in Britain among members serving between 1763 and 1783. This compares favorably to 40 percent of members of the British House of Commons between 1754 and 1790.

West Indians went primarily to Oxford and Cambridge at a time when the social composition of these universities was becoming more exclusively aristocratic. The Codrington Library at All Souls College (Oxford University), designed by Nicholas Hawksmoor, was endowed by Christopher Codrington of Barbados and the Leeward Islands. It contains his statue sculpted

TABLE 4   West Indians and North Americans at Harrow School, 1698–1776

Years	1698–1752	1753–1776
Antigua	0	10
Barbados	0	4
Jamaica	0	14
Nevis	0	3
St. Kitts	0	6
West Indies (total)	0	37
Maryland	0	1
New York	0	1
North America (total)	0	2

Source: W. T. J. Gun, *The Harrow School Register, 1571–1800* (London, 1934).

by Sir Henry Cheere. Some of the finest silver plate at Merton College (Oxford) was contributed by West Indians.[52] Scottish universities were also popular, reflecting the number of colonists in the islands of Scottish descent.[53]

West Indians also went to the Inns of Court in London to study law and train for the bar (see Table 6). Their numbers increased during the course of the eighteenth century: ten West Indian students went to Gray's Inn between 1675 and 1745 compared to twenty-seven between 1740 and 1775.[54] Twenty-three percent of members of the assembly and 28 percent of the council of Antigua were admitted to the Inns of Court among members who sat between 1763 and 1783.

A high proportion of members of the assemblies and councils in the British West Indies spent some stage of their education in Britain. They far exceeded the numbers from the southern plantation colonies in North America where, in the decade *before* the Revolutionary War, only 13 percent of members of the assembly of South Carolina were educated in Britain. In contrast, well over half the members of the assembly of Antigua, 31 percent of members of the assembly of Barbados, and over one-quarter of the assemblies of Jamaica and St. Kitts received some of their education in Britain. These proportions are an underestimate because of the lack of attendance lists for dissenting academies, private tutors, grammar schools, trade schools, and apprenticeships. Furthermore, it was this British educated-elite who dominated the island assemblies as speakers of the house and party leaders.

There was no comparable tradition of West Indians being educated in

Figure 5. *Anthony Morris Storer*, Robert E. Pine, 1767 (Provost of Eton, Eton College, Windsor). A leaving portrait of Anthony Morris Storer of Jamaica, who later became a major benefactor of the Eton College Library. It was traditional in the eighteenth and early nineteenth centuries for the headmaster to request portraits from the wealthiest boys, usually within two years of their leaving Eton.

TABLE 5   Members of the Assemblies in the British Caribbean and Southern Mainland Colonies Admitted to Universities in Britain and Europe, 1763–1783

	Antigua	Barbados	St. Kitts	Jamaica	Maryland	South Carolina
Aberdeen	0	0	0	0	1	0
Cambridge	12	7	3	7	3	3
Dublin	1	0	1	0	0	1
Edinburgh	2	0	2	0	1	3
Glasgow	2	1	1	1	0	0
Leyden	1	0	2	2	0	1
Oxford	4	8	6	15	2	4
St. Andrews	0	0	0	0	0	0
Total	22	16	15	25	7	12
Assembly Members	91	110	130	170	378	539
Percentage	24	15	12	15	2	2

Sources: Roll of Alumni in Arts of the University and Kings College of Aberdeen, 1596–1860, ed. Peter John Anderson (Aberdeen, 1900); Alumni Cantabrigienses, ed. J. Venn, 5 vols. (Cambridge, 1922–54); A Catalogue of the Graduates in the Faculties of Arts, Divinity, and Law of the University of Edinburgh Since Its Foundation (Edinburgh, 1858); Edinburgh: Doctors of Medicine, 1705–1845 (Edinburgh, 1846); List of the Graduates in Medicine in the University of Edinburgh, 1705–1866 (Edinburgh, 1867); The Matriculation Albums of the University of Glasgow, 31 December 1727 to 31 December 1897, ed. W. Innes Addison (Glasgow, 1898); Alumni Dubliensis, ed. George Dames Burtchaell and Thomas Ulick Sadleir (Dublin, 1935); English-Speaking Students of Medicine at the University of Leyden, ed. R. W. Innes Smith (London, 1932); Alumni Oxoniensis, ed. Joseph Foster (Oxford, 1888; London, 2nd ed., 1891); The Matriculation Roll of the University of St. Andrews, 1747–1897, ed. James Maitland Anderson (Edinburgh, 1905); W. A. Fuertado, Official and Other Personages of Jamaica from 1655–1790 (Kingston, Jamaica, 1896); A Biographical Dictionary of the Maryland Legislature, 1635–1789, ed. Edward C. Paufuse, Alan F. Jordan, and Gregory A. Stiverson (Baltimore, 1985); Biographical Directory of the South Carolina House of Representatives, ed. N. Louise Bailey (Columbia, S.C., 1981).

North America, but this was not for lack of trying on the part of the mainland colleges. Dr. John Witherspoon, the president of the College of New Jersey, published *Address to the Inhabitants of Jamaica and the other West India Islands, In Behalf of the College of New Jersey* (1772), urging West Indians to consider the advantages of sending their children to North America instead of Britain. The proximity of the mainland colleges allowed parents to make regular visits while being sufficiently distant to remove the temptation for their children to run home. These newer colleges were more concerned about their reputation than were the complacent institutions in Britain. West Indian students in North America were not likely to be subject to the same temptations to be

TABLE 6   Members of the Assemblies of the British Caribbean and Southern Mainland Colonies Admitted to the Inns of Court in Britain, 1763–1783

	Antigua	Barbados	St. Kitts	Jamaica	Maryland	South Carolina
Gray's Inn	8	1	0	2	0	1
Inner Temple	2	0	6	2	4	4
Lincoln's Inn	3	3	1	8	0	2
Middle Temple	8	11	6	6	11	16
Total	21	15	13	18	15	23
Assembly Members	91	110	130	170	378	539
Percentage	23	14	10	11	4	4

Sources: The Register of Admissions of Gray's Inn 1521–1889, ed. Joseph Foster (London, 1889); Register of Admissions to the Honorable Society of Middle Temple, ed. Sir Henry F. MacGeah and H. A. C. Sturgess (London, 1949); Records of the Honourable Society of Lincoln's Inn (London, 1896); A Calendar of the Inner Temple Records, ed. R. A. Roberts (London, 1933); W. A. Fuertado, Official and Other Personages of Jamaica from 1655–1790 (Kingston, Jamaica, 1896); A Biographical Dictionary of the Maryland Legislature, 1635–1789, ed. Edward C. Paufuse, Alan F. Jordan and Gregory A. Stiverson (Baltimore, 1985); Biographical Directory of the South Carolina House of Representatives, ed. N. Louise Bailey (Columbia, S.C., 1981).

found in Britain. The tutors were chosen on merit, not ministerial recommendation or family interest, as they were in Britain. West Indians also stood to benefit from the interdenominational character of mainland colleges.[55]

Despite these advantages, few West Indians were educated in North America. The Nevis-born Alexander Hamilton was untypical, having been educated at King's College (Columbia) in New York. One study identifies only eighteen West Indian graduates of mainland colleges between 1650 and 1790: twelve at Harvard, three at William and Mary, two at the College of Philadelphia, and one at King's College (Columbia University).[56] Philip Fithian wrote of the "many students from the West Indies" at New Jersey, but the biographical dictionary of alumni contains only three graduates connected with the West Indies between 1748 and 1768.[57] West Indian students in North America were invariably connected with religious dissenters or merchants.

The preference of West Indians for a British education was explained in an anonymous sharp rebuttal to Witherspoon titled Candid Remarks on Dr. Witherspoon's Address to the Inhabitants of Jamaica, And the other West India Islands &c. In a Letter to those Gentlemen (1772). The reply asserted that West Indians were better served in Britain thanks to the abundance of private schools and academies, which were "renowned throughout Europe." West Indians were better-off at the superior British universities whose excellence had been cultivated "by the Experience of Ages." They were taught by "the ablest Teachers in every Branch" in comparison to North America, where there was a scarcity of competent individuals owing to "the small Profits attending the Occupation."[58] Such considerations swayed the West Indian elite in favor of a British education until well into the twentieth century.

A British education became a requirement of entry into the professions in the West Indies. In Jamaica, an English legal training was required by law for professional practice. The professions in the West Indies consequently contained a much higher proportion of British natives than the professions in North America. The Scots found better professional opportunities in the Caribbean than in the Chesapeake and became a major group within the professions of Jamaica, except in the law (owing to the differences between the Scottish and English legal systems).[59] The British-dominated professions were the surest avenues into the planter class.

Medical graduates were generally British-trained because there were no medical schools in the British West Indies, unlike North America. Doctors did not share the same levels of formal education as lawyers in an age when the benefits of established medicine were not fully established. Nevertheless, many West Indian practitioners held qualifications from the Royal College of Physicians, the Royal College of Surgeons, and Surgeons' Hall. Scottish doctors were the best trained and dominated the ranks of the medical profession.[60] Like lawyers and doctors, the clergy were generally educated and ordained in Britain; the vast majority were Anglicans.

Furthermore, the local merchants and agents were often educated in Britain and spent their early careers in the islands before returning to Britain. A British education was similarly a qualification for such plantation offices as estate clerks, bookkeepers, overseers, and managers. (Robert Burns was appointed a bookkeeper on a Jamaican plantation and was ready to leave Scotland when he received news of the success of his first volume of poetry.) White skilled artisans were often trained in Britain. Of some one hundred and fifty goldsmiths and silversmiths active in Jamaica, no more than two or three were locally trained before 1800.[61]

The tradition of a British education bound the white elite to the mother country to an extent unparalleled in the northern colonies. The effects were apparent to a young Scottish woman visiting the Leeward Islands in 1775: "They form their sentiments in Britain, their early connections commence there, and they leave it just when they are at the age to enjoy it most, and return to their friends and country, as banished exiles; nor can any future connection cure them of the longing they have to return to Britain." Edward Long similarly observed that West Indians, after returning from their education in Britain, regretted their "exile from the . . . delights of London, from the connections of early friendship and perhaps from the softer attachments of love." They were alienated from their native countries and embraced the first convenient opportunity of going back to the scenes of their youth in Britain.[62]

*　*　*

The influence of this predominantly British-educated elite was uncontested within white society in the Caribbean. The planter and merchant elite dominated positions as council members, assemblymen, militia officers, vestrymen, deputy patent officers, judges, and justices of the peace. The rise of a white yeoman class to challenge the planter elite was inhibited by the concentration of wealth among the leading planters, the displacement of small planters by large planters, the practice of primogeniture, the capital required to start a sugar plantation, the limited access to education, the displacement of white skilled artisans by blacks, and the need for racial solidarity against the predominantly black population. There were not as many small planters in the islands as there were in North America. George Washington observed of Barbados that there were "few who may be called middling people" since they were "either very rich or very poor" in comparison to Virginia,[63] even though Barbados had the largest proportion of small landowners among its white population in the British West Indies.

A small number of proprietors owned the majority of the wealth in the British West Indies. Less than 7 percent of landholders owned over 50 percent of the land, servants, and slaves in Barbados in 1680. Thirty of these estates accounted for almost 80 percent of the land and 60 percent of the slaves in 1729. An elite group of 467 planters in Jamaica owned plantations of over one thousand acres and owned nearly 78 percent of the patented land in 1754.[64] The largest plantations contained just over sixty slaves before 1700. A plantation optimally contained between one hundred and three hundred slaves by 1776.

Large planters displaced small planters and "swallowed up by degrees all the little settlements around." St. Kitts was divided among 360 sugar estates in 1724 but 110 in 1783. Nevis had about one hundred planters in 1700, sixty-one in the 1770s, and fewer than three dozen by 1800. The Antiguan plantation of Daniel Mackinnon was formerly inhabited by one hundred poor whites. Jamaican planters engrossed more land than they were able to use, which impeded economic growth and limited opportunities for small planters. The process mirrored contemporary trends in Britain: "This extrusion of poorer settlers from their small possessions of thirty to one hundred acres has operated like the demolition of many small farms in Britain, to build up one capital farm."[65]

The planters also consolidated their wealth by not dividing their estates. They imitated the English gentry in using elaborate legal devices like entails to preserve the integrity of an estate. They practiced primogeniture: few planters chose "to parcel out their plantation[s] among their children, as is done in the Northern colonies because their properties are not easily severable; and therefore are transmitted whole and undivided to one child, to preserve them in the family."[66] Sugar plantations of more than one hundred acres benefited from economies of scale, whereas small plantations were less financially viable. The planters preferred to bequeath annuities, charged to the profits of the plantation, to younger sons and daughters who consequently had little need to reside in the Caribbean. The heirs of plantations that were divided frequently sold their shares, owing to the problems of administration.[67] Such practices were often unnecessary since few planters were survived by more than one heir.

The mean size of sugar plantations was two hundred to three hundred acres in the Leeward Islands and six hundred acres in Jamaica in the 1770s. Edward Long calculated that the average sugar estate in Jamaica with two hundred slaves and six hundred acres cost £19,027 sterling in 1774. The cost was higher in Barbados and St. Kitts. Rev. James Ramsay estimated that the purchaser of a three-hundred-acre estate in St. Kitts required at least £30,000 sterling in the 1770s. This represented a threefold increase in the value of the same estate over a forty-year period. This rate of increase is confirmed by the estimates of modern scholars for Jamaica.[68] The cost of slaves, the largest capital outlay, increased by an equivalent amount between 1741 and 1775. Slaves represented two-fifths of the total capital investment in the average sugar plantation in Jamaica in 1774.[69]

White artisans were being displaced by free colored people and slaves as carpenters, masons, millwrights, coopers, tailors, cobblers, coppersmiths, shipwrights, mariners, midwives, sawyers, distillers, boilers, bricklayers, watchmen, bakers, boat pilots, boatmen, porters, town criers, seamstresses, hairdressers, and blacksmiths.[70] Whites who possessed some capital became small planters engaged in raising cotton, coffee, cattle, ground provisions, ginger, plantain, pimento, coconuts, and ginger. They might also purchase slaves to hire out as jobbers. The poor subsisted on fishing, hired work, and retailing. There were no manufacturing opportunities for poor whites except making cotton hammocks, stockings, and horse nets, and they had few opportunities to acquire land in Barbados and the Leeward Islands. Barbados "was pestered" by the largest number of "white beggars, of both sexes, and of all ages," who were "covered only with filthy rags" and who became known in the late eighteenth century as "redlegs."[71]

Despite the extreme dichotomy of wealth within white society, there was no parallel in the islands to the social class struggle in North America about "who ruled at home," which gave such momentum to the revolutionary cause. Racial divisions transcended class divisions. "Unnatural or unnecessary subordination and inequality among whites, that approaches them to the level of their slaves" was dangerous when every white had "such absolute Influence" over the discipline of the slaves.[72] White creole society appeared at least more egalitarian than white British society. The white elites needed the support of the poor whites not only as functionaries on the plantations but also to serve in the militia against slave rebellions and foreign conquest. The white elite protected the interests of poor whites by legislating to curtail the economic enterprise of free colored people and slaves. They passed a growing volume of laws to prevent anyone of color from engaging in huckstering, cotton planting, and various trades, which reinforced the discriminatory legal and social codes already in existence.[73] The free people of color represented less than 2 percent of the total population of the islands but their economic success was a threat to the system of racial stratification so integral to a society where slavery was pervasive.

The stability and prosperity of the islands, wrote the agent for Jamaica, depended "upon keeping up a distinction of colour" and the law was "calculated for the maintenance of that barrier."[74] The poor whites derived satisfaction from their relative status to the blacks, which caused "every white man" to think "himself a man of first consequence."[75] They did not "condescend to work in the [cane] Field[s] with their Inferiors."[76] The slaves, not the lower-class whites, posed the greatest threat of revolt in the Caribbean. The political dominance of the often British-educated planter elite was virtually unchallenged by white small planters and artisans.

*   *   *

White racial solidarity was reflected in the almost complete ascendancy of the Anglican Church throughout the British West Indies, which again reinforced the cultural ties with Britain. The religious origins of the early settlers were as diverse as those of North America and the islands had comparable traditions of religious tolerance with "a Climate where it is well known, [religious] Bigotry does not exist."[77] However, the Anglican Church enjoyed a virtual monopoly in the British Caribbean on the eve of the American Revolution.

Rev. William Johnson of Barbados contrasted "the Varieties of Sectaries in most parts of the Continent" of North America with the islands, "where the Doctrine of the Church of England alone is Maintained & propagated."[78] Presbyterians were numerous, owing the large number of Scots, but they had "not a place of public worship" anywhere in Jamaica, which caused many to "acquire a habit of neglecting religious exercises, and finally [to] lose all sense of religion." William Scot gave up preaching to the Scotch dissenters in St. Kitts, "being in danger of starving," and was ordained an Anglican clergyman in Nevis. There were very few Quakers left in Jamaica who "openly profess themselves" and only one Meeting of at most five members in Barbados.[79] Irish Catholics were a major presence in Montserrat but "many of them had recourse to the Anglican church for baptism, marriages, and burials," and over half the Irish planter families "moved quietly into an ambiguous Establishment Protestantism."[80] There were Jewish communities in Nevis, Barbados, and Jamaica. The thousand-strong Jewish community of Jamaica built synagogues in Spanish Town and Kingston, but they were excluded from voting or sitting in the elected assemblies.[81]

Moravian and Methodist missionaries began to arrive in the mid-eighteenth century and pioneered small-scale conversions among people of color but made little impact among the white population of the islands. Like the Anglican Church, they preached obedience and submission to authority. The Moravian missions began in Jamaica (1754) and spread to Antigua (1756), Barbados (1765), and St. Kitts (1774). Nathaniel Gilbert, a prominent planter who was converted by John Wesley on a visit to England, introduced Methodism into Antigua in 1760. He was disappointed before his death that "the word seems to make more impression on some Mulattoes and Negroes than it does on the white people."[82] This left the Anglican Church almost unchallenged among the white population in the British West Indies before 1776.

White religious solidarity was broken only in Grenada and Dominica, where "the illiberal cries of difference in religion was raised for, the first time, in a [British] West India island." Following their acquisition from France in 1763, these islands were divided between British Protestant settlers and an older population of French Catholics. The British Protestant settlers discriminated against the French Catholics because of their desire to acquire the lands of the French, their fear of being outnumbered in the event of a future war against France, and their traditional xenophobia about the French. English observers blamed the anti-Catholic bigotry of the Scottish governor of Grenada and the large number of Scottish immigrants. Grenada well illustrated the importance of white solidarity, as the resulting religious and ethnic divisions among the planter classes created opportunities for slave resistance, which culminated in the great Fédon rebellion in Grenada in 1796.[83]

The Anglican Church was otherwise supreme in all the older British settlements in the Caribbean. It complemented a slave-owning society with its emphasis on hierarchy, authority, and obedience. Its latitudinarian philosophy suited the antifanatical and more often irreligious attitudes of whites. Apart from the work of the Society for the Propagation of the Gospel in Barbados after 1710, the Anglican Church ministered almost exclusively to the whites and upheld the social order: "A Slave . . . once Christened," wrote Rev. William Smith of Nevis, "conceits that he ought to be upon a level with his Master, in all other respectes." When Rev. James Ramsay broke with tradition by publicly instructing slaves in St. Kitts, he soon roused opposition and found that "he stood, in opinion, a rebel convict against the interest and majesty of plantership."[84]

There was no Baptist revolt in the Caribbean before the American Revolution, and there were no religious revivals comparable to the Great Awakening, which is frequently cited as a causal factor in the American Revolution. The religious tradition in the islands was thus one which stressed authority and order in contrast to the antiauthoritarian tradition of dissent in New England. It also reinforced the ties with Britain.

*   *   *

The formation of a white creole identity was also inhibited by the continued threat of foreign conquest, which reinforced ties with Britain. The Peace of Paris (1763) removed the French threat in Canada but not in the Caribbean. The Windward and Leeward Islands were especially vulnerable. Dominica was situated between French Guadeloupe and Martinique. Nevis, Antigua, St. Kitts, and Montserrat were visible from Guadeloupe. Because there was a history of French invasions, this threat made the islands dependent on Britain for military support and, in an era when the identity of the mother country was often defined in opposition to the national character of the French, it encouraged the white island colonists to view themselves as British.[85]

The rearmament of neighboring European colonies after 1763 made the British West Indies additionally dependent on metropolitan protection. France and Spain awaited an opportunity to revenge their humiliating defeat in the last war when the triumphant British had captured Guadeloupe, Martinique, and Havana. Count Etienne François de Choiseul, the French foreign minister, planned to retaliate by giving priority to the defeat of the British in the Caribbean. There were European war scares during the Turk Island dispute in the Bahamas of 1764 and the Manila (Falkland Island) Crisis of 1766–70. The Caribbean was likely to be a major theater of another European war in which the Bourbon powers were allied (Pacte de Famille) against Britain. France and Spain began to strengthen their military presence throughout the Caribbean, reforming and expanding their navies, which were crucial for control of the Caribbean.[86] Louis XVI took a personal interest in the navy and visited the dockyards to encourage construction projects. Charles III initiated a comprehensive series of administrative, economic, and military reforms throughout the empire, including an ambitious plan for fortifications in Cuba and Puerto Rico under the supervision of Marshall Alexander O'Reilly. France and Spain enlarged their armies in the Caribbean: France sent out massive reinforcements; Spain created colonial militias to support professional metropolitan troops. There were no comparable preparations by the British in the Caribbean, where the colonists became increasingly alarmed by the prospects of another war and lobbied for reinforcements.

The geographical isolation of the islands also restricted the development of a pan-national consciousness throughout the British West Indies. Jamaica was one thousand miles from Barbados. Communication among the islands was obstructed by trade winds and contrary currents. It was said that there was less communication between Dominica and Nevis than between Nevis and England.[87] Travel between the islands was less frequent during the hurricane months between July and October. The average voyage from Jamaica to Barbados or the Leeward Islands was longer than a voyage from the latter to England. Samuel Martin in Antigua apologized for his infrequent correspondence with a friend in Barbados because the "opportunities sailing between your island and here but rarely offer."[88] The islands were also notoriously provincial in their attitudes toward one another, and this particularistic spirit was a major factor in their failure to form a political federation.

*   *   *

I shall not argue that the close associations with the mother country and the absence of a developed creole identity were sufficient to explain the loyalty of the white island colonists during the American Revolution. Even the inhabitants of the thirteen mainland colonies that rebelled "strove to be Britons," and some historians argue that "they attained their political independence without ever declaring their common character or distinctive identity."[89] The leading revolutionaries also possessed close ties with Britain, such as the two Old Etonian signers of the Declaration of Independence, Thomas Lynch of South Carolina and Thomas Nelson of Virginia. Furthermore, West Indian loyalties were compromised by overlapping ties with their thirteen sister colonies.

Nevertheless, the social and cultural bonds discussed in this chapter predisposed the white island colonists to align with Britain during the American Revolution. We shall see that these conditions were reinforced by the military and economic dependence of the islands on the mother country.

2

Black Majorities

BEFORE THE OUTBREAK OF the American Revolution, the North American patriots came to regard the presence of British troops as a conspiracy by the imperial government to overthrow colonial liberties. In contrast, the white colonists of the British West Indies encouraged the presence of the British army and, with the exception of Barbados, petitioned the home government for ever larger peacetime garrisons. They did not expect the army to defend them effectively against foreign attack (for which they depended on the navy). Instead, they looked to the army as a vital instrument of white control over the majority black slave population. Slavery made the white colonists militarily dependent on Britain and was a critical factor in ensuring the loyalty of whites during the American Revolution.

Whites in the British West Indies regularly spoke of slaves as the internal or intestinal enemy. They wrote as a group besieged. Negrophobia was even more pronounced in the islands than in the southern plantation colonies of North America. The writings of white West Indians like Edward Long, Philip Thicknesse, Samuel Estwick, and James Tobin depicted blacks as violent, primitive, untrustworthy, and troublesome.[1] The usually paternalistic language of eighteenth-century elites, which so elegantly disguised the dynamics of class and racial struggle, degenerated into the language of conflict and hatred when talking about blacks.

Whites wanted the British army in the Caribbean because of the rising proportion of blacks and the threat of slave revolts. This was not paranoia; their fears were derived from both direct experience of slave resistance and the knowledge that conditions in the islands increasingly favored a successful slave rebellion. The ratio of whites to slaves in the islands was more pronounced than anywhere else in British America. The white population was simply too small to effectively police the slaves: one thousand troops and five thousand militia policed some two hundred thousand slaves in Jamaica before 1776. The disproportion between whites and blacks was alone "sufficient to keep the Island [Jamaica] in continual apprehensions."[2]

Figure 6. *Negro Dance in the Island of Dominica dedicated to Brigadier General Charles O'Hara*, Agostino Brunias, reproduced in Bryan Edwards, *The History, Civil and Commercial, of the British Colonies in the West Indies*, 5 vols. (London, 1794–1800), 3: verso 279. Slavery made the British Caribbean militarily dependent on Britain. Whites were a besieged minority in a majority black population.

Slave revolts occurred more often in the British West Indies than in North America, not only because of the higher proportion of slaves, but also because of the larger average size of plantations and their slaveholdings. Sugar plantations typically consisted of between one hundred to two hundred slaves in comparison to the twenty or so slaves of the tobacco plantations in the Chesapeake. The management of the sugar plantations was consequently more impersonal and less paternalistic with only a few white employees. Furthermore, the large average size of the sugar plantations created a hierarchical social structure with an emerging black creole elite of drivers, boilers, coopers, and carpenters who took increasing initiative in conspiracies.

Slave revolts were also more common in the islands because of the prevalence of absenteeism among the planters. The estates of absentees were supervised by professional managers, overseers, and attorneys, among whom there was frequently a high turnover. In contrast, absenteeism was rare in North America. Managers and overseers were less common in the southern mainland colonies. The assembly of Jamaica petitioned the king against absenteeism because it claimed that most revolts occurred on the plantations of absentees.[3]

Slave rebellions in the British West Indies were also more frequent than in North America because of the high proportion of African-born slaves who exhibited a much greater tendency to rebel than creole slaves before the American Revolution. They were predominantly male and they often possessed military skills since the majority were captured in warfare. Africans were more numerous in the islands where the planters continued to rely on the slave trade because the creole slave population was not self-sustaining and mortality rates were high.[4] Twice as many Africans were imported into the British West Indies than into North America before 1776. Africans outnumbered creole slaves in Jamaica until as late as the 1760s. Coromantees dominated the leadership of the slave revolts in the British West Indies. They came from the Gold Coast of Africa where the Ashanti federation had a highly developed military regime. They were particularly numerous in Jamaica, where they provided the leadership of the maroons, Tacky's revolt of 1760, St. Mary's revolt of 1765, and the Hanover revolt of 1776. Coromantees were listed separately in the censuses of Tobago as a result of their role in a revolt of 1770. Their reputation was so formidable that Barbados passed a law against their importation.[5]

Opportunities for slave revolts were especially great in the Windward Islands. The mountainous and thickly wooded terrain of these islands abetted resistance. Whites also suspected collusion from the neighboring French in Martinique and Spanish in Trinidad. Labor conditions were oppressive in these rapidly developing but heavily indebted new colonies. White unity was more fragile because of the antipathy between the French residents and British

Figure 7. *West India Washerwoman*, Agostino Brunias (Barbados Museum and Historical Society). African traditions and culture were more pronounced among the black populations of the British Caribbean than among those of North America with the exception of South Carolina. These traditions also affected the white population.

settlers in Grenada and Dominica, and the assemblies were subject to political stalemates. The British military presence was small with only about one thousand troops to garrison Grenada, Dominica, St. Vincent, and Tobago. They were dependent for naval support on the distant Leeward Island squadron in Antigua.

*   *   *

Whites therefore encouraged the presence of the British army because of their fear of slave revolts; there were as many as seventy-five aborted and actual rebellions in the British West Indies before 1837. There was no comparable history of slave revolts in North America. Slave conspiracies and revolts were especially frequent during the "most troubled decade in Jamaica's long history as a slave society" — the 1760s. They occurred during what is often portrayed as a critical decade in the evolution of slave culture when creole slaves began to predominate in all the islands and when healing cults "sprang up to offer in rapid succession an array of syncretic religions — Myal, Convince, and bush Christianity." The rebellions coincided with a major slave uprising in the Dutch colony of Berbice, which involved thousands of slaves, lasted more than a year, and came close to creating an independent black state.[6] They were also concurrent with the development of the crisis of imperial government in North America.

There were three major rebellions in Jamaica in the first half of the 1760s. The decade began with Tacky's revolt, which "was more formidable than any hitherto known in the West Indies" and one of the largest slave rebellions in the history of the island. It ended in the deaths of four hundred blacks and ninety whites. The leaders took an oath to try again, which they did, in a plan for three parallel uprisings across seventeen plantations in 1765. The revolt broke out prematurely and the "New Negroes" from Africa found that "none of the old [creole] slaves joyn[ed] them."[7] The following year, thirty-one Coromantees rose and killed nineteen whites on an estate.

A similar trend of slave unrest occurred in the Leeward Islands and Barbados where there was otherwise no history of major slave rebellions in the eighteenth century. In 1768 "a dreadful Conspiracy in Montserrat" was discovered a few days before its commencement or, according to a more sensational account, "only three Hours before it was to have been put into Execution." The plot "was deep laid, and must have long been projected, as they had furnished themselves with great stores of arms and ammunition, which they had concealed in the mountains." The conspirators planned the rebellion when the predominantly Irish planter elite celebrated St. Patrick's Day. They aimed to "destroy all White Men," delegating those blacks in domestic service to disarm the whites and torch the buildings. Fires "were to be their signal one to another" for slaves elsewhere in the island "to erupt into [rebel] parties." The plot would "have been fatal to the white inhabitants" but for its prior detection. The white colonists were inconsolable until the arrival of a naval ship and a company of troops from Antigua. Nine of the ringleaders were hacked, quartered, hanged, burnt, broken on a wheel, or starved on gibbets, and thirty conspirators were imprisoned.[8]

In the wake of the Montserrat conspiracy, there were a series of incidents and alarms in the other Leeward Islands. In 1769 many blacks "in their nocturnal Perambulations" threatened the total destruction of St. Johns in Antigua. Nevis introduced additional security precautions. With the threat of a Spanish war in 1770, an insurrection scare gripped St. Kitts, where there was "a grand plan, laid by the Negroes . . . to cut off every white man on the island" led by a slave named Archy who was to be king. The conspirators held an assembly, which they called the Free-Masons meeting, and were overheard drinking toasts to the "Success to their war and liberty." The signal for revolt was "a piece of lead handed from the one Negroe to the other" and the rendezvous was at Monkey Hill. Following the removal of troops to St. Vincent in 1773, "the Insolence and Irregularities of the slaves" in Antigua became more "flagrant and enormous."[9]

About the time of the Montserrat plot, a black woman was executed in Barbados for attempting to poison a member of the legislature who was also a magistrate. Her funeral was attended "with unusual Pomp by numbers of Negroes meeted together for the purpose," which was interpreted by the white elite as an "open violation of the Laws, a daring arraignment of the justice of the sentence by which she was executed and a most outrageous insult to the person . . . whose life had been endangered." The incident resulted in an order to magistrates to bury the bodies of executed slaves far out to sea. In 1773 in Barbados, according to a curious story that circulated in the English press, "a set of desperate ruffians, to the number of ten or twelve . . . entered into the most diabolical association . . . to destroy every person they met with." They signed articles of agreement and called themselves True Blue. They wounded and killed several people before being apprehended.[10]

The Windward Islands were the scene of the fiercest slave resistance with four rebellions in Tobago in the early 1770s. Coromantees led a rebellion at the beginning of the decade in which they successfully attacked the British barracks at Courtland Point where they captured ammunition and killed two soldiers. The rebellion lasted over a week and, but for the early military successes of the whites, the assistance from the other islands "would have arrived too late, and this flourishing colony would have been now in a state of Ruin." Some of the rebels evaded capture by cutting "one another's throats, and died . . . in each other's arms."[11]

In 1771, several insurrections occurred in northeast Tobago, where at least forty rebel slaves were "lodged in good Hutts and plentifully supplied with provisions, cloaths and ammunition." In March 1774, a revolt broke out on two estates in Queen's Bay, Tobago. Some fifty insurgents killed four whites and captured arms. Shelburne and Titus, "the principal conspirators," escaped capture and continued to live in the vicinity.[12]

*   *   *

The presence of maroon communities in Jamaica and the Windward Islands heightened the security concerns of whites, who sought protection from metropolitan troops. Maroon communities, autonomous societies of runaway slaves, were most developed on islands with mountains and woods that offered refuge, such as Jamaica, Dominica, St. Vincent, and Grenada. Maroons, who fought lengthy wars against regular troops and negotiated treaties, lived in inaccessible, fortified towns. These independent societies existed in Jamaica from the time of English conquest in 1655. There were two major groups of strategically located maroons in eighteenth-century Jamaica: the leeward maroons in the northwest and the windward maroons in the northeast. The maroons mounted the greatest challenge to white authority in Jamaica in a series of wars that reached a climax in the 1730s.

Although the maroons of Jamaica were weakened by the peace treaties with Britain of 1739, the white population continued to fear them. The very existence of maroon communities was an affront to planter power and exposed the limitations of colonial authority. Maroon societies remained an inspiration to slaves by suggesting viable alternatives to the plantation regime. Their guerrilla tactics commanded both admiration and trepidation among the whites: Edward Long thought the exhibition of martial skills by the Trelawny maroons before the governor in 1764 "more justly deserves to be styled evolution than any that is practiced by regular troops."[13]

The 1739 peace treaties were unpopular with both whites and maroons. Stephen Fuller, the agent for Jamaica in Britain, claimed that in the aftermath of the treaties the maroons were "supposed to be friends yet it was feared They would always side with the strongest." Whites suspected that maroons were likely to ferment a slave rebellion or to join an external enemy in toppling the government. Their fears were encouraged by maroon complicity in a slave revolt of 1742 and the unenthusiastic support of the windward maroons for suppressing the rebellion of 1760. An eyewitness to the great rebellion of 1760, Bryan Edwards, thought the role of the maroons ambivalent and even duplicitous. By 1769 the legislature of Jamaica spent £2,000 annually pacifying the maroon communities in the form of salaries for white superintendents, rewards to maroons for capturing runaway slaves, and bribes to rent allegiance.[14]

However, relations remained tense. The encroachment of white settlements and the appearance of land surveyors in maroon territory upset relations with the maroons. The white superintendents, appointed to reconcile differences and to police their charges, were the subject of official protests from the maroons. In 1773, the assembly complained that the maroons "had grown very formidable" in several districts of Jamaica "to the great terror of his Majesty's subjects in those parts who had greatly suffered by frequent robberies, murders, and depredations" in which the maroons "plundered all around them," causing the abandonment of several plantations and dissuading prospective planters from cultivating "valuable tracts of land" to the detriment of the island's trade and settlement.[15]

A maroon presence similarly caused anxiety among the British settlers in the Windward Islands. The British were still in the process of colonizing Grenada, the Grenadines, Dominica, St. Vincent, and Tobago before the American Revolution. Following the formal acquisition of Grenada in 1763, a maroon population of six hundred to seven hundred escaped French slaves began guerrilla campaigns. They intimidated the planters, who only traveled in small, well-armed groups and left guards at their houses because "the terror was so universal, and the danger so great." The maroons successfully fought against the British until 1771. Similarly in Dominica, runaway slaves were forming embryonic maroon communities by 1772.[16]

The Caribs of St. Vincent also made up autonomous societies whose presence similarly caused whites to seek protection from metropolitan troops. Tradition held that the Caribs were the descendants of the indigenous peoples of the eastern Caribbean who had intermarried with blacks following the wreck of a slave ship off St. Vincent in the late seventeenth century. They numbered between two thousand and six thousand in 1763, occupying prime land suitable for sugar cultivation, which white speculators attempted to acquire by hook or by crook. Tensions climaxed in the Carib War of 1772–73. The Caribs made formidable opponents, "more serious, than . . . [the British had] at first Apprehended," and they forced a negotiated compromise similar to the terms of the maroon treaties of Jamaica in 1739. The *Boston Gazette* hailed the Caribs as exemplary "in the glorious cause of Liberty." The failure of

Figure 8. *A Carib Family*, Agostino Brunias, c. 1780 (Yale Center for British Art, Paul Mellon Collection). The Caribs of St. Vincent were autonomous societies like the maroons of Jamaica whose presence made the white colonists militarily dependent on imperial protection. The British fought an inconclusive war against them in 1772–73.

the British army to crush the Caribs alarmed whites, who feared that this might encourage slave rebellions throughout the British West Indies.[17]

* * *

Fear of slave revolts and the presence of autonomous maroon communities, more than fear of foreign attack, explains the willingness of the white colonists to seek the assistance of professional troops from Britain. One-quarter of all the British troops serving in America were stationed in the Caribbean. Of twenty regiments in British America after 1763, at least five garrisoned the islands: Jamaica had two, Antigua had one, and Grenada, St. Vincent, Dominica, and Tobago shared at least two. Together, these five regiments represented a total force of nearly 2,500 men. From a British perspective, they were strategically located in the major islands: Jamaica was the jewel of the British Caribbean, Antigua boasted a naval dockyard, and the Windward Islands were vulnerable by their proximity to the French.[18]

Until the 1730s, the island colonists had shown little more support for troops than had their mainland counterparts in North America. During the mid-seventeenth century, friction between troops and civilians in Jamaica reached a "dangerous" level: "Jamaicans were never certain whether regular troops were intended for defense or repression." Governor Daniel Parke of the Leeward Islands was gruesomely murdered by planters in Antigua in 1710—the only colonial governor in British America to suffer such a fate. The grievances against him included his attempt to force the white inhabitants of Antigua to quarter his regiment. The dispute climaxed when he resorted to bayonets to force the assembly to adjourn. Of the seventy British regulars involved in defending the governor, forty-four were wounded in a bloody exchange.[19]

But in the 1730s, in response to the maroon wars in Jamaica and the slave conspiracy in Antigua of 1736, the island colonies began to want more troops. The legislatures of Jamaica and Antigua started to pay annual additional subsistence allowances to the local regiments.[20] The subsidy to the army in Jamaica varied according to rank. Officers received twenty shillings a week (an additional 45 percent of regular salary) and private soldiers received five shillings per week (an additional 100 percent).[21] The subsidy was extended in 1756 to army families: officers received an additional ten shillings a week for their wives and five shillings a week for each child; private soldiers received two shillings and six pence for their wives and one shilling and three pence for each child. The subsidy was thereafter increased.[22] Officers in Jamaica could also supplement their income with perks like those granted to the commanders of forts who received a farm and servants. The subsidy in Antigua consisted of fifteen pence a day for a lieutenant (an additional 16 percent of regular salary), one shilling a day for an ensign, six pence a day for a sergeant, four pence a day for a corporal or drummer, and three pence a day for the common soldier (an additional 150 percent).[23] It did not extend to senior officers, possibly because they were expected to have a sufficient private income or simply because officers above the rank of captain usually left the island at the end of a war. These arrangements continued in Jamaica until the beginning of the nineteenth century.

These allowances were guaranteed by the islands as part of an informal understanding with the home government in return for the assurance of permanent peacetime garrisons, which increased in Jamaica to six companies and in Antigua to at least five companies in the 1730s. The garrison in Jamaica doubled when the Forty-Ninth Foot was assigned to the island in 1745 and doubled again to two regiments in 1758. Permanent peacetime garrisons were similarly established in the Windward Islands with one regiment in Grenada, one in St. Vincent, four companies in Tobago, and five companies in Dominica in 1768.[24]

Whereas the North American legislatures increasingly expected Britain to carry the cost of imperial defense and resented having to contribute financially, the island colonies were ever more willing to support imperial garrisons. The legislatures of Jamaica and Antigua not only paid additional subsistence to troops but also built and maintained barracks, fortifications, hospitals, guard rooms, arsenals, powder rooms, kitchens, stables, and separate quarters for officers. Almost every parish in Jamaica built and maintained barracks at great expense in accordance with a law following Tacky's revolt in 1760. The assembly financed barracks in Kingston and Port Royal after 1766. New barracks for the army were completed at Rat Island in Antigua in 1762.[25]

The legislatures of Antigua and Jamaica paid the cost of transporting the troops with their baggage around the island or moving them between forts. They also contributed toward the cost of purchasing firewood, coal, candles, water supplies, bedding, tools, chamber pots, brooms, mops, pails, lanterns, tin kettles, and candlesticks. They even provided boats for the soldiers in the forts. From 1759 on, Jamaica paid the cost of officers' lodgings. The island legislatures further rewarded the army with special grants and bounties. Soldiers in Jamaica were permitted to buy rum free of local duties and received one hundred acres of provision ground in the country barracks, equivalent of at least one to two acres for each soldier. Jamaica paid for the maintenance and recovery of any soldier wounded or maimed in public service.[26] The assembly of Antigua voted sea stores and wine in gratitude to the Thirty-Eighth Regiment on its voyage back to Britain in 1764 and again on the return journey of

Figure 9. *A View on the Island of Antigua: The English Barracks and St. John's Church from the Hospital*, Thomas Hearne, 1775–76 (Yale Center for British Art). West Indian planters encouraged the presence of metropolitan troops to police the majority slave population. Military barracks were among the most impressive architectural legacies, which are otherwise rare because of the transient quality of life among British settlers in the eighteenth-century Caribbean.

the Sixty-Eighth in 1772. Antigua even paid a pension for every soldier who completed ten years of service.[27]

Slaves, sometimes known as "King's Negroes," were also provided for the use of the regiments. Many of these King's Negroes in Jamaica were former runaways who, by an act of 1757, became available for the king's service if their masters failed to claim them within a specified time. Some were even branded on the cheek or shoulder with the king's arrow — the Broad Arrow — which normally appeared on ordnance and imperial government property. Slaves served companies of troops in particular forts. In Jamaica, thirty-nine worked at Fort Augusta in 1764 and seven at Rock Fort in 1766. These slaves lugged stores and provisions to the forts, mounted and dismounted the guns, manned the fortress boats, and cleaned the barracks and hospitals. The seven slaves in Rock Fort brought provisions from Kingston and fished for one company of troops. A captain of the Forty-Eighth Regiment in Dominica warned the

Figure 10. Ruins of eighteenth-century army barracks at Shirley Heights, Antigua (Author).

secretary of state for war in 1776 that without the slaves he lacked sufficient reserves for both guard duty and transporting supplies.[28] This testimony echoed that of countless British commanders that slaves helped both to relieve the exhaustion of troops and to preserve their health.

The cost of the regular army ranked second only to the expenditure on fortifications in Jamaica and Antigua. The additional subsistence allowances to troops were remarkable given that they were first annually voted in a decade of recession (1730s). Jamaica spent from £50,000 to £60,000 on inland barracks between 1760 and 1763, reaching £100,000 by 1774, sufficient for 2,572 troops (prices are in local currency unless indicated otherwise). Antigua spent £10,000 sterling on barracks. Their quality impressed Lord Adam Gordon, the visiting colonel of the Sixty-Sixth Foot in 1764, who contrasted them with their dismal counterparts in Jamaica. In Jamaica, by 1770, the annual cost of the additional subsistence alone amounted to £16,500, exclusive of the cost of the regimental hospitals, the lodgings for officers, the salaries of fort commanders, and so on. The cost of the army was estimated at £18,000 in 1773. The parish of St. Dorothy in Jamaica complained in 1767 that all the parish taxes hardly covered the cost of accommodating a company of troops. Supplying water for troops in Antigua cost a good deal on an island susceptible to drought. The financial sacrifice was particularly impressive there, where the inhabitants already paid the 4½ percent duty that had originally been voted to Charles II as a perpetual grant supposedly in lieu of the cost of defense and the salaries of civil administrators.[29]

The insatiable demand for troops increased in proportion to the rising number of slaves. The island assemblies remained seemingly undeterred by both the often poor quality of recruits and the possible constitutional threat posed by the existence of a standing army in their midst. Both Antigua and St. Kitts requested entire regiments in 1738 and again in 1746. Montserrat, after losing a company stationed on the island in the early 1740s, tried to negotiate an arrangement during the 1750s. Antigua actually suspended payment of the additional subsistence to the Thirty-Eighth Foot in 1741 in protest over the decline of the garrison below the promised four hundred men. The assembly requested an additional regiment or the expansion of the existing regiment in the mid-1750s, and in 1756 the garrison reached a peak of seven hundred men. The assembly of Jamaica complained that the island regiment had fallen below the full complement, and its request for a second regiment in 1758 was granted. Both Antigua and Jamaica protested when the size of regiments was reduced and troops were withdrawn in 1763, leaving about four hundred and fifty troops in Antigua and nine hundred in Jamaica. The demand for troops was so great that Richard Pares concluded that "the obligation to supplement the soldiers' pay was the only thing which prevented the sugar colonies from calling upon the Government for unlimited military support."[30]

Only Barbados did not request troops or offer the inducement of additional subsistence allowances for a peacetime garrison, and its legislature stubbornly refused any support for a garrison even during the most critical phases of the American Revolutionary and the French Revolutionary Wars. The local assembly argued that the additional subsistence paid in Jamaica was not a voluntary grant but an imposed burden. It also eschewed the presence of an army for the "licentiousness of manners" among the troops and the potential abuse by an arbitrary governor. The British army did not regularly garrison Barbados until after the American Revolution.[31]

A large white population, lower rates of absenteeism, and a proportionally smaller black population made Barbados exceptional in the British West Indies. Its ratio of four blacks for every white was the lowest in the

British island colonies. The planters deliberately avoided the purchase of Coromantees, who played such a key role in the rebellions in Jamaica. The white
establishment showed "but little of that corporal dread of blacks which seems
to pervade some of the islands." They felt secure enough to leave their weapons
exposed where "the Negroes, if they are disposed to revolt, may easily furnish
themselves with arms." As William Dickson commented after the American
Revolution, "no island in the West Indies has been so long exempted from
insurrections as Barbados, the white inhabitants of which do not appear to
harbour any considerable suspicions on that head."[32] It was not until the slave
revolt of 1816 that the Barbados planters were rudely awakened from their
complacency. The windward position of the island also provided natural defense against enemy attack; the island was never conquered after British settlement in 1627.

Barbados "had perhaps the most developed internal military system in the
English West Indies [which] allowed the white community to become overtly
complacent about the security and legitimacy of its rule." The island boasted an
effective militia that was well equipped and regularly exercised. Between 1697
and 1702, the assembly spent £36,000 to bring two thousand disbanded soldiers from Britain as militia tenants to be distributed among areas where slaves
were concentrated. The militia mustered once every two months in the early
1770s. George Washington was impressed by the militia, which he found "well
disciplin'd and appointed to their several station[s] so that upon an allarm
every Man is at his post in less than two Hours." Governor David Parry
thought the large size of the militia made a military establishment unnecessary.
Sir John Gay Alleyne, the veteran speaker of the assembly, concurred that the
militia "is fully equal to her internal defence if properly brought into the field,
and led to action."[33] Good roads enabled the militia to mobilize quickly.

Except in Barbados, the white island colonists distrusted the reliability of
civilian militias to protect them against slave revolts and preferred to depend
on British troops. The white population of the islands was not large enough to
support a militia capable of both defending an island and policing the slaves.
The planters feared that the use of the militia left women and children prey to
their slaves because all adult males were liable for militia duty. Furthermore,
the militia lacked standardized equipment. Among the poorer white inhabitants and some free blacks, many were unable to afford the proper clothing
and arms.

The militia laws were frequently written by legislatures suspicious of
executive power to obstruct local governors who otherwise enjoyed considerable authority during martial law. The penalties for noncompliance were often
so minor or so laxly enforced that few men attended musters. Governors gave

commissions to favorites and the issue of brevet ranks allowed many senior planters to absent themselves permanently. Planters resented the demands of parades, reviews, and exercises during crop time. Distances were so great in Jamaica that it took a day simply to muster the militia without even beginning the drill. Governor Archibald Campbell of Jamaica, a general in the British army, remarked to Lord Shelburne in 1782 that "no lasting support can reasonably be expected from the Militia of a sugar colony, but that it must derive its permanent and sure defence from Regulars alone."[34]

*   *   *

Fear of foreign attack was secondary to fear of slaves and maroons in explaining the willingness of the planters to support imperial troops. The white colonists regarded the army as only a token effort at external defense, a modest deterrent against sudden invasion, and a reassuring presence. The army could at best hold out for a brief time until relieved by the navy and was never expected to match the much larger bodies of troops stationed in the neighboring Spanish and French islands. As one contemporary protested in a London newspaper, "every military officer" knew that the British troops in the Caribbean were "totally inadequate" for the defense of the islands.[35] The same writer wished the islands at the bottom of the sea to stop the toll on the lives of some of the finest troops in the British army, and he called on the planters to patrol the slaves themselves.

Throughout the eighteenth century, the white island colonists consistently expressed misgivings about the probable effectiveness of small garrisons and amateurish forts against a determined enemy. Stephen Fuller stated bluntly that it would give him "great uneasiness to see Jamaica depending only upon an army for her protection." The colonists even questioned the value of resistance in the face of a major enemy landing. St. Kitts and Nevis were almost abandoned by English colonists in the seventeenth century in the aftermath of warfare. The island colonies of all European nations in the Caribbean frequently submitted within hours rather than allow their plantations and property to be destroyed. By the mid-eighteenth century at least, the colonists were confident of generous terms of surrender by an enemy, whether French, Spanish, or British. A French governor of St. Domingue observed that resistance risked the loss of everything while, even if it was successful, "nothing would really be preserved besides the King's troops and a show of possession."[36]

The white colonists regarded the navy, not the army, as "the only efficient protection" against a foreign enemy, as they stressed again and again in private correspondence, memorials, remonstrances, and petitions to Britain. It was a maxim of their defense policy that the navy was "the first & principal security of the islands in general." Christopher Codrington the elder, a leading planter in Barbados and the Leeward Islands, noted at the beginning of the century that "all turns upon the mastery of the sea. . . . If we have it our islands are safe, however thinly populated." Without naval superiority, the army was stranded and immobile. Only a strong navy enabled the planters to ship home their sugar produce and to import the food provisions on which the islands depended. British strategy aimed at maintaining a superior fleet in the Caribbean with only token numbers of troops. Only the successes of the French navy in the Caribbean during the American Revolutionary War finally "shattered the prevailing [British] dogma that naval superiority alone guaranteed British West India security."[37]

The island colonists exhibited little interest in the deployment of troops in a wider Caribbean defense strategy. Their legislatures actually threatened to withdraw funds when local governors proposed fitting out expeditions outside the island. Jamaicans threatened to stop additional subsistence in 1753 when troops were stationed at Rattan (an island in the Gulf of Honduras) and the Mosquito coast (the Atlantic coast of Nicaragua). The legislature of Antigua complained again in 1772 when six companies of the second battalion of the Sixtieth (Royal Americans) left to quell the Carib revolt in St. Vincent. The assembly of Jamaica consistently refused to pay additional subsistence allowances to troops sent out on foreign expeditions. Governor John Dalling of Jamaica lost his popularity and was driven from office after his much criticized deployment of local troops on the mainland of Central America in 1779–80.[38]

Whites instead relied on the army to maintain their hegemony over the predominantly black population. Edward Long ridiculed the naïveté of a governor who had the temerity to suggest "that his majesty's troops were sent hither to guard the coasts, not to protect the internal districts from Negroe insurgents." Long reasoned that the primary role of the troops was to provide internal security against the possibility of a slave rebellion: "The men of property in this island pay an ample contribution, in order that it may be protected, *not so much from French or Spaniards*, as against the machinations of the many thousand slaves, which, in proportion as the settlements advance further and further into the heart of the country, grow the more formidable from their multitude." Nathaniel Phillips, a planter in St. Thomas in the East in Jamaica, stated the importance of the army explicitly in a letter in 1776: "2000 soldiers distributed in different parts of the Island would always keep the Negroes in good order, and prevent their entering into such diabolical plots. But without this strength we are very insecure."[39] The white colonists wanted troops to be posted inland, to guard against a slave insurrection, not along the coast where they would be better positioned against sudden foreign attack.

The planters openly admitted that they needed troops for domestic order among their slaves more urgently than for defense against a foreign enemy. Their primary concern with internal order and control surfaced in the preamble to an additional subsistence act in Antigua of 1755: "The several conspiracys that have been formed against us by our slaves have taught us the necessity of guarding against the like dangerous designs for the future and seems to be no means which will probably discourage such attempts or more effectually disappoint them than keeping up a body of regular and well disciplined Troops in a condition to act upon the most immediate notice of danger." Another petition, received by the Privy Council from Jamaica in 1764, insisted on the need for two thousand troops, "a number they apprehended absolutely necessary and scarce sufficient to secure and Preserve the Peace and tranquility of the Island from the secret Machinations and open Insurrection of their Internal Enemys."[40]

In 1770, an address of the assembly of St. Kitts to the king requesting two hundred troops similarly spoke of the principal concern with internal order:

Apprehensions of danger even from an external Enemy are Alarming but they are considerably Encreased when we reflect upon the number of slaves, now employed and absolutely Necessary for the cultivation of our Lands and for the Manufactures of this country; this Number amount to Fifteen Thousand Men, This considerable disproportion between the white Inhabitants and the slaves, the turbulent and savage dispositions of the Negroes ever prone to Riots and Rebellions place the peace, security and lives of your Majesty's white subjects in a very precarious and Alarming situation.

The assembly of Jamaica addressed the king in equally stark terms in December 1773: "Your loyal subjects of Jamaica are constantly exposed to massacre and desolation from an internal Enemy . . . our humble request for and reliance on your Majesty's gracious protection is grounded not more on the dread of an Attack from a foreign Power than on our constant apprehension of the revolt of our slaves."[41]

Army regulars played a critical role in maintaining white control over the slaves. Troops were used to chase and capture runaway slaves, for which they received special bounties or "mile money." Small patrols of five men commanded by a corporal toured Antigua on Sundays when slaves were relieved of their plantation duties. Troops were frequently dispersed for policing duties throughout the interior of Jamaica, and companies of up to fifty men were quartered in the different parishes to "keep the negroes quiet in the neighborhood."[42]

Troops were customarily used as "residents" in the maroon towns. One of the two regiments in Jamaica was always posted inland throughout the parishes and along the coast in the seaports. A system had developed in the 1760s whereby the older of the two regiments served in the most vulnerable inland posts, and the most recent regiment was stationed in Kingston and Spanish Town. This was unsound military practice: a concentration of troops in Spanish Town or Kingston better served the needs of training and effective defense against an external enemy. The practice of distributing the troops throughout the island was also expensive, requiring the duplication of hospital facilities, barracks, and officers at each post. The Jamaican legislature even refused to allow the troops to train together during the Revolutionary War. It consistently obstructed attempts by Governor Dalling to withdraw troops from the country posts.[43]

The legislature was concerned more with the policing of slaves than external defense. In suppressing slave revolts, troops faced unconventional tactics, especially the guerrilla warfare of the maroons, and frequently sustained serious losses and even defeats by slaves. After a terrifying experience in Antigua in 1746, when a company of soldiers was surprised by slaves, the Twenty-Ninth Foot became the only regiment in the British army to allow its officers to wear swords in the mess, which they continued to do for another hundred years. In St. Mary's Parish in Jamaica in 1760, troops of the Seventy-Fourth and Forty-Ninth Regiments mobilized quickly to make forced marches against one of the largest slave revolts in Jamaican history. During the encounter, a detachment of the Seventy-Fourth was caught off guard when rebel slaves attacked: "The centinels were shot, and huts in which soldiers lodged were set on fire . . . the Light of the flames while it exposed the troops, served to conceal the rebels, who poured in a shower of musquetry from all quarters and many of the soldiers were slain." Nevertheless, Edward Long attributed the successful crushing of the St. Mary's slave revolt to the presence and alacrity of British regulars. Troops in Antigua could be quickly deployed throughout the Leeward Islands. A detachment of the local Sixty-Eighth Regiment was sent in 1768 to Montserrat, upon suspicion of a slave conspiracy, where they remained over six months "till the inhabitants shall be freed from their apprehensions."[44]

Troops from Boston, Antigua, and Britain were rushed to St. Vincent to serve in the war against the Caribs in 1772–73. More than eight regiments were eventually engaged. By May 1773, 72 men had been killed and 80 had been wounded in battle; another 110 had died from disease and 428 were sick. Troops were often unable to win decisive victories against maroons, forcing the imperial government to make peace terms in Jamaica in 1739, St. Vincent in 1773, and Dominica in 1794.

Troops were used against slaves in Tobago in three separate revolts of 1770, 1771, and 1774. Several soldiers of the Seventieth Foot, along with members of the local council, were killed in action in Tobago in 1770. Five soldiers guarding the barracks at Courtland Point lost two comrades and their ammunition in an exchange with slaves. During a second insurrection on the north side of the island in 1771, soldiers were ordered to wear green jackets and trousers rather than the traditional red because — with a logic that evaded the rest of the British army — the "Glaring colour of the soldiers cloathing greatly hurts the service." Troops faced some fifty rebel slaves armed with cutlasses and gunpowder in 1774. The local assembly lamented to George III that the idea of freedom seemed universal among the slaves.[45]

The Royal Navy also played an important secondary role in quelling slave revolts: "The appearance of a ship of war, and the report of her being here, to assist us when necessary . . . may have a good effect in overawing & intimidating such negroes, as may be disposed to join these desperate wretches already in arms." Two British fleets patrolled the Caribbean, the Leeward squadron, and the Jamaican squadron, stationed respectively at English Harbour in Antigua and Port Royal in Jamaica. The fleets carried their own marines and regularly conveyed troops for use in amphibious attacks. Warships were formidable: a single broadside from a three-gundeck naval ship launched a volley of shot greater than the artillery fire of an army during battle. Jamaican whites depended on the fleet as a weapon against the slaves, "it being notorious that a fleet of Men of Warr stationed here would at all times yield more Effectual support in the Suppression of internal commotions than can possibly be derived from the present or even a much greater number of regular Troops." Warships sailed against the Jamaica maroons in 1733, a slave conspiracy in Montserrat in 1768, the Jamaica maroons in 1774, a slave revolt in the Bay of Honduras in 1774, and the slave revolt in Jamaica in 1776.[46]

The planter contention that the army was essential to the security of the islands is supported by the frequent incidence of slave rebellions following troop reductions. Tacky's revolt of 1760, one of the largest and bloodiest of the century, broke out after the reduction of troops in Jamaica for service in Guadeloupe. A revolt in St. Mary's Parish in Jamaica in November and December 1765 occurred when there were only eighteen troops on guard duty instead of a full company of as many as fifty men. The slaves were well aware that the garrison was reduced. The outbreak of the Carib War began after the reduction of the Thirty-Second Regiment in St. Vincent by four companies (between one hundred and two hundred troops). The absence of troops and naval ships in the Bay of Honduras (Belize) "meant that the settlers had little ability to control the slaves," paving the way for slave revolts in 1768 and 1773.

When the garrison at Tobago was halved in size in 1768, the two remaining companies of the Seventieth Foot were incomplete when the slaves rebelled in 1770. Only eighteen men could be spared from the garrison to go to the assistance of a besieged plantation. When the army in Tobago was distracted with an invasion scare in 1780, rebel slaves became more audacious.[47]

Historian David Geggus has similarly found a significant correlation between troop reductions and slave revolts in both the British Caribbean and the non-English-speaking Caribbean after 1783. Edward Long attributed the lower frequency of revolts in the French West Indies to their larger garrisons. Slaves and maroons often possessed accurate military intelligence of troop reductions, which they used in the planning of their revolts. Indeed, the correlation between troop reductions and slave rebellions is evidence of the slaves' sophisticated network of information, investment in long-term planning, and shrewd "political analyses of the power structures."[48]

*   *   *

With the exception of Barbados, the support for the army among whites in the British Caribbean was in dramatic contrast to the attitude of the North Americans before 1776. Nevertheless, the island assemblies did not shrink from exercising constitutional restraints over the army. They nurtured a confident political elite fully conversant in the discourse and rhetoric of the political opposition in both Britain and in North America. They reassured themselves that the grants of additional subsistence to the army were voluntary and therefore constitutional. Edward Long argued that the annual grant constrained the governor as the Mutiny Act constrained the king after the revolutionary settlement of 1689. Nonpayment could be used in bargaining with the imperial government, which did occur in Jamaica in the 1760s. The grants of additional subsistence often contained "tacks" (additional clauses or other unrelated bills).[49]

During the 1760s, the assembly of Jamaica demanded greater financial accountability from the army. It requested regular returns to ensure accuracy in the number of troops for whom subsistence was claimed. It changed the system of payment to ensure that the private soldiers actually received their subsistence from the officers and required more elaborate proofs of work performed by surgeons in the military hospitals. It also showed sensitivity to abuses of military authority. The assembly reacted sternly when in 1769 Captain John McDonald of the Sixty-Sixth Foot employed two of his soldiers to execute a civil writ and take possession of a plantation. When in 1780 large numbers of troops vastly exceeded the capacity of the barracks, the assembly of Jamaica voted billeting unconstitutional.[50]

The island colonies could also take comfort in the fact that the troops were answerable in peacetime to the local civil governors rather than a remote commander in chief like General Gage in North America. Furthermore, as Governor Sir Ralph Payne of the Leeward Islands acknowledged in 1775, the number of troops was too small to oppress the inhabitants, even if the colonists had shared "that wicked and turbulent spirit . . . as too notoriously prevails upon the Continent," since any "active and contriving Man might in a very Few Days imprison the greatest Part, if not the whole of the Battalion, which his Majesty has design'd for the security of this Government."[51] Payne might have illustrated his point by referring to the bloody fate of his predecessor Daniel Parke in 1710.

Yet for all their concern about constitutional niceties, the white island colonists were willing to compromise their civil liberties to retain the presence of regular troops to an extent that was unthinkable in North America. The troops could potentially be used to enforce imperial policy on unwilling colonists. Troops enforced the prohibition of the Spanish bullion trade in Jamaica in 1764 and the Stamp Act in Antigua in 1765–66. The British government gradually made the granting of an additional subsistence by the island assemblies a condition of sending troops and it did not station peacetime garrisons on islands that did not pay additional subsistence allowances before 1783. Britain was able to use the threat of withdrawing troops to bring the island assemblies to heel, as it did in Jamaica in 1771 and 1782. The arrangement was in reality a form of indirect imperial taxation and the assembly of Barbados said as much in 1780. Indeed, the assembly of Jamaica admitted "that the Public faith of this country is stated, and bound to your Majesty" in maintaining the troops.[52]

The relationship between the island colonies and the army had no parallel in North America, not even among the southern plantation colonies. However, the mainland colonies were not totally opposed to the presence of the army before 1768.[53] In particular, South Carolina faced security problems comparable to those of the islands and was initially receptive to British regulars. It was the only black majority mainland colony and the scene of the largest slave revolt in British North America — the Stono rebellion of 1739 — and was also threatened by neighboring Indian tribes. Furthermore, the disaffection of the western settlers caused violent dissension within the colony and the formation of the Regulator movement in 1768. Yet even South Carolina became a leading opponent of the quartering of troops in 1757–58 and again in the late

1760s. Colonel Henry Bouquet left a scathing account of service in the colony, complaining that "the Lawyers, Justices of the Peace and in general the whole people are eternally against us." In contrast to the British Caribbean, South Carolina's support for the army gradually diminished and the assembly only reluctantly granted assistance to troops.[54]

*   *   *

In 1770, the year of the Boston Massacre, when the army became the chief symbol of tyranny in North America, the British West Indian assemblies requested more troops to police their slaves and to provide defense against foreign attack. The legislatures of St. Kitts, Nevis, Montserrat, and Tobago petitioned the king for troops to be stationed in their respective islands, promising to grant additional support for the maintenance of the soldiers. The garrison at Antigua had traditionally protected St. Kitts, Nevis, and Montserrat but these islands now wanted their own troops. St. Kitts wanted a garrison of two hundred men and Montserrat wanted one hundred men. Despite the reservations of the council, the assembly of Nevis agreed to match the additional subsistence granted to the regiment in Antigua.[55]

In 1771 the assemblies of Dominica, Grenada, and again Tobago sent petitions to England requesting additional troops: the address from Grenada sought a permanent regiment and a detachment of the Royal Regiment of Artillery. In the same year the assembly committee for fortifications in Jamaica recommended doubling the size of the two regiments. In 1773 the Jamaica legislature made a combined application to the king for more troops and at the same time actually extended the additional subsistence allowance to cover widows of officers and men. A renewed application for troops was made in April 1774 in an address from Tobago to the king.[56]

The "conspiracy theory" — given such emphasis in the immediate causes of the American Revolution by the republican synthesis school of Bernard Bailyn, John Pocock, Pauline Maier, and Gordon Wood — was unlikely to be meaningful to the white colonists of the British West Indies who were exempted from some of the most offensive imperial policies and to whom the army was not a symbol of tyranny.

Slavery determined the relationship between the army and the white island colonists. The demand for troops on each island roughly corresponded to the relative proportion of slaves. The frequency of slave revolts clearly influenced Jamaica, but they do not explain the response of Antigua and the rest of the Leeward Islands, which had no corresponding history of rebellion. It was the high proportion of slaves in all the island colonies that created a white garrison mentality whose intensity reflected local racial demographic patterns. Even Barbados, which had the lowest proportion of slaves in the island colonies, gladly received troops as long as their expenses were met by the mother country. Slavery thus reinforced metropolitan ties and made whites a besieged minority dependent on Britain for their ascendancy.

3

The Sugar Islands

SUGAR, WITH ITS RELATED BY-PRODUCTS rum and molasses, was the primary crop of the British West Indies, where it dominated the economy more than tobacco did in the Chesapeake: "The islands, to a much larger degree than any of the mainland regions, remained highly specialized plantation colonies." The cultivation of sugar was ideally suited to the tropical climate of the Caribbean, and its distribution was facilitated by the island locations' cheap access to the sea and protection from the navy. Sugar production tripled between 1700 and 1760, and the islands accounted for 38.6 percent of all sugar production in the New World in 1766–70. There were some eighteen hundred sugar plantations in the British West Indies on the eve of the American Revolution.[1]

The emergence of sugar plantations shaped the social conditions (discussed in Chapters 1 and 2) that made the planter elite dependent on Britain. The labor-intensive requirements of sugar were the primary cause of the growth of a majority black population and "one of the harshest systems of servitude in western history."[2] The high capital entry costs of sugar plantations accounted for the concentration of land. Sugar fortunes enabled an increasing proportion of planters to become absentees in Britain and to send their children to be educated in Britain.

Sugar also made the planters economically dependent on Britain. For much of the eighteenth century, British sugar planters were unable to compete with the price of sugar offered by rival French producers. The inability of the islands to compete openly with the French was a cause of friction with North America, where northern merchants preferred to buy from the French West Indies. Only the monopoly of the British market allowed British sugar planters to flourish. Hence, while the mainland colonies were outgrowing the imperial economy, the island colonies were increasingly dependent on the discriminatory duties that guaranteed their monopoly of the home market. In the event of an imperial rift, economic self-interest dictated loyalty to Britain.

*   *   *

Sugar dominated the export-orientated plantation economies of the British West Indies, far exceeding the production of all other staples as the main export of the islands. Historian Richard Sheridan estimates that sugar, rum, and molasses represented 93 percent of the total exports of Barbados, 99 percent for Antigua, 92 percent for St. Kitts, and 89 percent for Jamaica in 1770. Yu Wu similarly finds that sugar and its by-products accounted for 85.88 to 90.17 percent of the total value of exports in Jamaica in 1769. Philip Coelho gives the lowest estimate, but he still finds that sugar represented three-quarters of the total value of exports of the British West Indies.[3]

The sugar monoculture reached its supreme expression in Barbados and the Leeward Islands, where "everything was sacrificed to the sugar cane . . . [as] a trifle to the principal object." The Rev. James Ramsay of St. Kitts left one of the most vivid descriptions of how gardens and slave plots were "grubbed up" for the reception of the master's sugar cane. Eighty percent of the land in Barbados in 1767 was devoted to sugar cane, the "principal object of the planters." Nevertheless, the sugar monoculture was never absolute. The islands also grew coffee, cotton, cacao, flax (for linen), cassava, bananas, figs, ginger, corn, pimento, aloes, limes, and tamarinds. They raised dye plants, including logwood (brown), fustic (yellow), brazilwood (red), and indigo (blue), as well as provisions for food.[4]

Jamaica and the Windward Islands had more diversified economies than those of Barbados and the Leeward Islands. They were more mountainous, with greater soil variations and differences in altitude, which made large areas of land unsuitable for sugar cultivation. Jamaica was so large that coastal access for inland areas was difficult. Grenada and Dominica had also inherited a more diversified agricultural system from the French. However, sugar and rum dominated the economies of even the most diversified islands on the eve of the American Revolutionary War.

A detailed study of the Jamaican economy asserts that "beginning in 1744 and continuing to 1769, the total proportion of all minor exports" in relation to sugar "was expanding," but the author treats rum as separate from sugar cultivation when it was derived from sugar cane. In reality, the reverse was true and the same study finds that "not counting the influence of the rise of rum in the trade, the proportion of minor staples" fell in relation to total exports by

10.45 percent between 1688 and 1769. Jamaican exports of cotton, indigo, cocoa, fustic, and lignum vitae fell before 1769.[5] Coffee did not become a major secondary crop in Jamaica until after the 1790s. Livestock pens in Jamaica rivaled sugar plantations in acreage, but the sugar plantations were the "means of increasing the penns, by enlarging the demand for pasturage and stock." Minor staples accounted for only 10.9 to 14.12 percent of Jamaican exports in 1769. They "constituted a small part of the Jamaica export trade in terms of quantity and proportion."[6]

Following the British occupation, sugar cultivation expanded rapidly in the Windward Islands, especially in Grenada, on the eve of the American Revolution. Over the years 1763–73 the value of the islands' exports to Britain increased from £62,915 to £859,981 sterling. Their exports rose as a percentage of the total trade of the British Caribbean from 3.1 percent in 1763 to 32.3 percent in 1773. Grenada became the second most valuable colony in the British Caribbean. Tobago was transformed from woods by the enterprise of "younger sons of Gentlemen of good families in Scotland" to become a producer of sugar, indigo, and cotton.[7]

The sugar planters enjoyed what economic historians have variously described as a silver age or an era of prosperity in the decade before the American Revolution.[8] West Indian planters benefited from both increased levels of production and the rise of wholesale sugar prices, which returned to the boom levels of the beginning of the century. The rates of exchange improved dramatically in favor of the islands and peaked in 1775. Jamaican exports to Britain more than doubled between 1750 and 1775 — rum exports rose from 1,851,481 gallons annually between 1763 and 1767 to 2,169,482 between 1771 and 1775, and sugar exports increased from 1,359,621 hundredweight annually during 1763–67 to 1,746,990 during 1771–75. The total value of exports from the British West Indies to Britain increased from £1,994,654 in 1763 to £2,666,052 sterling in 1773.[9] Sugar exports to Britain reached new heights on the eve of the American Revolutionary War but at the cost of making the planter elite more economically dependent on Britain.[10]

*   *   *

For much of the eighteenth century, the British West Indies were unable to compete with the price of rival French sugar and were therefore dependent on the protected market in Britain. The competition developed slowly, due to late French entry into sugar cultivation during the seventeenth century. After the 1720s, St. Domingue began to develop at a faster pace than Jamaica and produced more sugar than all the British islands combined at the beginning of the American Revolutionary War.[11] Although the price differential varied, British sugar prices were between one-third and one-quarter higher than those of the French.[12] The comparison was well known to contemporaries. In 1733 Rev. Robert Robertson of Nevis estimated a 30 percent disparity in prices. In the 1750s, Malachy Postlethwayt found British prices between 30 and 40 percent higher than those of the French. In 1766, a Jamaican planter told the House of Commons that British sugar was double the price of French sugar. In 1784, Lord Sheffield calculated that British consumers paid between 15 and 30 percent more for their sugar than other Europeans.[13]

The French West Indies enjoyed the advantage of large areas of virgin soil suitable for sugar. The economies of the French islands were more diversified, as well as more self-sufficient and less dependent on imported food. Small planters abounded in the French islands (in contrast to the British) and were often resident on their estates, which were more efficiently operated than absentee estates under wasteful management practices in the British Caribbean. Historian Lowell Ragatz has even argued that absentee management was the "fundamental cause" of the inability of British planters to compete with the French.[14] It is true that Britain charged higher duties on sugar than did France, but this does not explain the difference in cost because it was still profitable for the French to disguise their sugar as British and to pay duties in Britain.

Indeed, so great was the disparity in prices that an illicit inter-island trade developed in which French sugar was imported into Britain. In the seventeenth century, British sugar was cheaper than French and the illegal trade flowed from the English Caribbean to the neighboring European islands. The direction of this trade reversed during the eighteenth century — French sugars were smuggled into the British West Indies and reexported to Britain, accounting for 30 percent of French West Indian sugar sales. Dominica became a major avenue of this trade owing to its free port status in 1766. The trade was unpopular with the British planters, who legislated against it; one of the few examples of cooperation between the British islands was when the legislatures of Barbados and Antigua agreed to underwrite the cost of legal suits against anyone involved in the smuggling of French sugar. Jamaica tried to make it punishable by death, but the law was disallowed by the Privy Council in 1756. A law in Antigua in 1764 branded anyone engaged in smuggling foreign products an enemy to his country and unworthy of membership in a civil society.[15]

The failure of the British islands to compete with the French was apparent in their inability to succeed in the European market. In 1733 and 1739, British planters won important concessions from the Trade and Navigation Acts to export directly to Europe. The privilege, however, did not bring significant custom. Britain also granted drawbacks (partial reimbursements of duty) on sugar reexported abroad. Whereas reexports accounts for as much as one-half to two-thirds of sugar exports to Britain before 1700, they fell to a little over 4 percent after 1730. Furthermore, most of these reexports went to Ireland rather than Europe after the 1730s.[16] In contrast, France reexported about 70 percent of sugar imports: "The *raison d'etre* of the French sugar business was the re-export trade, as the small amounts of sugar consumed in France could scarcely justify such a large enterprise."[17] The French captured the market of continental Europe.

The British West Indies produced sugar at uncompetitive prices and therefore relied on the monopoly of the home market. Philip Coelho notes that "the only reason for selling exclusively in one market in a competitive world would be if the price received in Britain were higher than elsewhere." Coelho has deducted the cost of import duties to calculate the comparative price of sugar in the British and European markets based on prices in London and Amsterdam. His figures are based on the wholesale price of sugar in London and the price of muscovado sugar in Amsterdam. His findings confirm the higher cost of British sugar even with the deduction of the import duties. He estimates that sugar in London, less duties, cost at the very least 15 percent more than sugar in Amsterdam and more probably around 23 percent higher over a five-year period shortly before the commencement of the American Revolutionary War. It is consequently argued by some historians that the islands were a burden to the British economy and "if the West Indian colonies had been given away, British national income would have increased."[18]

*   *   *

The inability of the British West Indies to compete with the French not only made the islands economically dependent on Britain but it was also a cause of friction with North America. The British planters and merchants in the Caribbean were frustrated that North Americans purchased cheaper and more plentiful molasses in the French West Indies.

Prominent New England merchants were engaged in this illicit trade with the French West Indies, including Peter Faneuil, the patron of Faneuil Hall in Boston, and the Brown family of Rhode Island. New England was the best market for French planters owing to a prohibition against the import of molasses into France, which aimed to protect domestic brandy. Less than one-sixteenth of the molasses consumed in North America was imported from the British West Indies. Rum made from French molasses in North American distilleries was 25 to 50 percent cheaper than rum imported from the British

Caribbean, which the Rhode Island merchants thought "an advantage worth contending for." The trade with the French West Indies was vital to the economy of New England and even to the mainland colonies in general. John McCusker, in his comprehensive study of the rum trade, contends "that the export of rum contributed significantly toward righting the balance of payments of the Continental Colonies."[19]

Planters in the British West Indies resented the trade between North Americans and the French Caribbean. Early in the century, Rev. Robert Robertson of Nevis voiced a popular sentiment when he blamed the trade of mainland colonists with the French Caribbean for the "near approaching ruin of our sugar colonies . . . and the no less signal rise of the French." The planter lobby sought imperial intervention to destroy the trade and to give British planters a monopoly of the North American market similar to their monopoly of the British market. As early as 1704, concern that French molasses was displacing British West Indies molasses caused the British government to grant protected status, as an enumerated commodity, to molasses. If they had succeeded in suppressing the French molasses trade, they would also have destroyed the New England rum industry, which Gilman Ostrander argued was their real aim, "however much the sugar planters . . . insist[ed] that it was merely an effort to protect British molasses from foreign competition."[20] The illicit trade continued.

The British West Indies lobbied hard for the Molasses Act of 1733, to the fury of North Americans.[21] The act imposed prohibitive import duties in North America of five shillings per hundredweight on foreign sugar and nine pence per gallon on rum. However, since the mainland merchants imported little French rum or sugar, it was the six pence per gallon on foreign molasses that really rankled. The passage of the law provoked a storm of recriminatory pamphlets from the North Americans. They denied the capacity of the British West Indies to satisfy the demand for molasses in New England, claiming that the trade was necessary to enable them to defray their balance of payments with Britain. The dispute anticipated future struggles between the two interests.

The Molasses Act was a paper victory for the British Caribbean because it was not rigorously enforced and the illicit trade continued between the French and North Americans. The trade was difficult to conceal owing to the size of the hundred-gallon wooden hogsheads and also to the cheapness of molasses. Customs officials in North America evaded obeying the letter of the act by a process known as "compounding" or "composition." Officers possessed the right to settle with smugglers out of court when the value of seized goods was low. One option was to "compound," in which the owner of the seized goods paid one-third of their value, together with all duties and costs, and swore not to engage in future illegal trade. This required permission from the British Treasury whose "out-letters to customs commissioners show that hundreds of permits to compound were issued every year."[22] It was more common for officials to choose "composition," in which they simply agreed with local merchants on a nominal charge of about a penny per gallon on molasses. In addition, officers sometimes ignored the trade laws or accepted bribes.

The British West Indies continued to campaign against the French trade with North America after the passing of the Molasses Act in several ways. First, they argued that the illegal trade deprived them of a market and drained them of currency because the mainland colonists refused to accept rum and sugar in payment for provisions. Second, they passed their own laws to reinforce the Molasses Act, empowering commissioned vessels to seize ships engaged in the trade during wartime. Third, they petitioned England, which provoked the mainland colonists to accuse them of engaging in an imperial civil war. Fourth, they sent representatives to give evidence to various committees of inquiry conducted by the Board of Trade in 1750 and the Commissioners of Customs in 1759–63.[23]

Relations between the British West Indies and North America soured as French competition intensified during the 1760s. In 1763, the governor-general and the intendant of Guadeloupe allowed specific foreign imports, including lumber, provisions, and horses from North America. It was said that the French port at Môle Saint Nicolas in St. Domingue inveigled the whole North American trade, "which supplies them with lumber, and Provisions at a low Rate; and drains us of casks, and at the same time supplies North America with Sugar, Molasses, Rum, to the great distress of our West India Islands." The seizure of North American ships by the British navy in the West Indies gave "great satisfaction, as it may be the means for the future of inducing the Americans to Trade with Jamaica instead of Hispaniola." West Indians made "loud complaints . . . of the Injury they [the North Americans] do to the Mother Country and the sugar colonies in general by the notorious and clandestine Trade they are continually carrying on with the French Islands."[24]

West Indian and North American interests continued to clash when Britain began in earnest to enforce the Molasses Act during the closing years of the Seven Years' War (1754–63). The North American trade with the French West Indies had continued during the war with France. Insurance rates on shipping with the French Caribbean were openly quoted in North America. In 1759 the Board of the Commissioners of Customs reviewed the service in North America and prepared a report for the Board of Trade. In 1760 William Pitt the Elder launched an inquiry into the French trade and issued a circular letter to colonial governors to carry out the commissioners' instructions against the trade.

Customs officers in North America began to enforce the letter of the Molasses Act. The navy prosecuted seizures in West Indian vice-admiralty courts, especially in Jamaica where condemnations were easy. British and British West Indian privateers were even more effective than colonial officials in capturing North American ships trading with the French Caribbean.[25] In July 1763, the Treasury ordered absentee customs officers to return within a month to their posts in North America and it proceeded to dismiss officers for noncompliance. It threatened prosecution of officers practicing "compounding" and "composition" and offered rewards to informants who exposed disobedient officers. "The publication of orders for strict execution of the Molasses Act," wrote Governor Bernard of Massachusetts to a Treasury official, "has caused a greater alarm in this Country than the taking of Fort William Henry did in 1757."[26]

The colonial customs service was reorganized and its size increased. New instructions were sent to royal governors to be more active in enforcing the duties. The Royal Naval Squadron in North America was given a larger peacetime fleet and made responsible for enforcing trade legislation including the Molasses Act. The navy treated their orders "as declarations of commercial martial law, with themselves replacing, rather than aiding, the regular enforcement agencies."[27] North Americans associated these changes with the lobbying activity of West Indians.

*   *   *

The acrimony between the island and mainland colonists erupted over the Sugar Act of 1764, which revised the Molasses Act. This was the first overt imperial tax raised by Parliament in British America and it yielded the largest revenue of any imperial tax before the Revolutionary War. The act decreased the earlier duty on foreign molasses imported into North America from six pence per gallon to three pence, prohibited the importation of rum, and increased the tax on sugar imports from five shillings to one pound seven shillings per hundredweight. The government wanted to lower the duty on molasses to two pence per gallon but the West India lobby opposed the lower figure.[28] The act also introduced elaborate enforcement regulations and new trial procedures in the vice-admiralty courts. The Sugar Act was much more successfully enforced than the Molasses Act. The continental colonists believed that the sugar planters of the British West Indies were the main beneficiaries of the Sugar Act and they were convinced of their complicity in its passage.

North Americans saw themselves sacrificed "to a few West-India planters." In the "Statement of the Trade and Fisheries of Massachusetts" (1764), the merchants of Boston held West Indians responsible for the Sugar (Revenue) Act who "with no other view than to enrich themselves, by obliging the northern Colonies to take their whole supply from them; and they still endeavor the continuance of it under a pretence, that they can supply Great Britain and all her Colonies with West India goods, which is perfectly chimerical." A Rhode Island newspaper lamented that a great empire had been delivered to "a few dirty specks, the sugar islands: the Continent must henceforth move in the wake of the sugar planters of the British Empire." In his "Novanglus" column, John Adams wrote that there was not a man on the continent who did not believe that the northern colonies had been sacrificed to the superior interest of the West Indies in Parliament.[29]

It is erroneous for historians to argue that the Sugar Act was purely a tax, unrelated to the regulation of trade, on the grounds that a duty "can not be extractive and prohibitive at the same time" and that "the West Indian islands and the northern colonies were not in competition."[30] The act intended to raise a tax but it was, in the celebrated pronouncement of Edmund Burke, "a revenue not substantiated in place of, but superadded to a monopoly, which monopoly was enforced at the same time with additional strictness, and the execution put into military hands."[31]

The Sugar Act was not equally disastrous for the economy of the British West Indies, but it did impose some inconveniences.[32] The role of the West India lobby in the passage of the act was likely much exaggerated by the North Americans. The new customs procedures were cumbersome and bureaucratic for both North Americans and West Indians. The use of vice-admiralty courts to enforce the new regulations deprived all colonists of their right to trial by jury, to the benefits of common law, to open trials, to public statements by witnesses, and to cross-examination. The dilatory, vexatious, and highly expensive proceedings in the vice-admiralty courts deterred claims, forcing the aggrieved party to settle out of court. Furthermore, the Sugar Act disappointed West Indians who were rebuffed by the low duty on molasses, which enabled the trade to continue between North America and the French West Indies. The British planters were still unable to compete with the French, who simply absorbed the loss of the new duty and reduced the cost of their molasses.

Overall, however, the British West Indies benefited from the Sugar Act at the expense of North America. It was not until after the American War that they began to campaign for its repeal. The elaborate customs procedure of cockets and bonds established by the acts hurt the islands but they were not effectively enforced. French competition in molasses permitted by the acts was not ruinous because the British planters already converted most of their molasses into rum and their molasses exports were never very large. West Indians were delighted with the prohibition against foreign rum imports and the regulations enforcing it. Their largest export to the mainland colonies was rum and the act gave them a monopoly over the trade.[33]

The Sugar Act was a major obstacle to an alliance between the West India lobby and the North American lobby at the time of the Stamp Act. In a very revealing letter of December 1765, Stephen Fuller explained that "the Sugar Colonies however disposed to cooperate with [the North Americans] . . . in a repeal of the [Stamp Act] . . . are & will be very tenacious in the former [Sugar] Act. . . . This has hitherto hindered a conjuncture, and will in my opinion *prevent any future Conjunction between the Continental Proprietors to the Island Proprietors residing in England.*"[34]

In 1766 West Indians and North Americans clashed over the revision of the Sugar Act and the introduction of the Free Port Act. The Rockingham administration encouraged the two lobbies to find a compromise over the duties on North American imports from the French West Indies. The two sides initially cooperated and struck a deal in which the West Indians grudgingly conceded the North American request for a reduction of the earlier duty on foreign molasses from three pence to one penny. However, when the West Indians discovered that the North Americans, together with the sugar refiners and shipping interests, were lobbying for free ports in the Windward Islands, the agreement dissolved. William Beckford led West Indian opposition in London both to the reduction in the duty on molasses and to the free port scheme, which he argued benefited their competitors abroad and endangered their monopoly of the British market. His campaign diverted the energies of the North American lobbyists and forced them to abandon their own activism against the Currency Act of 1764. The defection of William Pitt and the hostility of the government left Beckford in an untenable position. Stephen and Rose Fuller tried to salvage the cause of the islands by negotiating a compromise with the North Americans, which led to a revised Sugar Act and a Free Port Act in 1766.[35]

The revised Sugar Act of 1766 deprived the British West Indies of the chance for a preferential molasses market in North America and imposed the same import duty of one penny on the molasses of both the British and French West Indies. However, the British West Indies also made "substantial gains." They were relieved from paying any duty on their sugar exports to North America, which enabled them to be more competitive, and the classification of all North American sugar exports to Britain as foreign reduced the possibility of cheaper French sugar being smuggled via Dominica and North America into Britain. The islands also won an extension in the rum excise charges in Britain from six months to a year after landing, which allowed merchants and planters additional time to wait for the optimum market prices before selling. The Free Port Act created two free ports in Dominica and three in Jamaica. The Jamaican free ports were more popular among the planters as a means to revive trade with Spanish America. Merchants in the other British islands resented their exclusion from the free port system while planters in general opposed free ports in Dominica. Merchants in Barbados and Antigua sought free ports of their own. Richard Sheridan concludes that the two acts "represented a substantial, although partial victory" for the West Indies but it was a victory dearly won.[36]

West Indians continued to blame North American trade with the French West Indies for the shortage of currency and for the glut in the coffee market. They found it especially galling that North American merchants and ship captains spent the cash earnings from the British Caribbean in the rival French and Dutch islands "to purchase of them the very same commodities which Jamaica produces." The issue vexed Edward Long, who proposed that the islands find an alternative source of supplies, preferably Britain or Ireland. Jamaicans grumbled about underweight coin from North America, especially those minted in Rhode Island. The coins were forged Spanish doubloons which, although minted in the correct alloy, were underweight. Unofficial meetings occurred throughout the island to discuss the problem. In 1770, following a complaint from the principal merchants and planters, the assembly of Jamaica made the importation of base and light coin a felony. The merchants of Jamaica placed adverts in newspapers in Boston and New York threatening retaliation against anyone caught forging coin. Coffee growers in the British Caribbean similarly resented the North American trade with Hispaniola. The collapse of the coffee market in Germany and the crisis of the coffee trade made the British West Indies monopoly of the North American market all the more necessary.[37]

North American attempts to win further concessions to trade openly with the French West Indies widened the breach with the British West Indies after 1766. The merchants of New York, followed by the merchants of Boston and the legislature of Massachusetts, protested that the sugar and molasses duties were excessively high. West Indians naturally thought the duties too low. A petition by the New York merchants effectively sought to export cheaper French sugar to Britain.[38] John Adams railed against the "collusion and combination" of the West India interest and the imperial government for attempting to subjugate North American commerce: "I know not why we should blush to confess that molasses was an essential ingredient in American Independence, many great events have proceeded from smaller causes." The division of the West Indian and North American lobbies over trade "greatly diminished" the "effectiveness" of colonial lobbies in "working for repeal of the Currency Act and for other colonial reforms."[39]

West Indians suspected that the continued opposition of the mainland colonies to imperial policy was partially motivated by a desire to evade sugar duties and to trade openly with the French. North American protests frequently targeted officials enforcing the Navigation Acts, which appeared to West Indians tantamount to an attack on the established system of imperial commerce.[40] Samuel Martin of Antigua, a leading opponent of the Stamp Act and Townshend Crisis (1767), began to associate the turbulence on the continent with a desire for unrestrained trade. Martin recalled the North American trade with the enemy during the Seven Years' War and called for a suppression of all illicit trade in North America as "a more substantial mark of British superiority over its colonies, than the little insignificant Tax upon Tea." He was convinced that the North Americans wished the ruin of the British sugar islands, and he ultimately advocated the seizure of all their shipping.[41] Jamaican planter Simon Taylor also accused North Americans of opposing the revenue acts in order to carry on their smuggling trade with the French Caribbean and Europe. Taylor thought their clamor about representation was a cloak to continue their illicit trade. West Indians continued to regard North Americans as "abettors of our most avowed enemies."[42] The issue of trade between North America and the French West Indies was a major obstacle to a united colonial alliance before the American Revolutionary War.

*   *   *

The British West Indies intervened in the revolutionary crisis only when threatened by embargoes in North America. Their trade with North America was important but inferior to their trade with Britain.

North America was a vital source of food and lumber imports, especially for Barbados and the Leeward Islands. It supplied corn, flour, rice, bread, biscuits, peas, and salted "fish unfit for European consumption."[43] These supplemented the diet of the slaves in particular. North America supplied the islands with casks to ship their sugar, cattle to work on the plantations, shingles for roofing, staves for making casks, and lumber for building. These supplies were increasingly imported in ships owned and built in the mainland colonies.

Provisions from North America were generally cheaper, more abundant, faster in arriving, and fresher than equivalent supplies from Britain. The trade

Figure 11. "A Map of the British Empire in America," Henry Popple, color engraved by William Henry Toms and R. W. Seale, 1733 (DeWitt Wallace Collection, Colonial Williamsburg, Williamsburg, Virginia).

relieved merchants and planters of keeping stores of food stocks, which were all too likely to spoil in a tropical climate. "The lumber and provisions of the American colonies," wrote Adam Smith, "were more necessary to the West India islands than the rum and sugar of the latter were to the former."[44] However, the importance of North American supplies to the British Caribbean varied between islands.

The Leeward Islands and Barbados relied on mainland food provisions for their "principal support" because sugar cultivation was so widespread and land for cultivating other crops so limited. As early as the 1640s, Barbados began to import food from the mainland colonies: Governor John Winthrop of Massachusetts noted in 1647 that "it pleased the Lord to open us a trade with Barbados and other Islands in the West Indies." In 1672, the island did not grow "one quarter [of the] Victuals sufficient for its Inhabitants nor any other necessaries for Planting." In the 1760s, Barbados did not grow enough provisions to feed its population for a mere two months. The Leeward Islands grew their own provisions until much later because the sugar revolution occurred later than in Barbados. In 1724, Governor John Hart was still able to write of considerable quantities of provisions grown in the Leeward Islands. Until 1750, St. Kitts grew most of its own food. By the eve of the American Revolutionary War, however, these islands "had the fewest internal resources."[45] Apart from small quantities of corn, their food production fell far short of their needs.

Jamaica and the Windward Islands were less dependent on provision imports from North America. Some of the major sugar regions of Jamaica imported food, such as the parishes of Vere and Clarendon in the southern coastal plain (which was almost a peninsula). However, the terrain of Jamaica and the Windward Islands was too mountainous and the climate too variable to be entirely suitable for sugar crops. Some of the lowland areas of Jamaica were too arid for sugar cultivation. Food crops were grown either in independent small holdings or within the plantation system. One study suggests that food imports "were sufficient to support only about a tenth of the population of Jamaica" and that the island became "more and more dependent on local food production," which made it increasingly self-sufficient. Staves, lumber, and shingles gradually replaced provisions as the major imports to Jamaica from North America. Nevertheless, the devastation of a hurricane could leave the island dependent on food imports, as happened in the last years of the American Revolutionary War.[46]

Planters in Jamaica and the Windward Islands encouraged their slaves to grow their own food, making them less dependent on imports from North America. The slaves became proto-peasants with their provision grounds, sometimes many miles from the plantation, and they also often reared fowl. Slaves in the Windward Islands received an allowance of imported grain and fish but they were expected to subsist chiefly on food from their own provision grounds, allotments, and kitchen gardens. Slaves sold some of their surplus produce at local markets and were so successful that the legislatures passed laws to restrict the practice of "higgling." Their activities foreshadowed the rise of peasant agriculture in the post-abolition period. Owing to the competition of the provision grounds of the slaves, pen farmers found it unprofitable to engage fully in food production.[47]

The British West Indies nevertheless valued their trade with North America and thus intervened in the imperial dispute between Britain and North America when threatened with economic embargoes and the loss of trade with North America in 1765–66, in December 1774, and throughout 1775. The Stamp Act riots in St. Kitts and Nevis occurred when the Leeward Islands were threatened with a famine from a virtual boycott imposed on them by the mainland patriots (see Chapter 4). Barbados assumed a leading role in the West Indian lobbying activity in London in 1775 after Congress had resolved to boycott all trade with the British Empire (see Chapter 6).

West Indians sought first and foremost to maintain the integrity of the British Empire and the status quo existing before 1776. However, in the event of an imperial rift, economic self-interest and security dictated loyalty to Britain. Unable to find an alternative market in North America or in Europe, the British West Indies had to depend on Britain.

*   *   *

Britain was the primary export market for the British West Indies. Britain imported two-and-a-half times as much sugar as France did from the French West Indies and consumed most of it, whereas France reexported large quantities of sugar to the rest of Europe. Between 1663 and 1775, the consumption of muscovado sugar in England and Wales increased twentyfold. Demand was ahead of supply and prices increased after the 1730s.

Rum consumption in Britain increased correspondingly from 207 gallons imported in 1698 to an annual average of two million gallons in 1771–75. Britain imported the best British Caribbean rum, including over 85 percent of the total rum exports of Jamaica between 1744 and 1769.[48] Additional quantities of rum were distilled in England from imported British West Indian molasses. The popularity of sugar and rum was related to the drinking preferences of the British, who liked sugar in their tea and coffee. The demand for sugar spread as its uses multiplied in medicines, jams, gingerbread, and chocolate. It revolutionized cake making. Sugar and rum were among the most impressive examples of the rise of consumerism in eighteenth-century British society. They were transformed from being luxuries to becoming part of the regular diet.

In addition to rum and sugar, Britain also consumed most other British West Indian exports. This was not solely because of the Trade and Navigation Acts, which were difficult to enforce against colonial opposition. The islands

Figure 12. *Parham Hill House and Sugar Plantation, Antigua*, Thomas Hearne, 1779 (Copyright © British Museum). Sugar was the primary produce of the British Caribbean. West Indian planters relied on the monopoly of the metropolitan market because they were unable to compete with the French West Indies.

found their best market in Britain. Only ginger sold in Britain for less than prices elsewhere in Europe. Thanks to the bounty paid by the imperial government, indigo enjoyed preferences like sugar in the home market. Cotton and coffee prices in Britain were comparable to prices in the rest of Europe. Following the crash of the German coffee market in 1773, even coffee producers began to become more dependent on the home market. Exports to Britain accounted for 90 percent of the total exports of Jamaica, compared with only 10 percent to North America.[49]

British West Indian exports to North America were slight in comparison to exports to Britain. For example, the total export market in molasses was "inconsiderable being less than ten thousand hogsheads per annum."[50] Yu Wu, in the most detailed study of the exports of any of the islands, found that

North American ports "provided relatively small outlets for Jamaican products." Jamaican exports to North America represented only 3.71 percent of total sugar exports and 12.34 percent of rum exports between 1744 and 1769. Barbados and the Leeward Islands exported a higher proportion of their produce than Jamaica to North America, in exchange for imported food from the mainland (on which they were more dependent). Barbados exported the largest proportion of its produce to North America, but this accounted for only one-quarter of the value of its total exports in 1770.[51]

The rum trade to North America disappointed the expectations of British planters who wanted it to defray the annual expenses of their plantations and to pay for imported provisions from North America.[52] The importance of rum exports to North America varied among islands and even among plantations. Planters were able to vary the relative proportions of sugar, molasses, and rum produced from sugar cane. Barbados distilled 50 percent more rum than other islands, partly to pay for particularly large food provision imports from North America. Some plantations in St. Kitts "produced little or no rum at all," and the Stapleton estates in Nevis produced almost no rum in some years.[53] The Rev. Robert Robertson of Nevis thought the importance of rum much exaggerated, claiming that total sales defrayed less than one-fifth of the annual expenses of a plantation. One inquiry found that rum exports to the mainland discharged the debt of only one-quarter of the imports from the middle colonies in North America and one-tenth of the imports from New England. Only one-ninth of all British West Indian exports went to North America.[54]

The great majority of the produce of the islands went to Britain and the volume of the total exports to Britain reached new heights at the beginning of the American Revolutionary War. The governor of Jamaica wrote that "almost the whole produce of the Islands . . . is remitted to Britain." In 1770 90 percent of the exports of Grenada, the second wealthiest island colony with total exports worth £506,709, went to Britain and Ireland. Over nine-tenths of sugar produced in the Leeward Islands was exported to Britain. The value of sugar exports to England and Wales rose from £630,000 per annum at the beginning of the century to an average annual value of around £2.4 million on the eve of the American War. British West Indian exports rose from 12 percent of total British imports (1701–5) to just over 25 percent (1771–75). For one and a half centuries, between the Restoration and the end of the regency period, sugar was the most valuable commodity imported into Britain.[55]

Thanks to the protective tariffs against rival European sugar, the British West Indies enjoyed a monopoly of the British market, and the burden of this preference fell on the British consumer. Depending on the quality of the sugar, the British West Indies paid between one-third and one-half of the duties charged on foreign sugars in the metropolitan market. Between 1768 and 1772, the years of our best data, they provided 97.3 percent of total sugar imports into Britain. In 1759 Joseph Massie estimated that British West Indian monopoly of the home sugar market cost the consumer £20,650,000 sterling over a thirty-year period. Historians have given varying estimates ranging between £382,250 sterling per annum to almost one million pounds sterling per annum.[56]

The British government supported this monopoly against the interests of the consumer because the islands conformed to the ideals of the Trade and Navigation Acts. The islands imported supplies and manufactures from Britain or from within the British Empire (except Ireland until 1780). They exported tropical goods to Britain and the rest of the empire (except Ireland) that were otherwise obtainable only from rival European powers. The islands helped to make the mother country more self-sufficient. The sailors and merchant ships used in the trade were a potential source of manpower and support for the British navy in wartime. The British government believed that the colonies contributed toward the growth of the domestic economy and that they were an essential source of national power.

Britain not only provided the necessary market for West Indian planters but also offered the best commercial facilities including insurance, the lowest shipping freights, the cheapest slaves, the longest credits, and the widest range of imports. The large planters developed a close relationship with merchants in Britain, who performed several services. They acted as agents, purchasing supplies and recruiting white employees for the plantations; as bankers for both the planters and local island merchants, offering goods on credit, providing loans, and accepting bills of exchange; as broker and commission men who marketed and sold the sugar on behalf of the planters; as intermediaries who paid the customs duties, freight charges, primage, wharfage, lighterage, warehouse rental, insurance, cooperage, weighing expenses, and the trade rate for the Society of West India Merchants; and as the personal representatives of the planters, lobbying government on their behalf, managing their legal business, and overseeing the education of their children.

Planter families often dealt with the same merchant houses over several generations. For example, the Payne family of St. Kitts and Nevis dealt with the Neaves of London from at least 1758 until the 1870s. The trade was gradually engrossed by a smaller group of merchants who specialized in sugar and who were primarily located in London and Bristol. Richard Sheridan identifies 55 merchant firms in London in 1774, of which 37 dealt primarily with the Lesser Antilles and 18 with Jamaica. Kenneth Morgan similarly finds 513 individual merchants in Bristol who imported an average of 26.5 hogsheads between 1728–32. Their numbers contracted to 163 merchants importing an average of 84 hogsheads per firm in 1763–67.[57]

Britain was the main carrier of slaves, for which the greatest demand was in the Caribbean. The purchase of slaves was the largest depreciation cost incurred by the planters, who replaced between 2 and 5 percent of their labor force every year. Malachy Postlethwayt thought the slave trade alone kept the West Indies subservient to Britain, "for while our Plantations depend only on Planting by Negroes . . . our colonies can never become independent of these kingdoms."[58]

*   *   *

Sugar made the islands increasingly dependent on the home market when the mainland colonies were rapidly outgrowing the imperial economy: "Without the preferential tariff [in Britain], the sugar industry [of the British West Indies] would not have existed in the long run."[59]

The extreme vulnerability of the planters to competition explains their ambivalence about British expansion in the Caribbean and their opposition to any reduction in British import duties on foreign sugar. Historian Marc Egnal has argued that an expansionist mentality distinguished the revolutionaries in North America. In contrast, the island elites were more hesitant about new acquisitions even when offered the chance of conquering neighboring islands. In 1740, for example, they resisted any movement to annex new sugar colonies. The West India interest was divided over the issue of retaining Guadeloupe rather than Canada during the peace negotiations with France in 1763. Rose Fuller and William Beckford, the two leading West India absentees in British politics, advocated the retention of Canada rather than Guadeloupe. Richard Pares argues that the only reason that other planters were willing to tolerate the annexation of French Guadeloupe was because the island was a thorn in the defense of the British islands and because sugar prices were higher than in 1740. It was not due to an expansionist mentality.[60]

Only their monopoly of the home market enabled the sugar planters to survive because they were unable to compete with rival French sugar. In 1753, John Sharpe, the agent for the Leeward Islands, warned the Board of Trade that it would entirely ruin the sugar colonies and stop all future investment if foreign sugar was allowed to enter the home market on equal terms. Rev. James Ramsay wrote that while Britain continued to give the islands the monopoly of her sugar market, "she will always preserve a check over them."

Edward Long confessed that the British sugar planters had flourished because of the hereditary preference in the home market rather than any peculiar excellence in their soil or extraordinary skill. Hence, Lord Sheffield concluded that the islands would neither attempt to become independent nor join the thirteen colonies while the preference in the British market continued and while they were unable to compete with rival producers.[61]

PART II

—

DIVERGENT
PATHS

4

Sons of Liberty?

THE BRITISH WEST INDIES diverged significantly from the mainland colonies in their response to imperial legislation during the 1760s. For example, Jamaica and Barbados complied with the Stamp Act even though it imposed the greatest tax burden on the Caribbean, not North America.[1] Their submission was mocked by the patriots in North America, where none of the thirteen colonies that rebelled paid stamp duty (except Georgia, briefly). The British West Indies accounted for 78 percent of the colonial stamp revenues.[2]

The submission of the largest and most populous islands to the tax was significant because it anticipated their loyalty a decade later (at the outbreak of the American Revolution), in contrast to the mainland colonies, where "The Stamp Act crisis was not merely an act in a much larger drama; it was nearly the drama itself."[3] The Leeward Islands resisted the Stamp Act but only after threats of an economic boycott by the patriots in North America. They risked a famine and the associated danger of a slave rebellion if they complied with the Stamp Act because they imported most of their food from North America.

After the repeal of the Stamp Act in 1766, the island colonies remained aloof from the growing imperial crisis until December 1774. There is no substance to claims that the islands "were active participants in the pre-Revolutionary struggle," that resolutions "of the West Indies legislatures rang with all the clarity of those on the mainland," or that "there had been considerable support for the American cause."[4] The British West Indies complied with the Townshend duties (1767) and the East India Tea Act (1773), unlike the mainland colonies.

West Indians conspicuously failed to join the pamphlet campaign against Britain. They did not set up extraparliamentary opposition groups like the Sons of Liberty, nonimportation associations, or committees of correspondence. In Britain, the West India agents, merchants, absentee planters, and members of Parliament were divided in their response to imperial reforms and to the rise of revolutionary resistance in North America. Their inactivity and prevarication contributed to the isolation of the North American lobby in

London. The response of the British West Indies to imperial policies in the 1760s anticipated their divergence from the mainland colonies during the American Revolutionary War.

* * *

The Stamp Act was the most controversial of a series of imperial measures introduced by the new ministry of George Grenville in the aftermath of the Seven Years' War (1756–63). This direct imperial tax levied throughout British America incited the first imperial crisis to unite all the thirteen mainland colonies in opposition to Britain.

The Stamp Act was imposed on public documents, printed items, and civil law documents including newspapers, almanacs, pamphlets, playing cards, wills, land conveyances, diplomas, commissions, and licenses. It was passed to help defray the cost of colonial administration and defense at a time when Britain's national debt had reached £129,500,000 sterling. After the expulsion of France from Canada, the British government reasoned that the mainland colonies were the chief beneficiaries of the war and that they ought to share the cost.

The Stamp Act raised what would become the major constitutional issues of the American Revolution. The North American colonists objected less to the size of the tax than to the threat it posed to their customary liberties. The precedent of a direct imperial tax endangered the future of the colonial assemblies, widely regarded as the bulwark of colonial liberties, which traditionally enjoyed a monopoly of the right to vote colonial taxes. The tax denied the colonists the right to trial by jury because evasions were to be punished in the vice-admiralty courts. It imperiled the future of the colonial press by charging particularly high rates on newspapers and undermined the economic independence of the colonists because it was to be collected in cash when the circulation of gold and silver coin was critically low following the postwar depression. Finally, the tax was associated with a standing army and with tyranny because the revenues were to pay the costs of a peacetime British army in North America.

Revolutionary organizations dubbed Sons of Liberty appeared in all the thirteen mainland colonies. They forced stamp distributors to resign and prevented the circulation of the stamp papers. They orchestrated violent protests in Boston, New York, and Newport. Nine North American assemblies passed resolutions defining their rights in defiance of the Stamp Act. In October 1765, nine colonies sent representatives to a Stamp Act Congress in New York City, which petitioned both Houses of Parliament and the king for repeal, stating

Figure 13. Three-shilling West India stamp, copy of stamp dated April 19, 1766 (courtesy of Adolph Koeppel). The Stamp Act imposed a greater tax burden on the British Caribbean than on North America. It contained duties discriminating against the islands that necessitated the printing of a special three-shilling stamp for the British Caribbean.

their constitutional objections in a declaration of rights and grievances. The colonists began a successful campaign against the importation of British goods.

The British government repealed the Stamp Act in March 1766, just one year after its passage. However, unwilling to give up the principle of parliamentary sovereignty and the right to tax, Parliament passed the Declaratory Act, which affirmed its right to legislate for the colonies "in all cases whatsoever" and which the British understood to mean the right to tax. Taxation became a symbolic issue for both sides in the imperial conflict: the British regarded the right to tax as symbolic of their right to govern the colonies whereas the mainland patriots regarded direct-imperial taxes as raised without their consent symbolic of tyranny.

*   *   *

The Stamp Act imposed the greatest tax burden on the British West Indies because it contained clauses that specifically discriminated against the islands.[5] These included a duty on "any probate of will, letters of administration, or of guardianship for any estate above the value of twenty pounds," which was double the rate for the mainland. The stamp duties on Crown land grants above one hundred acres were also double those levied on the mainland, while the charge on Crown land grants below one hundred acres was triple the rate on the mainland, necessitating the printing of a special three-shilling stamp for the British Caribbean. Thomas Whately of the Treasury, one of the architects of the act, argued that the difference actually made the tax more equitable because land was less plentiful and thus revenues were likely to be lower, but land was also more valuable in the islands.

The Stamp Act fell hardest on Grenada, Dominica, St. Vincent, and Tobago, where the Crown was in the process of selling extensive areas of land following the acquisition of these islands from France in 1763. In the Caribbean a flat rate of two shillings and three pence was charged on promissory notes and bonds regardless of their value, but the same rate was applied only to promissory notes and bonds worth over forty pounds sterling in North America. A stamp duty on public officials with an income of over twenty pounds sterling per annum was imposed exclusively in the Caribbean. Furthermore, the cost of stamps in the islands fell almost entirely on trade and litigation, not on the small volume of newspapers, books, pamphlets, and printed advertisements.[6]

The British government consequently allocated more stamps to the Caribbean colonies than to North America. The greatest single consignment of stamps to British America went to Jamaica. The government apportioned more stamps to the Leeward Islands than to any of the mainland colonies: it expected revenues from Antigua to be higher than North Carolina or Maryland. Charles Jenkinson, the treasury secretary, expected roughly equal amounts of stamp revenue from the populous North American colonies as from the Caribbean.[7]

The requirement that stamp duties be paid in cash was a problem in the islands, where coins were in short supply. None of the island colonies minted its own coin, and they were prohibited from importing coin from Britain. They were dependent on "casual importations" from abroad but foreign coin was overvalued because of the shortage. The stamp duties were levied in amounts "not correspondent with the current coin" of the islands, which meant that the colonists either purchased more than they needed or they paid more than the real cost.[8]

The shortage of coin was acute in Jamaica because of the closure of the bullion trade with the Spanish, "the only people that brought us money here for our British manufactures, and enabled us to make our remittances to England." Jamaica was the chief conduit of the Spanish bullion trade, which imperial officials traditionally overlooked because of its obvious benefits to Britain. This trade was hindered by the customs reforms of 1764. Jamaicans blamed their governor, William Henry Lyttelton, and West Indians in London blamed the government for a slump in the Anglo-Spanish trade. George Grenville tried unsuccessfully to undo the damage by permitting officials to turn a blind eye to the Spanish bullion trade. Nevertheless, Jamaicans continued to attribute the acute currency shortage to imperial interference with the bullion trade, although the causes were actually more complex.[9]

The revenues from the Stamp Act were intended to benefit the defense of North America, not the Caribbean. Although two regiments garrisoned the islands ceded from France in 1763, the ministry simultaneously reduced the military presence in the other islands by almost an equivalent number of troops. To the great dismay of the white colonists, Jamaica lost over half of its two thousand soldiers, and Antigua similarly lost half of its seven hundred troops in 1764.[10]

The Stamp Act fell "unequally upon the Sugar Colonies which already contribute[d] to the exigencies of Government by very heavy Taxes upon all the Commodities . . . exported to the Mother Country," when none of the mainland colonies paid "such heavy Taxes as those in the Sugar Colonies."[11] The assemblies of Jamaica and Antigua already paid high annual subsistence allowances for troops after the 1730s (see Chapter 2). Since the Restoration, Barbados and the Leeward Islands had paid the imperial government a 4½ percent duty, which amounted to an annual income of £40,000 to £50,000 sterling. This tax was originally voted in perpetuity to cover the cost of imperial defense and administration but the money was diverted by Britain for other purposes outside the Caribbean. The Windward Islands also paid the 4½ percent duty between 1764 and 1774. Jamaica granted a perpetual £8,000 per year toward the cost of government in the Revenue Act of 1728, although the fund was never diverted outside the island. All the islands voted their governors perpetual salaries on arrival.

In short, the Stamp Act required the islands to pay more for less when they already contributed toward the cost of imperial government. Yet their opposition to the act was much more tepid than the reaction in North America.

*   *   *

West Indians shared the objections of the mainland patriots to the Stamp Act. They, too, traced their constitutional liberties from their first settlement and claimed the inherited and customary rights of Englishmen. Samuel Martin of Antigua, an outspoken critic of the Stamp Act, argued that these inherited liberties were defended against the Norman yoke and Stuart tyranny. They were enshrined in Magna Charta, the common law, and the revolutionary settlement of 1688. Henry Duke, the solicitor general of Barbados, later recalled that the whole island opposed the Stamp Act: "It was an Invasion, they said, of the constitutional Rights of English Subjects." In addition to appealing to the British Constitution, the Barbados assembly also cited the authority of the charter granted to the island in 1652.[12]

Like the mainland patriots, West Indians maintained that only the elected assemblies had the right to raise taxes — "a Bulwark essential to the very existence of a British Constitution." Taxes raised "in any other manner would be destructive of this most essential Privilege of a Briton" and this was "so fully & clearly understood" that in Jamaica "ever since a civil Government was first established . . . no Money hath been raised upon the King's subjects in this colony but by their Consent given by their Representatives in the Assembly." The Barbados assembly had stated in 1740 that taxes "laid upon the inhabitants without the consent of their representatives" were invalid. Following the introduction of the Stamp Act, it claimed exemption from any "Internal Taxation of Government, but what is authorized by the representative Body of each society in concert with the representative of the Crown presiding over it . . . a privilege which we imagined the subjects of Great Britain had been entitled to in every settlement, however distant, of the British Empire as a birthright and blessing." "We think of the Doctrine of internal Taxations," wrote the agent of Barbados, "like our Brethren on the Continent."[13]

Like the mainland patriots, West Indians rejected the British argument that the colonies were virtually represented despite the power of the West India lobby in London. A tax "laid by Parliament to be levied in" Jamaica deprived the inhabitants of the "most essential right" to vote their own taxes "as we have no Representative in Parliament." Even Samuel Martin denied that the colonies were virtually represented, despite his own political influence through his oldest son who was a royal officeholder and an influential member of Parliament. Martin declared that the Stamp Act infringed on traditional liberties including the right to taxation by local representatives and the right to trial by jury. William Beckford, the most prominent West Indian in England, also rejected the British defense that the colonies were virtually represented.[14]

Some West Indians even asserted their right to resist if their traditional privileges were threatened by tyranny. Sir John Gay Alleyne of Barbados wrote, in a public letter addressed to a North American, "Our political creed on the point of Resistance to the Supreme Power of the State, in case of any imagined oppression of our several colonies, is the same as yours." Another Barbadian pamphlet proclaimed that wherever tyranny was attempted "all Opposition becomes lawful" and that tyranny was no more supportable by a group than by a single individual. Samuel Martin denounced the Stamp Act for treating the colonies "as Slaves, to arbitrary power: for Tyranny may be as well displayed by *many in conjunction* as by one man." He feared that compliance with the tax would set a precedent that, "if it were unopposed, there was no knowing where it would stop."[15]

The islands shared the country Whig ideology of the mainland patriots and the opposition parties in England. Both the mainland colonies and the island colonies sympathized with the plight of the English radical John Wilkes in their own constitutional struggle.[16] Most of the English and Irish in Jamaica were "early partisans of John Wilkes," and both St. Kitts and Grenada founded subscription societies to raise funds for him. The society in St. Kitts was cofounded by John Gardiner and John Stanley, lawyers who had attended the Inner Temple in London where they studied under Charles Pratt (Lord Camden), the judge who acquitted John Wilkes in the case of General Warrants. Gardiner, a native of Boston, acted as a junior counsel for Wilkes in the case against General Warrants in 1764 and subsequently defended Arthur Beardmore and Daniel Meredith, leading allies of Wilkes. Several of the islands corresponded with Wilkes, especially after the foundation of the Society of the Bill of Rights in 1769. However, unlike South Carolina, none of the island assemblies in the Caribbean voted money for Wilkes.[17]

West Indians were well aware of the political ideas of the patriots in North America thanks to regular communications and interchange. They corresponded with merchants and friends on the mainland and received pamphlets published in North America. They read James Otis and his *Rights of the British Colonies Vindicated*, and their newspapers carried copies of articles from the mainland press. West Indians even subscribed to North American newspapers: it was possible to renew subscriptions to the *Pennsylvania Chronicle* through one of the printers in Barbados. They received news from North American merchants, captains, sailors, agents, and visitors. The islands and mainland were separated by less than a week-long voyage. West Indian planters also witnessed events firsthand on visits to North America.

West Indian free blacks and slaves also learned of events in North America: domestic slaves heard the discussions of their masters; printers employed black typesetters and delivery agents for their newspapers; and black sailors, urban blacks, and networks of plantation slaves shared information. This was to become apparent to whites in the great rebellion in Jamaica in 1776 (see Chapter 5).

*   *   *

West Indian merchants and planters residing in Britain actively opposed the Stamp Act. At its introduction in March 1764, Beckford spoke against the act in the House of Commons, the only member reported to have done so. His effort to obstruct the bill by a procedural motion received support only from "West Indian gentlemen and a few others connected with America." Absentee planters and merchants, along with island agents, campaigned against the bill. They initially hesitated to send a petition because they knew that parliamentary procedure disallowed petitions relating to money bills. However, when they heard that the Treasury was claiming that "none of the colonies had any objection," they decided to petition the House of Commons as "a Monument of our unwillingness to submit to and our inability to bear such a burthen." On February 11, 1765, Stephen Fuller presented his own petition on behalf of Jamaica. On February 15, Rose Fuller of Jamaica announced the petition "of certain Persons interested in and trading to the Island of Jamaica" stating their inability to pay the tax.[18]

West Indian merchants and planters in London also played a role in the eventual repeal of the Stamp Act. Barlow Trecothick, one of the chief agitators for repeal in England, had commercial links primarily with North America but also with several of the islands; he had lived in Jamaica in the 1740s, and he led the absentee planters of Grenada in petitioning the Privy Council for a separate assembly in the 1760s. In November 1765, he warned the marquis of Rockingham that if North American ships with unstamped papers were seized, "our sugar islands will be deprived of their usual supplies of provisions lumber etc and perhaps be disabled from sending home their produce or even subsisting." This worried Rockingham, who was well disposed toward the islands. In December, the agent for Barbados urged Rockingham to allow North American vessels to enter West Indian ports without stamps. Rockingham promised to lay the issue before the Privy Council. Edmund Burke assured the agent "that the Marquis was very desirous to relieve us. That he detested the Stamp Act and had always opposed it. But that the party which made it were upon the watch to take every advantage of him; and if he was to Relax in any part of it, they would charge him with the miscarriage of the whole."[19]

Rose Fuller, an absentee West Indian planter and brother of Stephen Fuller, played a crucial role in influencing parliamentary opinion in favor of the colonies. As chairman of the American Committee in February 1766, Fuller gave priority to the evidence of opponents of the Stamp Act. The first witnesses to appear before his committee included many with interests in the West Indies: Beeston Long, chairman of the Society of West India Merchants; James Carr, a Jamaica merchant; and Henry Wilmot, the agent for the Leeward Islands. When George III gave his assent to the repeal of the Stamp Act, "the American and West-India ships" in the River Thames in London "hoisted their colours and fired Guns" in celebration.[20]

* * *

Although the Stamp Act was unpopular throughout the British West Indies, only the Leeward Islands resisted its implementation. There were riots in St. Kitts and Nevis on October 31, the eve of the enforcement of the Stamp Act, and again on November 5, which was the anniversary of both the Gunpowder Plot (Pope's Day) and the Glorious Revolution (when William III landed at Torbay in 1688). These riots were well planned and organized. They mirrored the rituals of the Stamp Act riots in North America with ceremonial processions, effigy burning, forced recantations by stamp officials, and the destruction of stamps. The riots were boisterous and violent: private houses and even the longboat of a naval ship were burned. The stamp distributor in St. Kitts was convinced that the riots were not spontaneous but covertly organized; he was "greatly surpriz'd . . . as I had not heard that even such a thing was intended: (so secret was the design kept)."[21] We lack information about the identity of the participants in the riots, though we know that they included sailors from North America. However, the scale of the riots in St. Kitts suggests involvement of over half the free white adult population. In other words, if contemporary estimates are accurate, these riots were proportionally equivalent to those of Boston and New York.

The riot of October 31 began when a crowd of three hundred to four hundred people gathered at about eight o'clock in the evening at Noland's Tavern in Basseterre, the capital of St. Kitts. Accompanied by the beat of a drum, they marched to the home of John Hopkins, a local merchant and deputy stamp distributor, whose house contained the stamps. On their arrival, the crowd shouted three huzzas and demanded the stamp papers, which they then ceremoniously burnt at his door. They forced Hopkins to resign his office and, after searching his house for more stamps, made him lead them to the home of William Tuckett, the stamp act distributor for St. Kitts and Nevis, who was hiding about three-quarters of a mile out of town.[22]

With drums still beating, the crowd seized Tuckett and paraded him to the public market, where they made him "swear never to have any further connection with the Stamp Papers, and that he had no commission (for that was most wanted to be burnt)." According to Tuckett's account, they knocked him to the ground when he dismounted his horse and were ready to murder him but for the help of "some Negroes" who knew him and rescued him "from the enraged populace." His escape was short-lived, as "500 white People at least" came after him and made him walk back to town. Weak from a fever, Tuckett pleaded with their leaders for his release but was gibed with "gross insults" and obliged to resign his office. He promised to announce his resignation in the newspaper "to avoid being suspended" on a gibbet.[23]

After finishing with Tuckett, the crowd rampaged through the streets of Basseterre to the office of the island secretary where, unable to find the keys, they broke open the door and burnt another "four or five quires of stamped paper." They walked to the island secretary's home "with great acclamations of huzzas" and went on to the office of the deputy provost marshal, where they burned another "quire" of stamps. Finally, they surrounded the custom house but were eventually persuaded to leave when the collector declared "over and over upon his word and honor" that he had no stamps inside. Disorder continued throughout the night with many "violences and Disturbances" against supporters of the act, who were subjected to "low and public Threats" and taunted with insulting language. As much as two thousand pounds sterling worth of unaccounted stamps were destroyed in the riots. Tuckett had collected only a little more than eight pounds in stamp revenue.[24]

During the night Tuckett fled across the seven-mile channel from Basseterre to his native island of Nevis. There, he again began "to distribute those badges of slavery." The St. Kitts Sons of Liberty followed him to Nevis where, in association with local supporters, they resolved that they would by "some stratagem, get and burn, or tuck him up," but Tuckett escaped their clutches. In a trail of destruction, they burned two houses and loaded the stamps in a navy longboat in order to make a larger fire.[25]

Violence did not subside in St. Kitts: "There is hardly a Man among them from the highest to the lowest who does not openly show his hearty Abhorrence of the Stamp Law." On November 5, a crowd reassembled in Basseterre to parade effigies of the stamp master and his deputy, which they then burnt in the common pasture. The evening concluded "with an elegant supper, Drums beating and the French Horns playing; and the last Toast was *Liberty, Property and No Stamps.*" In late November, opponents of the act prevented a new supply of stamps from landing and they intercepted the correspondence of the stamp distributor. Tuckett still feared revenge and even assassination. He found no one in St. Kitts willing to be his deputy or even to rent him a house. Defended by a small bodyguard, Tuckett resigned in St. Kitts but clung to his office in Nevis, remaining a figure of ridicule long after the repeal of the Stamp Act. Following the riots, business continued as usual without the stamps and no duties were collected. Ships cleared from both islands with unstamped papers. The governor offered a reward for information about the riots but met with no success. On the repeal of the Stamp Act, there was "great rejoicing" in St. Kitts.[26]

The other Leeward Islands also successfully opposed the Stamp Act. Montserrat ignored the duties, while Antigua reacted more ambivalently than the other Leewards but similarly succeeded in obstructing the payment of stamp duties. The absence of Antiguan stamp master William Otley in Britain and the late arrival of the stamps left the tax unenforced by the end of November. Governor George Thomas rather misleadingly assured the secretary of state that everything had gone quietly for the first three weeks of November. An unidentified stranger "walking down the Water Side, and seeing a Bale of them (*the stamps*) lying on the Wharf, altogether neglected for Three Days, took charge of, and distributed them" for about sixteen days. The *Antigua Gazette* was published on stamped paper for six weeks until late December, when the paper announced the resignation of the third distributor, who had acted for "about 16 days much against the inclination of the People."[27]

The presence in Antigua of both the governor of the Leeward Islands and the Sixty-Eighth Regiment explains why the inhabitants initially paid the duty "though sorely against their wills." On the arrival of the stamp papers, Governor Thomas promptly ordered two sentries to guard the home of the stamp distributor and commanded one hundred troops to protect the stamp papers. The governor observed in December "a general uneasiness and discontent in the People of all Ranks." Lieutenant Colonel Josiah Martin of the Sixty-Eighth later recalled that "many people who knew better" opposed the Stamp Act. Martin lamented that, in their desire to expose the servants of the Crown to public odium, people daily heckled and abused the sentries guarding the stamp office and even the men of the Sixty-Eighth Regiment. According to Martin, only the presence of the troops prevented rioting. As two Pennsylvania merchants wrote home from the island, "we could wish the people dare shew their dislike to (the Stamp Act) . . . here in the same open manner that they do on your side of the water, but they are over awed by His Majesty's Sixty Eighth Regt."[28]

Nevertheless, three successive stamp officers in Antigua quit before the end of December. Thomas Warner, although offered a personal bodyguard, resigned without even "being solicited," apparently having heard of the fate of Tuckett in St. Kitts and Nevis. William Atkinson, also secretary of the island, discovered that "not a man in the Island would keep the stamp officer company, though before he was universally beloved, so that he resigned his office." In January 1766, the merchant John Harper "found not the least Difficulty arising from my papers not being stamp'd." A correspondent of the *Virginia Gazette* found that ships "enter and clear . . . as usual" without stamped papers.[29]

The situation in Antigua changed again the following February, for reasons that remain unclear, when reports circulated that the tax was being enforced. This is corroborated by the existence of a document bearing a five-shilling stamp from Antigua dated February 15, 1766. Despite these reversals, no duty was sent back to Britain. The *Maryland Gazette* praised the island for having "to its great Honour, most loyally withstood this Pest, contrived against his Majesty's loving subjects." A 1772 British Treasury report on the Stamp Act revealed that there was an outstanding balance of £2,275 sterling for unaccounted papers. The "principal gentlemen, merchants and inhabitants" of Antigua joyously celebrated "the repeal of that badge of American slavery the late Stamp Act" at "a very elegant entertainment."[30]

*   *   *

The disturbances in St. Kitts and Nevis were exceptional in the British West Indies. The largest and most populous islands — Barbados and Jamaica — complied with the Stamp Act. Unlike the majority of distributors on the mainland, their stamp officials never resigned.

Although it paid the stamp duty, Barbados shared the general grievances against the Stamp Act. There were "loud complaints" in Barbados against the West India members of Parliament for failing to be more vocal in their opposition. In November 1765, the assembly sent an address to Governor Charles Pinfold, complaining of the irregular nature of the tax and citing their compliance with British requests for assistance during the last war. In December, the lower house resolved to send a joint remonstrance to the king but then desisted, owing to the opposition of the council. The agent for Barbados warned Rockingham that "Peaceable as we are, Distress will make us desperate — Barbados will be in confusion like Boston."[31] By December 1765, the collector of customs in Barbados was admitting North American ships without stamps. At the time of the repeal of the Stamp Act, Governor Pinfold thought the island "ripe for Disturbance." There was talk in the assembly of voting no local taxes for the support of government, including the governor's salary, and even of reducing sugar exports to Britain. Against the wishes of the British secretary of state and Governor Pinfold, the assembly unanimously refused to send an address of thanks to the king on the repeal of the Stamp Act.[32]

Although Barbados sympathized with those who opposed the Stamp Act, it still complied with its enforcement even though there was no resident stamp distributor. So great was the demand for stamps in Barbados that there was concern about running out of supply. One contemporary estimated that the island paid £2,500 in stamp duties, although official returns gave a total of £500. The *Barbados Mercury* and the *Barbados Gazette* were printed on stamped paper. One stamped Barbadian newspaper was "handcuffed" by an iron chain and triumphantly burned to loud cheers in "the Coffee House" in Philadelphia. Stamped papers from Barbados were also exhibited on a pole and carried by local Sons of Liberty through the streets of New London in Massachusetts.[33]

In January 1766, by a majority vote of thirteen to six, the assembly of Barbados bowed to the objections of the council and refrained from sending a memorial to the king "setting forth the difficultys and hardships the Island labours under on account of the Stamp Act." It accepted the compromise of a joint letter to their agent in London. An adulterated draft copy of the letter, containing a clause that condemned "the present rebellious opposition given to authority" circulated in North America, where it provoked a hostile pamphlet from Pennsylvanian lawyer John Dickinson. It was in vain that the Barbados assembly and its apologists protested that "incorrect copies had been sent abroad" and that the offensive clause was not in the official draft to the agent. As one of the members observed, it was not simply the clause that angered Dickinson, "but the obedience yielded by them to the lawful Authority of our Mother Country, in a case where they might have been tempted by a very notable Example of Resistance."[34]

In compliance with the Stamp Act, Barbados was "determined to seize all

Figure 14. *Charles Pinfold*, Thomas Hudson, 1741 (Yale Center for British Art, Paul Mellon Collection). Pinfold was governor of Barbados (1756–66) during the Stamp Act. Barbados paid stamp duty, in contrast to the thirteen mainland colonies with the brief exception of Georgia. Its compliance brought a sharp rebuke from Pennsylvania patriot John Dickinson, who addressed an anonymous pamphlet to the Committee of Correspondence of the Assembly of Barbados.

vessels coming without Stamp-Paper" from North America. The *Barbados Mercury* printed a tirade against the "Sett of Men [in North America], who, under the specious Name of Asserters of their Liberty, dare, contrary to all Laws human and divine, break out into the most outrageous Acts of Rebellion against their Sovereign Defender." The writer vowed that no hardship, however extreme, would "lessen in us that loyal Attachment we have to Perform of our most gracious sovereign, or that tender Regard we bear our Mother Country." The governor of Barbados reported that all was "quiet and easy" and that the act was "obeyed with . . . Readiness." On the repeal of the Stamp Act, Barbados "did not show the least sign of rejoicing," nor did the assembly express any regrets for its passive role. On the contrary, it later told the governor that "the part of submission which was taken by this colony in that memorable Trial of their obedience by the late Stamp Act, was indeed agreeable to the Soundest Policy in our state as well as the Result of a principle not easily to be shaken by the first, though too well founded cause of general Discontent." George III personally acknowledged the loyal compliance of Barbados.[35]

Jamaicans also made but nominal opposition to the Stamp Act. Following the closure of the Spanish bullion trade, they were displeased with the imperial government. In December 1764, on receiving news of the intended stamp duties, the committee of correspondence for the Jamaican assembly urged their agent in London to "employ your utmost Endeavorus and Abilities in such a way as to obviate and prevent this alarming measure." On February 15, 1765, Rose Fuller presented to the House of Commons a petition against the act from Stephen Fuller. John Howell, the stamp distributor in Jamaica, suffered "repeated Threats of Violence Torrents of Personal abuse and many other very disagreeable Circumstances." Howell believed that the people found the duties so "obnoxious" that the stamp office was only saved by the speedy removal of the stamps to a safe place in Spanish Town.[36]

Many Jamaicans rushed to complete business before the stamp duty came into effect; others deferred their legal business until its repeal; and still others evaded it. By the beginning of 1766, North American ships were clearing Port Royal without stamped papers. In February, Stephen Fuller submitted another petition on behalf of Jamaica to Parliament. Following the repeal of the act, there were elaborate celebrations in which the militia "fired three vollies as a *Feu de Joye*" and "prepared an emblematical flag, representing LIBERTY TRIUMPHANT and an odious STAMPMAN imploring forgiveness for his many notorious oppressions and extortions." Kingston was illuminated. Effigies of John Howell and George Grenville were hung on a signpost and burned.[37]

Yet for all the token resistance, Jamaica still paid more stamp duty than the combined total of the rest of the empire during the four and a half months the act was in force. The distributor believed that the revenue would have been much greater "had not the people conceived a repeal of the Law unavoidable which they inferred from the conduct of the N. Americans." Jamaicans might have avoided the act "with the greatest Ease immaginable" since the stamps were entrusted to two slaves whose master ordered them to run off if attacked; they carried the stamps some fourteen miles without interference. The Jamaican local admiralty courts prosecuted at least eight North American ships for carrying unstamped clearances. North American newspapers reported that the tax met no opposition and quipped "that the Inhabitants of the Town of Kingston fed so voraciously on them (*the stamps*), that not less than 300 of them alone died in the Month of November." After repeal, the secretary of state congratulated the governor on the absence of disturbances.[38]

*   *   *

The obedience of Jamaica and Barbados is surprising in retrospect because they were in a much stronger position than the Leeward Islands to make gestures of defiance against imperial authority. They possessed a lower proportion of slaves than the Leeward Islands, and their white population was growing while that of the Leeward Islands was declining. Jamaica and Barbados boasted assemblies jealous of their privileges which were often more assertive than the mainland assemblies before the American Revolution (see Chapter 5). Jamaica and Barbados were economically and militarily dependent on Britain but so were the Leeward Islands.

The failure of Jamaica to oppose the Stamp Act is frequently but unconvincingly explained in terms of local conditions. It is typically argued that the Jamaican assembly deflected its energy against the governor, with whom it was engaged in a bitter local constitutional struggle which preceded the Stamp Act (see Chapter 5). The assembly was prorogued for most of the time that the tax was in effect. In addition, Jamaicans were already accustomed to paying stamp duties under local laws to pay the cost of new defenses in the wake of the slave rebellion of 1760. The stature and personality of the stamp distributor, John Howell, also enhanced the successful enforcement of the duties. He was not a native of the region, in contrast to all the other stamp distributors except the officer in Georgia. He enjoyed close court connections through a German brother-in-law who was a confidant of George III. Howell was also provost marshal of Jamaica, which gave him special powers of arrest, and his office in Spanish Town was situated seventeen miles from the merchant community of Kingston, where opposition was likely to center. Finally, historians argue that

Jamaica was passive owing to slave unrest, which diverted attention from the Stamp Act in "the most troubled decade in Jamaica's long history as a slave society."[39]

However, such local considerations do not provide a sufficient explanation for the passivity of Jamaica toward the Stamp Act, nor do they explain the passivity of other islands in the British West Indies. It is true that the Jamaican assembly regarded its dispute with Governor Lyttelton as "a subject *of more importance* than [the Stamp Act] . . . in that it more immediately concerns us as striking at the very Vitals of our Constitution."[40] Yet, as we shall see in the next chapter, this represented a perverse order of priorities: the imperial tax posed a much greater threat to colonial liberties than did the actions of a governor. On other occasions Jamaicans had demonstrated that they were very capable of defending their interests and defying the imperial government.

The precedent of earlier local stamp acts in Jamaica did not make the imperial stamp duty any more palatable. Massachusetts had also introduced stamp duties but it fiercely resisted the Stamp Act. The earlier Jamaican stamp duties were "so *burthensome* and so oppressive to the People, that they became clamorous" and the legislature was forced to drop the tax. The local stamp duties in Jamaica were different from the new imperial duties in important respects and — a critical distinction — they were levied by the colonial assembly. The popularity of Howell had little to do with Jamaica's compliance with the Stamp Act — equally popular stamp distributors on the mainland faced opposition from colonists. The slave rebellion of 1765 broke out one month after the enforcement of the stamp duties and was quickly suppressed. The fear of slave revolt may well explain the unwillingness of whites to riot but it does not explain their failure to develop other strategies of opposition, such as pamphleteering.[41]

Furthermore, the obstacles that supposedly prevented Jamaica from opposing the Stamp Act did not exist in Barbados, which was especially well placed to oppose the imperial stamp tax because it had the lowest proportion of slaves, the oldest elected assembly, a higher proportion of resident planters, and the highest proportion of white settlers anywhere in the British West Indies. Barbados had no slave rebellions in the eighteenth century, and there was no resident garrison of British troops to police protests against the Stamp Act.

By concentrating on local conditions to explain the passivity of Jamaica and Barbados, the essential point is missed — the reaction of the Leeward Islands to the Stamp Act was abnormal within the British Caribbean. Jamaica and Barbados typified the natural inclination of the West Indies toward conciliation with Britain, which became more pronounced on the eve of the Revolutionary War. Indeed, even the riots in the Leeward Islands were primarily caused by external pressure from North America.

*   *   *

It is curious that the Leeward Islands were so much bolder than Jamaica and Barbados in their opposition to the Stamp Act. Dwarfed by Jamaica, they were in a much weaker position than the two larger sister islands. They were less economically diversified, relying almost exclusively on sugar cultivation and thus more dependent on the British market than either Barbados or Jamaica.[42] Their scattered white populations declined throughout the second half of the eighteenth century and their proportion of slaves was higher than in any other colony in British America. Slaves outnumbered whites by twelve to one in St. Kitts and fifteen to one in Antigua. A regiment of troops in Antigua was easily deployed throughout the Leeward Islands. Antigua also had a major naval dockyard at English Harbour from which ships were dispatched to the other Leeward Islands. These conditions made resistance among the white colonists more difficult in the Leeward Islands than in Barbados or Jamaica. Nevertheless, the Leeward Islands vigorously opposed the Stamp Act in contrast to the submissive stance of Barbados and Jamaica. Why?

The vulnerability of the Leeward Islands to economic sanctions by North American merchants explains their bold resistance to the Stamp Act. The Leewards, more than all the other islands, depended on the North American colonies for food. Sugar cultivation was so extensive and ground provisions were so rare that these islands imported essential provisions from the mainland, especially salted fish and corn to feed their slaves. The American Revolutionary War grimly demonstrated the dependence of the Leeward Islands on North America with famine and acute shortages unsurpassed anywhere in the Caribbean.[43] Alternative sources of supply proved too expensive, too distant, or simply insufficient. The Leewards faced a stark alternative in November 1765: resist the Stamp Act or suffer famine with the associated danger of a slave rebellion.

North American merchants boycotted all the British islands that complied with the Stamp Act. Tensions between the West Indies and North America were already high as a result of the 1764 Sugar Act (see Chapter 3), primarily because northern mainland merchants suspected West Indians of complicity in the passage of the act.[44] Stamp papers from Barbados and Jamaica were publicly burnt in North America, and radicals proposed starving the "Creole Slaves" by a virtual embargo.[45] They fumed, "Can no punishment be devised for Barbadoes and Port Royal in Jamaica, for their base desertion of the cause of liberty, their tame surrender of the rights of Britons, their mean, timid resignation to slavery?" They urged their fellow countrymen to deny the British West Indies "the comfortable Enjoyment of every delicious Dainty from us . . . till they are brought to a state of Despondency without any Thing but stinking fish and false Doctrine."[46]

North American newspapers demanded reprisals against "the *SLAVISH* Islands of *Barbados* and *Antigua* — Poor, mean spirited, Cowardly, Dastardly Creoles" by denying them "Fresh or Salt Provisions from any Son of LIBERTY on the Continent." The mainland patriots hoped to force the islands to recant "by withholding from them the Provisions that are necessary for their support" because it was important that "all the People who are to be affected by . . . [the] Operation [of the Stamp Act] should be unanimous [in opposition]." There was, in any case, a virtual economic embargo against the islands because "no Individual can be secure in his Property that sends thither a ship with unstamped clearances."[47]

North American merchants either blacklisted those islands that complied with the act or simply stayed away for fear that ships using unstamped papers were liable to seizure. They found out which island ports were open to ships without stamp papers through scouts and newspaper reports. They tried to both coerce and cajole the islands to resist; ships arrived from the mainland "loaded with threats of starving us Islanders." They altered their destination from Barbados to St. Kitts "upon hearing the scandalous news" of the enforcement of the Stamp Act.[48]

On December 20, 1765, Samuel Martin wrote that the Stamp Act had driven the Americans into French ports and that planters had no casks to ship sugar to England. On the same day, another Antiguan planter wrote that the island was in imminent danger of being ruined by famine because submission to the Stamp Act had reaped the wrath of the North Americans.[49] A couple of days later, a local trader warned that without the northward trade "the estates can never be supported," fearing that if conditions continued, "we are likely to be Miserably off for want of lumber and Northern Provisions as the North Americans are determined not to submit to the Stamp Act. . . . The Islands (nay the Merchants in England as our Remittances principally center there) will feel the Effects severely, for there is not one tenth of the lumber in the Islands that will be required for the next crop." Beeston Long testified before a committee of the House of Commons in February 1766 that Antigua faced starvation and ruin.[50]

The loss of North American food imports and the prospect of famine provoked fear of a slave rebellion in the Leeward Islands. It was always a danger that "the interval of want and expectation in the West India Islands may

unhappily be filled with famine, revolt, desolation, and massacre!"[51] Only the
Leeward Islands confronted the potential of a dearth so serious as to provoke a
slave rebellion if they complied with the Stamp Act. The fear of a slave famine
and a rebellion, which restrained protest in other islands, such as Jamaica and
Barbados, helped unleash the violent opposition to the Stamp Act in St. Kitts
and Nevis. This may explain the paradox that the Stamp Act riots in the British
Caribbean occurred in the islands with the highest proportion of slaves in
British America.

In resisting the Stamp Act, the Leeward Islands yielded to the economic
pressure exerted by the North Americans. The inhabitants of Antigua only
resisted the stamp distributor after the captains of two ships from New York
threatened to leave because their "orders were not to sell at any Island where
the Stampt Papers were used." Even Barbados was "alarmed at the Vengeance
declared against them, for so readily admitting the Stamp Law, and now begin
to Curse it heartily." In addition to northern economic pressure, the presence
of sailors from New England ignited the riots in St. Kitts and Nevis where they
"behaved like young Lions."[52]

The unique administrative structure of the Leeward Islands enabled the
inhabitants to defer to North American threats and thwart the enforcement of
the Stamp Act. The most scattered and loose-knit federal colony in the empire,
the Leewards had four deputy governors, four councils, and four assemblies (a
fifth in Tortola was added in 1774). As Governor Sir Ralph Payne noted some
years later, "The government is divided into an Archipelago of Islands extend-
ing between two and three hundred miles . . . which have distinct legislatures
and laws, and in fact Governments independent of each other, although under
one General and Chief Commander, it is perfectly impracticable to carry on the
very laborious Business of my Government, without a ready and easy communication with every District of it." From their traditional residence in Antigua, the governors had to hire vessels at their own expense to visit the other
islands, and local planters were often appointed as governors owing to the
unprofitability of the post. Deputy governors on each island theoretically
aided the governor, but they lived in England. In practice, the presidents of the
councils governed each island. This dilution of power severely undermined
colonial authority.[53]

Poor communications between the Leeward Islands were another impedi-
ment to executive control: "The distance of the several Islands . . . necessarily
created delays." Governor George Thomas blamed these distances for his taking over a year to reply to the secretary of state. He claimed that he was not even
aware of the appointment of William Tuckett as stamp distributor until after
the riots in St. Kitts. Thomas believed that if he had been better informed, "the

stamps might have been secured in the first [place], till the ferment in People's Minds should have subsided." Montserrat even denied having received any stamps and claimed ignorance of the act but this was deception. On the other hand, Tortola had no stamp master or stamps as late as January 1766.[54]

The successful resistance of the Leeward Islands was facilitated by Governor George Thomas. A former governor of Pennsylvania and a native planter of Antigua, Thomas lamely responded to the news of the riots in St. Kitts and Nevis by issuing a proclamation offering a reward for information leading to the seizure of the perpetrators. However, he frankly admitted that "where there is no general discontent, I have had little hopes of Discovery." He did not visit the turbulent islands, and he sent the most superficial account of the riots to London. He even encouraged the legislature of Antigua to petition Parliament against the Stamp Act.[55] By January 1766, he became distracted by private affairs: his daughter eloped with a member of the Antigua council whom the governor angrily dismissed. Thomas returned of his own accord to England at the beginning of June 1766.[56] The government of the Leeward Islands then devolved on the president of the council of St. Kitts, who claimed disingenuously that "no one suffered either in his person or Property" during the riots and therefore took no further action.[57]

The high rate of absenteeism among St. Kitts and Nevis planters may also have weakened the potential restraining influence of a local elite. Absentee planters owned half the property in St. Kitts by 1745. On visiting the island thirty years later, Janet Schaw found it "almost abandoned to overseers and managers, owing to the amazing fortunes that belong to Individuals, who almost all reside in England."[58] The proportion of land owned by absentees far exceeded that of resident planters by the time of the Stamp Act.

* * *

The resistance of the Leeward Islands notwithstanding, the reaction of British West Indies differed in important respects from that of North America during the Stamp Act crisis of 1765–66. No radical leader, such as a Samuel Adams or a Patrick Henry, became prominent in the Caribbean through opposition to the Stamp Act. Samuel Martin, the most outspoken critic of the tax in Antigua, was an opponent of the American Revolution. Sir John Gay Alleyne of Barbados, the aggressive champion of assembly rights, voted against sending a memorial to the king about the Stamp Act. He sat on the infamous committee of correspondence that defended the obedience of Barbados in reply to the pamphlet of John Dickinson. Even in St. Kitts and Nevis, the island assemblies showed little initiative during the crisis. Unlike the mainland colonies, they did not pass resolutions defining colonial rights and made no attempt at federation, like the mainland colonies did with the Stamp Act Congress. No revolutionary groups or committees existed outside St. Kitts and Nevis. There was no appeal to homespun clothing or any attempt to limit trade with nonimportation agreements. There was no denunciation of luxury and corruption against Britain.

In contrast to the North American press, the printing presses in the British West Indies were silent during the Stamp Act crisis. There were printers in Jamaica, Barbados, St. Kitts, Antigua, Grenada, and Dominica.[59]

At the time of the Stamp Act, there were three newspapers in Jamaica, two in Barbados and two in Antigua.[60] The printers in the Caribbean produced no political pamphlets critical of the Stamp Act. Unlike their counterparts in North America, the island newspapers paid stamp duty where the act was in force, and some of the printers in the Leeward Islands even tried to obtain stamps when they were unavailable. Their passivity was especially noteworthy because the tax threatened the very existence of newspapers by charging duties for every copy and every advert. Printers were obliged to purchase ready-stamped blank sheets for their newspapers from England at a cost likely double the sale price.[61]

The island colonies preferred to emphasize commercial and practical rather than constitutional objections to the Stamp Act. In March 1764, Rose Fuller initially expressed "his satisfaction in the plan of the Stamp Act" when it was introduced into the House of Commons. The absentee planters and merchants of Jamaica asked Stephen Fuller to draw up a petition to Parliament "that should be liable to as few objections as possible upon such an occasion." "In order that his Petition might give no offence," Fuller personally consulted Grenville and was shocked to hear from the minister of the "violent & inflammatory" style of some of the North American petitions. The final draft of the February 1765 petition questioned only the expediency of the stamp duties and avoided reference to the issue of direct taxation by Parliament. Fuller actually took up an invitation to suggest amendments to the Stamp Act. He advocated the removal or reduction of the duty on rum from the British islands, as well as the introduction of a six-pence per gallon duty on French brandy and tougher measures against smuggling in Britain. In a clever game of dividing the colonial agents, Prime Minister Grenville deflected Fuller with an absurd errand to make a personal survey of the coastline of Britain.[62]

The timid formula of avoiding any reference to rights was adopted by the assembly of Barbados, which instructed its agent to draw up a petition in which he was to avoid anything "in the stile and substance of that Representation that might give offence to those from whom only our Redress can come."

Indeed, not only did they leave it to the discretion of agent whether to introduce the question of principles at all, but they actually admitted that they were uncertain of the constitutional legitimacy of their case: "How far, indeed, we are intitled, by the constitution of England, or our own peculiar character, to an exemption from every other internal tax, than such as may be laid upon us by the representatives of our own people, in conjunction with the two other branches of our legislative body, we can not positively say." The committee preferred to seek repeal by a "humble submission to authority." As late as 1771, a member of the Barbados assembly still believed that the Stamp Act was merely "impracticable and inexpedient" but constitutionally legitimate. These sentiments differed so widely from those of the continental colonies that John Dickinson wrote that it was better to die than set such a precedent for perpetual servility.[63]

Even in the Leeward Islands, the assemblies avoided confrontation with Britain. The assembly of St. Kitts did not petition Britain against the Stamp Act, and the Nevis assembly denounced the riots in North America in an address to the king. In Antigua in December 1765, the legislature resolved to petition the king, "setting forth the several Grievances sustained by this Island in consequence of the late Act of Parliament," but the petition avoided reference to abstract rights. Furthermore, the assembly later reversed itself. The assemblies of St. Kitts and Nevis sent addresses of thanks to the king for the repeal of the Stamp Act, which many of their counterparts in North America refused to do because the repeal was regarded as a right rather than a favor.[64]

Dickinson's *An Address to the Committee of Correspondence in Barbados* (1766) incited replies in three pamphlets from Barbados which, although representing a variety of views, reflected the gulf between the British West Indies and North America. They were written by Kenneth Morrison, an Anglican clergyman, who came close to advocating passive obedience to any parliamentary ruling; Sir John Gay Alleyne, an admirer of Boston radical James Otis and later speaker of the assembly, who praised Barbados for its pragmatic and prudent response; and an anonymous writer, posing as a mediator between Morrison and Dickinson, who criticized the abuse of British parliamentary power and advocated parliamentary reform.[65] All three condemned the injustice of the Stamp Act; even Morrison thought it detestable.[66] Despite their different stances, however, they all emphasized that the act was passed with the authority of "legal garb" and was therefore entitled to respect.[67] They distrusted Dickinson's "zeal for natural rights."[68]

Alleyne charged that the Barbados's real crime, to North Americans, was its appeal to authorities other than the laws of nature. He mischievously quipped that "in such a well cleared and little spot," it was impossible for the assembly to appeal to the laws of nature with "no woods, no Back-Settlements to retreat to."[69] Morrison and Alleyne accused "the North American" of advocating violence and bloodshed.[70] All three authors expressed shock at the behavior of the patriotic mobs in America and defended the moderation of Barbados.[71] They all nevertheless tried to absolve the island from the "Jacobitical Taint" of extreme passive obedience.[72] Morrison and Alleyne were unable to resist commenting on the irony that the North Americans were celebrating the repeal of the Stamp Act when Parliament had failed to acknowledge the right of the colonists to tax themselves and had specifically asserted its own right to legislate in all cases whatsoever in the Declaratory Act.[73]

The North American patriots had understood the urgency of resistance, fearing that the act would enforce itself as Grenville had intended.[74] They therefore moved swiftly to compel distributors to resign and to block the circulation of the stamps before enforcement. By the beginning of November 1765, none of the island distributors had resigned, in contrast to nine out of thirteen in North America. By failing to act immediately, Barbados and Jamaica ensured the successful enforcement of the stamp duties among themselves.

The conciliatory response of Jamaica and Barbados was anathema to the mainland Sons of Liberty. To pay any stamp duty appeared to the mainland patriots to be both a tacit acknowledgment of Parliament's authority to tax the colonies and a fatal precedent. Furthermore, it broke the united colonial front that they held necessary to defeat the tax. On the other hand, the reaction of Jamaica and Barbados paralleled that of mainland loyalists like Thomas Hutchinson who privately disliked the tax but believed in submission to authority until the offending taxes were repealed.

* * *

After the repeal of the Stamp Act, there was a brief rapprochement between the British West Indies and North America: "The uproar of the colonies again the Stamp Act . . . [had] inspired the little West Indian communities with like jealousies, & apprehensions." Thereafter, however, the differences widened and relations cooled between their respective lobbies.[75] In 1767–70, the islands were mute in their response to the Townshend Acts, which occasioned the second great imperial crisis before the American Revolution. Britain again sought to assert its right to tax the colonies and make them share the cost of imperial government. Charles Townshend, the chancellor of the exchequer, introduced an imperial tax on selected imports into the colonies including glass, lead, paint, paper, and tea. In addition to covering some military and civil expenses, the Townshend duties aimed to pay fixed salaries to some royal governors and judges to make them independent of grants from the colonial assemblies. The tax made little commercial or economic sense because it amounted to a tax on British exports. Yet it enabled Britain to assert its right to tax the colonies while appearing to observe the distinction made by a minority of North Americans between the right of Britain to levy external but not internal taxes. The Townshend Acts also reorganized the customs' service and established new vice-admiralty courts.

In the House of Commons, a "significant number of West Indian MPs joined the attack on the new policy towards America," including William Beckford and Rose Fuller. In December 1768, Beckford made a motion for a full inquiry. He was at the summit of his political career as lord mayor of London and founder of the radical *Middlesex Journal*. In an effort to further discredit colonial policy, Beckford selectively leaked the correspondence of Governor Bernard of Massachusetts, giving the Boston radicals invaluable propaganda. In Parliament, Beckford twice tried to present petitions from the agent for Massachusetts against the Townshend Acts. It was largely through his influence that the London livery instructed its representatives to urge the government to "reconcile the unhappy Differences subsisting between the Mother Country and her Colonies." Mark Lovell, a West Indian merchant, was also prominent in persuading the livery to write a petition reciting the specific grievances of the colonies. In March 1770, Rose Fuller called for a complete repeal of the Townshend duties. In April, following the partial repeal of the duties, Beckford seconded a motion for the repeal of the outstanding tea duty. Beckford's death in June deprived the colonies of their best advocate.[76]

The spirited opposition of West Indians in Parliament and of the North Americans to the Townshend duties found no parallel in the British Caribbean. The islands did not articulate their grievances in pamphlets or in the press, even though their private correspondence suggests that they had constitutional objections to the Townshend Acts.[77] None of the island legislatures passed resolutions against the Townshend Acts nor did they petition Britain. They were unable to plead the excuse that their assemblies were not in session yet only the assembly of Barbados made an oblique reference to colonial policy in an address to the governor: "We cannot but lament the causes of those Jealousies which have for some time past disturbed the Minds of our fellow subjects upon the Northern Continent nor look with less impatience than themselves for the result of those more tender and deliberate counsels which shall restore America to its former general quiet by placing it as formerly in the full Esteem and Kindness of the Parent country." Yet "Good order and Tranquility" continued in Barbados despite "the pressure of those Burthens which have thrown our more numerous Bretheren upon the northern Continent into a flame." There were no nonimportation associations even against luxury imports from Britain. Jamaica and the Leeward Islands were rumored to have set up such associations but only after the repeal of the Townshend duties.[78]

*   *   *

The islands and their powerful metropolitan lobby successfully exploited their submission to imperial policies to plead preferential treatment from the home government. In 1768 Henry Frere, a member of the council of Barbados, wrote a history to show that "Barbados hath always preserved a uniform and steady attachment to Great Britain and therefore is intitled to the affection and indulgence of the mother country." He included obedience to the Stamp Act as "a late remarkable instance" of the loyalty of Barbados to Britain. After a fire in Bridgetown in Barbados in 1767, George Grenville urged Parliament to reward the colony that had "acted dutifully" during the Stamp Act crisis. Lord Hillsborough, who was notoriously unsympathetic to colonial rights as secretary of state for America, submitted a plan to the king to exempt the West Indies and Virginia from the Townshend duties "since they have already made ample provision for that purpose." Secretary for War Lord Barrington was even more emphatic that the islands should be rewarded for their submission to the Townshend duties: "Though they don't like taxes any more than their neighbours are they to be treated in the same manner as Boston?" Barrington proposed that the laws be enforced in the colonies that resisted but repealed in "those colonies that have submitted."[79]

British colonial policy increasingly discriminated against the North American colonies in favor of the British West Indies. Apart from the Stamp Act, Grenville's imperial reforms had not affected the islands as negatively as the mainland colonies. The Sugar Act was welcomed in the islands as the first step toward ending the illicit trade between rival producers in the French West Indies and North America (see Chapter 3). Grenville tried to undo the damage of his customs reforms to the Anglo-Spanish bullion trade through Jamaica. The Quartering Act of 1765 was of little significance in the islands where barracks were already sufficient for peacetime garrisons and where there was not a comparable problem of armies on the march owing to shorter distances. It was not even clear that the act applied to the Caribbean. The Currency Act of 1764 was limited to North America and was unopposed in the islands, which did not in any case print paper money. While Britain tightened restrictions on the trade of North America, it granted free ports to Dominica and Jamaica in 1766.

The Townshend Acts similarly did not affect the islands as much as the mainland colonies. The revenues were to pay the salaries of governors and judges in North America. The power to vote the salaries of governors was never so great in the islands, where the assemblies voted royal governors permanent salaries at the beginning of their tenure and not, as in the case of some of the mainland colonies, annual salaries. Barbados actually wanted the British government to pay the salaries of the governor and other colonial officials for which the legislature had voted the 4½ percent duty after the Restoration.

Britain exempted the West Indies from some clauses of the Townshend Acts. Skillful lobbying by Beeston Long, Rose Fuller, William Beckford, and Richard Maitland, the agent for Grenada, won the islands a last-minute re-prieve from the jurisdiction of the new American Board of Commissioners of Customs (1767) and the four new American vice-admiralty courts whose creation roused such hatred among the patriots, especially in Boston. These lobbyists represented to the Treasury the impracticality of placing the islands under the distant jurisdiction of officials in North America.[80] West Indian lobbyists in London also did nimble footwork to keep prerogative disputes in the islands out of Parliament (see Chapter 5). Perhaps sensing the opportunity to divide the colonial lobbies, the successive secretaries of state for America were unusually lenient toward the islands, after the creation of this new office in 1768.[81] The West Indies were unlikely to find a conspiracy theory credible when they had escaped the majority of those imperial policies that convinced the mainland patriots of a deliberate plan of tyranny by Britain.

*   *   *

The divergence of the island and mainland colonies during the Revolu-tionary War was thus anticipated in the Stamp Act crisis of 1765–66 and especially in the Townshend Revenue Act crisis of 1767–70. The November 1765 Stamp Act riots in St. Kitts and Nevis, although primarily a result of fear of economic reprisals by mainland patriots, belie the notion that the whites of the British West Indies were incapable of even token opposition to imperial policy. These riots were major in proportion to the size of the free population and occurred despite the dependence of these islands on the British sugar market, despite their having the highest proportion of slaves in British Amer-ica, and despite a powerful military presence in the region.

The passive response of the major island colonies Jamaica and Barbados to colonial reforms may well have misled the British government about the likely consequences of imperial policies. The failure of the islands to protest sufficiently against the Stamp Act may have deluded ministers at Whitehall into thinking that imperial taxes were capable of success. In a speech of March 1770, Lord Barrington, the secretary of state for war, used the acceptance of the Townshend duties in the islands and some of the mainland colonies to defend colonial policy.[82] West Indian whites did not engage in radical movements; the slaves mounted the fiercest resistance movements and were the real Sons of Liberty during the 1760s and 1770s.

5

Winning the Initiative

THE RISE OF ELECTED ASSEMBLIES is one of the major themes in the political history of British America and a "necessary part of any explanation of the background of the [American] Revolution."[1] The assemblies were often the focus of opposition to Britain during the revolutionary period and were the forums where many of the revolutionary leaders gained their formative political experience and articulated the revolutionary doctrines. These elected bodies contributed to the remarkable stability of the American Revolution by providing an organizational framework that was adapted and continued after independence. Their privileges and powers were a critical issue because they were so fundamental to the protection of colonial rights and privileges in general.

The rise of elected assemblies in the British Caribbean complemented the trend in North America.[2] They exhibited the same disposition to enlarge their sphere of influence and were often even more assertive than mainland assemblies when defending their privileges. As early as 1651, the assembly of Barbados denied the authority of Parliament to legislate for them in terms similar to those used by the thirteen colonies in 1774.[3] The Jamaican assembly was one of the most vigorously assertive in British America. In the 1670s, it led the struggle against metropolitan attempts to introduce a system of government similar to that of Ireland. For the next fifty years, it refused to vote a permanent revenue to the Crown and tried to obtain a statute of colonial rights, which "was notable because it was the last such attempt by any assembly before the disturbances that immediately preceded the American Revolution." Throughout the mid-eighteenth century, the Jamaican assembly refused to insert a suspending clause into any law: "None of the provinces which revolted in 1775 ever dared to oppose officially the suspending clause with as much vigor as did Jamaica." In 1757, it was the first assembly to be censured by the House of Commons.[4]

Although there were similar trends between the island and mainland colonies in the rise of the assemblies, this chapter finds important differences. Parochial disputes about corporate privileges actually transcended the larger

Figure 15. *Court House and Guard House in the Town of St. John's, Antigua*, Thomas Hearne, 1775–76 (Victoria and Albert Museum). The island assemblies exhibited the same disposition as those in the mainland assembly of Antigua met in the Court House in St. Johns. The colonies to enlarge their influence at the expense of the Crown. In the painting, the Sixtieth Regiment (the Royal Americans) mounts an honor guard for governor Sir Ralph Payne.

imperial crisis in the British Caribbean until December 1774. Unlike the situation in North America, tensions did not mount to a climactic breakdown between the island legislatures and governors in the 1770s. The island colonial leaders did not claim equality between the assemblies and Parliament, nor did they deny parliamentary sovereignty.

Indeed, the example of the island colonies demonstrates the inadequacy of explaining the American Revolution in terms of the rise of colonial assemblies. It is misleading to regard the prerogative struggles and the revolutionary struggle as synonymous. Such conflicts over jurisdictional issues inevitably develop from any situation of divided power, like the modern-day competition for influence between the president and the Congress of the United States. These exchanges were not necessarily the prelude to an independence movement and they continued in the Caribbean for the life of the assemblies. As Bernard Bailyn observes, an explanation of the American Revolution in terms of the rise of colonial assemblies "does not make the dynamics of the Revolutionary movement intelligible — it does not provide a basis for understanding what impelled it forward at the time and place it moved forward."[5]

* * *

The island assemblies continued to be assertive and to make bold constitutional claims throughout the 1760s. By 1769, the *St. James' Chronicle* in London reported that "scarce any Assembly in America or the West Indies is now sitting" and that "of Jamaica seems to have led the way for all the Leeward Islands, as that of Boston has done for all America." The *Middlesex Journal* also reported "that the oppressive measures of some governors in that part of the world [the West Indies], have so irritated the people, that they are careless under what government they live, so they can preserve their property."[6]

British ministers variously threatened to bring the internal affairs of Jamaica, St. Kitts, and Grenada before Parliament during the 1760s. London debating societies had motions about "the important question . . . of Grenada."[7] The Middlesex freeholders discussed the case of the three successive expulsions of John Adams from the assembly of Barbados. Lord Hillsborough complained that the affairs of St. Kitts appeared in "weekly publications" in Britain in 1770. "Even the minutest circumstances . . . of transactions in St. Kitts" became familiar to Lord North, the prime minister, to the duke of Grafton, and to Lord Weymouth. Rumors abounded that these issues were to go before the House of Commons "to ascertain the Rights and Privileges of Provincial Assemblies in future."[8]

In the 1760s, the Jamaican assembly led the other islands in asserting its privileges and in openly confronting the imperial government. In a dispute with Governor William Henry Lyttelton, the assembly made some of the boldest constitutional claims "to be found in the records of all colonial America, in spite of the fact that they had come from the island province, and not from one of the seceding thirteen."[9]

The dispute in Jamaica arose when the carriage horses of a prominent member of the assembly were seized by a law officer who was enforcing a civil writ for debt. The member argued that the seizure of his horses prevented him from attending assembly debates and that it was a breach of his right to freedom from arrest. He was supported by the assembly, which regarded freedom from arrest as an essential precondition for freedom of speech. It was a customary right that the speaker of the assembly had formally requested from the governor since 1677 and a privilege that also conformed to the practice of the House of Commons where it was emotively linked to the attempted arrest of the five members by Charles I in 1642. The assembly ordered the imprisonment of those implicated in the arrest and in the original suit.

The contest widened into a broader constitutional struggle over the relative judicial powers of the assembly and the governor. The imprisoned men chose not to appeal for their release to the assembly but to the governor in his judicial role as chancellor. Governor Lyttelton, a successful former governor of South Carolina and the grandson of a seventeenth-century governor of Jamaica, tried to avoid ruling on the legality of imprisonment by the assembly. He attempted instead to persuade the assembly leaders to release the men but he was rebuffed when the assembly ordered additional arrests. In another effort to avoid making a judgment on the constitutional powers of an assembly, he prorogued the assembly in order to free the men on the technicality that the powers of the house were in abeyance. He failed. The assembly ordered the rearrest of the men when it next met. Governor Lyttelton finally heard the case in chancery and ordered the release of the imprisoned men.

The assembly refused to conduct business until the chancery decision was reversed and, despite the dissolution of three successive assemblies, the impasse continued for some eighteen months. The assembly contended that its power to imprison was an essential safeguard of its privileges and its judicial role. It did not matter that the governor avoided a general ruling about the power of the assembly to imprison and that he only judged against the imprisonment in this specific case. The assembly was merely a cipher if the governor could reverse its judicial decisions in his capacity as chancellor. There was no precedent for an English court's overruling the House of Commons. The governor, on the other hand, believed that the assembly acted contrary to his royal instructions, which he regarded as superior to local customs. The

Figure 16. *William Henry Lyttelton* (1724–1808), Benjamin Wilson. Antony House (Photograph: Courtauld Institute of Art, Sir Richard Carew Pole). Lyttelton was governor of Jamaica at the time of the Stamp Act. He was involved in one of the most celebrated prerogative disputes with the assembly, which overshadowed opposition to the Stamp Act in Jamaica.

Crown, not the assembly, was the ultimate arbiter of colonial constitutional arrangements. The colonists regarded such a view as a recipe for arbitrary government in which their constitutions were subject to the whims of the Crown.

Both parties sought external support to end the deadlock. They both appealed to England. The assembly published its resolutions in the newspapers in Jamaica, its members nearly unanimous in their opposition to the governor. The bitter differences between the Spanish Town interest of the planters and the Kingston interest of the merchants were put aside in their common cause against Governor Lyttelton. The opponents of the governor, including the speaker of the assembly, continued to be reelected. They were undeterred by news of the displeasure of the king, the threat of parliamentary intervention, hints of direct imperial taxation and talk of the closure of the legislature. Such threats only stiffened their resolve not to become "traitors to posterity."[10]

Lyttelton eventually joined a succession of colonial governors who found their attempt to uphold royal authority undermined by the home government. He initially received support when the government agreed to pay the additional subsistence of the army, which was traditionally granted by the assembly. His conduct was approved by the Privy Council. But, with the advent of the new Rockingham ministry in England, he was ordered to pursue a policy of conciliation and he was simultaneously granted a leave of absence, which he took. The imperial government conceded the original issue by instructing future governors to extend freedom of arrest to the goods of representatives. In the presence of all members of the legislature and a thousand spectators, Governor Lyttelton's successor destroyed the offending pages of the chancery court register and the right of the house to commit was upheld. The victory of the assembly caused jubilation throughout Jamaica similar to the contemporary celebrations of the repeal of the Stamp Act in North America. But the assembly was still not satisfied. It produced an eighty-page report accusing the former governor of a deliberate "design of subverting the Constitution of our Government."[11] The report was translated into thirty-four resolutions, which were used as the basis for a memorial against him to the king. The dispute still did not end there.

The aftermath was in many ways the most significant phase of the controversy because the Jamaican assembly openly confronted the imperial government and opposed the express wishes of the king. It refused to reimburse the home government for the eighteen months of additional subsistence money paid to the army by the British Treasury when the assembly had refused to vote funds during its dispute with Governor Lyttelton. The assembly regarded these annual subsistence grants to the army as equivalent to the annual military subsidies voted by Parliament after the Glorious Revolution. The grants were an essential check on the executive power because they necessitated the regular calling of the legislature by the governor to vote money. The assembly argued that the funds from Britain had enabled Governor Lyttelton to rule arbitrarily.

In 1768, Lord Hillsborough, as secretary of state for America, ordered the acting governor to obtain reimbursement but neither a dissolution nor prorogation of the assembly achieved results. In 1770, Hillsborough warned of parliamentary intervention unless the Jamaican assembly complied. Governor William Trelawny did not publish the threat for fear of a backlash but he did communicate the personal wishes of the king that the government be reimbursed. The assembly was adamant in its refusal. It twice passed unanimous resolutions justifying its actions and wrote letters of defiance to the agent at Westminster. It sent addresses to the king in September 1768 and again in November 1770. The justices and vestry of the parish of St. Anne specifically instructed their representatives not to accede to any demand to reimburse the Treasury. In 1770, the agent for Jamaica requested a hearing on the subject before the Privy Council. Governor Trelawny concluded that the assembly would never reimburse the Treasury.[12]

Jamaica won the power struggle with the imperial government during the 1760s. The dispute over the reimbursing the home government for the army allowance occurred simultaneously with the stalemate over the Quartering Act in New York but Parliament did not suspend the intractable assembly of Jamaica as it did the assembly of New York in 1767. The issue was only resolved by the new ministry of Lord North, which simply allowed the question to lapse in 1771. The behavior of the Jamaican assembly in "defying the Privy Council . . . carried the defiance of royal authority to an entirely new level," which was only again attained in South Carolina and Massachusetts in the early 1770s.[13]

*　*　*

The privilege dispute in Jamaica raised fundamental constitutional questions about the boundaries of colonial rights and imperial power. It brought into sharp relief the issue of whether colonial rights were guaranteed by custom or whether, as the governor contended, they were dependent on the royal prerogative. The issue highlighted the ambiguous nature of imperial constitutional arrangements, the difference between practice and theory. There were competing colonial and metropolitan interpretations of the imperial constitution.

The colonists saw their constitutions as an accumulation of past usages,

Figure 17. *The Governor Going to Church*, unsigned, c. 1740s (Barbados Museum and Historical Society). The island governors, like those in North America, found themselves increasingly impotent in relation to the assemblies, even though the external trappings of power were impressive.

customary privileges, and local laws. They considered "instructions from the crown to the governor as recommendatory only, but not obligatory upon them." The imperial government, on the other hand, regarded its commissions and instructions to governors as binding. It made little attempt to revise its instructions to successive governors to take into account changes in the colonial constitutions. The commissions and instructions to governors were therefore at variance with colonial practices. The imperial government did not acknowledge the political gains and customary rights of the colonies. The implication of the metropolitan view was that the colonies had no "defence against the assaults of arbitrary power, no security for their lives, their liberties, or their properties" if they had "no constitution . . . but what the king is pleased to give."[14]

The assemblies sought to extend their influence because they continued to fear the prerogative powers of the governors. They sought to restrain what they perceived to be the exorbitant powers of the governor "as a bear is rendered an inoffensive animal by muzzling; or a viper, by drawing its fangs." Although governors despaired of the relative impotence of their office, the colonists saw every governor as a potential reincarnation of Charles I and James II. This was because the governors still possessed very broad theoretical powers including the power to summon, prorogue, or dissolve the assembly; the power to veto laws; the right to declare martial law during which their powers were greatly expanded; and the right to appoint and dismiss judges, militia officers, and senior law officers such as the attorney general. Whereas the chances of royal tyranny in England were remote after 1688, they appeared all too real in the colonies. The colonists tried in vain to obtain a comparable political settlement and similar constitutional guarantees to those won by the House of Commons in 1688. Their best protection against the ambitions of a governor was an independent assembly: the "temple of Liberty" and "the only solid foundation of British liberty."[15]

The colonists looked upon their disputes with local governors as epic struggles mirroring those of the House of Commons against the Stuarts. They were "playing out roles and operating within a conception of politics that derived directly from the revolutionary situation in Stuart England." The colonial pantheon of heroes included such seventeenth-century English parliamentarians as Sir John Elliot, John Hampden, John Pym, and Sir Edward Coke. The seventeenth-century constitutional struggles occurred in England when many of the first English emigrants left for the Caribbean and when the English colonies were in their formative stages of development. The rhetoric of the seventeenth-century English parliamentarians continued in the colonies long after it had ceased to be an animating force in British politics. Its survival

Figure 18. The King's House, Spanish Town, Jamaica (Author). The residence of the governor in Jamaica was much larger than the governor's palace in Williamsburg. This was a reflection of the contemporary importance attributed to the West Indies by Britain. The mansion gave an illusion of power that was much more circumscribed in practice.

in the colonies during the eighteenth century is explained by the similarity of the colonists' political circumstances with those of seventeenth-century English citizens. There was consequently "a strong predisposition to interpret virtually all political conflict as struggles between prerogative and liberty."[16]

In addition, the colonists claimed a theoretical basis for their power, impelling them to make greater political claims for their assemblies. They took for granted that they possessed the inherited rights of Englishmen and were entitled to the same respect and advantages as their fellow subjects in England. They traced these rights from Magna Charta (1215), the Petition of Rights (1628), and the Bill of Rights (1689). They looked back to a mythical Anglo-Saxon constitutional balance that fell victim to the Norman Yoke in 1066 and to the Stuarts. They insisted that they could not "be subjected to laws repugnant to those of England, and are no more liable to be governed by mere will of the King than if they had remained in England."[17] They cast themselves as defending traditional rights against the invasion of colonial governors, rather than assuming new powers, which was important in a society that venerated continuity with the past.

Following the common-law tradition of Sir Edward Coke, the assemblies enlarged their powers by appealing to precedents, traditions, and statutes in both their own and other colonies. According to the attorney general of Barbados in 1740, practices and customs which were "general, and . . . long continued [became] in a manner Lex Loci [and were] not at once to be overthrown merely because they happened to be various from those of England." The privileges so acquired compensated for the lack of formal constitutional guarantees by Britain. These customary privileges were "the *natural Inheritance* of every representative Body of a free People or every such Body will be found, upon Trial, to be a *form* without a *substance*, whose Powers are inadequate to the End for which it was created." They were "absolutely necessary to support their own proper authority, and to give the people of the colony that protection against arbitrary power, which nothing but a free and independent assembly can give." The colonists cited not only their own precedents but also those of other colonial assemblies. The assembly of Grenada "very Early got upon the subject of their Privileges which . . . they meant to Establish as largely as possible from those of any British colony of which they had knowledge, whether in North America or the West Indies."[18]

The assemblies also enlarged their powers by claiming that they were analogous to the House of Commons. They found in the journals of Parliament "precedents by which Legislatures in the Colonies conduct themselves." The colonists collected parliamentary procedure books and adopted the customs, procedures, and forms of the House of Commons "by whose model their own Assembl[ies were] constructed and destined to the same general Purposes." They not only copied internal procedures but claimed the same privileges and powers because "the assembly . . . holds the same rank in the system of their constitution, as a British house of Commons does in that of the mother country." Their imitation of the House of Commons reflected the tendency of colonial elites both to emulate British society and to defer to metropolitan standards in judging the quality of their own societies. They despaired that "our constitution . . . is far from being agreeable to the spirit of the English constitution" but the very inadequacies of the analogy only made contemporaries all the more determined to close the gap and reproduce the metropolitan model. The conscious imitation of the House of Commons not only influenced procedure but "prescribed explicitly and in detail a whole set

Figure 19. Grenada mace, 1781 (detail showing arms of the colony), reproduced in Sir Harry Luke, *Caribbean Circuit* (London: Nicholson and Watson, 1950), plate xxvi. The mace was a symbol of parliamentary independence the British West Indian assemblies copied from Parliament. The Grenada mace portrayed slaves and oxen operating a sugar mill which graphically demonstrates how the planters saw no contradiction in the coexistence of slavery with their own freedom.

of generalized and specific institutional imperatives for representative bodies, a particular pattern of behavior for their members, and a concrete program of political action."[19] They even copied the mace of the House of Commons, which symbolized parliamentary independence.[20]

The rise of colonial assemblies consciously mirrored the early history of the House of Commons. Colonial assemblies, too, won the initiative and enlarged their sphere of influence at the expense of the executive in a series of constitutional struggles against the governors and councils reminiscent of the prerogative disputes between the House of Commons and the Crown. This was the primary preoccupation of the British West Indian assemblies where local prerogative disputes eclipsed the imperial issues that so concerned North Americans.

*　　*　　*

The Jamaica privilege dispute inspired other islands to define their rights and privileges during the 1760s. In June 1767, Sir John Gay Alleyne, on assuming the speakership in Barbados, requested the privileges of the assembly in conformity with those of Jamaica and the British House of Commons. He recalled that Governor Lyttelton had dissolved the assembly of Jamaica on one occasion for failing to request its privileges. His request was not only an innovation in procedure but also the first time that the legislature had formally claimed freedom of members from arrest. Except in the case of tie votes, Alleyne simultaneously relinquished his right to vote in conformity with the practice of the speaker of the House of Commons.[21]

Alleyne proceeded to introduce other innovations, including new procedures for the presentation of bills to the council and for the passage of money bills, all modeled on the House of Commons. Alleyne was familiar with the Governor Lyttelton dispute and with a pamphlet, published at the height of the controversy, titled the *Privileges of the Island of Jamaica Vindicated* (1766), which he thought "a masterly Piece, and written upon an extensive View of the subject." His request for privileges was ridiculed in a pamphlet titled *A Short History of Barbados* (1767), written by Henry Frere, who was a member of the council and who asserted the unwavering loyalty of Barbados to Britain. Alleyne wrote a reply accusing Frere of promoting "a Doctrine of the most abject and undistinguishing submission to our Governors." The two men subsequently fought a bloodless duel.[22]

The assertion of privileges was echoed throughout the smaller islands of the eastern Caribbean. The normally quiescent assembly of Montserrat refused the request of the council to prosecute one of its members, citing that doing so would be contrary to freedom of speech. In 1770 the assembly moved to impeach two judges for negligence, and when it was ordered by the governor to erase these proceedings from its minutes, the assembly reaffirmed its right to impeach, citing the House of Commons. The two judges resigned.[23] In the opinion of the acting governor of the Leeward Islands, there was a "growing Disposition in the Assemblies of these Islands to extend their privileges beyond what . . . [was] consistent with the nature of their Establishment and the intention of the Government."[24]

The assemblies of the Windward Islands (Grenada, Dominica, St. Vincent, and Tobago) were especially turbulent. In January 1768, the speaker of the new assembly of Dominica demanded the "usual Privileges enjoyed by the British Colonies." It soon became entangled with the council over its sole right to adjudicate disputed elections. Governor Robert Melville threatened to deport troublemakers as criminals to Britain and prorogued the assembly. In 1774, it voted the right of members to freedom from arrest and imprisonment, which it extended to "four days before meeting."[25] The new assembly of St. Vincent contended with the governor over the right to appoint a registrar of deeds. It passed resolutions against the governor's adjournment as "illegal Arbitrary and Tirannical."[26] It tried to make itself sole auditor of the public accounts to the exclusion of the council.

*   *   *

The assemblies of the British West Indies were triumphant in their prerogative struggles in the 1760s except in St. Kitts and in Grenada, where the white inhabitants were split over who should control the assembly. These divisions were much more damaging than the traditional rivalry of merchants and planters and were reflected in the high membership turnover. Grenada had the highest membership turnover in British America as opposing parties jostled for majorities in the elections.[27] St. Kitts, despite having a long established assembly, experienced a sharp rise in membership turnover.

In October 1768, the assembly of St. Kitts passed a resolution excluding members of the council from voting in assembly elections.[28] It invoked the practice of the House of Commons, which excluded members of the House of Lords from voting in their elections in order to maintain the separation of powers. This was indeed the practice in Jamaica but not in other islands like Grenada or Antigua. In St. Kitts the small size of the electorate gave the votes of council members considerable influence over the composition of the assembly. Like the contemporary debate over the expulsion of John Wilkes from Parliament, the event inspired an unusual privilege dispute in which colonists challenged the power of the legislature and accused the representatives of acting arbitrarily.

When the assembly removed three new representatives by disqualifying the vote of a council member, seven representatives walked out. The remaining members, acting as a bare quorum, ordered the arrest of the seven dissidents, who were subsequently imprisoned for sixteen days and expelled with an order to pay court costs. The action polarized the island. The protagonists were supported by rival newspapers, with Daniel Thibou's *St. Christopher Gazette* acting as the voice of the assembly and Thomas Howe's *Charibbean and General Gazette or Saint Christopher Chronicle* advocating the cause of the seven rebel members and the council. The division became more emotive when one of the expelled members died twenty days after his release, which his doctors attributed to his imprisonment. The quorum in the assembly proceeded, quite unabashed, to imprison John Gardiner, who had acted as a lawyer for the seven dissident members. The assembly even attempted to indict the printer of the opposition newspaper for libel against their leader.[29]

The supporters of the seven rebel members likened the division to one between a party of debtors who continued to sit as representatives and a party of creditors who had opposed the right of the assembly to discount the votes of council members: "Allowing for a few fugitives from each to the opposite side, it was credit and property against debt and poverty." The claim is supported by an analysis of the membership of the two parties confirming that sitting members were socially obscure while the expelled members and the council members were among the wealthiest inhabitants. John Stanley led the party of debt and used his influence as a lawyer to protect several debtors. They remained in power by gerrymandering elections partly thanks to the appointment of Stanley as registrar of deeds, which enabled him to rearrange land titles to give his supporters more votes. These actions were sanctioned by his relative, Governor William Woodley, and later by the acting governor, Richard Hawkshaw Losack. The governors sent scant information to Britain, where Lord Hillsborough and the Board of Trade admitted that they did not have the "least intelligence" of the matter.[30]

Led by Stanley, the party of debt and poverty, which dominated the assembly, had a specific agenda that aimed to benefit indebted planters and lower-class whites. They wanted to discourage the latter from emigrating — a particular concern in the Leeward Islands. They also aimed to decrease local interest rates from 8 to 6.5 percent; to curb public expenditure, including the repeal of the costly Basseterre water act; and to restrain the economic activities of free people of color who competed with the lower-class whites.[31] These policies widened the rift.

The case of St. Kitts was one of the few examples in which a colonial assembly was successfully disciplined by the imperial government. In June 1772, the Privy Council affirmed the right of the council members to vote in elections and permitted the continuance of court actions against the assembly. It ordered the governor to keep the assembly "more within the legal Bounds of a provincial council." The party of debt soon unraveled. Daniel Thibou, the printer whose newspaper was the voice of the party of debt, left the island to live in St. Croix, where he founded the *Royal Danish American Gazette* (1770). Between June and September, six members suddenly quit their seats and power was restored to the party of credit. The assembly consequently endorsed the judgment of the Privy Council, which was fully entered into its journals after the successful completion of related lawsuits in October 1778. The Rev. James Ramsay later recalled that Stanley's intrigue was "impotent to prevail in the Privy Council" and that "law and Britain conquered."[32]

Like St. Kitts, Grenada was "in a kind of civil war for several years" in what became the most celebrated political controversy in the British West Indies in the 1760s.[33] It was the subject of five pamphlets and much newspaper commentary on both sides of the Atlantic. Following the acquisition of the island from France in 1763, many of the British Protestant settlers came into conflict with the French Catholic inhabitants. As in Quebec and French Canada, the presence of a non-English speaking, Catholic, white European population posed an urgent problem of integration for the imperial authorities. The numerous small French planters were in the majority and they were permitted to vote. The British planters had larger properties and were more likely to be absentees; they commanded fewer votes.

After 1768, in an effort to assimilate a conquered people, the British government relaxed its discriminatory rules against French Catholics. It permitted French subjects to be nominated for a prescribed number of positions as councillors, assemblymen, judges, and justices of the peace. They were only required to swear allegiance to the king and they were exempted from the Test Act (oath against transubstantiation). At the same time, candidates elected with the support of the French won control of the assembly. It was bold experiment when Catholics were still excluded from political office in Britain.

The policy of tolerance was opposed by the more zealous of the British Protestant subjects who contended that the alteration of their constitution by the Crown prerogative was illegal. In a period when popular anti-Catholicism and Francophobia were among the defining national characteristics of the British, they associated French Catholicism with tyranny. They wanted to maintain their monopoly of power. The Protestant council members blocked measures of the French elected assembly. When two French Catholics were

admitted to the board, six councillors walked out in protest. The British Protestants threatened civil disobedience rather than submit to laws and taxes
passed by a body they portrayed as the organ of the French Catholics.

Governor Robert Melville was sympathetic to the opposition of the British subjects and he attempted to impede the new imperial policies until his
removal in 1771. He was the son of a Scottish minister of a religious sect "not
remarkable for comprehensive charity" and he was formerly a member of an
anti-Catholic club in Edinburgh.[34] During the elections of 1766, he had used
various means to prevent the election of Catholics or those chosen by French
subjects. When they nevertheless triumphed in the election, he dissolved the
first assembly. He obtained a favorable majority at the next election, which
voted him a large salary. The British Protestants also passed a draconian militia
act with twenty capital offenses that denied Catholics any rank above private
and an election act requiring that all candidates be Protestants. Their delibera-
tions may have alienated some of the wealthier resident and absentee British
planters who had supported the imperial experiment in religious toleration.
When the latter combined with the French subjects to elect a hostile assembly
in 1768, Governor Melville returned to Britain where he defended his administration before the Privy Council and where he remained until 1770.

The Protestant subjects of Grenada published a paper titled "Constitutional Declaration" in which they called for a return to the original constitution of the island to exclude French Catholics from office or for a constitution
settled by Parliament. They boycotted the legislature and refused to pay taxes,
causing a state of virtual paralysis between 1768 and 1774. They were supported by the judiciary, which ruled against the confiscation of slaves for the
nonpayment of tax. One of the judges was the elder brother of John Wilkes, to
whom toasts were made to "Grenada Wilkes, the British constitution and no
dispensing power." A less pliable judge was burned in effigy.[35]

Events in Grenada gained notoriety in Britain and North America where
popular anti-Catholicism and Francophobia identified government policy
with the tyranny of the Stuarts. The secret enemies of the British constitution
aimed "to undermine and subvert the grand principles of the revolution [of
1688], on which is founded all civil and religious freedom."[36] While the French
Catholics bewitched the administration into granting unconstitutional concessions, "our Protestant Brethren in North America . . . have not been able to
obtain the smallest favor."[37] To save posterity from civil and religious slavery,
"a minute enquiry into the present state of . . . Grenada, [was] an object of the
highest importance." If the prerogative powers of the Crown were able to
force Roman Catholics into the legislative body of Grenada, "may not they by
the same power be forced into the Councils and Assemblies of colonies more

extensive and more important?" The proceedings were "exactly similar to those [which] exasperated all good subjects against the Ministry and Council of James the II," which led to the Glorious Revolution of 1688.[38]

*   *   *

Tensions between the lower houses and the royal governors did not lead to a climactic breakdown in the early 1770s, as they did in North America. The assemblies had emerged victorious from the disputes of the 1760s, except in St. Kitts and Grenada where divisions among the membership frustrated any chance of success against the imperial government. D. H. Makinson finds that the political issues in Barbados were characterized by their parochial nature and the fervent declarations of loyalty before 1775. Michael Craton and James Walvin find that in Jamaica "faction evaporated in an era of good feeling characterized by votes of loyalty to the British Crown" and "imperial reforms went unchallenged" before 1774. Even in Grenada, the governor reported the island to be in a state of tranquillity in 1773–74.[39]

The difference between the island and mainland colonies was reflected in the extraordinary popularity of Governor Sir Ralph Payne in the Leeward Islands. The mainland patriots found the political sentiments of Governor Payne so offensive that the *Virginia Gazette* claimed that Lord North wrote his inaugural speech to the assemblies in the Leeward Islands. The paper found it "difficult to determine whether" the speech "ought to excite our contempt or our Indignation!" Yet the assembly of Antigua rejected a motion to dissent from the governor's unreserved praise for the home government. The members were unable to "restrain our expressions of attachment to him, as the true representative of the royal master."[40]

In April 1775 when the first skirmish of the American Revolutionary War occurred at Lexington and Concord, the four assemblies of the Leeward Islands (St. Kitts, Antigua, Nevis, and Montserrat) all honored the departure of their governor with addresses of thanks and requested his immediate return. The assembly of Antigua sent a "loyal" petition to the king thanking him for appointing Sir Ralph Payne and for the "continued state of union and tranquility . . . when other governments have been rent by faction." Their petition was reprinted by the Purdie and Dixon *Virginia Gazette* without comment. The assembly of Antigua voted the governor a gift of "a handsome small sword, richly and elegantly decorated [and] . . . set in diamonds" at a cost of one thousand pounds. The island's enthusiastic endorsement of Payne illustrates the gulf that existed between the British West Indies and North America. The popularity of his governorship was mirrored among governors in the other islands of the British Caribbean.[41]

In North America, a new series of assembly prerogative disputes arose throughout the mainland colonies even during the so-called period of quiet when the partial repeal of the Townshend duties brought a temporary lull in imperial conflict between 1770 and 1773. Prerogative disputes occurred in Georgia, Maryland, and North Carolina, and were most pronounced in Massachusetts and South Carolina. Legislation was interrupted for over two years in Massachusetts. The assembly in South Carolina passed no annual tax bill after 1769 and ceased to pass any legislation after February 1771. A controversy over the subscription fund for John Wilkes had led for all practical purposes to the breakdown of royal government in the colony.[42]

In contrast, parochial politics in the British West Indies transcended the larger imperial dialogue until the eve of the Revolutionary War. The local prerogative disputes were, of course, related to the broader colonial search for a viable constitutional settlement in which the rights of the colonists were safeguarded "against the preponderant power of the Mother Country." But the assemblies of the British West Indies never moved significantly beyond these internal disputes to participate in the wider imperial debate. Jamaica and Barbados did indeed send letters to their agents opposing the Stamp Act but this was a tame response, as John Dickinson of Pennsylvania recognized when he charged the assembly of Barbados with negligence for having left such an important issue to their agent.[43]

Some historians attribute Jamaica's passivity to its preoccupation with the dispute with Governor Lyttelton and to the dissolution of the assembly for much of the period of the Stamp Act, but this explanation is far from satisfactory.

From the perspective of the patriots in North America, the assembly of Jamaica was perverse in giving a local privilege dispute priority over the Stamp Act. Although Jamaica sent instructions to its agent to oppose the stamp tax, it was generally "unattentive to the new resolution of the British Parliament, to force successive local taxes upon us, without out our consent."[44] The instructions to the agent were primarily concerned with the privilege dispute even though the Stamp Act involved more fundamental issues and affected all the colonies in British America. The threat of an imperial tax was much more explicit than that posed by Governor Lyttelton, who had tried to compromise with colonial leaders and tried to avoid a judgment that raised broader constitutional questions. The mainland patriots understood that a direct imperial tax threatened to make the colonial executives independent of representative government by enabling them to raise revenues without the consent of the colonists. They understood that the very existence of assemblies was at issue.

The assembly of Jamaica had not only failed to pass resolutions against the Stamp Act but it remained silent about the Townshend duties and other imperial policy initiatives until the eve of the American Revolution. This silence was mirrored by all the island legislatures and also by contemporary pamphleteers of whom nothing was heard before December 1774. Indeed, imperial issues were so disregarded that the assembly of Barbados wanted to reduce the salary of its London agent because "there is at this time so little for an agent to do." It was dissuaded by the speaker — Sir John Gay Alleyne.[45]

Alleyne argued that an agent was necessary "to Distinguish when to join our Interest with our Northern Brethren in one common cause, or when to stand upon Seperate Ground for our advantages or to prevent an Injury." He thought it a bad idea not to have an agent "at a time too when our Brethren of the Northern Continent have been zealous and happy enough to engage on their side not only a Franklyn but if the papers do not Misinform us a Burke and Barré in their service, men of the first Rate Political Abilities in the kingdom." In August 1774, the governor reported that Barbados was more concerned about the dry weather than about the crisis in North America.[46]

The leadership of the island assemblies failed to unite against the passage of laws that triggered the American Revolution — the Coercive Acts of 1774. In Antigua, Samuel Martin — an outspoken opponent of the Stamp Act and the Townshend revenues — condemned the "Boston firebrands" and the "mad" resolutions of the new Congress at Philadelphia. In "A Friendly Memorial to the North Americans" in the *Antigua Gazette*, Martin tried "to convince them of their folly, madness and ingratitude."[47] The most considerable men in the Leeward Islands, "best vers'd in the Traffick with the Continent of America, and in the knowledge of its inhabitants," believed that the Boston Port Act would reduce the rebels "to a due subjugation to the Laws, and to a proper sense of their Dependence on the Mother Country." In Jamaica, Simon Taylor felt that "after what the Americans have done Britain cannot give up the Point it would only be making them more arrogant than they are at present and I look on them as dogs that will bark but dare not stand when opposed loud in mouth but slow to action."[48]

The inactivity of the assemblies was reflected in behavior of the West India lobby in London, which contributed to the isolation of the North American lobby. The Society of West India Merchants actually lobbied the government in support of the drawback on tea in 1772 and of "continuing the Exportation of Tea from Great Britain to Ireland, & the Colonies as a national concern" despite the tea tax, the last remaining tax of the Townshend duties. An anonymous correspondent in the *Public Ledger* criticized the West India lobby for failing to be "alarmed sooner" by the situation of North America and for failing to take any action to prevent the "Destruction of the British Empire." In March 1774, the Society of West India Merchants met to consider "the new regulations affecting Boston" but determined upon no other action than to instruct "Rose Fuller, Richard Pennant and Richard Oliver to inform the chairman [Beeston Long] of any further proceedings in Parliament which may in their opinion affect the interests of the sugar colonies, & to use their best endeavours to get time allowed for the further consideration thereof."[49]

A former champion of the North American cause in Parliament, Rose Fuller was so outraged by the Boston Tea Party that he proposed levying twenty thousand pounds on Boston to indemnify the East India Company. Fuller nevertheless opposed the Coercive Acts and moved for a repeal of the tea duty, but he began to equivocate on colonial issues and soon gave total allegiance to the government. The agent for Massachusetts was disappointed that the West Indian merchants were too divided to organize effectively against the Coercive Acts. In May 1774, "some West Indians" joined the North American representatives at the Thatched House Tavern to protest against the Boston Port Bill, which closed the port of Boston to all commerce, but the interest was not united. At a time when there were between twenty and fifty members of the House of Commons with interests in the West Indies, there were only twenty-four votes against the third reading of the Boston Port Bill.[50]

Stephen Fuller voiced no opposition to the Coercive Acts. During the passage of one of the acts — the Massachusetts Regulating Act — he "consulted most of the Jamaica Gentleman upon the subject, and also the West India Merchants, who, are altho of various opinions in regard to several clauses of the Bill, did not chuse to step forth in opposition to it, as a matter not immediately affecting them." He regarded the Quebec Act as "just and fair and will not hurt us." He similarly did not oppose the Revenue Act because "the Merchants and Planters tho' of various opinions all agreed not to act in it as not immediately affecting us." The passive behavior of the West India interest was typical of the London merchant community in general in 1774. Edmund Burke thought that the intervention of other groups in support of the North American lobby might have averted the crisis and led to the adoption of more conciliatory policies. The West India lobby contributed to the fatal isolation of the North American lobby in Britain.[51]

The Jamaica assembly claimed in December 1774 that "for several years" it had "lamented this unrestrained exercise of legislative Power" by Parliament; it had hoped for the "interposition of their Sovereign" to avert a calamity. No doubt West Indians did expect justice to prevail and the offending imperial acts to be repealed. Yet their quiet suffering in "deed and silent sorrow" was deliberate and cannot simply be attributed to a sudden loss of nerve. The passivity of Jamaica can hardly be ascribed to lack of courage since the assembly willingly risked confrontation with Parliament in its refusal to reimburse the British Treasury for the payment of troops under Governor Lyttelton. It had openly ignored the explicit instructions of the Privy Council and the wishes of the king. It was more exposed to imperial wrath in this local dispute than if it had united with the mainland colonies against the Stamp Act. The passivity of the assembly reflected major differences between the British West Indies and North America.[52]

*   *   *

The assembly leaders in the British West Indies were not "a small knot of busy, unscrupulous lawyers, of the same type as, though with less ability than, the eminent Samuel Adams," nor were they "infected by the spirit of rebellion."[53] They shared more in common with such contemporary political leaders in Ireland as Henry Floud and Henry Grattan. They sought to direct the internal affairs of their colonies and to obtain local autonomy while deriving the economic and military benefits of membership of the British Empire. Many of them were educated in Britain and later returned to live in Britain (see Chapter 1).

They preferred to leave the issue of parliamentary sovereignty undefined. They recognized the right of Parliament to regulate trade and wanted the mainland colonies to abide by the Navigation Acts. Unlike the patriots in North America, they specifically denied any claims to their assemblies' equality with Parliament. Nicholas Bourke of Jamaica, one of the most sophisticated writers on constitutional issues in the East Indies and author of the *Privileges of the Island of Jamaica Vindicated* (1766), considered the power of an assembly "like that of all other bodies thro' the British Empire . . . subordinate to that of a British Legislature, which is and must, in the nature of things, be supreme over all the British dominions . . . I contend not for an equality of the colonies with the mother country; they are, and in the nature of things must be dependant upon it." Jamaicans thought it "better to be Slaves to a British parl[iamen]t than to [be] the dependant of a Minister." They continued to revere the House of Commons as "the Constitutional Judges of the Rights of British Subjects, however remotely Situated from their Mother Country," and they trusted the wisdom of Parliament to "decide in a Constitutional Manner . . . the Nature and Extent of their [the colonies'] Privileges."[54]

The champions of colonial rights in the British West Indies continued to acknowledge the subordination of their assemblies to Parliament even at the height of the imperial crisis with North America. In 1773, Sir John Gay Alleyne told the assembly of Barbados that their rights and powers "must not be poorly disclaimed and given up on the one hand," nor should they be "too freely and wantonly put in force on the other." He continued, saying that "we cannot in the nature of things be supposed to possess the same degree of power they [the House of Commons] do." In speaking against Alleyne, Henry Duke nevertheless conceded "that this House has not all the Power of a House of Commons; I admit." Edward Long, the most astute of contemporary commentators, thought that "acts of parliament are obligatory" and he hardly mentioned Parliament in his *History of Jamaica* (1774).[55]

In 1776, Alleyne told the assembly of Barbados that the king in Parliament is "supreme over the colonies." The Jamaica representatives spoke of their veneration "for the name of Parliament, a word still dear to the heart of every Briton" and their unquestioning obedience to the trade acts "as the salutary precautions of a prudent Father, for the prosperity of a wide extended Family." Even when opposing an imperial act for the registration of slaves in 1815, the Jamaica assembly resolved that it had "always acknowledged the power and authority of Parliament to make all laws necessary for the general benefit of the empire," and they were not "disposed to capriciously raise difficulties about the exact limits between this constitutional jurisdiction and the rights of internal legislation." They were less willing to make an explicit declaration of colonial rights in 1774–75 than was the Barbados assembly in 1651.[56]

The islands' recognition of parliamentary sovereignty separated them from the mainland colonies. North Americans advanced the "extravagant doctrines" that the colonies were "even independent of Parliament altogether." In 1773, Massachusetts made "an unequivocal rejection of Parliament's supremacy." By the following year, such views were becoming common orthodoxy in political essays like those of James Wilson of Pennsylvania and Thomas Jefferson of Virginia. Their acknowledgment of the right of Parliament to regulate the trade of the empire "was so qualified as to be scarcely an offer at all."[57] Even the conservatives advocated a new imperial relationship in the plan of union.

In 1774 all the colonial assemblies won vital confirmation of their constitutional rights against the Crown prerogative in Lord Mansfield's judgment of *Campbell v. Hall*.[58] The ruling had little relevance for North Americans, who were then more concerned with the power of Parliament, but it excited interest in the British West Indies where the colonists still thought in terms of prerogative struggles with the Crown, not Parliament. The case involved the right of the Crown to levy the 4½ percent duty on the exports of the Windward Islands (Grenada, Dominica, St. Vincent, and Tobago), which was raised by order of the Privy Council (July 20, 1764) with neither the consent of the colonists nor the authority of Parliament. Alexander Campbell was a British planter who had served in the assembly of Grenada and who had brought a suit against William Hall, the local collector of the duty, for gathering a tax raised without the consent of the colonists. Lord Mansfield found in favor of Campbell, ruling that the Crown had divested itself of the right to tax when it promised to grant an assembly in a proclamation of October 7, 1763. The power to levy taxes consequently resided with the assembly or Parliament. The judgment relieved all the Windward Islands from paying the duty. Subsequent attempts by governors of the Windward Islands to persuade the assemblies to vote the 4½ percent duty were unsuccessful. The judgment had far-reaching constitutional implications because it suggested that the Crown could not alter the constitution of a colony retrospectively, following the grant of an assembly. The judgment reaffirmed a central contention of the assemblies that their constitutional rights were not subject to the whim of the royal prerogative and that the colonists could not be treated as conquered subjects after the granting of their assemblies.

*   *   *

The divergent responses of the British West Indies and North America to the new imperial policies were reflected in the differences in their political and social structures. The British West Indian assemblies were more oligarchical than those of North America. Only the assembly of Barbados survived without interruption into the twentieth century. The assemblies of the other islands voluntarily disbanded themselves during the mid-nineteenth century rather than admit black representatives. The opposition of the planters to a broader franchise among both whites and blacks, for much of the eighteenth century, meant that the legislatures were but mere tools of the plantocracy and shadows of representative government.

The narrow representation of the island assemblies reflected the racial composition of the society and the concentration of landownership that attended the sugar revolution. The exclusion of blacks and people of color made voting rights very restricted in a population where whites were such a minority. As late as "the year of liberty" (1776), Antigua passed a law prohibiting people of mixed race from voting. Like the House of Commons, the West Indian assemblies remained ambivalent about public opinion even among the white minority. In 1768, the assembly of Grenada voted to exclude strangers other than those introduced by members or by the speaker. In 1770, the assembly of Barbados voted by a narrow majority to prohibit members from discussing debates with outsiders, although it reversed itself the following year, confining the rule of secrecy only to the clerk. As late as 1777, Barbados voted to continue to lock the doors of the House during debates.[59]

Although there was a higher ratio of members to voters in the islands than in the mainland colonies, the proportion of eligible voters in the islands was lower. The franchise was no more restrictive than it was in the southern mainland colonies, but the proportion of voters was lower than that in the mainland colonies because of the small size of the free white population in the islands, the concentration of wealth, absentee landlordism, and the lack of a large class of small planters. Barbados had proportionally one of the largest electorates in the islands owing to the size of the white population and greater number of small landowners. The elections in Barbados were well contested with canvassing and "some double Returns (even in the smallest Parishes)." Yet, only about 20 to 25 percent of white adult males were qualified to vote.[60]

Jamaica restricted membership to representatives with minimum earnings of £300 per annum or a gross wealth of £3,000. Jews made up 8 percent of the white population but were excluded from voting in Jamaica until 1832. Free colored people were similarly excluded. The distribution of seats left towns and new areas of population inadequately represented. True to the political philosophy of the age, the white elite equated the possession of liberty with the possession of landed property, which supposedly enabled voters to exercise independent judgment. They were critical of the allocation of seats but only because it did not accurately reflect the distribution of landed wealth.[61]

Although the emphasis on the representation of landed property was common throughout British America, it produced absurd distortions among the island electorates. It was not unusual for one vote to determine an election in some constituencies, especially in the smaller islands of the Lesser Antilles. The electorate was so small in St. Kitts that it had "thrown the Elections in some parishes into the hands of two or three People so that the Assembly is in Danger of becoming a Junto, influenced by the private views of a few individuals." This was particularly true of the parishes of Saint Mary Cayon, Saint Peter Basseterre, and Christ Church Nichola Town because of high rates of absenteeism and the presence of large sugar plantations. The single vote of Samuel Crooke, the only freeholder among forty-six white adult males in Saint Mary Cayon, determined the return of three members in the elections of 1768 and 1770. Saint Mary Cayon did not return a member, "there being no Freeholder to poll" owing to the death of Crooke in 1772. Because candidates and voters were able to participate in the elections of all the parishes where they held minimum freeholds, the single vote of Samuel Crooke's son determined the election of five members in 1773.[62]

With 66 percent of white adult males enfranchised, Grenada was unusual because of its more diversified economy and larger number of small property owners. However, the majority of the electorate were French Catholics who were permitted only three seats in the assembly. Furthermore, the British Protestant subjects gerrymandered elections so that candidates were returned without their knowledge and elections were held without a published summons. The assemblies of Jamaica and Antigua were able to continue indefinitely without elections unless dissolved by the governor. The assembly of Antigua held no elections between 1770 and 1781. This tendency toward oligarchy was reinforced by intermarriage among the planter, merchant, and professional classes. Questions were "decided by Votes of one, or two Family Compacts." Even in Jamaica, the assembly was "generally led by one or two principal Men."[63]

The plantocracy were primarily interested in their own hegemony and only secondarily interested in the legislatures as vehicles of their power. The assemblies "in the sugar islands represented only the master class."[64] Their rise and fall was inextricably linked to the rise and fall of the planter classes.

PART III

THE IMPERIAL CIVIL WAR

6

The Crisis of American Independence

THE ONSET OF THE REVOLUTIONARY CRISIS occasioned a shift in the political posture of the islands and their London lobby. Toward the end of 1774, the British West Indian assemblies and the West India lobby in London belatedly interceded to persuade the imperial government to adopt a more conciliatory policy toward North America.

These futile protests were not the climax of a cumulative opposition movement in the islands but rather a spontaneous reaction to the economic threat posed by the nonimportation and nonexportation resolutions of the Continental Congress in September 1774. The imminent loss of food imports from the mainland provoked fears among the white elite of a famine and the associated danger of a slave rebellion. These fears were heightened by the actions of the slaves who took advantage of the imperial crisis to intensify their own struggle for freedom, which climaxed in the great Jamaican rebellion of 1776. The planters and their lobbyists therefore tried to avert a war that promised them no benefits but serious risks.

There was no republican shift in the political ideology of the British West Indies. Planters continued to think of liberty in traditional hierarchical terms, defining rights narrowly as privileges associated with property and corporations and preferring a traditional rhetoric of customary rights and privileges rather than universal abstract rights. They did not speak the language of natural rights and equality. They did not appropriate the republican language of virtue to claim moral superiority over the corruption of the mother country. They did not attempt to widen the franchise. They did not try to disestablish the Anglican Church. They did not expand their concept of education to advocate broader opportunities even among the white population. In 1776 the plantocracy exhibited no sudden wish to change or improve their societies.

The posturing of the island assemblies and their lobbyists on behalf of the North Americans in 1774–75 ceased in 1776. It is significant that the Continental Congress did not offer the British West Indies the option of signing the

Articles of Confederation but left open a provision for Canada. The patriots rebelled without "once calling on the West Indians to declare their sentiments [and] . . . without once proposing whether they would join with them in their . . . race for liberty."[1]

*   *   *

It was not until December 1774 that the British West Indies tried to intervene to avert the crisis in North America. The Jamaican assembly petitioned George III in words and sentiments that were almost indistinguishable from those of the patriots in North America. The petition began with the familiar recitation that the colonists enjoyed the same rights as Englishmen and that the abrogation of these rights by the parent state "destroys that confidence, which the people have ever had and ought to have, of the most solemn royal grants in their favour."[2]

The Jamaican petition repudiated parliamentary sovereignty over the internal affairs of a colony. It even repeated the mainland conspiracy theory that there was a "plan" to enslave the colonies. This "plan [was] almost carried into execution" by the British government, which abused the rights and property of the colonists, having encouraged "the murder of the Colonists" by taking away their rights of trial by jury and sending "fleets and Armies . . . to enforce those dreadful Laws." The petition called upon the king to intervene.[3]

The Jamaica petition elicited letters of thanks from the Connecticut House of Representatives and from the Continental Congress. In the only formal invitation ever extended by the mainland colonies to the British West Indies, Connecticut asked Jamaica to join them in a committee of correspondence in the belief that the British government was likely to be impressed by "the representations of so respectable a body as the Assembly of your large and important island." Congress expressed its "warmest gratitude for your pathetic mediation on our behalf with the Crown."[4]

Congress acknowledged its regret at the necessity of adopting trade sanctions that hurt "friends, who have never offended us, and who were connected with us by a sympathy of feelings, under oppressions similar to our own." It nevertheless thought it unnecessary to apologize "to the patriotick Assembly of *Jamaica*, who know so well the value of liberty; who are so sensible of the extreme danger to which ours is exposed; and who foresee how certainly the destruction of ours must be followed by the destruction of their own." It urged the Jamaicans to convert "your sugar plantations into fields of grain" to supply themselves with the necessaries of life and punish Britain.[5]

The Jamaican petition created a stir. A copy was printed by William and Thomas Bradford in Philadelphia, and its arrival in London caused a political storm. Arthur Lee told Sam Adams that Jamaica carried "vast weight" in Britain and that the petition "gives therefore great alarm." The mild evangelical earl of Dartmouth, secretary of state for America, was furious at "so indecent, not to say criminal, Conduct of the Assembly" and he warned of possible dire consequences. The government took care to see that it was never debated in Parliament. Governor George Johnstone, former governor of West Florida, asked the government why the petition was held back from the public eye. He succeeded in provoking a debate about which papers the government was required to lay before Parliament. The prime minister denied that the petition was deliberately withheld and claimed that it was under consideration by the Privy Council.[6]

The West Indian agents, absentee planters, and merchants in England also began to mobilize. At the beginning of January 1775, a group of absentee planters approached the Society of West India Merchants to suggest combined action in response to "the very alarming situation in which the West India Islands are now placed by the late American proceedings."[7] On January 18, at a well-publicized joint meeting at the London Tavern in Bishopsgate Street, Rose Fuller moved for a joint petition to Parliament "as the only probable means of warding off impending ruin."[8] He proposed a cautious petition that confined itself to warning of the disastrous impact of a war on the economy of the British West Indies.

Even the modest proposal to send a petition met with opposition. Two merchants spoke against it: one favored postponing a petition until the islands actually experienced scarcities due to the loss of trade from North America (doubting the will of the North Americans to impose economic sanctions); the other argued that it was unnecessary to petition Parliament because the facts were already known. Fuller replied that "the majority of them [members of the House of Commons] were not apprised of the magnitude of the *American* business as a national concern."[9]

The petition was restrained in tone and avoided discussion of the merits of the imperial dispute. It was proposed that the petition not mention Congress, because it was not a body recognized by the British government, but instead that it refer only to "a Meeting held at Philadelphia, called a Congress." A London alderman feared that this might appear "an oblique censure on the Americans" and advised against offending either the Americans or the British. Rose Fuller suggested a compromise formula—"a meeting held at Philadelphia." The final version was a victory for the moderates because it adopted the compromise to read "a Meeting held at the City of Philadelphia." It emphasized the financial importance of the islands to Britain and predicted the ruin of the islands in the event of their losing the North American trade.[10]

As the government prepared to declare New England "in an actual state

RICHARD GLOVER ESQ.ᴿ

Figure 20. *Richard Glover* (?1712–85), T. Holloway after N. Hone, for *European Magazine*, 1786 (Author). Richard Glover was hired as a professional lobbyist by the West India Merchants and Planters in a desperate last minute bid to stop the British war against America in 1775. Glover gave evidence to a committee of the House of Commons to demonstrate the ruinous economic consequences for the British Caribbean of a war with America.

of rebellion," the West India lobby cooperated with the London North American merchants in simultaneous petitions to the House of Commons.[11] It sought support from "All other Members of Parliament interested in, and immediately connected with the sugar colonies." The petitions, along with petitions from numerous other localities and groups, played a major role in the strategy of the opposition parties. They consequently received a cold reception from the government, which referred them to a committee that Edmund Burke called the "committee of oblivion" because it consigned "everything the merchants could allege to entire oblivion."[12] The West Indian and North American lobbies then petitioned the House of Lords, where they met the same fate. Thereafter the two interests separated.[13]

Richard Glover represented the West India merchants and planters before a committee of the House of Commons. He was a leading member of the merchant community, a poet, and a politician with no apparent ties to the West Indies. His experience in advocating merchant causes spanned some thirty years, including representing the North Americans in the 1760s. In March 1774, Glover appeared before the committee with two witnesses: George Walker, an absentee planter and agent for Barbados, and John Ellis, an absentee planter from Jamaica who had been very active in "bringing the West India merchants and planters to a right sense of their situation."[14]

Glover stressed the importance of the islands to the British economy and their potential ruin in the event of a war with America. His only overt criticism of the government was the suggestion that a policy of coercion was unlikely to dissuade the patriots from their present course. His argument, together with the evidence and the original petition, was published in two thousand copies of a pamphlet distributed to every member of Parliament.[15] But these efforts were to no avail. The committee did not report and the petition was not debated. The West Indian attempt to mediate between Britain and North America was too little too late: war broke out with the first skirmishes at Lexington and Concord in April 1775.

Throughout 1775, the white island colonists and their lobby in Britain became more agitated about the growing imperial crisis. In June, the assembly of Grenada petitioned the king to "terminate the Contest which now subsists between your Parliament and your provinces of *North* America." It deplored "the horrors of a Civil War already manifested in the effusion of blood of our Countrymen and *friends on both sides.*" Unlike the Jamaican address, the Grenada petition "contained no Principles or Expressions tending to encourage or approve [the] Rebellion." Nevertheless, the governor immediately dissolved the assembly but its New England–born speaker was already on his way to Britain with a copy of the petition.[16]

There was a brief upsurge of British West Indian support for America in mid 1775. In June, a Rhode Island merchant found that there were "many friends" of the American cause in Jamaica among "the English Irish and Creole planters as well as the Common people." He had heard that "all the English Irish and Creole Planters" were willing to donate generous sums of money "to the suffering people of the Colonies." The London press reported that there was discontent in Antigua "on account of the oppressive laws carrying on against the Americans." Governor Valentine Morris of St. Vincent blamed North American sea captains and newspapers for misleading the island assemblies with the "delusive sounds of liberty and independence."[17]

Yet even at this critical juncture, West Indians were bitterly divided over the issue of America. Planters fought duels over the imperial question, resulting in the deaths of two men in St. Kitts. The *Barbados Mercury* reprinted an article from the *New York Gazette* condemning the extremism on both sides. West Indians were divided but generally opposed to British policy and the drift toward war in America. In October, West Indians in London signed both antigovernment and progovernment petitions but they were more numerous among the ranks of the opposition.[18]

In November and December 1775, the West India interest in London rallied in opposition to the Prohibitory Bill in which the British government proposed to prohibit all trade with the rebel colonies. Johnstone warned the House of Commons that "you will starve the islands, and uniting them in the same cause with North America, drive them into revolt also." The West India planters and merchants formalized their association in a joint standing committee of forty-three members, called the Society of West India Merchants and Planters. They again petitioned Parliament. Nathaniel Bayly, an absentee Jamaican planter, distinguished himself during these debates, describing it as "madness" for the ministry to "put the nation to so immense an expense of blood and treasure." He warned of the consequences of a war for the West Indies: "In order to wreak the revenge of a vindictive ministry on the Americans, you are now going to ruin all the plantations in the West-India islands."[19]

West Indian opposition to British policy in North America continued until well into 1776. In February, the assembly of Barbados petitioned the king about the prospect of a famine in the event of a war with America. In March, Admiral Gayton of Jamaica complained that it was impossible to persuade local courts to give judgments against North American ships and that there were "too many friends of America in this island." Jamaican Bryan Edwards wrote a poem commemorating the heroism of General Richard Montgomery, who was killed by the British during an attack on Quebec in December 1776. Governor Hay of Barbados claimed that "there are but too many among these

West Indians who would have been very glad to have dispersed any bad news" about the fate of British forces in North America.[20]

At least one-third of Jamaicans were said to be in favor of the Americans. It was reported that the inhabitants of St. Kitts "continue warmly attached" to the cause of North America and "that their reigning toasts are *Washington*, *Lee*, and *Independency* to America." Copies of Tom Paine's *Common Sense* circulated in Jamaica. The contents of the pamphlet were sufficiently known for Admiral Gayton to write an absurdly pedantic letter to the *Jamaica Gazette* refuting the figures given by Paine for ship building in North America. In July, Governor Lord Dunmore of Virginia advised Germain that "the Rebels receive all their information" from the Caribbean, where "it is first sent to the British Islands and from hence to St. Eustatia [St. Eustatius]."[21]

Samuel Estwick, the subagent for Barbados, published a pamphlet opposing the British war for America. Estwick reiterated the now familiar theme of the ruinous economic consequences of the war on the islands and the importance of the North American trade to their survival. He denied that Parliament had any right to tax the colonies and refuted Blackstone on parliamentary sovereignty, which he believed to be circumscribed by the fundamental rights of the people. He declared the war pointless, accusing the ministry of conspiring to start the war to enrich themselves and the Scots.[22]

An anonymous series of letters appeared in the *London Evening Post* by "the West India Merchant" who traded with the Windward Islands. The author protested against the war although he did not enter into a constitutional debate. He admitted that he failed to sign the West India petitions of the previous year, pleading that he was deceived by the confident language of the government who promised an early British victory. The thrust of the letters once again stressed the disastrous economic impact of a war in the Caribbean owing to the importance of the North American trade and the inadequacy of alternative sources of supplies. He cautioned that the loss of this trade would lead to famine and even a slave rebellion, another familiar theme. He accused the ministry of ignoring the interests of the islands, which stood to gain nothing from the war.[23]

*　*　*

The British West Indian intervention of 1774–75 was not the climax of a cumulative opposition movement in the islands, but rather the islands' spontaneous reaction to the threat of losing their trade with North America and the associated danger of a slave revolt caused by famine. The petitions and lobbying were incited by the nonimportation and nonexportation resolutions of the

Continental Congress in September 1774. These sanctions were due to come into effect respectively at the beginning of December 1774 and September 10, 1775. Congress delayed the prospective date of the nonexportation agreement by nine months in order to canvass the support and mediation of the British West Indies.[24]

The British West Indies were also reacting against the policies of the British government, which aimed to end all North American trade. In January 1775, British ministers spoke of retaliation against the North American colonies with the possibility of military intervention and an embargo of North American trade. In March and April, the threat became a reality when Parliament passed two Restraining Acts against commerce with colonies in rebellion. In September, the British admiralty ordered the commanders of the two squadrons in the Caribbean to start seizing North American ships that contravened the Restraining Acts. In December, the government imposed an economic boycott against North America in the Prohibitory Act.

Most British West Indian petitions cited the interruption of trade with North America as their chief motive in soliciting the mediation of the king or Parliament. In January 1775, Rose Fuller emphasized to the joint meeting of the Society of West India Planters and Merchants that they "grounded the necessity of a petition . . . on the two resolves of Congress." The petition began by explaining that "the planters and merchants are exceedingly alarmed at an agreement and association entered into by a Congress held at the City of Philadelphia in North America, on the 5th day of September 1774." Richard Glover wrote that the nonimportation and nonexportation agreements occasioned the petition of the West India merchants and planters to Parliament.[25]

The radical petition of Jamaica in December 1774 is often cited as crucial evidence to support the contention that only the threat of coercion or the impracticality of a revolt prevented the islands from joining the mainland colonies. One historian likens the petition to the Declaration of Rights; another describes it as "a ringing endorsement of the emerging colonial view of the distribution of authority within the empire."[26] However, both the timing and the content of the petition make it suspect as evidence of British West Indian support for the American Revolution because it was passed after the announcement of the nonimportation and nonexportation resolutions of the Continental Congress.[27]

Governor Sir Basil Keith of Jamaica downplayed the petition. He noted that it was passed by the minority mercantile faction from Kingston who waited until the departure of the planters (the Spanish Town interest) for Christmas. Only twenty-six of the forty-three members were present. The assembly sent the petition hours before the annual prorogation, despite the opposition of the speaker and a movement in rural areas against "the surreptitiously-obtained petition." The governor was emphatic that "it did not reflect the opinion of the colony as a whole." Governor Keith was right and wrong. His excuses about low attendance might equally have applied to resolutions against the Stamp Act in Virginia. Nor was his dismissal of the petition as the work of a minority party persuasive since the same Kingston faction soon afterward became the majority party within the assembly.[28]

Nevertheless, Governor Keith was correct to see that the petition was not a political manifesto for Jamaica. The assembly had simultaneously renewed its request "in the most forcible manner" for more troops from Britain. Moreover, the members voted their usual additional subsistence for the two regiments that garrisoned Jamaica. The day that they passed their controversial address, they voted five hundred pounds for the military hospital at St. Jago de la Vega. According to one local merchant who was sympathetic to the revolution, "the Sentiments so Nobly Expres'd by our Assembly . . . in their Address to the Crown [were] . . . by no means the general sense of the People" and the majority of Jamaicans gloried in the downfall of America.[29] Nor did the petition sour relations with the governor.

Loyalty in Jamaica was said to be as pronounced as rebellious sentiments "in the unhappy American colonies." A nonimportation party was set up in Jamaica, but it met "with little success." The leading merchants of the island "strongly opposed the general resolutions of the Americans." Within six months of the passage of the petition, Governor Keith reported that the inhabitants felt concern and regret over the imperial crisis but they hoped that "their Misled fellow subjects will forthwith see their Error and acknowledge the supreme Legislature of the Mother Country."[30]

The British West Indies had belatedly intervened in the imperial crisis in an attempt to avert the American war. It was a last-ditch effort to jolt the British government into adopting a conciliatory policy to prevent the imminent breakup of the empire and to win a reprieve from the economic sanctions imposed by the Continental Congress. West Indians had avoided, for the most part, ideological arguments in preference for economic objections to the war. They stressed the importance of the North American trade for their very survival and the inadequacy of alternative sources of supply and predicted dire consequences for the economy of the islands in the event of a war with America. West Indians were primarily concerned with economic self-interest and with their own security in the event of a famine among their slaves. Governor Lord Macartney of Grenada, one of the shrewdest contemporary observers, concluded that economic arguments weighed more than political ideas in the response of the white island colonists to the American Revolution.[31]

*   *   *

The British West Indian intervention in the imperial crisis was also motivated by an upsurge in slave resistance. Slaves were the first victims of the severance of food supplies from North America because their diet was traditionally supplemented with imported salt fish and guinea corn from the mainland colonies. In March 1774, John Ellis of Jamaica told the House of Commons that a famine in the islands might occasion a slave revolt. By 1776, newspaper reports circulated in London that slaves were dying in the islands due to the food shortage.[32]

Slaves and maroons took advantage of the imperial crisis in a remarkable spate of resistance movements on the eve of the American Revolution. Their response created greater urgency among the planters to end the imperial crisis and helps to explain the flurry of lobbying activity in 1774–75. In March 1774, a slave revolt broke out in Queen's Bay in Tobago. The slaves of Sir William Young and the late President Stewart, two of the highest-ranking officials and wealthy planters, killed three white men and captured some weaponry. They were joined by other slaves, making about fifty in all. In April, seven slaves in Tobago seized a ship, killing a crewman, and sailed for refuge to the Spanish mainland. The assembly of Tobago lamented that "the idea of regaining freedom seems to be universally spread amongst our slaves in all parts of the colony."[33]

In August, a slave woman called Attea betrayed a plan for a revolt in Westmoreland in Jamaica. She testified that Gold, "a Gunman in the great Rebellion in the year 1760," who was the head driver of an estate, and Warren, who was regarded as the headman on another estate, planned to rise and kill the white people. The following year, five slaves were tried in Jamaica for murdering their master: one was hung after being given two blows to the neck and breast with a pestle; another was burnt alive; and a third was hung, "his head afterwards cut off, and fixed on a pole"; two others were transported. A plot against another planter was foiled and the "three ringleaders were immediately hung up."[34]

In March 1775, maroons in St. Vincent launched a series of raids and attacked a party of surveyors, killing one. In an encounter with British troops, they left a lieutenant dead and other soldiers wounded. They were encouraged by the Caribs in what the white inhabitants feared was the prelude to a second Carib War.[35] At the same time, the assembly of Nevis offered a reward for information "about the cutting down of a gibbet [suspending] . . . the body of a negro near the race ground." It also recommended the prosecution of three "fellons accused of helping slaves to escape to Martinique." In September, the assembly forwarded intelligence to the governor about a group of slave rebels in Montserrat who planned to escape to Puerto Rico.[36]

Fear of the maroons among white Jamaicans reached heights unparalleled since the end of the 1730s. In April 1774, when the North American patriots began military exercises in preparation for the war against Britain, the white colonists believed the maroons to be in open rebellion, "the Maroons Negroes having assembled together and taken to arms, on the Northside of this Island." Admiral Sir George Rodney, the commander of the Jamaican naval station and a naval hero, sent two warships to Port Antonio because these "late Disturbances prove they [the maroons] have still a strong Inclination to be troublesome, the late Reduction of them was more owing to the timely arrival of two frigates . . . detached (by Lucky accident of a strong windward current) near their settlements, than to any internal force, that could have been opposed to them." It was not until October that Rodney felt sufficiently confident to recall the *Maidstone* from Port Antonio back to Kingston.[37]

A violent outbreak involving the windward maroons occurred simultaneously on the south side of Jamaica. The party of maroons landed at Old Harbour in search of a runaway slave. R. C. Dallas claimed that these maroons were probably intoxicated and that they feared that they were about to be repelled by the local inhabitants. The disturbance began when the captain of a merchant vessel called out to one Captain Thompson that the maroons were about to kill one of his slaves. A struggle followed in which Thompson fired a shot at the maroon leader, Captain Davy, which missed "or doubtless Mr Thompson and the Gentleman with him, would have been instantly cut to Pieces." Sam Grant, one of the maroon commanders, returned fire, killing the slave who had rushed to protect Thompson.[38]

The maroons then retreated through a crowd of sailors and were pursued to shouts of "Stop the Murderer!" Captain Townshend, the master of a Bristol ship, caught up with Sam Grant and began to whip him. After repeated warnings, saying, "I don't want to hurt you," Grant shot Townshend and escaped to the maroon town of Scott Hall. The incident provoked "a general Alarm throughout the Island, as if the maroons had revolted as many weak and wicked Reports were raised on the occasion." The colonial authorities negotiated a truce with the maroons and acquitted Grant.[39]

∗ ∗ ∗

The posturing of the island colonists on behalf of the North Americans in 1774–75 virtually ceased by August 1776. This was also true in London, where pro-American sentiment "was evidently on the wane." In June 1776, an address of the assembly of Grenada admitted that the island initially accepted that the North Americans were fighting a war to claim redress of grievances but that the subsequent conduct of the patriots revealed "that redress of Grievances had been the pretext [and] . . . Independance the Object of their pursuit." After leaving the West Indies in June, an anonymous planter wrote a pro-government pamphlet to refute the petitions of the previous year and to demonstrate that the islands were able to survive without provisions from North America.[40]

The unpopularity of the American cause was reflected in the hostile treatment of captured Americans in the British West Indies. Silas Deane warned Robert Morris that American patriots "were not safe in Antigua and Barbados if they were known to be friendly to the continental Interest." He claimed that the island colonists "exult in the prospect or rather [the] hopes of a total reduction of the colonies by the Administration" because they expected to confine "American Commerce in the West Indies absolutely to the English Islands." An American merchant in Dominica fled when his belongings were seized and "it was likewise said that all the monies lying in the hands of the merchants in the English islands belonging to America, will be taken hold of by proclamation."[41]

Antigua, the island formerly most closely connected with North America, was especially zealous in arresting anyone suspected of "attachment to the American cause," such as Charles Hobby Hubbard of Boston. Hubbard was "apprehended and confined to Gaol upwards of six Months, a great part of the Time in a Dungeon" after his ship was forced to land by a storm and letters to "the leaders of the American faction" were discovered in his mattress. Another five "friends of the Congress at Philadelphia" were arrested at Gray's Tavern in St. Johns, Antigua. They were subsequently imprisoned "for speaking Treason, and aiding and abetting the cause of the said Congress." There were not "a great many Persons of such Principles" in Antigua.[42]

Antiguans arrested and executed a man who, "falsely imagining that he might declare his mind here as freely as he did in England, being a favourer of the Americans," had publicly condemned the government. He was taken into custody where a body search revealed papers from British merchants to members of Congress. His punishment was particularly severe because he had tried "to inflame the minds of the people against the government, which might be a means of overturning all order and regularity in this island, and throwing us all into the greatest consternation." An indignant Captain Robert Campbell complained of gratuitous unpleasantness when his ship *America* was condemned by the vice-admiralty court at Antigua. He was imprisoned for over eight weeks "with fellons, at a short allowance of raw provisions, which were . . . dressed by the common Negro Hangman" and he suffered "continual insults and the utmost contempt, being shunned by the men with whom he had been acquainted, who would scarcely deign to speak to him."[43]

There was an outburst of loyal rhetoric and petitions in the British West Indies in 1776. Six hundred and three "friends of government," a high proportion of the adult white population, dined at a tavern in Antigua where they drank twenty-one toasts to the royal family, the government, colonial officials, and military commanders in North America, "success to his Majesty's Arms in America," and finally "Confusion to the Congress." This was a far cry from only two years earlier when local planters had refused to do business with one of the East India ship captains who had transported the infamous tea cargo to Boston.[44]

"Many Gentleman of Large Estates & property in the different West India Collonies . . . expressed their surprise" that the government did not ask them to supply slaves for military service in North America. The inhabitants of Nevis presented British troops with fifty hogsheads of rum "to inspire [them] with courage to beat the Yankee Rebels." Two former members of the assembly of Jamaica offered their advice to the government on how to crush the rebellion in North America.[45] Some of the large planters in Jamaica were willing to provide a thousand slaves for military service on the mainland, "such is their detestation at the present Rebellion in America." A loyal planter wrote that the safety of Jamaica was in jeopardy from both the slaves and the foreign islands until the "sons of sedition [in America] are checked."[46]

The island assemblies began to send addresses to Britain affirming their loyalty to the king. These addresses were generally pro forma but they began to include clauses specifically denouncing the rebellion in North America. In December 1775, Jamaica led all the islands in sending a declaration of loyalty to the king in which it also requested more troops. George III replied by publicly expressing his pleasure at the dutiful behavior of the Jamaican assembly. In December 1776, the assembly passed another loyal address, proclaiming that "it must be and is our desire as well as our interest, to support maintain and defend your Majesty in your just rights, with the greatest loyalty and affection, and thereby render ourselves truly deserving of your Royal favor and protection." They again asked for more military assistance. Their tone was now very different from that of their radical petition of December 1774.[47]

The Windward Islands were more forthright in their denunciation of the American Revolution. In February 1776, Tobago sent an address to the king in which the assembly expressed the deep concern at "the Rebellion in twelve of the North American Provinces." It advised the king that it "most ardently

Figure 21. *Nancy Hallam as Shakespeare's Cymbeline*, Charles Willson Peale (DeWitt Wallace Collection, Colonial Williamsburg, Williamsburg, Virginia). Loyalist refugees from North America found safety in the British Caribbean. The American Company of Comedians were the most exotic group to flee to Jamaica after the Continental Congress banned theatrical performances (October 1774). The celebrated troupe was founded by Lewis Hallam.

wish[ed] that the measures taken for suppressing it may have their desired effect." In March, St. Vincent sent an address of loyalty to the king, and Grenada followed suit in April, reversing its criticism of the previous year by expressing its regret at the rebellion in North America and "the violent and unjustifiable proceedings of the people of those Colonies [who] . . . forced your Majesty to the painful necessity of reducing them to a proper obedience by Coercive means." The assembly allowed that the mainland colonists had experienced "oppression" from the king's ministers but that their sufferings did not "justify the proceedings of the revolted provinces."[48]

Grenada asked the king to conclude the war quickly by both military power and conciliatory gestures. In the event of "crushing the present Rebellion," they appealed to the king to both "maintain the supremacy of Parliament" and preserve the rights of the colonists in order to avert the danger of future despotism. Also in April, the assembly of the British Virgin Islands sent a loyal petition to the king, speaking of its abhorrence at the "desperate and unnatural Rebellion formented by designing Men in your Majesty's American colonies." This "very Loyal Address" later made them the object of reprisal by the rebel colonies. In June, Lord Macartney wrote of Grenada that "I have the satisfaction to find them [the people] more reasonable in their sentiments & more respectful in their language, than they were formerly supposed to be."[49]

Another indication of British West Indian loyalty was the welcome extended to loyalist refugees from North America. The most exotic group of loyalists were the actors of the American Company of Comedians, who relocated to Jamaica after the Continental Congress banned theatrical performances (October 1774). This was the celebrated troupe founded by Lewis Hallam. As early as February 1775, actor David Douglas led the company to Jamaica, where they opened with a performance of *Romeo and Juliet* in Kingston in July. In October, several families arrived in Jamaica from North America "on account of troubles in their own country." In March 1776, following the flight of Governor Sir James Wright, many loyalists quitted Georgia for the West Indies and the Bahamas. American loyalists in the West Indies influenced local opinion, such as Douglas, who, in partnership with Alexander Aikman, became the king's printer for Jamaica. They published the *Jamaican Mercury and Kingston Weekly Advertiser* beginning in 1779, which they renamed the *Royal Gazette* in 1780.[50]

*   *   *

Why did the posturing of the island colonies on behalf of North America in 1774–75 cease in 1776? The conservative backlash against North America was in part caused by the great Jamaican slave rebellion of 1776. The rebellion was led by skilled creole slaves who, the governor wrote, "never were before engaged in Rebellions and in whose fidelity we had always most firmly relied." They included black drivers, coopers, distillers, millwrights, penkeepers, cartmen, carpenters, and cooks. Jamaica had "never been in such imminent Danger since the English conquest."[51]

The slave leaders confided their plans to no more than two "chiefs" on each estate in the parish of Hanover, in northwest Jamaica, where most of the planters were recent settlers with new plantations and where there were "more sugar works than some [parishes] of three times the extent." Furthermore, the Hanover black-white ratio was an extraordinary twenty-five to one. From Hanover, the leaders aimed to incite an island-wide insurrection beginning in late July. The revolt broke out prematurely. It did not cause immediate panic and the governor thought the danger almost over when he received notice of a general rebellion. The governor declared martial law during which the noise of trumpets and drums beating to arms filled the air, "rousing the most insensible human beings" and causing terror. He placed an embargo on all shipping including the sugar convoy, a drastic measure because it hurt the credit of the island among the merchant community in Britain. The leeward maroons at Trelawny Town were suspected of involvement in the rebellion. Governor Keith found them "restive" during the rebellion and warned of the "very high idea the slaves entertain of them."[52]

The revolt widened when some of the conspirators spread the word elsewhere on the island. In the parish of Vere, on the south side of Jamaica, two slaves were tried and convicted for attempting to obtain guns with the intent to rebel. At Montego Bay, someone tried to poison the market water with arson. At the request of the governor, Admiral Gayton sent two ships to the port of Lucea in Hanover to quell the rebellion. Panic ensued for almost seven weeks. The governor called off martial law even though he was not confident that the danger had passed. Of 135 slaves subsequently tried for the rebellion, 17 were executed, 45 transported, and 11 suffered "severe corporal punishment." Some of those executed were burnt alive and others gibbeted.[53]

The 1776 Jamaican rebellion was a direct consequence of the American Revolution. The loss of food imports from the mainland colonies, together with a severe drought, provoked the slaves to rebel because, according to Pontack of the Blue Hose Estate in the parish of Hanover, "they were angry too much with the white people, because they had taken from them their bread." A report in an English newspaper claimed that American emissaries encouraged the slaves, giving them ammunition and guns. Silas Deane, an American diplomat, had indeed advocated American support for an uprising of the Caribs in St. Vincent and a slave revolt in Jamaica.[54]

Several planters blamed the ideology of the mainland patriots for the revolt. The Rev. John Lindsay, rector of the parish of St. Catherine and Spanish Town, wrote to Dr. William Robertson (the principal of Edinburgh University who became a distinguished historian of the Revolutionary War), attributing the participation of creole slaves to "disaffected" whites who openly expressed their sympathy for the mainland patriots at their dinner tables. Lindsay pondered the impact on slaves who heard some whites praise "the Blood spilt by Rebells extoll'd as precious drops" and heard "Men toasted into Immortal Honours for Encountering Death in every form, rather than submit to Slavery." A merchant asked, "Can you be surprised that the Negroes in Jamaica should endeavour to Recover their Freedom, when they dayly hear at the Tables of their Masters, how much the Americans are applauded for the stand they are making for theirs." His correspondent agreed and replied, "We are too often unguarded in our conversation when our Servants are present."[55]

Slaves hardly needed to import ideas of liberty; the favorable circumstances created by the outbreak of war was the primary cause of the Jamaican rebellion in 1776. The slaves planned the rising to coincide with both the removal of British troops from Jamaica to North America and the withdrawal of naval ships escorting the merchant convoy to Britain against the new menace of American privateers: "The taking away the few soldiers we had left, at a time when there was a great scarcity of provisions . . . was the chief cause of the late conspiracy among the Negroes in Hanover."[56]

The Jamaican revolt dramatically illustrated the dependence of the white island colonists on the presence of the British army to police the slave population. The revolt began when the Fiftieth Regiment, representing almost half the military force on the island, was about to embark for North America as reinforcements for General Sir William Howe. Nine of the total ten companies were already onboard the troop transports where they were awaiting the other company before sailing from the Hanover port of Lucea for service in America. The military strength of the island was consequently reduced to about 360 soldiers and some parishes were left totally denuded of any protection by regulars.[57]

The slave conspirators recognized that there were fewer troops on the island "than at any other time in their memory" while their own numbers had increased. They knew that "the English were engaged in a desperate war, which would require all their force elsewhere [so that] . . . they could not have a better opportunity of seizing the country to themselves." They knew that the British troops were scheduled to depart before the end of July and that naval ships were due to escort the troops and the homeward-bound convoy. Governor Keith—apparently fearful that his report to the secretary of state would appear too far-fetched—apologized that "this train of Reasoning may seem above negro comprehension."[58] Later examinations of the conspirators uniformly supported the evidence that the rebellion was planned around the anticipated departure of the soldiers.[59] An inquiry by the assembly of Jamaica concluded unanimously that the withdrawal of the troops, upon which the slaves had "placed their strongest hopes," was the primary cause of the conspiracy.[60]

The garrison mentality of the white island colonists intensified in the aftermath of the Jamaican slave rebellion and contributed to the backlash against the American Revolution. A letter from Barbados, written at the time of the Jamaican rebellion, described the slaves there as "in a state of rebellion." In September 1776, the president of the council of St. Kitts sought the help of the British navy when he suspected that the fires on two or three plantations were part of an intended slave insurrection. Others suspected slave involvement in the great fire in Basseterre, the capital of St. Kitts, which caused over £200,000 sterling worth of damage and was widely believed to be arson. Montserrat increased its guards to check the "outrages" committed by slaves and to apprehend any slave found without a ticket after 8:30 at night. Whites in Antigua stayed up all night to prevent a slave uprising. Some estate owners sent their wives and daughters back to England for safety. In December, four slaves in Montserrat were executed for attempting to murder their master. Maroons in Grenada were committing "outrages and Depredations [of the] . . . most alarming Nature." There was "seldom a week passes but we hear of some estate being plundered by them."[61]

*   *   *

The posturing of the white island colonists on behalf of the North Americans in 1774–75 also ceased in 1776 because of the effects of the American War in the Caribbean. It became treason to openly avow sympathy for the North Americans after the king proclaimed them in rebellion on August 23, 1775. It was not safe to express political sentiments in correspondence.[62] The North Americans were no longer fighting a war for the redress of grievances but a war of independence that was less comprehensible to the island colonists, whose self-interest dictated their loyalty to the British Empire.

American privateers intercepted the trade of the islands, which "naturally incline[d] those who were their friends to become their enemies" in the British West Indies. In November 1775, Massachusetts led the other provinces by issuing commissions to privateers and by setting up prize courts. In March 1776, the Continental Congress also began to issue commissions. It initially tried to exempt the property of the British Caribbean from seizure but found the distinction unworkable. In July, it passed a resolution for the confiscation of the property of the British "and particularly the inhabitants of the British West Indies" taken at sea.[63]

Congress sent agents to neutral islands in the Caribbean of whom the most distinguished was William Bingham. Arriving at Martinique in late 1776, the twenty-four-year-old Bingham was instructed "to feel the Pulse of the French Government, to know whether it beat towards American Independancy" and to procure "if possible . . . 10,000 good Musquets, well fitted with Bayonets . . . for General Washington." After his disembarkation, Bingham watched his ship, *Reprisal*, engage in "the first battle fought by an American ship in foreign waters" against H.M.S. *Shark*. The fort guns at Martinique fired on the British naval ship, which was forced to disengage.[64]

American privateers such as *Oliver Cromwell*, *Rattle Snake*, *Pilgrim*, *Scourge*, *Manley*, *Hampden*, *Bunker Hill*, *General Washington*, *Black Prince*, *Revenge*, *Retaliation*, and *Reprisal* cruised among the British islands where their names became infamous. They were armed and refitted in North American ports and in the French West Indies. A privateer like *Governor Trumbull* was crewed by a 150 men with 24 guns.[65] They hovered off the popular sailing routes near Martinique, northern Cuba, and the southern coast of Florida, and they even awaited the West India trade in the English Channel.

Some American privateers were bold enough to launch raids on the outer ports of the British islands where they cut merchant vessels and fishing boats from their moorings "in sight of the inhabitants" and where they mounted landing parties. They briefly invaded Nassau (New Providence) in the Bahamas in 1776 and twice tried to capture Tobago in 1777. St. Anne's Bay in Jamaica experienced almost daily alarms of an imminent enemy landing and several ships were snatched from their moorings. A raid against Speights Town in Barbados netted fishing boats and slaves valued at £2,000. John Pinney of Nevis was stunned to witness, from his own breakfast table, a St. Kitts–bound brig taken by a privateer off his plantation wharf. He protested that the islands were "subject to be pilfered and robbed by Pirates in the night, who may, with ease, carry off our slaves to the utter ruin of the Planters."[66]

It was all the more galling for the British planters that American privateers found sanctuary in the islands of rival European colonies in the Caribbean. Privateers fitted out at Martinique, where William Bingham held court with their captains at the American Coffee House. Bingham issued blank commissions for privateers, which meant that less than one-third of the crews of some of the privateers were Americans and most were French. He "took an early & active part in the arming of Privateers . . . to annoy and cruize against British Property," with a view toward provoking a war between Britain and

Figure 22. Miniature of William Bingham, Charles Willson Peale (Frick Art Reference Library of the Frick Collection). William Bingham was agent to Congress at Martinique between 1776 and 1779. He secured supplies for the Continental Army and attempted to involve France in the war against Britain.

France "by sowing the Seeds of Jealousy & Discord betwixt them, & by affording them matter for present Resentment, & renewing in their Minds the objects of their antient Animosity." Bingham reported home that "every [British] W India Gazette abounds in abuse & invective" against the French commander at Martinique for assisting the American privateers.[67]

In February 1776, the British admiralty revived the convoy system to protect the West India merchant fleet against American privateers. In June, the first convoy sailed for Britain. Thereafter, they sailed every year from St. Kitts, the rendezvous of trade from the eastern Caribbean, and from Port Royal in Jamaica. They sailed between June and October. The convoys were large, infrequent, and easily delayed, consisting of as many as 350 ships. The convoys out of London were sometimes so large that the West India merchant ships blocked the Thames.[68] The convoys provided only limited protection from the attacks of the American privateers.

British West Indian merchants pursued their own solution to the problem of privateers in a hostile backlash against the American revolutionaries. They soon began to arm their own vessels to annoy "his Majesties Rebellious Subjects." Antigua took the initiative. By January 1777, the Antiguan sloop *Reprisal* had taken three American vessels and it was said that "seven others will be ready to sail from the Island . . . before the end of the present week." The owners of the *Reprisal* declared that they were "zealously disposed to assist in reducing his Majesty's rebellious colonies in America to lawfull obedience." The owners included prominent merchants and planters in the assembly. Antigua and Tortola led the other British islands in arming ships against American privateers.[69]

Disdainfully known as "pirateers" in the United States, these armed British West Indian vessels "made amazing Havock among the Rebels." They typically carried three or four guns and ten to twenty men. Governor Burt of the Leeward Islands believed that they were "of infinite more service" than the navy in intercepting the trade between the neutral islands and the United States. Their success was acknowledged by the mainland colonies, who despaired that the "present trading vessels to the Continent tho' armed can not make resistance against the pirateers that are very numerous in these seas." Nicholas Cruger, an American resident of the Danish island of St. Croix, advised his correspondents to warn their ships to stay clear of Tortola, where a number of vessels were lost to "Pickeroons, who carry from 4 to 68 guns & small guns & about 20 to 309 men."[70]

A correspondent of George, Lord Macartney wrote that the "report of letters of reprisals being granted [in the British Caribbean] had already discouraged trade to America" and that insurance rates had risen 5 percent on

trade between the neutral islands and the United States. The pirateers consequently became the objects of retaliation by the Americans. As early as April
1776, the *Virginia Gazette* denounced the practice of pirateering and especially
criticized the Antiguans: "They are most cruel and unjust wretches existing;
for they condemn a vessel, if she has only the name of being once in America."
Robert Morris wrote to Silas Deane that he hoped the Antiguans would live to
repent. As late as 1782, Congress planned a retaliatory raid against Tortola.[71]

American privateers were not deterred by these countermeasures, and
they continued to disrupt the plantation economy and compound the effects
of the loss of North American trade for the British West Indies. It became
dangerous to sail across the Atlantic and even between islands. American
privateers took an estimated 25,000 hogsheads of sugar aboard ships sailing
from the British Caribbean in 1776. Two captured ships from Barbados alone
were reckoned to be worth £20,000. By February 1777, the American privateers had taken some 250 British West India merchant ships, contributing to
the collapse of four major West India merchant companies in London.[72]

*   *   *

The British West Indies stood to gain nothing from the American Revolutionary War. They dreaded the approach of a conflict in which the colonies
were wrenched apart in what contemporaries commonly termed a civil war.
They wanted most of all to maintain the integrity of the empire and blamed
extremists on both sides for the war. They wanted "a happy reconciliation."[73]

The island colonists repeatedly stressed their desire for the war to end
quickly. William Payne Georges, the agent for St. Kitts, described the frustration of the colonists, after every detail of the conflict had already been
discussed and analyzed: "Nothing new remains by me to be added to the
subject, beyond my sincere wishes for its speedy and favourable Termination."
Some colonists, such as John Nelson, an attorney for the estates of Catherine
Stapleton in St. Kitts and Nevis, were confident that the mainland colonies
would return to their former allegiance and that they would soon supply the
islands again. At the same time others, such as John Pinney of Nevis, fore-
saw "nothing but distress & ruin." One Barbados planter thought that the
promise of a bold stroke toward victory during the summer campaign was "all
imagination."[74]

The British West Indies eagerly desired a settlement between the con-
testants. There were many trimmers who wanted to offend neither Britain nor
the United States. Some advocated appeasing the United States, "at least [to]
convince our neighbours, that we are not *inimical* to their interests [and] not

[to] furnish *reasons* for an hostile disposition on her part nor provoke her just resentment." In 1778, they were tempted by an offer of neutrality from Congress, which the Society of West India Merchants considered but found impractical.[75]

West Indians supported the 1778 British peace initiative led by the earl of Carlisle. The commission was empowered to negotiate directly with Congress and to offer the suspension of all colonial acts passed since 1763. However Britain was unwilling to grant the independence of the United States and was negotiating from a position of weakness with the imminent declaration of war by France. West Indian hopes of reconciliation were dashed and they became frustrated spectators in a war that promised them nothing but trouble.

7

The Groans of the Plantations

THE BRITISH WEST INDIES stood to gain nothing from the American Revolutionary War. The war became a source of grievance in the islands especially after it was apparent that Britain was unlikely to achieve a quick victory. The British defeat at Saratoga in 1777 "had a considerable influence on many" of those colonists whom the governors had "considered as the best affected" but who turned against the war. West Indian whites "did not altogether approve of the mode of proceeding" in the conduct of the war and increasingly opposed the government that had "precipitated the nation into a war, for an object they knew to be unobtainable," and that had falsely "lulled the islands with the assurance of protection."[1]

This chapter examines the impact of the American War on the British West Indies, arguing that the war was unpopular among the white colonists because it interrupted trade and caused plantation profits to plummet to their lowest levels of the century. The war was also a source of grievance because the islands were inadequately protected by the British government, whose resources were overstretched owing to the escalation of the American War into a global conflict after 1778. Whites resented the necessity of arming colored people and blacks on an unprecedented scale, which they regarded as a dangerous expedient.

Despite these hardships, only a minority of the colonists supported the American Revolution, and West Indians in general were divided over the mildest gestures of opposition to the government. West Indians who opposed the war were more concerned about the sacrifices it inflicted on the islands than the legitimacy of the Americans' cause. Their frustration was increasingly shared in Britain.

* * *

The "fatal consequences" predicted by the merchants and planters at the outbreak of the war were "in a great measure experienced" during the course of the war.[2] West Indians had feared severe shortages of food and supplies following the loss of imports from North America. Their failure to find alternative sources of supply as abundant and, more important, as cheap was a source of grievance against the war.

The Leeward Islands were affected the worst by food shortages because "of their close proximity to islands held by foreign nations, the extent to which the sugar monoculture was practiced [and] their dependence on external food supplies." In 1777, the Leeward Islands petitioned their governor for urgent relief to sustain them through the late summer and early autumn. The late summer months were known as the hungry season, even in peacetime, because of food crop cycles and the hurricane months. The legislature of Montserrat expressed concern that the conditions of famine might lead to a slave revolt. Governor Burt of the Leeward Islands "feared a Risque of Insurrections among the slaves" and responded by opening the ports to provisions from neutral islands carried by British ships.[3]

His measures failed to save the lives of three to four hundred slaves in St. Kitts. Nevis lost much the same number to diseases caused by malnutrition. Antigua lost over one thousand slaves. Some twelve hundred slaves, as well as some whites, died in Montserrat where "for three successive Days Hundreds of People came to Town in search of . . . a Morsel of Bread & returned Empty."[4]

Barbados also suffered acute shortages in the early years of the American War. In 1776, the poorest whites gathered in flocks to find food and to pick "the most wretched of all fruits of the earth, to eat for their subsistence." A simultaneous smallpox epidemic killed hundreds of blacks and some whites. The inhabitants were "starving — many families not having the common necessaries of life." Governor Hay downplayed the extent of the problem in order to prevent the opposition parties in Britain from using the crisis as an argument against the American War. He even allowed the army to purchase the few remaining provisions, which "spread an alarm of famine" and alienated the assembly. But his claims of plenty were contradicted by General Sir William Howe, the British commander in chief in North America (whose father was a former governor of Barbados), whose scouts found provisions scarce: "They have not . . . a single cask of salt provisions on the Island . . . [and] are in the greatest want of . . . provisions."[5]

Indeed, Governor Hay belied his own charge that the shortages were a myth when he asked the navy to permit merchants to trade with the neutral islands because Barbados was "in great distress for want of support for their negroes . . . which distress is likely to increase dayly, as long as this unhappy contest between the Mother Country and the North American colonies subsists." Nevertheless, he continued to deny the distress to the home government. He told Lord George Germain that "it is wicked to talk of famine, in the most plentiful Island of all the West Indies" and that prices had remained stable for the past three years. Yet visitors found Barbados "in a starving Condition" in 1777. There was a particular shortage of flour, of which there were "not 20 barrels on the island" on the eve of war with France. However, Barbados became the storehouse of the British West Indies for the army and navy in 1778. The Leeward Islands received no such relief. They were again threatened with starvation in 1779.[6]

The subsistence crisis was greatest in Antigua, where shortages were compounded by a prolonged drought. Between the summer of 1779 and the autumn of 1780, one-tenth of the slaves on the Parham estate of the Tudway family in Antigua died (primarily from dysentery). The remaining slaves were too frail to process the sugar crop. Those slaves "who were intrepid enough to venture on to neighbouring cane pieces to steal and pillage, were either killed by the watchmen or chopped and mangled in so severe a manner, that they were laid up in the sick houses for a length of time." There were cries of "Give us water quickly, or we die." One-fifth of the 38,000 slaves died between 1778 and 1781.[7]

*   *   *

The lowest plantation profits of the eighteenth century, together with widespread debt, were a major source of planter opposition to the American War. J. R. Ward estimates that plantation profits averaged about 10 percent throughout the century but that the "years of the American War of Independence were miserable" with an average profit of 2.3 percent in Barbados, 2.4 percent in the Leeward Islands, 3 percent in Jamaica, and 7 percent in the Windward Islands. His calculations are corroborated by evidence from other plantations. Joshua Steele, a conscientious resident planter, earned less than 1.25 percent on one thousand acres in Barbados between 1773 and 1779. "The American Revolution was extremely destructive of the profits" of the Codrington plantations run by the Society for the Propagation of the Gospel on Barbados. It was also a period of increasing difficulty for John Pinney of Nevis, but his plantation continued to make money with an average profit of 4.9 percent between 1779 and 1783. Samuel Estwick estimated the profits on a plantation in Jamaica, costing £28,000 sterling and producing one hundred hogsheads of sugar annually, to be about 4½ percent between 1775 and 1780.[8]

The low plantation profits reflected the rise in plantation expenses and wartime inflation, which fluctuated between 35 and 600 percent.[9] In October 1777, corn sold in Antigua for sixteen shillings a bushel when it "used to be sold for 3s 6d." Salt provisions were four times dearer than their usual price. There was no rice. In April 1778, beef was four times more expensive in Jamaica than in French Martinique. The price of flour increased fivefold in less than four years in Barbados. There were 500 percent increases in the cost of many articles in Grenada. To compensate for the rise in prices, the wages of free skilled artisans and the hiring of slaves rose during the war. Labor costs in St. Vincent rose threefold by 1781. These exorbitant prices were "fatal to the planting business."[10]

The low profits and the rise in plantation expenses were, in part, a consequence of the closure of trade with North America, which deprived the British West Indies of the cheapest source of staves, hoops, lumber, oil, shingles, cattle, flour, rice, and salted fish. The planters were unable to import casks of the same size and quality as those imported from North America, "those from Europe being very brittle, and apt to crack." The lack of casks to contain dry food caused waste. The cost of staves to make casks and puncheons more than doubled during the course of the war from an average of eleven shillings to twenty-six shillings. Planters were unable to find cheap cattle to work the sugar mills and to carry produce inland. They could not boil lime for the manufacture of sugar. They lacked shingles to repair and build their houses and sugar works.[11]

Furthermore, the planters had to compete with the army and navy for supplies and food. In 1776 Sir William Howe, the British commander in chief in North America, and Lord Dunmore, the governor of Virginia, sent officers to the islands to find military stores and provisions. Prior to the conquest of St. Lucia in 1778, General Grant purchased food for his five thousand troops "at any price" in Barbados, the Grenadines, and St. Vincent. "Astonishing Quantities of all kinds of live and dead stock" from Barbados were consumed by the army and navy. In December 1781, Admiral Samuel Hood sent frigates to St. Kitts and Antigua to collect as many provisions as possible because his fleet had only a twenty days' supply of bread. The arrival of a British fleet tripled prices in Barbados in 1782.[12] These fleets were the size of small cities in population.

The activities of enemy privateers and fleets also aggravated the rise in prices and the shortage of supplies. They caused the disruption in trade, increases in insurance charges, higher freight rates, shipping shortages, convoy delays, and severe financial losses for many individuals. American privateers made two to three captures a day off the Windward Islands in 1777. They intercepted almost all the supplies from Britain to Tobago in 1777–78 and captured the most valuable vessels in the Jamaica fleet in 1777. They twice captured the outward-bound convoy from Britain to the Leeward Islands and

TABLE 7   Charges on a Hundredweight of Sugar Shipped from Jamaica to Britain

	Before the war	1781
Cask and shipping	1s	2s
Freight	3s 6d	8s
Duty	6s 4d	11s 8½d
Port charges	1s	2s
Commission on sale	1s 1d	1s 9½d
Insurance	1s 1d	11s 7½d
Total	14s	37s 1½d

Source: [Samuel Estwick], Considerations on the Present Decline of the Sugar-Trade (London, 1782), 51.

most of an outward-bound convoy to Jamaica in 1780. As early as 1777, it was estimated that privateers had caused £1,800,000 sterling of damage to the trade of the British West Indies.[13]

Insurance rates rose from a peacetime level of 2 percent to a wartime high of 28 percent. John Pinney of Nevis preferred to take the risk of not insuring his freight but dividing his produce among several ships. Nevertheless, he still lost £1,000 worth of goods in a year despite distributing goods among six vessels. It was almost impossible to insure a ship that was not part of a convoy. The rise in insurance rates alone was "precipitating things into a state of general bankruptcy."[14]

In addition to the rise in insurance rates, freight rates increased "so enormously high" that planters were "reduced to great difficulties" (Table 7). The loss of North American merchant ships, the captures by privateers, the high rate of insurance, the risk of the voyage, the rise in the wages of seamen, and the demand for ships for army transports caused a shortage of both ships and crew, thereby doubling the peacetime freight rates in 1777. The Society of West India Merchants took legal action against shipmasters after freight rates increased again in 1781. Sugar freight increased from three shillings, six pence per hundredweight to 10 shillings, six pence per hundredweight.[15]

Plantation profits were further diminished by British import duties on sugar and rum, which the government increased to finance the escalating costs of the war. Import duties almost doubled their peacetime level before the end of the war. The assembly of Jamaica petitioned against the import duties and even went so far as to stop work on the fortifications in protest against new duties in November 1781. Stephen Fuller, the agent for Jamaica, expressed amazement at the duty's passing through Parliament "without a single word said against it" and without warning, "like a thunder clap upon us all." Fuller believed that the duty caused merchants to withdraw credit and recall debts from the West Indies.[16]

While planters contended with an increase in their expenses, the market for their rum declined with the loss of the North American market. Although secondary to sugar, rum sales were a useful source of additional revenue. Jamaica "did not feel the want of the market" because it supplied the army and navy, which "created a consumption equal to the surplus [of rum not sold to Britain]." However, total sales from the British West Indies to England fell from 2,305,808 gallons in 1776 to 1,207,421 gallons in 1781. Rum prices were depressed in England. The sale of rum hardly repaid "the Labor that attends it" and there were dire forecasts that "a total decay of that once valuable produce will follow."[17]

As plantation expenses increased, sugar production fell. British West Indian sugar exports fell to half of their prewar levels by almost one million hundredweight in 1781. They averaged £3 million before the war but only £2,647,000 sterling during the American War. Selwyn Carrington finds that Jamaica exported 51,218 casks of sugar to England in 1774–75, compared to only 30,282 casks in 1782–83. Barbados shipped 6,929 casks of sugar to England in 1774–75, compared to 2,804 casks in 1779. Antigua shipped about 20,000 hogsheads of sugar in a satisfactory year but it produced less than 4,000 hogsheads in 1779 and 1783.[18]

Planters found it difficult to obtain credit to cover their losses because the war precipitated the collapse of several prominent London merchant houses. Four firms stopped payments before mid-1777, leaving their planter clients without supplies. Among those firms that survived, merchants like Houseton and Company became timid and cautious, resolving to "restrict trade to the West Indies." A merchant in St. Kitts reflected that he was easily able to borrow £5,000 on his own personal security before the war but he now found it more difficult to borrow even £500. It also became more expensive to borrow money with minimum interest rates rising to 6 percent.[19]

The Windward Islands were still reeling from the credit crisis of 1772. Two thousand acres of land were abandoned in Dominica before the end of 1777. Lord Macartney "did not know a single British subject [in Grenada] out of debt." Most of the produce remitted home merely discharged debts and brought no returns. The members of the assembly of Grenada were "much embarrassed in their Circumstances, and rather to be considered . . . as Stewards and Managers for Mortgagees in London and Holland, than as the real owners of the Estates they possess." Estate debts in Grenada and the Grenadines amounted "to a sum of Two Millions sterling and an interest of near £15 per cent (including charges) . . . paid for the greatest part of it."[20]

Was this just another case of the groans of the planters heard throughout

the seventeenth and eighteenth centuries? I believe not. The low plantation
profits were insufficient to pay the 5 percent or more interest rates on debts
owed by many of the planters before the war and "without which, it is well
known, this business cannot be carried on." These low net profits on capital
were insufficient if properties were "incumbered with any debt, legacy, or
annuity," leaving "very little for the subsistence of the owner and his family; no
savings against calamitous years; or for improvements."[21]

The attorney general of Jamaica privately confided that "all the Planters in
the Island are so embarrassed in their Circumstances, & many of them so many
thousand pounds worse than nothing, that they would willing be subject to
any Power, which might rid them of debts." In October 1776, a London
newspaper claimed that several hundred absentee planters living in the neighborhood of Cavendish Square were preparing to return to the Caribbean
"owing to loses." The majority of plantations in Barbados were mortgaged by
mid-1777; two-thirds of the estates and property were owed to merchants in
England. Sir John Gay Alleyne, the speaker of the assembly, owed thousands
of pounds to London. Debtors fled aboard government packet boats, merchant vessels, and naval ships.[22]

The small sugar planters were more vulnerable than the large planters for
several reasons: they were less able to raise credit among metropolitan merchants; less likely to have provision lands for their slaves and often more
dependent on purchases from America; and less able to replenish stocks of
slaves or to rebuild sugar works during the war. The price rise was "oppressive
to the opulent [but] on the inferior planter, it . . . [was] intolerable." The
majority of taxpayers were middling people who were too poor to pay.[23]

Many planters consequently did not replenish their slave stock, leaving
the future profitability of the plantations in jeopardy: "For an estate in sugar is
like a machine when out of order, it is not easily repaired." Barbados was "some
thousands [of slaves] below the requisite stock" by the end of the war, virtually ceasing to retain imported slaves. Antigua only retained 9 slave imports
in 1779 and 132 in 1781, compared to 1,137 in 1775.[24] Planters were deterred
from purchasing slaves "while Provisions were so scarce" and when sale prices
increased by 71 percent between 1775 and 1791. The slave trade declined by
one-quarter in the early years of the war, with twelve out of thirty leading slave
companies in Liverpool ceasing operation before 1778.[25]

Creditors foreclosed on debts, causing, for example, "many of the finest
plantations" in Barbados to be "desolated by the cupidity of rapacious, relent-
less creditors." If plantations were heavily mortgaged, the owners were forced
to sell at a fraction of the original cost. In 1777, John Pinney of Nevis calculated that estates were selling for one-third of their prewar value, while the
value of estates in Barbados fell by one-third of their prewar value. One planta-

tion in Tobago was purchased at £9,000 before the war and sold for £6,000 during the war. West Indian property in general fell to half of prewar values after the declaration of war by France in 1778. Slaves in Barbados "were sold at public auction for less than half their value, and transported to the Dutch settlements." A judge in Barbados even proposed a bill to suspend "the proceedings of the courts of justice, and of the marshal's office, for a limited term of years" to protect debtors.[26]

The dissolution of the plantation empire of the Price family in Jamaica dramatically illustrates what happened to many West Indian planters. As early as 1753, the family became indebted to London merchants for the purchase of slaves, land, supplies, and buildings. Unable to repay the loan, they were eventually forced to mortgage and remortgage their plantations. On the death of Sir Charles Price in 1772, the estates were "already disastrously compromised, but it was the onset of the American War which brought about the final collapse." His son continued to borrow at illegal compound rates of interest and would see "most of the family estates not simply mortgaged, but leased, sold, or seized to satisfy impatient creditors" before 1788.[27]

Frustrated by their inability to relieve their misfortunes, planters and merchants wrote of their fear of imminent ruin and their desire to sell up.[28] At the beginning of the American War, one Jamaican planter had "great hopes that good will arise" from punishing the patriots and making the islands more economically self-sufficient, but by 1781 he warned that the war threatened to inflict "everlasting ruin." He was ready to leave the island for "some other Government where we may be able to make shift to live, and not be held in Egyptian Bondage."[29]

However, even with profits at their lowest level of the century, some plantations continued to thrive throughout the war, such as those of the Beckford family in Jamaica.[30] But even the Beckfords suffered lower profits because of the war.

*   *   *

Another reason the British West Indies were critical of the war was because they were inadequately protected by the imperial government against internal slave rebellions and external attack. Whites felt themselves neglected and defenseless owing to "the concentrating of our national force to the single point of North America." There was "a general Murmur of discontent . . . heard buzzing thro' every part of Jamaica, that so little Attention [was] paid to its safety & defence from the mother country."[31]

They were inadequately protected because the British navy was overstretched after 1778. It was numerically inferior to the combined opposition of

COUNT DE GRASSE
Taking a peep in the west Indies.
Sold by W.Humphry. N.227 Strand.

Figure 23. "Count De Grasse Taking a Peep in the West Indies," 1779 (copyright © British Museum). British satire of the French naval superiority. The resentment of British planters to the weak presence of the British navy became a major grievance against the home government.

TABLE 8   British Forces in America and the West Indies, November 1779

North America	35,921
Canada	7,469
West Indies	7,796
Total	51,186

Source: State of the forces in America and the West Indies, November 1779, vol. 20, f. 15.

the United States in 1775, of France in 1778, of Spain in 1779 and of the Netherlands in 1781. There were often fewer naval ships than British islands in the eastern Caribbean. The colonists were bewildered by the presence of superior enemy navies, the movements and relative strength of the respective national fleets became a matter of acute local anxiety. The very sight of sails on the horizon occasioned numerous false alarms.

The British army was so dispersed in the Caribbean that "scarcely one island could resist the lightest of attack." In 1778, it had dwindled to fewer than 1,060 men fit for duty, in contrast to the French islands, where there were 8,000 troops. The army was not supplemented by German mercenaries (often called Hessians in histories of the United States) owing to a stipulation in their contracts prohibiting them from service in the Caribbean. The successes of the last war evaporated as one island after another fell to the French (Tables 8 and 9).[32]

In September 1778, Dominica became the first British island to fall to France during the American War. It was defended by only a company of forty-one troops and a small militia, which were easily overwhelmed by a force of over two thousand men. There were no casualties on either side. The twenty-five-mile distance from Martinique was so short that the French were able to conquer Dominica "before the news of the expedition could reach Admiral Barrington," who was, in any case, under orders to remain in Barbados to join a secret British expedition to conquer St. Lucia. The fall of Dominica enabled the French to consolidate their own colonial possessions and to divide the British islands in the eastern Caribbean.[33]

In June 1779, St. Vincent capitulated to the French without a shot fired. There was not an artillery officer on the island or "any who knew the great gun or mortar exercise." There was "not twenty barrels of [gun] powder in the island," the stores were empty, and "provisions almost out." The white inhabitants dared not resist the small French force because of the presence of the Caribs against "whom resistance would not only have been fruitless, but would have drawn inevitable destruction on the colony." The French landed less than two miles from Kingston, where there were only forty-four British

TABLE 9   Distribution of British Troops in the West Indies, 1779

Jamaica	1,866 (August)
Antigua	1,256 (October)
St. Kitts	1,701 (October)
St. Lucia	1,417 (September)
Grenada and Tobago	259 (June)
Onboard the British fleet	1,003 (July)
Total	7,502

Source: State of the forces in America and the West Indies, November 1779, vol. 20, f. 15.

soldiers. The British were outnumbered fifteen to one by the combined force of the French and Caribs. Most of the seven companies of British troops in St. Vincent were defending the twenty inland posts against the runaway slaves and Caribs. The British fleet of Vice Admiral Byron was escorting the convoy beyond St. Kitts.[34]

Nine days later, the French seized Grenada, which was the largest sugar producer after Jamaica in the British West Indies. Governor Macartney made a brave defense with a force of only one hundred and fifty regulars and three hundred militia against three thousand French troops. The free blacks and people of color hastened his surrender by deserting the garrison. The captives included the radical politician Richard Oliver, who had resigned as an alderman of London to go to the island "on suspicion of what would happen."

Britain was unable to reinforce the West Indies because it faced the threat of French invasion at home in the summer of 1779.[35] The British fleet did not appear until two days after the surrender of Grenada but it was inferior to the French fleet owing to the arrival of a squadron commanded by La Motte Picquet, which was able to enter Martinique unopposed during Byron's absence in St. Kitts. After an indecisive sea battle off Grenada, a shattered British fleet left to refit in St. Kitts. It made a shocking sight when it landed the dead and wounded. The decks of the *Grafton* were "entirely covered with Blood" and the *Prince of Wales* had "ninety-five Holes intirely through her Sides."[36] The condition of the British fleet left the way open for Admiral D'Estaing to attack any of the remaining British colonies in the Caribbean.

D'Estaing boasted that he did not intend to leave George III enough British sugar "to sweeten his tea for breakfast by Christmas." The French "were so sure of the conquest of *all* our Islands" that they had already prepared the capitulations "to be granted to *each*." D'Estaing spent late July "playing the duce among the [Leeward] Islands . . . Barbadoes, Antigua, Montserrat, and Nevis, were at the mercy of the French for about ten days."[37] Five French ships taunted Montserrat where the fort guns at Plymouth exchanged fire, hitting the decks of the largest ship while cannonballs "flew about, and some reached up into the Country." The French paraded ship by ship before the British fleet off Basseterre in St. Kitts but, finding them "formed in the Line of Battle . . . and protected by our Forts," they left without firing a shot.[38]

The British West Indies were unprepared for such humiliation. They regarded themselves as the source of British power and expected their defense interests to be given absolute priority. They still basked in the memories of the victories of 1759. It was a maxim of their defense policy that the British fleet was their only true security against foreign attack. The colonists were unable to understand the loss of naval superiority, which left them exposed "as if we did not belong to Great Britain." Planters in the Leeward and Windward Islands protested against the relegation of their defense interests within the Caribbean for the protection of St. Lucia and Jamaica. West Indians became increasingly disaffected with every British reversal.[39]

The island assemblies and the West India interest in London lobbied incessantly for reinforcements. They regularly petitioned the King and Parliament, and delegations of the West India merchants and planters routinely met with government ministers including Lord Sandwich (first lord of the admiralty), Lord Weymouth (southern secretary of state), Lord Amherst (secretary of state for war), Lord George Germain (secretary of state for America) and Lord North (first lord of the Treasury). There were also private appeals like that of Philip Gibbes, who owned "considerable property" in Barbados and wrote about his fears for the safety of the island to Germain. Thomas Charles Bunbury, a member of Parliament for Suffolk, became preoccupied with the fate of his property in Grenada and told Thomas Walpole in May 1781 that "not a day has elapsed, and hardly an hour . . . that I have not either in person, or by letter, solicited one, or other, of his Majesty's ministry."[40]

Each twist of the war brought a new round of lobbying activity. In response to the fall of Dominica in 1778, lobbying became more intense. Following the loss of St. Vincent and Grenada in 1779, the West India merchants pressed Germain "in the most urgent manner for immediate and effectual succour, to prevent the utter Ruin of many Planters and Merchants." With the French fleet much superior in the West Indies in the summer of 1779, the absentee merchants and planters of Jamaica made three separate applications to Germain, warning that "upon every Hours delay the safety & Property of themselves & their Brethren in Jamaica are left exposed to the Continuance of known & imminent danger." The West India lobby and the islands inundated the ministry with petitions and requests for reinforcements.[41]

Alarmed by the superiority of the French in the Caribbean, the West India interest in London assumed a more confrontational posture toward the gov-

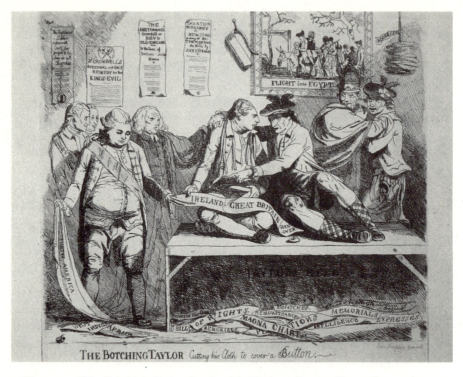

Figure 24. "The Botching Taylor Cutting his Cloth to Cover a Button," 1779 (copyright © British Museum). Antigovernment satire of Prime Minister Lord North destroying the British Empire. He is depicted as a tailor with pieces of cloth at his feet inscribed "West Indies" and "Africa." A strip of cloth beneath the table reads the "Petition of Jamaica," a reference to the numerous petitions from the island he ignored, including the infamous petition of December 1774.

ernment in 1782. They began to enlist the support of merchants in the outports in their lobbying campaigns and to make public appeals through the newspapers. Nathaniel Bayly and Richard Pennant, the chairman and deputy chairman of the Society of West India Merchants and Planters, were both opposition members of Parliament and outspoken critics of the American War. They were both absentee planters who won control of the society from the merchants whose earlier passivity they derided.

*   *   *

The inadequate military protection of the islands increased the probability of slave rebellions, a further grievance of the white colonists against the war. In a speech before the House of Lords in 1780, the marquis of Rockingham declared that the military forces in Jamaica were insufficient even to quell a domestic revolt of the slaves and that "there was no Species of Danger to which . . . [the white colonists] . . . were not subjected."[42] In reality, such fears were exaggerated. After the rebellion in Jamaica in 1776, there were no major revolts in the British West Indies until the 1790s. Nevertheless, slaves engaged in alternative forms of resistance.

With French entry imminent in 1778, it was rumored in St. Kitts that some slaves had planned to rise on Easter Sunday "to murder the Inhabitants, to deliver the Island to the French, or any Persons who would make them free."[43] The governor placed the island under martial law for several days. His critics ridiculed the alarm because an inquiry failed to produce any proof of danger, but the governor remained convinced that the threat was real.

After the hurricane in 1780, slaves went "plundering in every part" of Bridgetown in Barbados. The colonists were "afraid that as soon as the storm ceased, the negroes would rush in from the country, and taking advantage of the general consternation, would commit great violence." The army "formed themselves into regular watches, and constantly patroled the streets throughout the whole night." At the same time, the governor of Jamaica "was obliged to march a regiment to reduce [the slaves] to order" and to quell what the press described as an insurrection.[44]

There were stories of enemy agents conspiring to encourage revolts among the slaves. Spanish agents "landed at some of the country ports privately" in Jamaica and "travelled through the body of the country." They masqueraded as prophets who "could dry up the sea, and remove the high mountains." They claimed to have the power to "raise the dead and destroy all the living." They successfully "tainted the Minds of all the Negroes," causing twelve hundred of Sir Charles Price's slaves to lay "down their hoes and bills" and refuse to work. They spread rumors of a plot against the British by the French and the Americans. An investigation uncovered some two dozen guns, loaded with three bullets each, at the house of a free black person in Spanish Town. Discovery of the Spanish agents terrified many people in Jamaica. It was true that American diplomat Silas Deane wanted to incite rebellions among the slaves in Jamaica and the Caribs in St. Vincent to "oblige Great Britain to withdraw part of her forces from the continent [of America]."[45]

A weak British military and naval presence assisted slave resistance in the Windward Islands. Naval ships rarely visited these most southerly islands during the course of the war. Their garrisons were poorly fed; those in St. Vincent were close to mutiny. The French slaves of French masters and the free colored French population in the British Windward Islands conspired with the neighboring French islands. Almost all the colored people in Grenada deserted the British garrison to join the French army when the island was invaded in 1779.[46]

Maroon communities revived throughout the Windward Islands during the war, becoming so considerable in Dominica that they became a formidable postwar force against Britain. These runaways became increasingly daring as the war progressed. Runaways in Tobago launched regular raids on plantations from the beginning of the war until the island's conquest by France in 1781.[47] During the British occupation of St. Lucia, the planters were "terrified to death, by a large body of Runaway negroes [who were] arm'd, & have plundered & drove from their Plantations some of the first people." Runaway slaves in St. Vincent were joined by slaves from as far away as Barbados, Martinique, St. Lucia, and Grenada.[48]

The Caribs in St. Vincent were undefeated and wanted revenge after the Carib War of 1773–74. They blamed the British for the shortage of food and encouraged the "large bands of runaway negroes" who became "very formidable" in number. They gave intelligence to American privateers and "were very partial to their French neighbours." They "knew the use of firearms" supplied by the French. In June 1777, the British army successfully intervened to avert a joint attack by Caribs and maroons, but many of the conspirators escaped into the depths of the woods. During the invasion of the island in 1779, the Caribs and maroons hastened the British surrender by rallying to the French. When the British attempted to retake St. Vincent, the Caribs began "burning every Plantation they came near, & killing whites and Blacks."[49]

In Jamaica, a gang of runaways led by "Three Finger'd Jack" (Captain Bristol) mounted daring raids. The gang consisted of about forty men and eighteen women who settled "in the recesses of Four-mile Wood in St David's." They were chiefly Congos and, it was said in the London press, "especially formidable to mulattoes who they swore to kill." Their animus toward mulattoes (if the reports are true) was probably a reaction to the mulatto regiment used against runaway slaves. Ever larger rewards were offered for the capture of the leader, dead or alive. The exploits of Three Finger'd Jack were so famous that he later became the subject of literary narratives and plays.[50]

*   *   *

The inadequacy of imperial defense necessitated the arming of unprecedented numbers of people of color and slaves, another reason why white island colonists opposed the American War.

The planters were unhappy about the necessity of recruiting people of color on such an unprecedented scale. They were more reluctant than other

Europeans in the Caribbean to deploy black troops owing to the higher proportion of slaves in the British islands. The acute white manpower shortages necessitating the arming of blacks also posed a threat to the white minority, who lived in constant fear of a slave rebellion. Furthermore, the arming of blacks contradicted the alleged inferiority of subject peoples. It undermined the essential myth of European racial superiority, which justified imperialism and slavery. Military service offered blacks status and recognition within slave societies that systematically sought to deny their very humanity. Slaves, as Orlando Patterson forcibly reminds us, theoretically did not possess traits of honor and courage, the qualities of a good soldier.[51]

There were numerous precedents for arming slaves, dating from the earliest times of European settlement in the Americas. Free blacks and free coloreds served in the colonial militias, and slaves took part in the British offensives in the Caribbean during the Seven Years' War. It was an expedient long advocated by imperial officials. Europeans crudely calculated that the use of blacks spared the lives of white troops and saved money. In short they performed those duties which "no *European constitution can stand long*."[52]

The British found the use of black troops irresistible during the American War when resources were overstretched and when the use of regular troops in the Caribbean deflected resources from the war for America. White troops suffered catastrophic levels of mortality in the tropics owing primarily to malaria and yellow fever. During the American War, 11 percent of troops died during the voyage aboard troop transports to the Caribbean. The annual mortality rate of soldiers in the Caribbean was 15 percent, compared to 6 percent of those stationed in New York and 1 percent in Canada. Without firing a single shot, the British lost 3,500 troops in three and a half years in Jamaica. Of the 1,008 men of the Seventy-Eighth Regiment stationed in Kingston in 1779, only 18 were still alive in 1783. Of 7,000 troops sent to the island, only 2,000 were fit for duty in April 1782.[53]

After the fall of Dominica in 1778, the recruitment of blacks became a matter of urgency in the British West Indies. They became active participants in the American War, in which they served as soldiers, militiamen, sailors, laborers, pioneers, and nurses. They were conscripted to construct fortresses on a scale greater than the largest plantation field gangs: two thousand slaves worked on the fortifications in southeast Jamaica. "Several companies of free Mulattoes and Negroes . . . joined [the Jamaica] militia in keeping guard" in the countryside in place of regular troops who were concentrated in Kingston. Five percent of the slaves of St. Kitts were conscripted to build entrenchments and breastworks. In the event of an invasion, the governor planned to organize them into armed parties to act as foragers and to attack the enemy at night.[54]

Two percent of the slave population of Grenada was rotated to work on

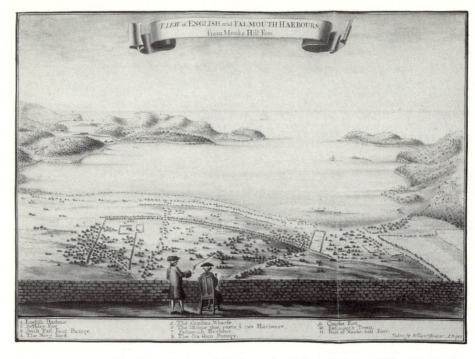

Figure 25. *View of English and Falmouth Harbours, from Monks Hill Fort*, William Brasier, 1757 (John Carter Brown Library of Brown University). English Harbour, the dockyard of the British fleet in the eastern Caribbean, also refitted occasional ships from the British squadron in North America.

the harbor batteries.[55] Black artificers worked at the naval dockyards in English Harbour (Antigua) and Port Royal (Jamaica), where they repaired and careened (a process of turning the ships' hulls on their side for cleaning) British naval ships. These two dockyards were central to the British war effort. They kept afloat not only the warships of the two naval squadrons in the Caribbean but also occasional ships from the squadron in North America.

In 1778, with the entry of France into the America War, the governor of Jamaica created a separate British army regiment of free blacks and free coloreds. William Ricketts, William Lewis, and Nathaniel Beckford, commanders in the militia, championed the idea. They contended that people of color and blacks exhibited an "extraordinary alertness in Military manoeuvres." The blacks were "used to the climate and enured to Labor, and fatigue," as natives of the island, and they were less susceptible to diseases, enabling them to march "as occasion required." They were also familiar with the local terrain,

Figure 26. The Admiral's house at English Harbour, Antigua (Author). English Harbour is a perfectly preserved eighteenth-century dockyard and a symbol of the importance of British naval superiority to command of the Caribbean.

making them both of "service against any Invading Enemy" and "a better safe Guard" against a slave revolt. They could pacify the interior of the island and encourage the new settlements for the benefit of the island.[56]

Although the new regiment was "equalled by none in whole Island, except the Regulars, for military discipline," it was quickly disbanded because of the opposition of the West India lobby in London. Stephen Fuller argued that there were only nine hundred potential recruits of whom "you can not depend upon more than Five hundred." He warned that "the free negroes & mulattoes are not to be trusted in corps composed of themselves only, & the incorporating of them with the whites will not be endured."[57]

When the French navy gained superiority in the summer of 1779, the invasion scare in Jamaica occasioned the revival of schemes for two light infantry regiments of free blacks and free coloreds. Governor Dalling suggested that the regiments be raised solely for defensive purposes. He thought it necessary to offer the inducement of four-month furloughs "as the free people are all Tradesmen."[58] Nathaniel Beckford personally lobbied Germain, who warmly welcomed the scheme.

However, a meeting of the planters and merchants associated with Jamaica in London rejected the plan, finding "the expediency of the measure as connected with the general welfare of the Island appears very doubtfull and may at the present crisis prove dangerous and delusive." In deference to the determined opposition of the West India lobby, Germain reluctantly refused to give his consent to the free black and colored regiments in Jamaica. Meanwhile, Governor Dalling had already created one regiment of 48 colored men. This regiment marked a new departure, as these men were now part of a professional force, salaried like army regulars, better equipped, and under army discipline, "which distinguishes the soldier from the citizen" in the militia. However, the governor was again forced by the British government to disband the regiment.[59]

In April 1782, in a significant reversal caused by the threat of foreign invasion, the Jamaican assembly approved the establishment of regiments of free blacks and people of color. George III supported the enterprise and the home government permitted a third regiment to be added. By November 1782 officers "were raising recruits with great alacrity" and Governor Archibald Campbell of Jamaica sent recruiters to Charleston (South Carolina) to raise the third battalion of free blacks and free colored people. A visitor to Jamaica remarked on the fine appearance of these corps: "A large regiment is here made up of strong, able bodied, effective men, Negroes and Mulattoes, who are equalled by none in the island, except the Regulars, for military discipline."[60]

Governor Campbell was a long-time proponent of the use of black troops. He was a veteran of the Guadeloupe campaign where Barbadian slaves had acted as auxiliaries in 1759. At the beginning of the Revolutionary War, Campbell had proposed raising a regiment in the West Indies of 1,400 "stout Active Negroes" to suppress the revolt of the thirteen colonies and to encourage the desertion of slaves from the patriots. Campbell had previously commanded in North America where his successful conquest of Georgia was guided by a black scout called Quamino Dolly. Through his influence, Jamaica conscripted 5,130 slaves during martial law in 1782.[61]

The prospect of freedom for slaves was used as a powerful inducement for loyal service, which was a major reason why planters were so opposed to the idea. Edward Long had thought the bestowal of freedom a necessary condition of arming slaves: "Before slaves are entrusted with arms, they should either receive their freedom, or a conditional promise of it, as the reward of their good behaviour; that so the memory of that valuable prize, liberty, . . .

may inspire them with courage and fidelity." Governor Campbell and a council of war, composed of members of the assembly, ordered that "all Negro, or other slaves, who shall behave well, shall be recommended to the legislature for their freedom." Three hundred copies of the orders were printed and distributed throughout the island. The adjutant general in Jamaica predicted that slaves would be motivated by "the Attainment of their own freedom." It was an attractive prospect in the British West Indies, where manumissions were rarer than in the French and Spanish Caribbean.[62]

Slaves acquired increasing military importance in both combatant and especially noncombatant roles. "Trusted" slaves were armed throughout the British islands with cutlasses and bills. During the invasion scare of 1779, the Barbados legislature voted to arm slaves. St. Kitts stepped up defense precautions with the passage of an act to conscript slaves for public works. Two to three hundred slaves labored constantly on the great fortress of Brimstone Hill in St. Kitts. They built a cistern to hold ninety thousand gallons of water and carried provisions. In 1780, Antigua armed one thousand slaves and hired one thousand more for two hundred days on the public works. Antiguan slaves worked on the defenses around English Harbour where they raised batteries and redoubts. On this dry island, one of their most arduous duties was carrying water and fuel for the British troops.[63]

In Barbados large bodies of slaves "were armed with swords and spears. The free negroes had firearms, were well cloathed, at their own expense, and made a very good appearance." The free black and free colored militiamen "made a far better appearance, and were far better disciplined (being more susceptible of discipline) than any white corps in the island." One general even offended "the white militia by expressing his preference for the free people of colour." One in every forty Jamaican slaves worked on the island's fortifications in mid-1782. There were five thousand slaves "so employed . . . [at] a charge to the inhabitants of £3,000 per week."[64]

The desperation of the navy for manpower enabled many black recruits to join the crews of warships. The navy suffered the mortality rates of the army but it did not have the luxury of simply merging ("drafting") regiments because warships required a minimum number of sailors. The navy even had to resort to carrying army regiments onboard as crew members and marines. Admirals complained of high desertion rates among seamen lured away by high-paying merchant ships and privateers, rum and "black wenches." Admiral Hyde Parker of the Leeward Island squadron reckoned himself twelve hundred men short with another six hundred sick in Barbados in 1779. The naval press gangs risked civil lawsuits if they seized white sailors, as Admiral Young discovered in the Leeward Islands in 1777.[65]

There were so many blacks enlisting in the British navy that Admiral

Young, probably in deference to the planters, gave orders to limit the number of black sailors per warship to four "to do laborious duty, that might prove hurtful to white men in this climate." These recruits included runaway slaves like eighteen-year-old Johnny of Barbados, who was suspected of being "employed on board some of his Majesty's ships on this station, when commanded by Admiral Rodney." The site of the naval dockyard at English Harbour in Antigua facilitated "more frequent" escapes "than ever known heretofore" and generally by the "most valuable slaves."[66]

Antiguan planters were prevented from repossessing their slaves from the navy "at the risk of their persons . . . and some have actually undergone the most injurious treatment from the licentious and uncontrolled behaviour of the seamen." They protested to the home government that "every person of that complexion is to be supposed a slave, till, authentic legal proofs to the contrary are produced, this is a maxim so very trite, so very obvious to the meanest capacity, that to suppose it to have escaped the observation of any man, is to consider him almost devoid of common understanding."[67]

The Revolutionary War advanced one of the most remarkable careers of a colored man who rose to the rank of captain in the Royal Navy. The life of John Perkins of Kingston, Jamaica, illustrated the opportunities military service offered to free people of color and the resulting rising level of expectations. Perkins was "from his youth, engaged in the sea service, and was in actual and constant duty in his majesty's navy" from the commencement of the American Revolutionary War. In 1775, he became the pilot of the flagship of the Jamaica squadron. He soon rose to command a schooner tender, the *Punch*, when he did "the utmost of his power, [to] harass and annoy the enemy, and captured no less than three hundred and fifteen prizes and made upwards of three thousand prisoners."[68]

Governor Campbell "and the inhabitants of the island of Jamaica" recommended Perkins to Admiral Rodney. Campbell later recalled that he was "not less admired by his superior officers in Jamaica, than respected by those of the enemy." In 1782 Admiral Rodney promoted Perkins to lieutenant in command of the *Endeavour* in recognition of his "gallant behaviour in taking . . . [a] French sloop with so many officers on board." The gesture illustrated not only the remarkable courage of Perkins but also the confidence and maverick qualities of Rodney. Perkins regularly reconnoitered St. Domingue and Cuba to obtain intelligence for Admiral Sir Peter Parker, who found the information "at all times authentic . . . when the island was threatened to be invaded." However, with the war over, Perkins's commission was not confirmed by the admiralty in London until 1797.[69]

The most novel military developments in the deployment of blacks occurred in British-occupied St. Lucia, which was captured from the French in

1778. The military commanders did not have to justify the use of black troops to either a hostile civil government or an elected assembly. Brigadier General Edward Mathew obtained slaves from New York, Charleston, and Africa for service with the army in St. Lucia.[70] He had previously commanded a British expedition in Virginia where he had used 1,500 slaves. He helped to assemble the core of the first permanent black army regiment in the British West Indies.

The arming of slaves was regarded by whites as a double-edged weapon that threatened to undermine the system of deference within the racial hierarchy of the British West Indies. As Stephen Fuller explained in 1778, "The arming of the Domestic Negroes is a policy . . . promising relief for the present, but pregnant with future evils."[71] The French discovered the truth of his prophecy, arming slaves and free blacks in much greater numbers than the British. These trusted black and colored French soldiers participated in the siege of Savannah in 1779. They included men like Henri Christophe and André Rigaud, the future heroes of the St. Domingue (Haiti) Revolution.

The opposition of the white colonists to the use of black troops was not an effort to sabotage the British war for America but a consequence of their traditional antipathy toward arming large numbers of blacks. Historian Sylvia Frey suggests that British interests in the Caribbean restrained the policy of arming slaves in North America.[72] The necessity of such expedients highlighted the inadequacy of imperial protection and was a source of planter opposition to the war in America.

*   *   *

The American War was the cause of numerous grievances in the British West Indies, but opposition to the war did not amount to support for the American Revolution, just as was true in Britain. The governors were tempted to dub all critics of the war as republicans and rebels, but few whites in the British West Indies actively supported the American Revolution. Governor Dalling likened the assemblymen in Jamaica to "the Emissaries of an American Congress." Governor Burt of the Leeward Islands wrote of the "ignorance of a Narrow Minded Parsimonious Gallo-American Assembly" in St. Kitts. Governor Cunningham of Barbados claimed that the greater part of the population of Barbados was "tinged by American, and Levelling Principles which seem to pervade this Part of the British Dominions." However, such accusations were freely used to brand opponents and did not carry much weight. The same "vile calumny [of rebel sympathies] was whispered about GOVERNOR HAY [in Barbados]" because he was "unwilling to disgrace the King's Commission by granting it to every picaroon who applied for it."[73]

The governors equated island inhabitants' opposition to the governors with support for the American Revolution. In St. Kitts, Governor Burt described Sir Gillies Payne as "a strong North American Partizan," a curious remark because Payne had left St. Kitts for England before the appointment of Burt as governor of the Leeward Islands. On the other hand, Payne owned estates in Sandy Point, neighboring a plantation belonging to Burt, a native of St. Kitts. Payne was a successful litigant in a protracted case against Burt which went before the Privy Council. Payne was also the cousin of the very successful governor of the Leeward Islands who preceded Burt.[74]

Payne had left his estates under the management of the Tyson family, whom Governor Burt claimed were "the most violent Asserters and Propagators of American Principles, warm propagators of Every intelligence favorable to America." The Tysons had supported Payne in the lawsuit against Burt. John Tyson was paradoxically appointed an assistant justice by Burt, who later claimed that Tyson had declared, "What do I care for a Royal Instruction tis no Law: a Royal instruction is nothing to me." Tyson was also said to be a friend of two merchants accused of acting as agents for Congress in St. Eustatius.[75]

Burt dismissed him as assistant justice but only *after* Tyson had ruled against Burt in the land dispute with Payne. He also acted after the assembly refused to reimburse him for his expenses when Tyson was the speaker of the assembly. Burt claimed that he had waited before dismissing Tyson until "an old very old claim I had pending against Sir Gillies Payne was over . . . least it should have been said I wanted to get rid of him as an opposer or to pack a Bench." This was how it was interpreted by his successor, who thought Tyson well attached to the Crown and "who never heard Governor Burt [give] any reason for displacing him neither do I think it was in his power to give such support with any degree of Justice."[76]

Although the accusation of republicanism was sometimes used indiscriminately, a minority of whites in the British West Indies did support the American Revolution. The disaffected in Jamaica "*impudently assumed the appellation of Patriots.*" Many Jamaicans were "not the most loyal subjects, and consequently not favourable to . . . [loyalists]" from America. There were "Rebel friends in Kingston, of whom there are but too many of influence and property." There were American agents who "started to create and promote the seeds of division among people of no mean authority" in Barbados, where they worked for William Bingham of Martinique.[77] The *Antigua Gazette* even published a letter encouraging the colonists to join the Americans. Michael Kean, a lawyer in St. Vincent, publicly supported the Americans by "wishing them success, giving entertainments when the Americans gained any advantage, [and] toasting their Generals." He called his residence Faneuil Hall, which was a rendezvous of the radicals in Boston.[78]

Men accused of treasonous activities with North America latterly escaped conviction in the West Indies. For example, Mr. Resolve Smith of St. Vincent was "acquitted of the charge of writing contumacious and Rebellious Letters" and found "guilty only of a misdemeanor," despite the evidence of intercepted correspondence and orders for his trial from Britain. He was defended by Kean, who "by prostituting his professional knowledge, and abilities, so successfully perverted all evidence, and circumstances of accusation, as to obtain his acquittal." "Noted for his Attachment to the Americans," Dr. Benjamin Clifton, a physician in St. Kitts, was accused of relaying correspondence from the board of war in Virginia to a Mr. Birch in Antigua. Clifton was prosecuted by "the civil powers" but by some "manoeuvre he escaped."[79]

The revolutionary supporters shared some common characteristics. They tended to be "closely connected by Relationship and trade with North America"; to have "formerly lived in America, & imbibed no small portion of her levelling spirit"; and to be "persons born in America — many of whom from interested motives, or otherwise, have lived in" the islands during the war. They were most likely to be merchants.[80]

Those "completely ruined in their fortunes" were also more likely to support the American Revolution. "The American spirit prevails amongst many in these islands and is derived from the same source . . . the great debt contracted in England." There were "not . . . a great many Persons of such Principles" in Antigua "but all that are Adherents of the Congress here are involved in Debt to Great Britain" and they hoped that "Independency will pay the Whole for all of them." Poor whites were also likely to support the American Revolution. The American faction in St. Kitts "Poisoned the Minds of many of the lower inhabitants" who were "neither opulent, numerous or of any Rank."[81]

Rebel supporters were for the most part outmaneuvered by the loyalist majority at the beginning of the war, especially on those islands with the closest ties to North America, such as Antigua and St. Kitts. They never gained the ascendancy in the British Caribbean that the patriots did in the mainland colonies.

* * *

Far from wholeheartedly supporting the American Revolution, West Indians were divided over the mildest gestures of opposition to the home government, in spite of the financial strain of the war and the inadequacy of imperial protection. These divisions had hampered the lobbying activity of the West India interest in London in 1774–75 and continued throughout the American War.

The divisions were reflected within the West India lobby in London. In a debate in the House of Commons in December 1779, the opposition West India members attempted to shame the government by exposing the defenseless state of Jamaica during the invasion scare of September. Richard Pennant, an absentee planter of Jamaica, moved for all the petitions from the Jamaica and West India lobbies to be laid before the House of Commons. Lord Rockingham made the same motion in the House of Lords.[83] The motion was defeated but Pennant rebounded to lead a sally against the government in January. He charged that the neglect of Jamaica was sufficient grounds for the impeachment of Germain, causing the prime minister to cry, "Impeach now!" Pennant presented a petition allegedly from absentee merchants and planters of Jamaica that was critical of Germain. The tactic split the West India lobby between those who wished to work with the government and those who wanted to publicly embarrass the government.

However, the ploy of the opposition West India members was foiled when Germain replied that the petition did not represent the views of all Jamaicans resident in Britain. Germain cited a counterpetition with sixty-one signatories, which complained that the original petition was not drawn up at an open meeting of the West India lobby and that it was "premature because we place confidence in Lord George Germain's assurance of future protection." John Fuller, the brother of the agent for Jamaica, spoke in defense of Germain, asserting that "many other considerable Planters, as well as himself" refused to sign the original petition, "satisfied that the Defense of Jamaica had not, and would not be neglected." Lord Rockingham's use of the original petition similarly backfired when Lord Onslow retorted that it did not represent "the unanimous Opinion of the Merchants concerned in the Object of it, he himself, in Concurrence with many very respectable Gentlemen, having signed a Protest, intimating the strongest Disapprobation of it." The opposition West India members never again tried to break with the rest of the lobby.[84]

8

Rule Britannia

ALTHOUGH THE BRITISH WEST INDIES avoided confrontation with the home government, there was a virtual political stalemate between the island assemblies and the civil governors at the height of the American Revolutionary War. The source of opposition to the governors was not, as historians have claimed, "the pro-republican ideology of a large number of the inhabitants" who supported the American Revolution.[1] Nor did internal political wranglings prevent the islands from supporting defense measures or assisting the imperial government.

Even during the worst years of political deadlock in the islands, the assemblies voted significant contributions toward defense, which was remarkable given the economic strain of the war and the inadequacy of imperial protection. The British West Indies continued to make fervent declarations of loyalty to Britain and to denounce the American Revolution. The West India lobby in London assisted the British government in waging the war for America. Furthermore, the virtual stalemate between island assemblies and governors ended as the war evolved into a patriotic struggle against the ancient enemies of Spain and France.

Indeed, the British West Indies played a major role in the American Revolutionary War. Their defense interests ranked high among the priorities of the British government and deflected resources from the war for America. The failure to provide sufficient protection was due to overstretched resources, not lack of commitment.

* * *

There was virtual paralysis in the government of the British islands at the height of the American War. The royal governors were variously obstructed by the island assemblies over taxes, the building of fortresses, the organization of the militia, and the declaration of martial law. Governor Valentine Morris of St. Vincent, Governor John Dalling of Jamaica, and Governor James Cunningham of Barbados were recalled by the home government owing to the clamors of the colonists. Governor William Mathew Burt of the Leeward Islands was equally unpopular but he died in office in a state of delirium. He was transfixed in the final year of his life by premonitions of his imminent death, "which he frequently mentioned," and there were rumors that he had been poisoned.[2]

The governors were authors of their own difficulties to some extent. They were more dogmatic, irascible, and inflexible than their predecessors when circumstances required otherwise. This was no coincidence: they were appointed by the government that had opted for war against America. Their supercilious view of colonial rights mirrored that of their political patrons in Britain. Governor Burt was suspicious of all colonial assemblies "where arises opposition to Government." Governor Morris "was infatuated almost to the point of fanaticism" with the idea of packing the legislature in order to bridle the opposition and to elide "turbulent members." Governor George, Lord Macartney of Grenada had written an unpublished pamphlet on the right of Parliament to tax the American colonies in which he had argued that "Representation . . . is not essential to Liberty." Both Governor Dalling and Governor Cunningham had wanted a military command, not a post in civil government, which predisposed them to clashing with the assemblies.[3]

In the midst of the American War, Governor Burt advocated the reform of the entire colonial administration to enhance the authority of the governor. He proposed that governors be given more control over colonial patronage, including the appointment of patent officers, and that they be given sole authority over the officials in their government. He contended that if the governor won the power of appointment and became the fountainhead of patronage, "no opposition would Ever be started, in my opinion, to the Measures of the Crown abroad."[4] He urged that his plan be instantly implemented. He had no sense of political timing.

The autocratic personalities of the island governors contributed to the political impasse experienced by most of the islands at the height of the American War. Governor Dalling was candid about his personal failings but "found it almost impossible to brook criticism from others, or even to accept honest differences of opinion." Governor Burt was "something of the martinet" who possessed an "irascible temper." He was infamous in the House of Commons for his dull ponderous speeches in which he harangued and rambled against his opponents.[5]

The governors' disdain for colonial rights was reflected in their policies. Governor Morris and Governor Burt both spent their own money on defense preparations without first obtaining a vote of taxes from the assembly, being well aware that only the assemblies had the right to initiate tax bills. They excused themselves, claiming an emergency following the fall of Dominica in 1778, but the assemblies thought otherwise and were unwilling to set a precedent. Neither governor was refunded, causing deadlock in St. Vincent and St. Kitts. They hoped to be reimbursed by the home government, but they had not sought prior approval and were thus refused by the Treasury. Burt wrote pathetically to Lord Germain that the debt was "too much for my family to stand charged with."[6] He was eventually given a "loan" by the home government but Morris was abandoned. Morris was already in serious financial trouble from gambling, an extravagant lifestyle, and his unsuccessful bid for a seat in the House of Commons. He was subsequently sued by creditors for the money he had spent on defense preparations and eventually died a ruined man in Britain after five years of imprisonment for debt.

Governor Morris and Governor Burt compounded their problems by their inept attempts at a resolution. Burt wrote to his attorney general seeking advice on how to punish the assembly but the letter was leaked to the press, causing a furor. He dismissed the house clerk, who was the son of the speaker. The assembly refused to do business for much of the time before Burt's death in January 1781.[7] Governor Morris attempted to enlarge the assembly membership in order to obtain a house willing to reimburse him and to vote him a permanent duty to supplement his salary. His action raised the possibility of a governor's arbitrarily changing the composition of a house and it violated the tradition that assemblies determine their own electoral practices. Morris was recalled by the home government but he ignored his orders and continued a lame administration until the conquest of the island by France in 1779.

Governor Cunningham arbitrarily introduced higher fees to supplement his salary, which caused political deadlock in Barbados. The fees were fixed by custom and were charged for services involving the governor. The assembly regarded the new fees as an illegal tax, similar to the ship money levied by Charles I. It argued that the fees violated the charter of the island and colonial rights. The assembly demanded his recall, and the agent threatened to bring the matter before Parliament.[8] Thereafter, civil government almost broke down until Cunningham was recalled in 1782.

The governors revealed themselves to be equally high-handed in their treatment of other royal officials. Governor Dalling quarreled over prize money (the reward from captures) with Sir Peter Parker, who commanded the naval squadron in Jamaica. It was a damaging dispute, considering that collaboration between the governor and the admiral were vital for the defense of the island and for the success of overseas campaigns. Dalling exceeded his authority by dismissing Attorney General Thomas Harrison as advocate general for refusing to prosecute Admiral Parker. He defied the orders of the admiralty in London to reinstate Harrison and even removed four assistant judges who appeared sympathetic to Harrison.⁹ Like Governor Morris in St. Vincent, Dalling ignored his recall by the home government. His behavior was brazen in the extreme.

Governor Burt surpassed the other governors in quarreling with fellow royal officials. A dispute with John Felton, the inspector general of customs, degenerated into an acrimonious debate about their relative jurisdiction over trade and revenue. He alienated Aretas Akers, the speaker of the assembly, by challenging the right of patent officers to make appointments and by illegally imposing his own candidate as deputy casual receiver of St. Kitts. The rift would have serious consequences in his relations with the assembly.¹⁰

Burt had an absurdly inflated view of the role of a governor, which he regarded as "in an inferior degree [equivalent] to Command in Ireland" or equal to the supreme military commanders in Europe. He claimed supreme command over all British troops stationed in the Leeward Islands. This led to a damaging series of confrontations with several senior officers, whom he resented for treating him as "a Barrack Master subordinate to Lieutenant Colonels." He was embroiled in various disputes with the military over packet boats (which carried official dispatches to Britain), flags of truce, letters of marque for privateers, and prisoner exchanges. His behavior "paralyzed the service in that area" and impeded preparations for the recapture of St. Vincent. Burt caused Major General John Vaughan to threaten resignation as the commander in chief of the British army in the Lesser Antilles. Burt, in a rare moment of self-criticism, acknowledged that his "Zeal may Perhaps precipitate me too far."¹¹

The governors alienated the colonists by launching overseas campaigns that sacrificed the defense of their own islands. Governors Dalling and Cunningham were both army officers who were openly frustrated by their civil duties and warmed at the prospect of military commands. Neither Governor Burt nor Governor Morris possessed military experience but their ambitious schemes for overseas campaigns were equally grand. They wanted to repeat the successes of the last war against France and to harass the Spanish empire in a policy reminiscent of that of Queen Elizabeth I.

Their plans for overseas campaigns were unrealistic, because they failed to appreciate the implications of a weak British navy for the amphibious warfare of the Caribbean, and the insufficient number of British troops. The plans did not allow for the impact of disease and the high mortality rates, which afflicted all offensive operations in the tropics. Nor did they consider how the new conquests were to be garrisoned and defended when British resources were already so thinly stretched. Furthermore, their plans involved removing troops from the remaining British islands, which were already inadequately defended.

Governor Dalling's overseas campaigns were the primary cause of his irreconcilable breach with the assembly in Jamaica. Dalling envisaged using local volunteers, black troops, indigenous peoples, and army regulars in a ludicrously ambitious series of campaigns against Spanish America. Dalling had served under General James Wolfe at Quebec, where he was wounded scaling the heights of Abraham, but he lacked the experience of independent command. He jeopardized the security of Jamaica by removing troops for overseas service when the island was defended by fewer than thirteen hundred regular troops fit for duty in 1779–80. There were even bets in the financial district of London that "Jamaica . . . will be in the hands of the Spaniards by the first of July (1779)." Dalling went "from being one of the most popular characters a twelve month ago that perhaps ever was in this country . . . [to] the reverse."[12]

Dalling's first expedition aimed to avenge Spanish successes against British settlements in the Bay of Honduras. In October 1779, Dalling achieved the capture of Fort Omoa, the most important fort in the bay. The victory was short-lived, however: disease decimated the British troops and the fort was retaken by the Spanish in November. Dalling was undeterred and embarked on an even wilder plan. His objective was no less than to divide the Spanish Empire in the Americas and to open commercial routes with the Pacific by an expedition through Central America. He boasted that by securing possession of the St. John River and Lake Nicaragua, a single force could take all of Spanish America.[13] In April, a second expedition successfully laid siege to the castle of San Juan, the strongest fort guarding the entrance of Lake Nicaragua, but the campaign again came unraveled and the fort was retaken by the Spanish.

Dalling's campaigns were a fiasco and permanently embittered his relations with the assembly, which demanded his recall. His defeats resulted in a spectacular loss of life, which weakened the defense of Jamaica. Only 380 men out of the original 1,800 survived the campaign. Six of the nine officers lost their lives. Only 10 of the 200 crew members survived in the *Hinchinbroke*, which had escorted the expedition under the command of Horatio Nelson. Germain acknowledged that the expedition was "ill concerted and worse executed" and a "waste of . . . Public Money." He pronounced it an "entire failure" in which "no Public Benefit has been derived from the loss of so many brave men." Even after his recall by the home government, Dalling pressed ahead with plans for the conquest of Curaçao.[14]

Governor Burt also pursued various "idle foolish projects" for overseas campaigns. On the eve of the French conquest of Grenada and St. Vincent, he

Figure 27. *Governor John Dalling* (National Portrait Gallery, England). Dalling was acting governor of Jamaica in 1772–74 and governor in 1777–81. His decision to send troops abroad in a wild scheme to capture Spanish America alienated the planters in Jamaica who petitioned Britain for his recall. As for most of the British islands, there was a virtual stalemate in the politics of Jamaica at the height of the American War.

predicted a year of British victories more impressive than those in 1759. He proposed the conquests of Martinique, Guadeloupe, St. Bartholomew, St. Martin, and Puerto Rico. His bravado encouraged Germain in an offensive strategy, but the army commanders dismissed the reports as "too sanguine" in their prospect of "some capital stroke."[15]

Germain, the secretary of state for America, censured the conduct of the governors in the West Indies. He was displeased with Governor Burt's tampering with the patronage rights of patent officers. He upbraided him for allowing a private quarrel with a planter in Antigua to escalate into a constitutional question that disrupted the public service and threatened to raise issues that the government might have to concede. He overturned his appointment of a solicitor general while Admiral Rodney overruled Burt on the exchange of prisoners. Germain rebuked Governor Burt for arrogating to himself powers over the army and interfering with details when he was forbidden to do so. Germain asked him to use discretion in the exercise of his powers as commander in chief and ordered him to obtain the approval of the military commanders "of every military matter if possible before you undertake it."[16]

Germain had forbidden the governors of the Windward Islands from urging "in any *peremptory*" manner, the payment of the 4½ per cent duties" and "to avoid even any risque whatever" of a dispute over the duties with the assemblies. Governor Shirley in Dominica dropped the issue but Governor Morris tried to pack the assembly to pass a bill to levy the duty, a disastrous move. Germain was critical of Governor Cunningham for charging high fees for official services and for not accepting the salary offered him in Barbados. Germain was also displeased with the inflammatory nature of his speeches. In conversation with the island agent, Germain "very freely condemned the governor's conduct."[17]

The governors in the British West Indies had stuck rigidly to the letter of their instructions when the home government had become more conciliatory and more flexible in its dealings with the remaining colonies. The paramount goal of the imperial government was to win the war, even at the cost of political concessions. The governors were out of step with their superiors, who wanted the governors to work in harmony with the legislatures and to avoid unnecessary entanglements.[18]

*　　*　　*

The governors were not exclusively to blame for their political difficulties; they were victims of the ambiguities of the imperial constitution. We discussed earlier the discrepancy between the theoretical powers of the governors, embodied in their commissions and instructions, and their authority in practice. The governors had to deal with rival departments of the imperial government, which often countermanded one another, causing chaos within a colony. The governors were consequently at odds with other colonial officials who were answerable neither to them nor to the secretary of state for America. Germain acknowledged the deficiencies of the imperial constitution but he warned that this was no time to make changes.[19]

The British government was inconsistent in its own interpretation of the colonial system. It refused to reimburse Governor Morris for his private expenditure on defense but it repaid the governors of other colonies who had similarly spent their own money in the same circumstances. It repaid those governors who were politically better connected and commanded more vital colonies like Lord Macartney in Grenada. It was only after the governors had become embroiled in stalemates with the assemblies that Germain ordered them to be more conciliatory, even at the expense of giving up their prerogative rights. It is little wonder that governors felt "lightly sacrificed" by the imperial government while being subjected to "the scoff and derision of turbulent and nearly rebellious Colonists."[20]

The policy of launching unrealistic offensives highlighted the shortcomings of the chief architect of the American War, Lord George Germain. Germain encouraged the island governors not only to "preserve and protect" their colonies "but to act offensively" against the enemy. On the eve of the expedition to St. Johns, he told Governor Dalling that "your Ideas . . . coincide entirely with the opinions entertained here." At the same time he expected Dalling to defend Jamaica and to reinforce West Florida (Pensacola). He even encouraged him to consider campaigns in New Orleans and in the Mississippi River. Germain encouraged the army to retake the French-occupied British islands and even to attack Puerto Rico. Germain did not micromanage his subordinates but left it to their discretion to decide the "objects . . . most for the advantage of the Public." He gave them too much latitude, in fact, enabling him to deflect criticism by arguing that his policies failed because they were badly implemented. His actions were already under scrutiny after the debacle of the British defeat at Saratoga in 1777 and the stigma of his own court-martial for failing to obey orders to lead a cavalry charge at the Battle of Minden in 1759.[21]

The governors inevitably clashed with assemblies whose quest to win the initiative and to usurp executive powers made constitutional disputes a characteristic of all eighteenth-century wars in the British West Indies. The assemblies sought to eclipse the influence of the governors over taxation, expenditure, the militia, martial law, the tenure of judges, the appointment of public officers, and the right to determine their own internal procedures. The assemblies were similar to those in the past in seeking as much autonomy as possible within the British Empire. Their assertiveness was an essential means by which the balance between local and imperial interests was adjusted. Even an assembly composed of American loyalists in the Bahamas vied with Governor Lord Dunmore after his relegation from Virginia.

The governors were bound to collide with the assemblies that sought to win control over the introduction of martial law. The French conquest of Dominica in 1778 triggered the issue of martial law, the main source of the rift with Governor Morris and the beginning of the troubles of Governor Dalling. The assemblies resented the tremendous powers acquired by the governors during martial law, which included the command of the militia, courts-martial, the confiscation of property, the imposition of embargoes, and the conscription of slaves. The assemblies also wanted more influence over martial law because it was expensive. Jamaica lost almost five weeks of crop time in some parishes during the martial law in the summer of 1779, costing the island about £20,000 a week or the equivalent of the annual peacetime additional subsidy for a regiment of regular troops. Five thousand slaves were conscripted to work on the fortifications during martial law in Jamaica in March 1782. The colonists suspected that the governors introduced martial law as a pretext to augment their personal authority when there was no real emergency.[22]

The assemblies in St. Vincent and Jamaica denied the sole authority of governors to declare martial law and asserted new constitutional claims. The assembly of St. Vincent refused to vote taxes in opposition to martial law, which caused Governor Morris to spend his own money on defense preparations. Governor Dalling imposed martial law almost continuously for three months, but the assembly protested that martial law "if continued [will] end in the total ruin of this country." His power to declare martial law and select his advisers was challenged by the assembly. The governors lost to the assemblies, which subsequently won greater influence over the process of martial law in the revised militia acts in St. Vincent (1776), Grenada (1778), and Jamaica (1779). The assemblies similarly sought control over the maintenance and building of fortifications. The assembly of St. Kitts began its dispute with Governor Burt when he refused to concede his powers over expenditure on fortifications. The Jamaican assembly won tenure for judges and the right to nominate judges in 1781, an important victory because of the long-standing grievance that the judiciary was extremely vulnerable to the political whims of a governor who was previously able to appoint and dismiss them.[23]

The governors confronted assemblies that were especially cautious about

expenditure, as they witnessed the economic strain and the inadequate imperial protection that characterized the American War. The burden of defense
increased the cost of local taxes and reduced the productivity of the plantations. The planters had little control over the dramatic wartime rise in their
expenses except for local taxes. It was little wonder that they wanted to "with-
hold their consent to any expense, they can avoid" and to obtain greater
accountability from governors for the expenditure of their taxes.[24] There was a
correlation between low levels of plantation profits and opposition to voting
taxes for defense. For example, Antigua voted generous supplies for most of
the war, but it was less willing to vote taxes in the last years of the war because
of the constant drought and a fall in exports.

Barbados was more reluctant than the other islands to contribute to the
cost of defense. This was partly because it was the most creolized and independent of the islands but also because it suffered the lowest average profits in the
British West Indies during the American War. The hardship of the war was
preceded by years of declining profits, lower productivity rates, and decreased
production due to soil erosion. In addition, prior to the war, Barbados had
exported about one-quarter of its produce to North America. J. R. Ward
estimates that Barbados plantations averaged the lowest profits (2.3 percent)
during the American War, insufficient to pay off interest rates of at least 5
percent on debts when a majority of the planters — two-thirds according to the
governor — were in debt. Sir John Gay Alleyne, the speaker of the assembly,
was one of the largest planters but even he was also heavily in debt.[25]

Furthermore, Barbados was severely affected by the hurricane of 1780.
The island suffered an estimated £1,300,000 worth of damage, including the
loss of 4,000 slaves and 8,000 head of cattle.[26] One company of London merchants lost £80,000. Hundreds of plantation buildings were destroyed, such as
398 windmills, which cost between £1,000 and £8,000 each. Bridgetown,
which "but a few hours before had been one of the best towns in the West
Indies [was] converted into little better than one confused heap of ruins."[27]
The "houses, public buildings, forts, batterys and churches (were) all de-
molished." The assembly refused to vote any taxes in the aftermath of the
hurricane.[28]

Barbados also resisted defense expenditure in protest against paying
higher rates of imperial duty. The assembly had voted a 4½ percent duty in
perpetuity when Barbados was the richest colony in the British Empire in
1663. The assembly increasingly resented the duty, which was originally voted
to pay the cost of defense and administration but was used for other purposes
by Britain. The injustice of the duty became especially apparent when competitors in the neighboring Windward Islands were exempted from paying the

duty by a judicial decision in London in *Campbell v. Hall* (1774). The aggravation was greater still when a new inspector of customs began a more rigorous system of collection and removed traditional allowances for leakage in 1776. (Antigua simply refused to comply with the new system by threatening not to ship its sugars.) Barbados alone paid the duty under the new method of collection.

In July 1780, the assembly of Barbados reduced the salary of the incoming governor in protest against the 4½ percent duty, but the affront to the new governor caused the worst political crisis in the British West Indies. The idea of reducing the salary of the governor was mooted over a decade earlier and there were previous precedents. The assembly was given the impression by its agent that the home government was to commute and eventually abolish the duty, but it was disappointed to find that no such orders accompanied Governor James Cunningham when he arrived in 1780. Cunningham naturally took the reduction of his salary as a personal affront and sought to make up the loss by introducing a set of arbitrary fees. According to one source at the time, the "deduction of Cunningham's salary was the cause of all subsequent disturbances in his administration." The result was a total deadlock in which the assembly was the most obstructive of any island.[29]

Barbados was the least tractable of all the islands during Cunningham's administration (1780–82). The assembly refused to make any contributions toward defense, even after the fortifications were almost leveled by the hurricane of 1780. On hearing the news of Yorktown (1781), the assembly had refused to vote any additional funds for defense although it professed to be "deeply affected with the unhappy surrender of the troops under their brave general Lord Cornwallis" and alarmed by the "intelligence respecting the French fleet." Admiral Rodney was so impatient with the inadequate defense preparations that he publicly accused the inhabitants of Bridgetown of being "inclined to the American interest" and of keeping up "a constant correspondence with the Enemy at Martinique."[30]

Lord George Macartney was the only governor to escape political deadlock primarily because he allied himself with the majority party in the assembly. He supported the British settlers who had opposed the integration of the French inhabitants and was condescending about the French, whom he distrusted and believed could "never be incorporated with our people." He befriended George Leonard Staunton, the champion of the British Protestant settlers, despite earlier suspicions that Staunton supported the Americans, and appointed him his private secretary and attorney general of Grenada. The partisan tone of his administration was apparent in the address of thanks on his departure that contained thirty-two British names but no French. His social

Figure 28. *George, Lord Macartney [1737–1806] with Sir George Staunton*, L. F. Abbott, 1784 (National Portrait Gallery, England). Macartney was governor of Grenada between 1776 and the conquest of the island by France in 1779. He was the only governor among his contemporaries to enjoy good relations with the colonists. His friend Staunton was reputed to be a supporter of the American Revolution but was nevertheless appointed attorney general of Grenada.

and political stature also helped, as "the only Governor . . . [in the West Indies] that can pretend to [have] personal character or influence." Germain regarded him as a model, "for no administration of government has been more meritorious than his Lordship's."[31] However, his success was bought at a high price. Macartney did not win support among the French population who betrayed the British during the invasion of the island in 1779.

* * *

Despite the political impasses experienced by most islands, the British West Indies contributed significantly to their own defense during the American War. The sums voted were remarkable given the economic strain of the

TABLE 10   Annual Expenditure by Jamaica Assembly

	Grant (Jamaica £) (includes perpetual annual revenue of £9,000)	Increase after 1768
1768	£44,000	
1772	53,300	£9,300
1775	85,300	41,300
1776	110,000	66,000
1777	84,200	40,200
1778	98,200	54,200
1779	120,900	76,900
1780	153,000	109,000
1781	141,000	97,000
Total		£493,900

Source: [Samuel Estwick], *Considerations on the Present Decline of the Sugar-Trade* (London, 1782), 53.

war and the inadequacy of imperial protection. For example, Jamaica was generous in its defense expenditure (Table 10); its assembly spent more than £71,567 on forts alone in 1778 and an "unprecedented" additional grant of £70,000 in 1779. These grants were exclusive of the £9,000 annual perpetual revenue and the £38,000 parochial taxes levied "for the rector's stipend, salaries to parish officers, repairs of church, bridges, parochial barracks, and highway's; maintenance of paupers, &c &c." Extraordinary taxes were greater than ordinary taxes in Jamaica after 1779. These included a double poll tax, charged at five and a half times the normal rate, and a double deficiency tax. Between 1775 and 1781, the assembly voted £484,600 in excess of the peacetime expenditure, of which most went toward "fortifications, barracks, and other military services, exclusive of £1,250 per annum issuing out of the perpetual revenue to like uses." The national debt was more than £282,260 in 1781.[32]

Antigua spent more than £87,929 on defense over the course of the war, a sacrifice for an island suffering the effects of a prolonged drought, an epidemic of dysentery, the loss of one-fifth of its slave population, and three disastrous years of sugar crops. Almost without credit, the island was forced to borrow £20,000 sterling from the imperial government. It was understandable that the assembly eventually refused to grant the requests of the army, whose commander falsely concluded that the merchants and a considerable number of the planters were "attach'd to the Rebellious Americans." Governor Burt thought the accusation absurd, insisting that members were compelled to refuse the request due to the distresses of the island. He added that there were none more ready to testify their zeal and affection to the king than the inhabitants of Antigua.[33]

At the time of its rupture with Governor Burt, the assembly of St. Kitts voted unprecedented defense subsidies. The assembly resented criticism when the members "were proceeding with the greatest unanimity upon Business of the Highest Importance." Far from refusing to pay for military stores, it "passed every account of expense incurred on that Head and for the repairs of the forts and fortifications." In December 1778, the assembly cheerfully concurred "in voting such sums of money as was necessary for the payment of seamen and other British subjects who were to be employed in the Forts and Batteries of the Island." The following April, the assembly voted to relieve the militia by hiring one hundred seamen to man the forts and fortifications. It voted a bounty to all seamen who entered the Royal Navy, for which the legislature received a personal message of thanks from Vice Admiral Byron. In June 1779, the assembly voted a reward to any constable who found and returned able seamen to the navy.[34]

Before the arrival of Governor Cunningham, Barbados had voted £6,000 for the forts and fortifications. Although such expenditures ceased during Cunningham's administration, "volunteer associations . . . undertook the reparation of their dismantled fortifications." Bridgetown "raised a liberal subscription" emulated in "Speight's [Town], Saint James's, Ostin's and Reed's bay." The alacrity with which the island was put into a state of defense impressed Admiral Rodney, who wrote that it did "them honour, and is very meritorious, as the greatest part is done by public subscription."[35]

The white colonists willingly voted money for regular troops to deter foreign attack and to police the slaves, and the islands constantly sought more troops from Britain. Jamaica extended the additional peacetime subsistence allowance to all the new regiments. Although it tried to limit subsistence to 2,650 men, it later relented at an annual cost of £65,000. In return for 1,500 reinforcements, St. Kitts offered to "make a sufficient and immediate pecuniary provision." It provided slaves to land the army and to transport equipment and established a troop hospital. Some representatives even made their private houses available as barracks. According to Colonel Christie, St. Kitts was "so far from adopting refractory measures, that they grant cheerfully every assistance."[36]

Barbados voted provisions for the British fleet and army in St. Lucia in 1778 and again in 1779. Every planter with fifty acres of land or town dweller with an equivalent rent was required to provide twenty-five pounds of meat or twelve pounds of poultry for the army. Indeed, the levy was so "cheerfully received by all ranks of people . . . that . . . at least treble the levy will be exported." In February 1780, the assembly of Barbados voted unanimously to provide barracks for the army. Struggling with a prolonged drought and starvation among the slaves, there was "a little wrangling" in Antigua over expenses but it was "all in good humour."[37] Antigua spent £45,000 building two barracks for the army.

Despite all this apparent goodwill, the colonists were reluctant to spend money on fortifications because they regarded external defense as the responsibility of the imperial government and believed that the building of fortifications lulled the home government into a false sense of optimism. They had long held that fortifications were a useless deterrent without naval superiority.[38] Forts helped avert pirate attacks and "keep the slaves in awe" but they provided only momentary protection against foreign attack until the arrival of "that succour and relief which only ships can supply." "Even [army] officers" declared that "it would be better to surrender to an enemy, than to attempt to save a colony by retiring to the interior parts of the country." Some colonists were ready to capitulate immediately because the "sovereignty of the Island is nothing to them if their Houses are burnt." Their attitude did "not proceed from any disaffection but [from] fear their families . . . might be exposed to the insults of Negroes." They believed that the sacrifices of the war must be proportionate to what was at stake. To their minds, the only real security was a superior fleet.[39]

The colonists were not overly confident about their forts, which were often poorly constructed and inappropriately located. The building materials were usually inferior, especially in wartime owing to scarcity and high prices. The guns were too close together, stone pavements were dangerous, walls were too low, and parapets and ditches were insufficient. The combination of the climate and neglect caused the fortresses to decay quickly as wooden gun carriages rotted, magazines leaked, honeycombed ordnance rusted, gunpowder decomposed, canon became positively dangerous, bored soldiers committed acts of vandalism, articles were pilfered, and windows broken. Sponges, ladles, and rammers to operate guns were lost or stolen. Most of the forts were in a ruinous condition throughout the British West Indies on the eve of the American War.

Colonists were opposed to building new forts because there were already too many forts and not enough gunners, which "could actually be more harm than good." There was an elaborate system of fortifications on each island, including batteries along the coasts, forts defending important towns, and places of refuge (deodands). There were well over three hundred fortresses in the British Windward and Leeward Islands. In the Leeward Islands, the colonists were convinced that the forts were useless because of the small number of whites and their inexperience in firing canon. The fortifications on Brimstone Hill were too large for St. Kitts, with its diminutive white population. In Jamaica, there were more "forts, bastions, and other works than could have been manned in case of a siege during the war."[40]

The colonists were also apathetic about spending money on fortifications because they were a major source of public expenditure, especially during the inflationary period of the American War. They were built with the labor of conscripted slaves, which represented an additional cost to the planters. Engineers and local builders often took large percentages, and the whole process was riddled with corruption. The bricks had to be imported from England while lime for building was scarce and prohibitively expensive during the American War. "The whole wealth" of Barbados "laid out in the repairs of fortifications" was still not enough to provide adequate protection.[41]

The white colonists were suspicious of the reliability of fortresses because they received so many conflicting opinions about their location and design. The governors and military commanders, with almost ritualistic regularity, were critical of the defense works of their predecessors: "Great sums of money . . . [were] expended for forts and fortifications" in Jamaica and yet there was "not a single work to answer the immoderate expence" by 1779.[42] Fort Augusta was the only one "in the least respectable, where thousands and tens of thousands [had] been sunk," but "its original bad construction [could] never be rectified." After the American War, the assembly of St. Kitts resolved that the fortifications were found wanting and "by no means contributive to the safety and defence of the Island." The construction of Fort George in the parish of St. George in Barbados was abandoned because the assembly could "not discover its utility" and preferred "to sacrifice what it had already cost, rather than raise new taxes for its completion."[43]

* * *

The political impasse in most islands did not prevent the white colonists from making regular declarations of their loyalty to Britain during the American War. Even at their most fractious, the assemblies vied with one another in protestations of loyalty. The evidence of addresses and petitions must of course be treated with care since they were often pro forma with "all the Guilded Glare of Adulation usually attendant on Addresses."[44] However, the declarations of the assemblies were not mere exercises in political relations because their zealous language risked alienating the United States by denouncing the American Revolution.

In February 1777, the parish of Westmoreland in Jamaica congratulated the governor and the king on the success of the British army against "the Provincial Insurgents" and "that deluded people" whom they hoped "will soon be brought back to their Duty."[45] Governor Shirley affirmed the support and loyalty of Dominica for Britain. In May, Antigua addressed George III as the "best of sovereigns" and denounced the "wanton and unnatural Rebellion" in North America. The same month, the council and assembly of Montserrat independently denounced the rebellion in North America. In October, the governor of Barbados testified to the "steady loyalty and affection" of the island to the king. Even Kingston, the radical urban mercantile center of Jamaica, sent a "dutiful" address to Britain. The assembly of Jamaica passed a resolution of thanks for the gift of a pair of portraits of George III and Queen Charlotte from the widow of Governor Trelawny. In contrast, patriots in the United States destroyed or disfigured any images of the royal family.[46]

In 1778, all the Leeward Island legislatures sent petitions of loyalty to the Crown. Governor Burt regarded these addresses as sincere expressions of their zeal and attachment to Britain. The council of St. Kitts "deeply regret[ed] the infatuation of their deluded fellow subjects in America, & lamented[ed] their Perseverance with in a Rebellion so Calamitous, & Unnatural" and wished that "they may renounce the Bondage of Anarchy." The council and assembly of Nevis similarly scorned the "unnatural Rebellion." Montserrat expressed its "Indignation at the attempt of Rebellious Americans to disturb the public peace and Tranquility." The assembly of Antigua voted to prosecute the *Antigua Gazette* for a disloyal article. In December, the assembly lambasted the "daring and unnatural Rebellion" and wished that "Prosperity and Triumph . . . avail the British army" in North America.[47]

After "a general and full meeting . . . at the court house," the inhabitants of Montego Bay in Jamaica formed a loyal committee "to draw up an address to his Majesty, offering their lives and fortunes in support of his Crown and dignity, against the daring rebellion in North America." The inhabitants of Jamaica were "strenuous and spirited in their support of the British government." The Barbados legislature similarly expressed its "unshaken loyalty to the best of sovereigns" and declared its "abhorrence of those unwarrantable practices on the continent of America which have since broken out into an unnatural rebellion." They regretted "the delusion of those unhappy people, who have been seduced to exchange their former unbounded happiness for the destructive consequences of a ruinous state of anarchy and confusion." Governor Cunningham spoke of the continuing tradition of loyalty in Barbados to Britain, and another colonial official boasted of "silencing all Rebellious Clamours" in Barbados.[48]

In 1780, "the patriotic inhabitants" of Basseterre in St. Kitts raised "a liberal subscription [for] his Majesty's service," aiming to "strengthen the hands of the great naval Officer Admiral Rodney." The council of Nevis described George III as "the best of kings." Antigua was "loyal, zealous [and] strongly attached to the Crown" despite the "woeful, miserable & wretched state of the Island." In the midst of its struggle with Governor Cunningham, the assembly of Barbados proclaimed its loyalty to the king and its attachment to Britain, rejoicing "at the success of the Br. army in N. America." At the height of the conflict with Governor Dalling, the assembly of Jamaica issued proclamations of loyalty and attachment to Britain. Admiral Sir Peter Parker also thought that the "Jamaican people [were] well disposed to government." Theatrical performances in Jamaica were sometimes concluded with the patriotic strains of "Rule Britannia."[49]

The press in the islands was loyalist. In Jamaica, the *Royal Gazette* was edited by Alexander Aikman and David Douglas, both loyalist refugees from America. Formerly the *Jamaica Mercury and Kingston Weekly Advertiser*, the paper was renamed and the royal arms placed on the masthead "to mark the devotion of it to royalty." Similarly, the *Gazette of Saint Jago de la Vega* and the *Freeport Gazette or the Dominican Chronicle* in Dominica also bore the royal crest on their mastheads. In St. Kitts, Thomas Howe published the *Royal Charibbean Gazette or, The St Christopher Universal Chronicle*, which mocked the "tyrannic yoke of Congress." His paper angered the mainland press for its "abusive Pieces . . . reflecting on the Governor and People of St Eustatius on Account of their supposed Partiality for the American States." According to the satire of the mainland press, Howe drew particular venom as "a Genius little known in the topographical World" and "a Servant to the miserable English Caraibeans." Both his sons served in the British armed forces. When his health and financial affairs deteriorated during the war, his popularity was evident from a public subscription to send him to England. Funds were donated by Aretas Akers, the speaker of the assembly, and many of the leading planters.[50]

*   *   *

The American War in the British Caribbean evolved into a patriotic struggle against the ancient European enemy of France and Spain. In an era when a British identity was often defined in opposition to the national character of the French, the colonists regarded France as an "arbitrary power" and the French as "haughty, imperious and perfidious . . . Enemies." The colonists became more resolute in their opposition when they learned of the "wantonly oppressive and tyrannical manner" of the French in occupied British islands: in

Dominica, the French governor was said to have behaved like a perfect Nero and the French were blamed for a fire that destroyed the capital town of Roseau; in Grenada, the French ordered the confiscation of the land of absentees; in St. Vincent, the French seized slaves from the plantations; and in St. Kitts, the inhabitants of Basseterre were forced to illuminate their windows on the birthday of St. Louis.[51]

The islands' hostility toward the French also incorporated suspicion of the Americans. In article seven of the alliance of 1778, the United States agreed to cede to France any islands captured in the British West Indies. As Governor Burt told the assembly of St. Kitts in 1779, "this consideration abstracted from the love and duty we owe our sovereign, will alone be sufficient to determine our resolves on the most vigorous defence." Congress even contemplated a combined strike against the British West Indies. It seemed that France and Spain held out freedom to the United States in order "to deprive us of these colonies . . . and rob England of her sugar."[52]

* * *

The stalemate between the assemblies and the governors ended during the final years of the American War. In November 1781, Colonel Archibald Campbell replaced Governor Dalling in Jamaica. Dalling left a difficult legacy: the militia seldom trained; the assembly had voted to end work on the fortifications in protest against the increase in sugar import duties levied in Britain and refused to provision additional troops; and riots broke out against the inequitable distribution of hurricane relief money given by Parliament. Governor Dalling "had unfortunately lost the confidence of the people," which Campbell aimed to regain "by arts of address and liberality." He succeeded in becoming "one of the most successful governors of the period."[53]

Campbell was a distinguished soldier who had been wounded during the Seven Years' War at the conquest of Quebec in 1759. James Boswell, Samuel Johnson's biographer and Campbell's legal adviser, praised "his activity, his application, his command of accurate expression." Campbell led the reconquest of Georgia during the American War and boasted that "I have ripped one star and one stripe from the Rebel flag of America." He had already acted as lieutenant governor in Jamaica when he succeeded Dalling. The earl of Shelburne appointed him, although he was "a gentleman who he never saw in his life, for no other reason than that he thought the safety of the island depended upon his abilities and exertions." He later became governor of Madras and the deputy to Lord Cornwallis in India.[54]

Campbell succeeded where Dalling had failed, even though pursuing

Figure 29. *Sir Archibald Campbell* (1739–91), by George Romney, c. 1792 (National Gallery of Art, Washington, D.C.). Campbell was governor of Jamaica in 1781–84. He obtained many of the changes desired by his predecessor but obstructed by the colonists, including the formation of three black and colored regiments of soldiers.

similar policies to those of his predecessor. He introduced a new code of martial law that included a court-martial and the death penalty for betrayal or "encouragement of rebellion." The new code impressed Shelburne, who observed that the same changes "had so recently caused such dread" in Jamaica. The militia made "rapid progress" that exceeded the "most sanguine expectations" of the governor and "astonished the most dejected subjects among us." Campbell obtained generous grants for the construction of fortifications, the building of new barracks, the temporary housing of troops, and the extension of the additional subsistence allowance to all new regiments. He was consequently able to implement an elaborate system of fortifications and defense works.[55]

Campbell was even able to succeed where Dalling had failed in Central America. He sent a small force which, in combination with a larger force of settlers and Mosquito Indians, took Black River and secured British control of the Mosquito Shore. He even established three battalions of colored and black troops (see Chapter 7). His success was especially remarkable given the anger of the assembly at the increase in sugar duties in Britain in 1782.

The political impasse in other islands similarly thawed with the death of Governor Burt in February 1781 and the recall of Governor Cunningham in June 1782.

*   *   *

Even during worst years of political deadlock in the islands, the West India lobby in London facilitated the British war for America. For example, the West India planters and merchants in London raised a subscription of £5,000 sterling to offer generous bounties for two thousand recruits for Jamaica, who were known as Colonel Rainsford's Jamaica Regiment.[56]

At the request of Lord George Germain, the West India merchants provided shipping for troops bound for the Caribbean. Stephen Fuller calculated that they saved the government £10 sterling for every soldier. They transported 8,500 troops in merchant ships, which freed the equivalent of 15,000 tons of shipping for the government to use for other purposes. Fuller's recognition of the reciprocal nature of lobby politics, the quid pro quo necessary for influence with government, was highlighted in his request to the assembly of Jamaica for military intelligence with which to barter with the ministers.[57]

With the exception of Barbados, the British West Indies appointed agents who were associated with the home government. Dominica (1777–78) appointed playwright Richard Cumberland, who was secretary to the Board of Trade and a close friend of Lord George Germain. The Virgin Islands appointed John Pownall (1776–77), a former undersecretary of state in the American department and commissioner of excise, who was regarded by Benjamin Franklin as hostile to the colonies as early as 1766. Pownall also held the patent of provost marshall of the Leeward Islands, where he jealously guarded his rights, even against the governor.[58]

Stephen Fuller was genuinely fond of Germain and chided the Jamaican committee of correspondence for a letter that "seemed not to place that confidence in his Lordship which I know he merits at your hands." His partiality toward Germain did not hurt his own standing in Jamaica, where the assembly unanimously reelected him as their agent in November 1780. He relished the failure of opposition parties in England to undermine Germain and wrote to Governor Dalling of Jamaica, "It gives me great Pleasure to find that during their long inquiries in the H of Commons they have been able to fix no stain whatever upon his Lordship." Fuller wanted to name a company of artillery destined for Jamaica in honor of Germain, remarking that such gratitude "may encourage ministers in our service."[59]

Only Barbados did not play the game and suffered accordingly. Samuel Estwick, the agent for Barbados, was a known opponent of the home government. He was an opposition member of the House of Commons and the author of a pamphlet that opposed the American War. His patron in Parliament was the earl of Abingdon, who was "a strong friend of the Americans." His appointment did not win the island friends in government; as one contemporary observed, "if an agent, for so weak a place as Barbados, was in opposition to the Ministry, he would expect to obtain nothing from the government." Barbados consequently received less consideration than the other islands from Britain. The legislatures of Barbados and Jamaica simultaneously requested the removal of their unpopular governors, but only Jamaica was initially successful, although, according to Samuel Estwick "the case of Jamaica is as nothing in comparison with that of Barbados." Germain punished the island for its inadequate support of defense by withholding military stores and ammunition.[60]

*   *   *

Outside Barbados, the compliance of the British West Indies with the home government paid political dividends. The agents, merchants, and planters enjoyed ready access to senior ministers throughout the war. Stephen Fuller spoke of the warmth with which Germain "embraces every proposition for the benefit of the colonies." Fuller felt that "no man upon earth wishes better to this country" and insisted that "we have had an active advocate & steady & preserving friend in his Lordship." In sharp contrast to the earlier experience of North American agents, West Indian agents found government departments amenable to requests for information. When they assembled their case for Parliament in 1775, they found that the clerks of the customs house went to "extra Trouble & Dispatch in making out very distinct accounts of the Imports into the Sugar Islands from the northern colonies."[61]

The British government attempted to mitigate the economic impact of the war on the islands in several ways. In 1776, the Society of West India Merchants won the right to negotiate the dates of convoys with the admiralty, in contrast to previous wars when such matters were left to the authority of the naval commanders. The following year, the home government permitted the export of corn and tobacco pipe clay (which were useful in the making of muscovado sugar) to the Caribbean. Upon receipt of a petition from Barbados, the government sent out provisions of beef, pork, and flour at prime cost and free of freight charges. In 1779, Antigua borrowed £20,000 from the British Treasury and "the British government endorsed the measure in spite of its novelty." In 1778 and 1780, the government also relaxed trade restrictions between Ireland and the West Indies. After the devastation of the hurricane in 1780, Parliament voted relief funds of £80,000 sterling to Barbados and £40,000 sterling to Jamaica. Except for the grant to South Carolina in 1740, this was the first time that Parliament had voted relief for a natural disaster in British America. George III personally donated five thousand pairs of shoes for the poor in the Jamaica militia. In 1781, Lord North granted new drawbacks (the repayment of import duties on reexportation) on sugar, which Fuller believed would allow British planters to undercut French refined sugar in foreign markets.[62]

The support of the government also assured the planters of victory over the sugar refiners and sugar bakers in Britain in 1780. Alarmed by decreasing sugar supplies and rising prices, the refiners contested the cherished British West Indian monopoly of the home market by seeking permission to refine foreign prize sugars (sugars captured from the enemy). The West India interest lobbied intensively for the continuance of the "exclusive Privilege of supplying the British consumer" with the support of Prime Minister Lord North. The West India interest won (142 to 62) against a motion for taking the request of the refiners into consideration. They won again against the refiners by an even larger margin the following year.[63]

The British government even made political concessions to the islands that their agents had not asked for. In 1778, it promised to withdraw the imperial duty on tea and to waive the claim to levy internal taxes in the colonies, which it had offered to the United States in the Conciliatory Proposals.

*   *   *

Britain also gave consideration to the defense of the Caribbean, which although regarded as insufficient, deflected resources from the American War. George III and his ministers persisted in the war in part because of their belief that the loss of the thirteen colonies inevitably entailed the loss of the British West Indies. They regarded the possession of the island colonies as essential for generating the wealth to wage the war and for sustaining national greatness.[64] It was widely accepted that "the Loss of America will be the Loss of these Islands, and perhaps may make the British Empire totter to its very Foundation." George III thought it better to risk an invasion of England than to lose the sugar islands, without which it was "impossible to raise money to continue the war." British strategy placed the defense of Jamaica second only to domestic security and gave it priority over the war for America. With the prospect of a French war, the British government agonized over whether to abandon the mainland war to launch offensive operations in the Caribbean.[65]

Following the declaration of war by France in 1778, Britain subordinated military activities in North America for objectives in the Caribbean. The British relinquished Philadelphia, then the largest city in the United States and the capital of the Revolution, primarily to free five thousand troops for the conquest of St. Lucia. Sir Henry Clinton, the British commander in chief in North America, warned that the loss of these troops to the West Indies, together with the redeployment of troops in Florida and Canada, might force him to abandon his headquarters in New York for Halifax. He was left with less than fourteen thousand troops. Clinton was promised the return of his troops, and he blamed their absence for his subsequent failure to aggressively engage the continental army. The abandonment of Philadelphia for St. Lucia also contributed to the failure of the Carlisle Peace Commission because it was a resurgence in hostilities.[66]

St. Lucia became the main station of the British fleet and army in the Lesser Antilles. It was the gateway to French Martinique with its view of Fort Royal Bay, the base of the French navy in the Americas, and possessed a fine harbor in Gros Islet Bay that was more spacious than the narrow anchorage at English Harbour in Antigua. The Rev. James Ramsay, a keen observer of naval matters, thought it "worth the whole of these [the Leeward Islands] in time of War."[67] The British regarded St. Lucia as their most important military post and they gave its defense priority over their other islands in the eastern Caribbean.

Figure 30. *Barrington's Action at St. Lucia, December 15, 1778*, Dominic Serres, 1780 (National Maritime Museum, Greenwich, London). The British gave up Philadelphia, the capital of the American Revolution, for the small sugar island of St. Lucia in 1778. St. Lucia was the gateway to the headquarters of the French fleet in the Americas at Martinique.

The defense of Jamaica was especially important. Germain later recalled that his very first act as secretary of state for America was securing "the safety of Jamaica" by sending out supplies of canon and powder. Between August and September 1778, Jamaica was gripped by an invasion scare soon after Governor Dalling sent troops off the island to Central America. Dalling sent an urgent request for assistance to British headquarters in New York. Clinton ordered Lord Cornwallis and four thousand British troops to embark for Jamaica. The reinforcements sailed for almost a week before another dispatch from Jamaica brought news that the alert was over. D'Estaing had sailed via St. Domingue to collect more troops for North America where he intended to retake Georgia. The Jamaica invasion crisis was a remarkable moment because it demonstrated that the British were willing to defend the island at all costs, even at the risk of sacrificing the war for America.[68]

Leaving Clinton to make do with existing forces in North America, Britain continued to reinforce the Caribbean. In 1779, Britain sent Major General

John Vaughan with four brigadier generals and two regiments to reinforce the eastern Caribbean. In 1780, Brigadier General Garth went with an additional four regiments to Jamaica. There were eight brigadier generals commanding in the eastern Caribbean, a remarkable reflection of the importance attached to these islands. In 1781, George III permitted one of his oldest elite household regiments to go to Jamaica, observing that "this country now feels the value & importance of her island colonies." The British also kept a larger naval presence in the Caribbean than in North America. The British military presence was still insufficient to please the colonists but it represented a major diversion of resources from North America.[69]

The French alliance with the United States in 1778, together with the entries of Spain (1779) and Holland (1780), escalated the war in the Caribbean, becoming what Horatio Nelson called "the grand theatre of actions." The Caribbean was central to French strategy, which aimed to disrupt British trade and revenge the defeat of 1763. The Americans believed that a British defeat in the Caribbean "will put our affairs on a favourable footing, and . . . will effect the full completion of all our wishes, in securing the independence of America." The Caribbean, as a major theater of the American Revolutionary War, would play a decisive role in the war and in the events that led to the British defeat at Yorktown.[70]

PART IV

THE DIVISION OF BRITISH AMERICA

The Other Road to Yorktown

THE PATRIOTIC CAUSE IN NORTH AMERICA was sustained by military supplies from the Caribbean. The patriots lacked the resources to manufacture the materials necessary to wage war, especially gunpowder, of which local stocks were exhausted within the first nine months of the conflict. The Continental Congress and the state governments responded to the shortage of ammunition by sending agents to Europe and to the neutral islands in the Caribbean. In association with private merchants and sympathetic governments, the agents procured gunpowder and other military supplies: 90 percent of all gunpowder discharged during the first two years of the war was imported from overseas and much of it came from the Caribbean.[1]

The French, Dutch, Spanish, Danish, and even the British islands in the Caribbean all supplied the revolutionaries in North America. It was a constant lament among the governors of the British colonies that "The Genius of all West Indians without distinction, seems turned to piracy and freebooting."[2] The trade flowed primarily through the French Caribbean until the entry of France into the American War; then it was diverted through neutral islands, primarily Dutch St. Eustatius. British strategists blamed the trade for their failure to win the American War and attempted to suppress it with the conquest of St. Eustatius by Admiral Sir George Rodney at the beginning of February 1781.

This chapter examines the extent to which the British West Indies were complicit in supplying the American revolutionaries and the extent to which their involvement was motivated by sympathy for the American Revolution. It is often alleged that the opposition to Admiral Rodney after the capture of St. Eustatius was orchestrated by the neighboring British islands sympathetic to the American Revolution. This chapter offers a more compelling explanation. It finds that it was the subsequent plundering of St. Eustatius by Admiral Rodney that provoked such criticism because it set a dangerous precedent for retaliation in British islands occupied by the French.

Indeed, the United States was primarily supplied by the French Caribbean and later the Dutch Caribbean, not the British West Indies. We can identify some British West Indian merchants who were sympathetic to the American Revolution, but such trade was generally pursued for profit, not political principle. Illicit trade with the enemy was not isolated to the Revolutionary War but was a common characteristic of warfare in the Caribbean. Finally, the behavior of Rodney at St. Eustatius and his related failure to intercept the French fleet of Admiral François De Grasse led directly to the British defeat at Yorktown and the loss of North America. The strategic consequences were far greater than the insignificant supplies received by the American patriots from the British West Indies.

*   *   *

At the beginning of the American War, the French Caribbean was a major conduit of supplies to the Continental army. On Martinique, in an operation parallel to the modern drug trade (which often runs the same routes), the gunpowder was divided into small quantities among light crafts, such "as Virginia Pilot Boats [which] . . . steal out in the night [and which] . . . sail much too fast to be caught by any" of the few sluggish British naval ships. William Bingham, assisted as agent for Congress by Richard Harrison, masterminded these activities on Martinique, which "ever since the commencement of the Rebellion [was] . . . considered by the Americans as their chief magazine and asylum in these seas."[3] Bingham appointed other American agents throughout the Caribbean in St. Domingue (Haiti), Guadeloupe, St. Eustatius, and Curaçao. These agents, together with private traders, played a vital role in supplying the Continental army through the Caribbean.[4]

With the entry of France into the American War in 1778, Martinique lost its advantage as the neutral port that cloaked the illicit trade with America. Bingham requested his recall and subsequently left Martinique for the United States in June 1779. The agents had become little more than consular officials, and the opportunities for private ventures were much diminished. Martinique was replaced by St. Eustatius as a neutral trading entrepot for the Americans.

The Dutch island of St. Eustatius is widely thought to have been the first foreign port to salute the flag of the United States.[5] The guns of Fort Orange returned the salute of the *Andrew Doria*, one of the first four ships of the Continental navy, which was flying the red-and-white striped rebel flag (the Grand Union Flag that preceded the Stars and Stripes). The salute was witnessed by the British in the neighboring island of St. Kitts, where the newspaper carried a full report "wherein many *scandalous and illiberal reflections* [were] cast . . . on the Americans." The captain of the *Andrew Doria*, with a

Figure 31. View of Dutch St. Eustatius from the British fortress at Brimstone Hill in St. Kitts (Author). St. Eustatius was a major source of military supplies for the patriots in North America. Its guns fired the first foreign salute to the flag of the United States, which the British observed from the fortress at Brimstone Hill in nearby St. Kitts.

copy of the Declaration of Independence, was "most graciously received by his Honour [Governor de Graff] and all ranks of people" in St. Eustatius.[6]

Situated among the northern Leeward Islands, St. Eustatius was less than seven square miles in area. Its wealth "as a place of vast traffick from every quarter of the globe" was derived from its status as a free port and its geographical proximity to the islands of other European powers.[7] Without its trade, it was a mere rock whose infertile land produced less than six hundred barrels of sugar a year.

Janet Schaw, a Scottish visitor to St. Eustatius on the eve of the Revolutionary War, was entranced by the diversity of merchants vending "goods in Dutch, another in French, a third in Spanish, etc. etc. [each wearing] . . . the habit of their country." She described the island as a grand market where she found "rich embroideries, painted silks, flowered Muslins, with all the Manufactures of the Indies. Just by hang Sailor's Jackets, trousers, shoes, hats etc." She marveled at "the variety of merchandize in such a place, for in every store you find every thing, be their qualities ever so opposite." Schaw treated herself to some excellent French gloves and "English thread-stockings cheaper than I could buy them at home."[8]

St. Eustatius prospered during the American War. Merchants' dealings with the North Americans were "so general and done in so publick a manner, as to be no secret to any person in the West India Islands." The trade included the sale of guns, powder, rifles, and ammunition, often purchased by Dutch firms from France and Belgium. Some 235 American ships visited the island between 1776 and 1777. William Bingham made trips to St. Eustatius as the agent for Congress at Martinique. The agent for Maryland at St. Eustatius enthused that he was "on the best terms" with the governor, who expresses "the greatest desire and intention to protect a trade with us [and that] . . . our Flag flys current every day" in the port. American agents in Europe found it safe to send their mail home via St. Eustatius.[9]

After French entry into the war, St. Eustatius became a major source of supplies for the North Americans and the French. It was not unusual to see two hundred ships at anchor on any day there. Storehouses were rented for as much as £1,200 sterling a year. An armed convoy of forty to fifty French merchant ships visited the island every other week to buy provisions for Martinique and Guadeloupe. The North American patriots exported 94,000 pounds of indigo and 12,000 hogsheads of tobacco to St. Eustatius to purchase military and naval supplies. The American trade was "immense," with between seven and ten ships arriving every night and regular fleets of ten to thirty sail. The French similarly obtained vital supplies for their navy and their island colonies in the Caribbean. Jacques Texier, a French agent in St. Eustatius, corresponded "with the several French Governours, and [was] . . . most rancorous in his hatred of G[reat] Britain."[10]

The British government was incensed at this "nest of Spys and Rogues who carry'ed on a Clandestine Trade, with the French and the Rebels." It regarded St. Eustatius as the storehouse of the French and Americans—"not properly a colony [but a] . . . nest of outlaws, or at best Adventurers from every State [selling] . . . provisions, cloathing, and all naval and warlike stores . . . to the Rebels, and Enemies of Great Britain." The British believed that the French and Americans were only able to sustain "the War in that Quarter of the World" because of "the Supplies they had received from St. Eustatius." British officials watched helplessly from neighboring St. Kitts where they observed the trade at close range. Diplomatic pressure on the Dutch government achieved nothing but an unenforced ban on gunpowder sales and the recall of the governor, who was back in office within a year.[11]

In December 1780, Britain sent orders for the immediate capture of St.

Eustatius, whose trade was a major factor in the simultaneous declaration of war against the Dutch. The attack was directed by the British commanders in the eastern Caribbean: Admiral Rodney and Major General John Vaughan. It occurred before the inhabitants of St. Eustatius were even aware of the outbreak of war between Britain and the Netherlands.

*   *   *

On February 3, 1781, St. Eustatius surrendered unconditionally to the combined British forces. It was said that the blow "was as sudden as a clap of thunder [and] . . . wholly unexpected."[12] The island was incapable of resistance, with only a garrison of less than sixty men and a single Dutch frigate against fifteen British warships and three thousand troops. The British success was bolstered by the pursuit and capture of a merchant convoy that had left the island before the attack. The British proceeded to capture most of the remaining Dutch territories in the Caribbean, including the islands of St. Martin and Saba and the South American colonies of Demerara and Essequibo (which make up modern Guyana). They also took French St. Bartholomew.

In the meantime, the British commanders engaged in the indiscriminate plunder of St. Eustatius. They continued to fly the Dutch flag over St. Eustatius to trick unsuspecting enemy ships, of which "the largest proportion belonged to America." They ordered a general confiscation of all private property, including clothing, petty cash, and even food. The broad arrow, the sign of British government property, was marked "on every store particularly on iron chests." Wallets and pockets were searched; gardens and even graves were dug for hidden treasure; houses were ransacked; and slaves and horses were seized. Merchant inventories, accounts, and letter books were confiscated, and warehouses were locked. Every necessary of life was withheld "for the space of twenty days, before the retail shops were permitted to be reopened." The cabinets of the Dutch governor and his wife were broken open and "every Thing valuable" taken. One inhabitant who pleaded for food was told by the British quartermaster general, "Not a Mouthful; must you be told a second Time — not a Mouthful!"[13]

The commanders did not distinguish between friends and foes. Edmund Burke evoked the scene: the "Sentence of Beggary was pronounced indiscriminately against all." The inhabitants were daily paraded according to nationality in preparation for exile. Only the Dutch sugar planters were spared, except Governor De Graff, "the first Man that insulted the British" by saluting the American flag, who was sent as a prisoner to England and whose plantation was seized. The Americans were ordered to leave and were made to gather on the beach within the afternoon to board boats. Even loyalist refugees from America were "forced to seek bread wherever they could find it."[14]

The commanders treated all the British inhabitants at St. Eustatius as smugglers, an erroneous assumption because Britain had permitted a limited trade with the neutral islands. Parliament had passed an act in 1780 to specifically encourage British merchants to import tobacco from neutral islands, including those of the Dutch. British ships had sailed with valid clearances from the major ports of Britain and Ireland for St. Eustatius, and British residents in St. Eustatius had included refugees from the British islands occupied by France and "unfortunate traders . . . driven down by losses in business" who had "preserved their faith to their creditors and their allegiance to their country."[15]

It was scandalous behavior when even the British army in North America and in the Caribbean had made purchases from St. Eustatius before the conquest in 1781. British naval officers had sold prizes at St. Eustatius, which were sometimes resold to the patriots in North America. Governor Burt had armed and fortified St. Kitts with supplies from St. Eustatius following the fall of Dominica in 1778. The British Leeward Islands had lessened the "miseries of actual Famine" when they imported provisions "formerly received from North America" in the years 1778 and 1779. The slaves of Antigua might have "perished had they not been fed from St. Eustatius."[16]

The British commanders admitted their ignorance to Germain when they declared that "we military men . . . cannot be suppos'd to be so well vers'd, in the Laws of Nations, or the particular Law of Great Britain." Yet, despite specific orders not to touch "the Property of British subjects, lawfully exported thither" and despite the request of a delegation from St. Kitts for commanders to obtain more information before condemning all property, Admiral Rodney went ahead with the sale of confiscated goods. He eventually conceded that "a few, a very few may have been less guilty of those atrocious practices and may have legally imported the goods . . . from Great Britain." He even began to restore their property but changed his mind and resumed the sale.[17]

The Jews suffered the harshest treatment even though some of them were British. The Jewish community at St. Eustatius was made up of some 350 Sephardic and Ashkenazim members. With the support of their brethren in Curaçao and Amsterdam, they had built a synagogue, which they called Honen Dalim, meaning "the one who is merciful to the poor," of which there are still remains in St. Eustatius.[18] Janet Schaw first met orthodox Jews on her visit to the island before the war, some of whom were victims of persecution in Europe. One had been tortured in France, where "he was stretched on the wheel and under the hands of the executioner [until he had] . . . hardly a joint in its place." Another had suffered for eighteen months under the Spanish inquisition "till he has hardly the semblance of a human creature remaining," after which he was dumped in a street at night.[19]

The conquest of St. Eustatius was "a day of desolation to the community at large & Jews in particular." The Jews shared in the common "Loss of their Merchandise, their Bills, their Houses, Clothes, [and] Provisions" but they alone suffered the separation of families and the banishment of their men who were not even told the destination of their exile. They "petitioned, intreated, implored, [and] remonstrated against so hard a sentence, but in vain." They were not allowed to keep their personal possessions, in contrast to the Americans, Dutch, and French. Those found withholding petty cash were set apart for punishment. The 101 adult male Jews were assembled under guard and had the linings of their pockets ripped open and their "cloaths torn in pieces to search for concealed money" before thirty of them were "hurried off the island, destitute of everything, to solicit the cold charity of Antigua, and St. Kitts." The rest were locked in a weighing house for three days; they were released just in time to witness the auction of their belongings.[20]

Some of the banished Jews were American loyalists who had escaped North America. One had been persecuted by the French for his "partiality to the English," but this did not spare him from mistreatment by the British commanders. He was taken prisoner despite his "very infirm state of health" and died two days later. Myer Pollock was also taken prisoner despite having been "stripped of all his worth" in Rhode Island for importing British East India tea and despite having lost his brother and brother-in-law in the British cause. He had been left to raise their two families, as well as to care for his mother and his sister. When he tried to conceal some money from his British captors at St. Eustatius, he was separated for additional punishment. Samson Myers, the secretary to the synagogue and a loyalist refugee from Norwalk, Connecticut, suffered a similar fate. These instances go unremarked by the biographers of Admiral Rodney.[21]

The indiscriminate plunder by the British commanders at St. Eustatius violated the spirit and customs of the laws of war, which were "generally understood" to allow a conquered people "the enjoyment of their property" as subjects of the victorious state. This was at least the convention toward fellow Europeans. (This was the practice of the French toward the occupied British islands during the American Revolution.) The British commanders at St. Eustatius had set a precedent which critics feared the French might imitate if any more of the British islands "should hereafter have the misfortune of falling into the Enemys power." The commanders exceeded their instructions which, although giving them discretion over seizures, did not permit a general confiscation. Germain clarified his original instructions when he ordered the commanders not to mistreat the inhabitants and not to take the "Property of English subjects lawfully exported to St. Eustatius." His orders were disobeyed.[22]

*   *   *

Not even the friends and allies of the British commanders at St. Eustatius felt able to exonerate them for their indiscriminate plunder following the conquest. Rev. James Ramsay, a former naval surgeon who was close to the commanders and whose brother-in-law was agent for the sale of the goods, admitted that "the clamour raised on the proceedings at Statia is very great and it must be confessed, that the hardships imposed on individuals, in many cases, have been scandalous, in most unnecessary, and in all so notorious, that it is in vain to attempt to palliate, or conceal them." Ramsay wrote as if in a state of shock. He had tried to persuade the commanders that force was unnecessary since they had already achieved their objective of cutting the trade of the enemy. His words unheeded, he despaired that "the national character, and the honour of the service have received wounds, that will not easily be healed." Nevertheless, out of "regard for both Commanders," Ramsay advised Germain on how to make the defense of the action of the commanders before Parliament.[23]

There is no doubt that the behavior of Rodney at St. Eustatius in part "sprang from his unshakable belief that the English merchants were traitors." Rodney was the dominant of the two commanders. Major General Vaughan had played a leading part in the controversial burning of Kingston in New York in 1777, but he deferred to Rodney throughout the conquest of St. Eustatius. Rodney loathed St. Eustatius as a nest of "Robbers, Adventurers, Betrayers of their Country and Rebels to their King [who] . . . had no right to expect a capitulation or to be treated as a respectable People." The inhabitants were "Traitors to their King, and Parricides to their Country . . . mixed with Jews, and Dutch who, regardless of the Treaties subsisting between Great Britain and Holland, had traitorously conspired, and for years supported the Public Enemys of the state, and the Rebellion of our divided colonies." He felt justified that "a perfidious people, wearing the mask of friendship, traitors to their country, and rebelling against their king deserve[d] no favor or consideration."[24]

Rodney was fully convinced that but for the "Treasonable Correspondence [of St. Eustatius] . . . the Southern Colonies [of North America] must long since have submitted" to Britain. It was an "island inhabited by Rebellious Americans and their agents, disaffected British factors who from base, and lucrative motives, were the great support of the American Rebellion." He fumed that this "rock of only six miles in length, and three in breadth, has done England more harm than all the arms of her most potent enemies, and alone supported the infamous American Rebellion." He maintained that commerce alone had sustained the American Revolution and that "an end to commerce, is an end to [the] Rebellion."[25]

Furthermore, Rodney believed that St. Eustatius had robbed him of a victory against the French fleet in which the balance of the American War might have turned dramatically in favor of Britain. On April 17, 1780, Rodney had fought an indecisive naval battle against the French fleet of the Comte De Guichen. After the battle, St. Eustatius had sent "two vessels loaded with cordage and naval stores and full of carpenters to meet the [French] fleet," which otherwise might have lost eight of their ships for refitting at St. Domingue. The merchants of St. Eustatius had simultaneously denied the British fleet supplies because they claimed that their stocks were depleted. This lost opportunity to defeat the French rankled with the admiral for the rest of his life.[26]

His patriotic fervor, however, was mixed with a large element of greed. Admiral Hood, who witnessed the plunder following the conquest, predicted that Rodney and Vaughan would "find it difficult to convince the world that they [had] not proved themselves wickedly rapacious." Rodney was unscrupulous in financial matters. He was born to genteel poverty and brought up on the charity of distant relatives. He had made a fortune in the Seven Years' War but it was quickly dissipated by his lavish lifestyle and gambling. He had ruined himself in one of the most expensive electoral contests of the eighteenth century and was subsequently reduced to the status of a fugitive debtor in France.[27]

Humiliated by creditors and imprisoned for debt, Rodney was in Paris at the outbreak of the American Revolution. The British government was reluctant to appoint him to a command but found the best-qualified senior officers unwilling to serve under the unpopular Lord Sandwich. Rodney secured his release from prison thanks to a gift of money from a French nobleman. On reaching Portsmouth, he narrowly escaped imprisonment when his son bailed him out with a legacy from a relative. St. Eustatius represented the best chance for this sixty-two-year-old naval commander to make a fortune from prize money and to leave his family in comfortable circumstances. The first month of sales of the plunder of St. Eustatius netted over £100,500.[28]

Rodney's abject situation was suddenly transformed with the conquest of St. Eustatius. As he wrote to his wife, "I shall be happy as, exclusive of satisfying all debts, something will be left for my children. . . . My chief anxiety is,

Figure 32. *George, Lord Rodney* (1719–1792), Sir Joshua Reynolds (National Maritime Museum, Greenwich, London).

that neither yourself nor my girls shall ever be necessitous, nor be under obligations to others." His private letters to his family were euphoric with promises of a new London home, "the best harpsichord money can purchase" for one daughter, a marriage settlement for his oldest son, a commission in the foot guards for a younger son, a dowry sufficient for another daughter to marry the earl of Oxford, and a settlement of the debts of his prospective noble son-in-law. "The lares of St. Eustatius were so bewitching," wrote Sir Samuel Hood, "as not to be withstood by flesh and blood."[29]

Eighteenth-century warfare still possessed features of the medieval practice of private profit from the plunders of war. The loot was euphemistically called "prize money." In a period of inadequate salaries and no pensions, officers and men expected rewards in the form of prize money, which was distributed according to rank. Like the planters and the majority of white creoles, naval and military officers anticipated making quick fortunes in the Caribbean before returning to Britain.

It was disingenuous for Rodney to plead that he was unaware of the likely benefits of his capture, because the royal grant of prize money was a mere formality following a naval capture. Commanders traditionally received one-eighth of the entire value of the captured goods. This gave the two commanders each one-sixteenth of all the possessions in St. Eustatius.[30]

The object of the commanders at St. Eustatius "was rather to increase their pecuniary emoluments, & those of their dependents, than to promote the national" interest. In the month following the capture of St. Eustatius, Rodney and Vaughan held "a grand military fair" in which seized goods were auctioned to buyers of any nationality. Naval and military stores were included in this sale after "it was represented that permitting these articles to be included would *promote the sale of other* goods." Sales to the French were "so notoriously flagrant" that the officer onboard the British flagship, "under whose stern they necessarily passed," asked visitors "not—*from where came ye*; but *have ye money on board?*" Captain Harvey "was appointed to see the Purchasers, with their Commodities, clear" of British privateers. The French and Americans were able to purchase stores from the British at St. Eustatius 50 percent cheaper than they had purchased them from the Dutch. Meanwhile, the British commissioner of the dockyard at Antigua complained that the admiral was sending him unsuitable materials at inflated rates. Rodney countered that the commissioner and storekeepers were angry because they received a lower commission on cheaper goods.[31]

Rodney's behavior also suggests anti-Semitism. The most recent historian of the episode finds no evidence of anti-Semitism in his background, but for what other reason would Rodney have discriminated against the Jews in

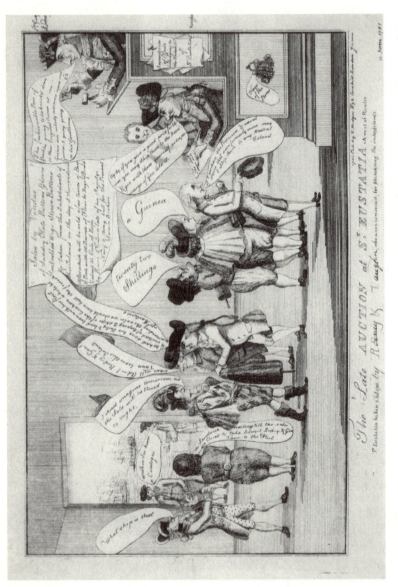

Figure 33. "The Late Auction at St. Eustatia" (Copyright © British Museum). British satire of Admiral Sir George Rodney and General John Vaughan after the conquest of St. Eustatius, when they arbitrarily confiscated goods and sold them as prizes to buyers of all nations including the enemy.

punishing them more harshly than others? It was said that Rodney was unaware of the treatment of the Jews until it was too late, but this claim was
contradicted by several witnesses. He himself wrote of apprehending "a Rascal
of a Jew [who] has hid a chest of 5000 joes in a cane patch." The Jews might
have suffered more but for Vaughan, who eventually succumbed to requests to
allow those remaining "time to settle their affairs," and who gave them permission "to return, and arrange their little matters."[32]

Earlier in his career as a naval commander in Jamaica, Rodney had lashed
out against Jews who conducted a "pernicious and Contraband Trade" at
Kingston, where he insisted that "particularly the Jews" traded illegally with
the Spanish. He confiscated two of their ships, which were subsequently condemned for sale in the vice-admiralty court. The "Sons of Israel, who are
possessed of most of the ready money in [Jamaica]," met with a lawyer and
considered making an appeal. None of the correspondence of other naval
commanders in the Caribbean made such special mention of Jews.[33]

*   *   *

The behavior of the British commanders provoked an immediate outcry
against the illegality of their proceedings at St. Eustatius. Only hours after the
capture of St. Eustatius, a delegation of British merchants from St. Kitts arrived to claim property. They sent the commanders a lengthy memorial, which
was presented by the solicitor general of St. Kitts. They even threatened to
arrest the admiral if he should set foot in St. Kitts. They began legal proceedings against the commanders in both St. Kitts and Britain. In Amsterdam,
as many as forty thousand people rioted in protest against the plunder of
St. Eustatius.[34]

As news of the activities of St. Eustatius reached London, the Society of
West India Merchants and Planters collaborated to send a petition complaining of the behavior of the commanders to the king. The society printed the
petition in order to appeal to a broader external constituency, a tactic increasingly employed during the war. A delegation met with Germain. The
merchants were particularly concerned about the possibility of retaliation by
the French, especially considering the fact that Grenada, Dominica, and St.
Vincent had already fallen to France. The merchants of St. Eustatius had
requested that France indemnify their losses out of the incomes of plantations
in occupied British islands.[35]

Edmund Burke brought the issue of St. Eustatius before Parliament but
his motion for copies of the royal instructions relative to the disposal of captured property was defeated. Undeterred, Burke began to prepare a case

against Rodney, a dress rehearsal for his more famous prosecution of Warren Hastings. He renewed his appeal for copies of the instructions and made a motion for a committee of inquiry. In February 1782, supported by Charles James Fox, Burke made his final appeal when he presented the petition of one of the Jewish merchants who appeared in person to present his case. Samuel Hoheb, an elder of the Jewish community who was a native of Amsterdam and twenty-five-year resident of St. Eustatius, was left without a shilling after the conquest and was too impoverished to bring legal proceedings against the commanders.

The initiative thereafter passed to the law courts where the admiral faced suits until his death in 1792. The ninety claims of near £300,000 far exceeded the value of his prize money. The claim of one British merchant amounted to £70,000. In 1786, the claimants won a judgment for reimbursement, not according to the value of the sales conducted by the commanders, but for the full original value of the goods. The French merchants at St. Eustatius were similarly reimbursed. Rodney was forced to return their household goods and slaves while he was in St. Eustatius. The British government later paid them two million livres compensation.[36]

The biographers of Rodney have blamed the success of the English legal suits on the disappearance of crucial evidence: the merchant letter books and ledgers seized at St. Eustatius. They argue that the loss of these papers by the British government was contrived by political enemies of Lord North who won power in the final year of the war in the new government of Lord Shelburne. The fate of these papers must remain a mystery, but it is more likely that Rodney's own political patrons, upon finding that they contained nothing to help his case but rather the reverse, arranged for their disappearance. Merchant papers rarely contained accounts of smuggling activities and illicit trade. The British commanders had ordered the sale of the captures without investigating these papers and they had simply assumed the guilt of the merchants.[37]

Some of the merchant papers were examined two months after the capture by an army officer who found "nothing material or improper" in their contents and returned them to the owners. The rest were shipped to England where George Jackson, acting as counsel for the admiral, found them incomplete and confused. Rodney made no attempt to use these papers before their disappearance to defend himself in Parliament or in the admiralty court.[38]

The fiasco of the British conquest of St. Eustatius continued when the convoy containing much of the treasure was seized by the French during its shipment to Britain. St. Eustatius was later retaken by the French with the remaining proceeds of the plunder, together with pay for the British forces in North America, in November 1781. It was even rumored that this last humiliation was deliberately planned by Rodney to destroy the evidence against him.[39] St. Eustatius was soon replaced as a conduit of illegal trade by the Danish island of St. Thomas and by British islands under French occupation.

*   *   *

Rodney used improper methods to enrich himself but his contention that many British merchants were guilty of illicit trade is undeniable. British merchants were active in contraband trade in all the neutral islands: "All the world knows that the English colonies were more interested than any other in the commerce of St. Eustatia." British merchants represented about 38 percent of the population of St. Eustatius and they were in the majority in Danish St. Croix. A list of burghers in St. Eustatius at the time of the conquest included Abraham Marchineau and James Dougan of St. Kitts, Henry Dickson of Antigua, Thomas Tobin of Nevis, and Henry Taverner of Barbados. There were also other names common to the surrounding British islands — John Martin, John Meynard, Joseph Manchester, Sean Louis Menard, M. L. Walrond, John King, and Clement Challenger.[40]

The archaeological remains in St. Eustatius reflect the preponderance of British manufactured goods in the material culture of the island. There was even an Anglican Church in St. Eustatius "built . . . by the English Merchants," who paid the clergyman a regular salary. These resident British merchants were typically unmarried single men seeking their fortunes; contraband trade was the fastest way to get rich quickly. English was widely spoken in the neutral foreign islands: the newspaper in St. Croix, for example, the *Royal Danish Gazette*, was printed in English by an ex-printer from St. Kitts.[41]

Merchants in the British islands were also engaged in supplying the enemy, especially those on the smaller islands of the eastern Caribbean. Merchants in St. Kitts and Antigua exported Irish salt and provisions to Guadeloupe and Martinique, which otherwise risked "being literally starved." The British officer commanding in Antigua exclaimed that "the Truth is, the Mercantile people are mostly Smugglers in Trade not only with St. Eustatia, but with the French Islands." "Our own merchants even of the best reputation," wrote the governor of Grenada, "will not scruple to trade with our Enemies, or engage in any commercial adventure, however prejudicial to the public Interest, if they can derive from it any private advantage." In the eastern Caribbean, Colonel Gabriel Christie thought it "a very great misfortune that the French Islands are so contiguous, for every English Island is in fact a St. Eustatius, or mart of supply, to the Enemy."[42]

However, the British islands were a minor source of supplies to the United States, which imported most of its military stores from continental Europe or from the French and Dutch West Indies. This was less risky. At the beginning of the war, Germain sent intelligence to the governor of Jamaica that the island was supplying gunpowder to the patriots. The *Kingston Gazette* alleged that every barrel of available gunpowder in Jamaica was "swept away . . . and chiefly expended in the slaughter of many a brave Englishman" at the first battle of the Revolutionary War at Bunker Hill. Congress exempted military stores from its embargo against the British West Indies and encouraged merchants "to estimate a generous price" for gunpowder, arms, and stores. This resolution circulated "in printed form among the trading people [of the British Caribbean] . . . to induce them to supply Gunpowder &c to the North Americans."[43]

The rumor of a gunpowder trade in the islands gained currency because colonial officials remained uncertain of the law and most did not immediately take action. Vice Admiral James Young was quick to act in the Leeward Islands but he was opposed by the governor of St. Kitts. It was yet another example of the demarcation disputes between rival officials over their respective jurisdictions: the admiral had earlier questioned the governor's right to issue letters of marque to privateers. In Jamaica, the admiral was slower to react. Nevertheless, the British civil authorities in the Caribbean thought it impossible that gunpowder was exported in any quantity from the islands because private supplies were too low.[44]

In a few cases the illicit trade was politically motivated, especially among "Ill-disposed Americans settled in [the British Caribbean]."[45] One of these, Eliphalet Fitch, was a Boston native and a merchant in Kingston, Jamaica, where he imported provisions and timber from North America, cordage and cloth from Britain, and reexported slaves to Cuba as the agent of the Spanish Royal Asiento Company. Fitch was an experienced smuggler; before the American War he used the slave trade as a cover to export British manufactured goods to Cuba.

During the early years of the American War, Fitch supplied naval and military intelligence to the patriots while arranging prisoner exchanges with the Spanish. He met Francisco Miranda, who is better known as a Venezuelan revolutionary but was then a Spanish official in Jamaica. Fitch contracted with Miranda to supply large quantities of military materials to the Spanish. The flags of truce, used for the exchange of prisoners, were the most convenient covers for contraband trade in war. The scheme was helped by the quarrel between Sir Peter Parker, the British admiral, and Colonel John Dalling, the governor of Jamaica. Fitch was able to pretend that he had received permission for flags of truce because the governor and the admiral were not speaking to each other.[46]

It was a "stupendous fraud" and it was almost impossible to keep secret.[47]

Fitch not only provided provisions and naval equipment but also armed ships Miranda purchased with money allocated by the Spanish authorities for the exchange of prisoners. Miranda was gazetted from the Spanish army for his role and fled to the United States while Fitch was investigated but evaded prosecution. The materials supplied by them played a key role in the Spanish conquest of Nassau (New Providence) in the Bahamas in 1782.

The line between patriotism and treason was thin. When an American agent arrived in St. Kitts with two thousand dollars to purchase woolen clothing, the merchants "who to a man, are all, by profession, opinionated in favor of government, smiled at the sight of the dollars [and] . . . suspending their loyalty, they supplied the American agent every thing he wanted." Aretas Akers was a good example of opportunism. He was one of the wealthiest merchants in St. Kitts, who was reputed to have supplied the southern patriots in the United States. He was friendly with agents for South Carolina, Virginia, and in St. Eustatius and was said to have loans and merchandise worth £40,000 to £50,000 in St. Eustatius in 1781. He was a prominent public figure as speaker of the assembly, deputy receiver of casual revenues, deputy provost marshal, and an assistant judge. He had lobbied in London against the American War because of the potentially adverse economic impact in the British West Indies and he had led the opposition to Governor William Mathew Burt in St. Kitts, but he was not sympathetic to the American Revolution.[48]

On the contrary, Akers played an important role in the American War on behalf of the British. He was the supply agent for the navy in St. Kitts, where he fitted out the fleet of Vice Admiral John Byron, declaring that "my sole motive for Engaging in the matter, was the service of the fleet; for the commissions which I shall charge, will not be much more than will pay my clerks for their Extra trouble." He "held first place in Admiral Lord Rodney's favour & patronage" and supplied him with critical naval intelligence. He made a personal loan for the fortifications and for paying the gunners in St. Kitts. Rodney appointed him agent for prisoners of war and later appointed him agent for the auction of the seized goods at St. Eustatius.[49]

The case of Aretas Akers was more typical than that of Elipahlet Fitch in the British West Indies where contraband trade was motivated more by profit than political principle. The trade was so openly mercenary that Governor Burt thought that the merchants were prepared to "export our Provisions, starve us & supply, through the Dutch at St. Eustatius, the French Islands." The practice was not isolated to the Revolutionary War but was a common characteristic of all wars in the Caribbean. As a visitor observed after the war, the islands were "particularly adapted to clandestine traffic [which] was not of modern date here, for [as] long back as the administration of General Daniel

Parke (1706–10), it was carried on with avidity." This illicit trade also operated
out of Britain. The Irish merchants of Cork notoriously supplied salt and
provisions to Martinique and Guadeloupe via St. Eustatius. Smuggling was
endemic to the maritime empires of Europe; money knew no patriotism.[50]

*   *   *

The conduct of Admiral Rodney at St. Eustatius had strategic consequences far greater than the insignificant illicit trade of the British West Indies
because it contributed to the British defeat at Yorktown and the loss of North
America. Rodney remained at St. Eustatius for three crucial months, during
which he ceased to pursue further military operations. His presence was hardly
necessary because "without its trade" the island was "a mere rock . . . neither of
real nor relative importance." He was preoccupied with the details of the sales
of the captured goods and the safe return of his loot to Britain. He called off a
proposed expedition against Dutch Curaçao and Surinam, excusing himself
with intelligence of the sailing of a French fleet for the West Indies, although
his deputy claimed that the decision was made before receiving what turned
out to be a false report.[51]

These setbacks were incidental compared to the failure of Rodney to
intercept the French fleet of Admiral de Grasse. British strategic policy in
North America was predicated on a superior British naval presence. French
naval reinforcements were shadowed by fleets from Britain or from the West
Indies. Rodney was expected to intercept the imminent arrival of a French fleet
before it reached Martinique but he delegated this task to Admiral Sir Samuel
Hood. Rodney remained at St. Eustatius. The two commanders quarreled
over the location of the British ships stationed to intercept French entry into
Martinique.

Hood suspected that Rodney positioned him to protect the convoy of a
hundred prizes from St. Eustatius rather than to oppose the reinforcements
from France. Rodney had ordered Hood to move from the windward (between Dominica and Martinique) to the leeward (between St. Lucia and
Martinique) of Martinique. Hood complained that "doubtless there never
was a squadron so unmeaningly stationed as the one under my command, and
what Sir George Rodney's motive for it could be I cannot conceive, unless it
was to cover him at St. Eustatius."[52] These were not retrospective criticisms
but ones he had repeatedly expressed to Rodney. His fears were justified by
events when Admiral De Grasse outmaneuvered him by sailing the windward
route to Martinique.

In defense of Rodney, there were valid strategic reasons to reposition

Hood. In 1779, Vice Admiral Byron had kept the windward position urged by Hood but was unable to prevent the reinforcement of Admiral D'Estaing at Martinique. It was difficult to patrol the entry to Fort Royal Bay in Martinique, either from the windward or the leeward, owing to the sudden changes in currents and winds. Furthermore, Rodney was misinformed by intelligence reports from Britain that underestimated the size and importance of the French fleet. Nevertheless, the suspicion must remain that mercenary motives caused him to reposition Hood while he remained with part of the British fleet at St. Eustatius.

After a brief interlude at Martinique, De Grasse sailed via St. Domingue for Virginia. Rodney made no effort to pursue him but again delegated the job to Hood. Rodney appreciated the portentous implications of the departure of De Grasse for North America and was well aware that he intended to make for the capes of Virginia, "where I am persuaded the French intend making their grand effort." The British government had assumed that Rodney was to follow De Grasse, taking with him three British regiments from the Caribbean. After some equivocation, Rodney instead ordered Hood to go to America while he sailed for Britain.[53]

Rodney may have decided not to follow De Grasse to Virginia because he understood the hopelessness of the British position, but such behavior was uncharacteristic of a man undaunted by the challenge of battle against a superior fleet. He himself blamed ill health for his inaction: he suffered acute gout and prostate trouble but the pain often subsided in the thick of battle. Only the previous month, he had insisted that while he had "Vigour of Mind sufficient to . . . give Orders" he would pursue the French fleet "let them go where they will."[54]

It is more likely that his real motive for not pursuing De Grasse to Virginia was his desire to answer his critics in Britain about the conquest of St. Eustatius. His first priority on arriving in Britain was not his prostate surgery but an unannounced visit to the king to justify his behavior at St. Eustatius. He hurried from Plymouth to Windsor, where he astonished and embarrassed the king, who had just returned from hunting and was unprepared for this unexpected visitor. Dismayed by newspaper accounts of what had occurred in St. Eustatius, George III deflected the admiral by pleading fatigue.[55] Rodney turned to Parliament to resume his seat and to answer his political opponents in person. As news of the surrender of the British forces at Yorktown reached London, Rodney was defending himself against Edmund Burke in the House of Commons.

With the land forces of George Washington and Comte de Rochambeau, De Grasse encircled Lord Cornwallis and his British troops at Yorktown. His fleet blockaded the mouth of the Chesapeake, preventing the British army from either retreating or receiving reinforcements by sea. Sir Samuel Hood and Admiral Sir Thomas Graves, the commander of the North American naval squadron, were unable to dislodge the French fleet in the naval battle in the Chesapeake, sealing the fate of the British army at Yorktown and the outcome of the American Revolutionary War. The British defeat was, of course, due to a variety of factors, but Rodney had deprived the navy of a superior commander by his absence in Britain. He had also contributed to its numerical inferiority by sending ships to Jamaica and by returning with three warships to escort some of his plunder to Britain.

*   *   *

Rodney was successfully prosecuted by several litigants from St. Eustatius after the American War, but why did he not face more serious consequences when his private avarice may have helped contribute to the British defeat at Yorktown? It was because he emerged as one of the few heroes of a disastrous war following his great victory over the French at the Battle of the Saintes in April 1782.

The British surrender at Yorktown is traditionally regarded as the closing chapter of the American Revolutionary War, but it marked the escalation of the conflict in the Caribbean. The French and Spanish prepared a grand attack on the remaining British islands, primarily targeting Jamaica. For the first time since the British conquest of St. Lucia in December 1778, the war in the Caribbean overshadowed the North American theater. Britain hastened the evacuation of troops from the southern states for service in the Caribbean, which were accompanied by Charles O'Hara, the general who surrendered the sword of Lord Cornwallis at Yorktown.

Yorktown had left the French free to concentrate their military resources on offensive operations in the Caribbean. News of the British defeat in Virginia reached the Caribbean in November 1781. The French governor of Martinique, the marquis de Bouillé, seized the moment to recapture British-occupied Dutch St. Martin and Saba. He ended the debacle of the British occupation of St. Eustatius in a brilliant coup against the unprepared garrison that outnumbered his own force.

In the meantime, Admiral De Grasse had rejected the request of George Washington to remain with the French fleet in North America after Yorktown, having already overstayed his orders from France to go to the Caribbean. His arrival at Martinique gave France naval superiority over the British. His prime object was to combine with the Spanish fleet in the grand attack on Jamaica.

Figure 34. *The Battle of the Saintes*, April 12, 1782, Nicholas Pocock (National Maritime Museum, Greenwich, London). Rodney's victory at the Battle of the Saintes in 1782 helped secure Jamaica for the British Empire.

French troops at Martinique daily practiced embarking and disembarking, preparing for another campaign. The French flagship carried "50,000 pairs of handcuffs, and fetters . . . intended to confine the negroes" in Jamaica.[56]

The French attack on Jamaica had to await reinforcements imminently expected from France under De Guichen and the arrival of Don Solano from Spain. De Grasse, in concert with the marquis de Bouillé, consequently confined activities to the eastern Caribbean, primarily St. Lucia. Ever since its loss to the British, the French had tried several times to recapture this strategically important island with its proximity to Martinique. In December, De Grasse twice attempted an attack on St. Lucia, sailing off the island for six days in the first instance and attempting an actual landing at the end of December.

It was only after abandoning his original design on St. Lucia and preliminary to the planned offensive against Jamaica that De Grasse chose St. Kitts. In

The VILLE DE PARIS, Sailing for Jamaica . or Rodney Triumphant.

Figure 35. "The Ville De Paris Sailing for Jamaica, or Rodney Triumphant," Gillray, 1782 (Copyright © British Museum). Cartoon celebrating the victory at the Battle of the Saintes in which Rodney is depicted sailing on the back of the French admiral De Grasse toward Jamaica.

early January 1782, accompanied by substantially the same French fleet and troops that had played such a critical role in the British defeat at Yorktown, De Grasse began the invasion of this island of only sixty-four square miles.

St. Kitts made the most determined resistance of any British island during the American War. Some three hundred and fifty members of the colonial militia joined the garrison of British regulars at Brimstone Hill. For five weeks, they were totally cut off and unable to contact the British fleet. They were bombarded and cannonaded night and day by the surrounding French artillery. The garrison occupied an area not even two hundred yards in diameter and faced the fire of twenty-three canon and twenty-four large mortars. Their resistance bought time in delaying the planned invasion of Jamaica and in allowing Admiral Hood to be reinforced by Rodney, who returned from England with his fleet in January.[57]

On the day that the House of Commons debated Conway's motion

Figure 36. Rodney Memorial, Spanish Town, Jamaica (Author). The statue of Rodney by John Bacon was housed in a splendid octagonal temple linked by curving white colonnaded walkways to two office buildings that flank the monument on either side.

against the "further prosecution of offensive warfare on the continent of North America," rumor of the fall of St. Kitts reached Britain. Charles James Fox made devastating use of the loss of "the most important island remaining to us in the West Indies, except Jamaica," to lash the ignominious ministry who would "not be satisfied till they had mangled and destroyed the last miserable tenth" remaining of the British Empire. Lord John Cavendish feared that "the great and splendid empire of Britain was nearly overturned; calamity, disgrace, and disaster were pouring from us from every quarter; and the measure of our misfortunes was likely to be soon completed by the loss of all our dominions in America and the West Indies."[58]

The loss of St. Kitts marked the lowest ebb of the American War for Britain. The rumor of its loss, along with another concerning the loss of Minorca, haunted the last three weeks of the government of Lord North. It fed the fears of wavering independent members that the ministry was incapable of saving anything, and it justified the warnings of opposition members that

Figure 37. Rodney Memorial, Spanish Town, Jamaica (Author). It was appropriate that the most impressive and most costly public monument in Jamaica commemorated the victorious admiral whose victory had preserved British rule in the Caribbean during the American Revolution.

Britain risked the loss of the West Indies. The successes of the previous war seemed to be frittering away as one island fell after another. The French even recaptured the Dutch mainland colonies of Essequibo, Demerara, and Berbice (Guyana). Contemporary cartoons lampooned the government, such as "The Royal Hunt or Prospect of the Year 1782," published in February, which featured the devil saying, "I am sorry we have lost St. Kitts." Official confirmation of the loss of St. Kitts was still hourly awaited the day that Lord North resigned as prime minister.[59]

As politicians fretted over the future of the remaining British colonies in the Caribbean, Rodney became the savior of the British Empire when he defeated the French fleet at the battle of the Saintes (April 9–12, 1782). In a passage of islands between Dominica and Guadeloupe called Les Saintes, Rodney intercepted the French fleet on its way from Martinique to join troops in St. Domingue for the invasion of Jamaica. He captured Admiral De Grasse and his flagship, the *Ville de Paris*, along with four other ships with the siege artillery intended for the invasion of Jamaica. The victory caused an outburst of euphoria in Britain and helped the British obtain generous terms from France in the peace of 1783.

The victory at the Saintes won Rodney immunity from public censure for his actions at St. Eustatius. The new government had already ordered his recall and sent out a successor before receiving news of the Saintes, but it made quick amends by giving him a peerage as Lord Rodney of Rodney-Stoke. It ended the hearings against him and voted him the thanks of both houses of Parliament. Edmund Burke personally congratulated him for "such very splendid & such very substantial service to his country . . . [and denied any] personal animosity," telling others that he could crown the admiral with laurels. Burke and Fox were ridiculed in one satire for dropping the case of the Jews of St. Eustatius. They were portrayed playing musical instruments including the Jew's harp "found in the breeches['] pocket of the *St. Eustatius Israelite!*"[60]

Rodney was also celebrated in the British Caribbean, where the victory of the Saintes became a major anniversary until it was eclipsed by Nelson at the battle of Trafalgar in 1805. Jamaica commissioned one of the finest sculptors in England to commemorate Rodney. The merchants of Kingston and the planters of Spanish Town competed for the location of the monument, which survives today in the center square of the old government capital at Spanish Town.

It was appropriate that the most impressive and most costly public monument in the British West Indies commemorated the victorious admiral whose victory had preserved British rule in the Caribbean during the American Revolution.

Conclusion

Revolutionary Legacy

THE AMERICAN REVOLUTION DIVIDED British America with important implications for both the West Indies and the United States. In *Capitalism and Slavery* (1944), Eric Williams contended that the American Revolution was "the beginning of [the sugar colonies'] uninterrupted decline."[1] Influenced by the work of Lowell Ragatz, he argued that the profitability of West Indian plantations declined as a result of the disruption of the American War and the virtual loss of trade with the United States after 1783. He concluded that the decline in the profitability of sugar and slavery was a primary cause of the abolition of the slave trade in 1807 and the Emancipation Act of 1833.

The American Revolution did indeed weaken the foundations of slavery in the British West Indies but the causes were political, not economic. Contrary to the view of Williams, the postwar plantation economy remained profitable with almost an 11 percent rise in sugar production and a little less than 3 percent rise in rum production. John McCusker estimates that the average annual value of the crop rose from about £3,300,000 sterling before the war to about £4,200,000 sterling in the mid-1780s. Productivity per slave rose from £6.89 worth of sugar in the early 1780s to £8.38 worth of sugar in the mid-1780s. Exports to Britain were greater in the postwar decade than in the prewar decade: McCusker finds that "West Indian exports to Great Britain in the 1780s, on a per capita constant value basis, were 9.5 percent higher than they had been in the 1760s and early 1770s."[2]

Studies of individual plantations indicate that they remained profitable. After the American War, Nevis planter John Pinney continued to receive returns of 9 percent from his Mountravers plantation. In the decade after 1783, Worthy Park estate in Jamaica produced "at least the £10 a year per slave which Bryan Edwards gave as a rule-of-thumb for efficient operations and up to three times that amount in the mid war years." Nathaniel Phillips, "like other Jamaican planters . . . made a sizeable profit in the boom years of the early 1780s" and returned to Britain "with about £20,000 in ready capital" in 1789. The Taylor estates in Jamaica increased their production by 48 percent and income by 69 percent, which "more than kept pace with . . . rising costs of production." The Codrington Estates of the Society for the Propagation of the Gospel in Barbados averaged profits of £1,953 per year and a total profit, in the postwar decade, of £19,533. The younger William Beckford made £7,000 pounds from one of his estates in a single year after the American War. He boasted that he was "growing rich" and that he intended "to build towers, and sing hymns to the powers of heaven on their summits." He commissioned James Wyatt to design Fonthill Abbey, "the most astonishing private house ever to be built in England."[3]

J. R. Ward acknowledges that the American War was a miserable period for the planters but finds that "profits recovered well in the next decade" with estimated average returns of 6.4 percent in Jamaica, 5.3 percent in Barbados, 12.1 percent in the Leeward Islands, and 15:5 percent in the Windward Islands between 1783 and 1791. This gave an average of 8.5 percent profits throughout the British Caribbean compared to a 10 percent average for the century.[4] Without a fall in absolute demand in Britain, the British West Indies were unlikely to suffer decline while they enjoyed the monopoly of the home sugar market.

The 1791 slave revolt of St. Domingue (Haiti) helped the economy of the British plantations. It briefly gave the British planters a virtual monopoly to the European market. London merchants were optimistic about the future of the plantations and willingly advanced credit on "a very much greater" scale in the last decade of the eighteenth century. Their continuing optimism was apparent in the early nineteenth century when they commissioned the building of the great West India Docks in London for the reception of the trade of the British West Indies. Their belief in the future of the plantations was shared by British policymakers who exhibited no decline of interest in the Caribbean.[5]

*   *   *

It was the weakened political leverage of the planters after the war, not economic influences, that prevented the planters from successfully defending the slave trade. The changed circumstances of the postwar years left the planters on the defensive against imperial measures prejudicial to their interests. West Indian demands for a full resumption of trade with the United States clashed with the traditional mercantilist principles of colonial policy, which opposed a trade whose balance did not favor Britain.

The planters were "thunderstruck" at an order in council restricting trade with the United States on July 2, 1783. Robert Thompson, the manager of the Stapleton estates in St. Kitts, wrote that the restrictions "took place very unexpectedly, and at a time when there was little Lumber or Provisions in the Island." Simon Taylor, a Jamaican planter, accused the home government of seeking the ruin of the plantations and of treating "the inhabitants as their Gibionites [the citizens of Gibeon in ancient Palestine who were condemned to be the hewers of wood and fetchers of water]."[6] The trade restrictions not only remained but were extended and strengthened by an act of Parliament in 1788.[7]

West Indian whites vigorously opposed the restrictions on trade, especially in Barbados and the Leeward Islands, which were more dependent than the other islands on imports from the United States. Some protestors were killed by troops during the violent demonstrations in Barbados. A spate of antigovernment publications and handbills circulated in Antigua where London radical Richard Oliver chaired an extraparliamentary meeting that passed strong resolutions against the restrictions. There was a series of riots in St. Kitts "of a . . . Rebellious nature" in 1784 and in 1785, during which a crowd tarred and feathered a customs officer. The president of St. Kitts flew an Irish flag on St. Patrick's Day.[8] The local legislature refused to offer rewards for information about the riots and a grand jury threw out a bill of indictment against the leaders. The merchants of Nevis brought a suit against Horatio Nelson, then a young naval lieutenant and commander of the *Boreas*, when he seized four American merchantmen off Charlestown. Their threats forced the future victor of Trafalgar to remain onboard his ship in harbor for three months for fear of mob revenge and may have prompted him to make a politically useful marriage to the widow of a planter.[9]

In contrast to their passive behavior between 1766 and 1774, the colonists exhausted every official channel to obtain the removal of the trade restrictions after 1783. The Jamaican assembly requested open trade with the United States from the governor. It instructed Stephen Fuller to forcibly oppose any restrictions of trade with the United States. It sent a separate address to the king. Half the parishes of Jamaica petitioned the assembly for open trade with the United States in November and December 1785. The assembly collected copious information and data to demonstrate the importance of the American trade. The assembly of Barbados also petitioned the king for open trade with America in 1784.[10]

The Society of West India Merchants and Planters in London lobbied vigorously against the restrictions. They passed resolutions for open trade with the United States in April and again in November 1783. In February 1784, they submitted a petition to the King for the "free intercourse between the . . . sugar colonies and the United States of America" on American ships.[11] In May, they ordered a series of resolutions against the restrictions on trade to be printed and distributed to all members of Parliament and merchants in the principal trading towns. Finally, in May 1785, they urged Parliament to set up a committee of inquiry into the regulation of trade with the United States.

In contrast to their silence about imperial policy before 1774, West Indian pamphleteers and writers were very active after 1783. Members of the London West India lobby led the charge. The authors included James Allen, secretary to the Society of West India Merchants and Planters, Bryan Edwards, and Edward Long. The petitions of Stephen Fuller on behalf of Jamaica were printed, and a spate of articles by West Indians appeared in British newspapers.[12]

West Indians thought it unfair that Britain permitted British residents to trade with the United States but not the British West Indies. They argued that the trade was essential for their prosperity and even for their survival. The United States was a convenient and cheap source of food and lumber for which alternative sources of supply were more expensive, irregular, and inadequate. The United States was an outlet for rum exports for which there was not a sufficient market in Britain. British ships were larger, less dependable, and less frequent than American ships. Beginning in 1780, a series of six hurricanes in seven years, in which some fifteen thousand slaves perished in Jamaica, demonstrated the necessity of imports when ground provisions were destroyed.

In attempting to win exemption from the Navigation Acts to trade with the United States, West Indians challenged the traditional mercantilist principles of colonial policy that had attempted to enforce a balance of trade favorable to Britain and to encourage the expansion of British shipping. The postwar conflict of interests weakened their political influence in Britain.

*   *   *

The American War also led to a decline in the impact of the West India lobby in London. The strength of the lobby was the envy of the North Americans before 1776. It thereafter diminished, however, because the lobby was no longer able to appeal to the traditional harmony between their self-interest and the interests of the mother country, the basis of its influence before 1776. Furthermore, wrote Eric Williams, "every important vested interest in England" formerly aligned with the West India lobby "one by one . . . came out" against the West Indies.[13] The changed configuration of imperial politics in the postwar period pitted the West India lobby against the mercantilist system and against formerly allied interests.

A strict imperial trade policy was supported by groups who were formerly allies of the West Indies but who now formed a coalition of vested interests in opposition to their lobby. The British shipping interest, including ship-builders and shipowners, wanted the monopoly of the carrying trade with the West Indies. The navy wanted West Indian trade to be carried exclusively in British ships in order to build up a "nursery of seamen" to serve in war. Merchants and economic interest groups in Ireland, Canada, and Britain wanted to supplant the Americans in the trade of the British West Indies. The East India interest began to lobby for entry into the home sugar market and posed a threat of new competition. In addition, the abolitionists became the most formidable domestic opponents of the planters after the war with a brilliantly conducted propaganda campaign.

These hostile interest groups were critical of the higher price of British sugar in comparison to that of French sugar and attacked the British West Indian monopoly of the home sugar market. The British sugar refiners continued their campaign to weaken the West Indian monopoly of the home market and were supported by representatives of the East India Company, who wanted to gain equal access to the British market.[14] Free trade theorists used the monopoly to argue that colonies were a burden rather than a benefit to the national economy. The Rev. Josiah Tucker and Adam Smith had advanced such arguments even before the American Revolution. Opponents of the planters were able to pose as the champions of British consumers. The 1788 parliamentary inquiry into the slave trade devoted a large segment of its report to a discussion of why French sugars were cheaper than British.

The organization and lobbying techniques of the West India interest in London had developed in response to the adversity of the American Revolutionary War, but its influence began to diminish at war's end. The Society of West India Merchants was gradually displaced by a coalition of merchants and planters who kept their own minutes and formed a separate standing committee during the closing years of the Revolutionary War (1782–83).[15] Stephen Fuller directed the activities of the West India lobby with the skills of a professional lobbyist. It was now a formal body rather than a collection of individuals who relied on private political contacts: the chairman continued "the tradition of giving West Indian advice to Prime Ministers, though it was as a spokesman of an organised interest rather than as an individual."[16]

However, their lobbying techniques employed a more confrontational approach with appeals to a wider public and assumed a more shrill tone. The lobby published and circulated political pamphlets, using the press to publish them, and launched signature campaigns. Lobbyists began to formally orchestrate their parliamentary friends: the papers of Stephen Fuller include a 1781 list of "colony" members in Parliament.[17] There were earlier examples of similarly sophisticated methods but these were now sustained within a more formal structure. It was no longer sufficient to act as a discrete insider lobby that relied on a cozy relationship with government.

The tactics and skills acquired during the war were employed to full effect against the abolitionists, but never with quite the same triumphal illusion of power that the lobby commanded before the American Revolution. They were snubbed in their campaign to reduce the domestic sugar duties and to open the trade with the United States. The very restructuring of the West India interest and the more visible nature of their campaigns indicates that the hidden hand, the low-profile approach of insider lobbyists, was no longer sufficient.

*　*　*

The American War left the planters on the defensive against an increasingly vocal free colored population who challenged the racial structure so essential for the functioning of the slave system in the Americas. The war elevated the status of colored peoples in the British Caribbean, who, along with slaves were able to exploit the war to assume more visible roles as peasant farmers, soldiers, and religious evangelists. They became more essential to the economy as peasant farmers following the virtual loss of imports from North America. Their success was facilitated by the postwar restrictions against a full resumption of trade with the United States. Free colored farmers and slaves even extended credit to indebted planters who were consequently frustrated by their "diminished command of their world and greater vulnerability to forces beyond their control."[18] The free colored population and the slaves won a greater share of scarce local currency.

The majority of free colored men and large numbers of slaves had also served in some military capacity. The most distinguished was John Perkins of Jamaica, whose career was unique not only as a colored British naval officer in the eighteenth century but also as the only officer to spend his entire career on one station without ever visiting England (see Chapter 7). The rise of such men during the war undermined the racial assumptions of a slave society that aimed to enforce the inferiority of colored people and to deny their humanity.

The free colored population used their military service as a pretext to demand increased civil rights. For example, the distribution of relief money from the imperial government was a source of great bitterness among the free colored population of Hanover County and Westmoreland after the hurricane in 1781. They were told that the money was intended for the white population only. The men argued that their former military service and their payment of the same taxes as whites entitled them to more equitable treatment and a fair share of the hurricane money. They petitioned the lieutenant governor and the assembly of Jamaica, expressing their disbelief that "the humanity and charity of the British nation could mean to exclude a large body from receiving a part of the benefits of their donation, so generously conferred on the distressed, because their skins are brown." They reminded the Jamaican assembly that they had loyally performed their "militia duty, as good citizens, and in arms, as soldiers, they have always done, and are still ready to do, their utmost in defence of the British constitution, and the honour of their most gracious sovereign, their native country, and the liberty and property of others, as well as their own." They complained that they had endured great expense clothing themselves in regimental dress and protested that "their zeal and loyalty, instead of meeting with encouragement, [was] treated with contempt, and insult offered instead of relief."[20]

The American War also swelled the number of free colored people in the British West Indies. Slaves were manumitted in reward for military service, including black loyalists from North America. John Pulis has identified nineteen men and nine women who were former members of a black pioneer corps serving in North America and who were registered as free people in the parishes of Kingston and St. Catherine in Jamaica. He has similarly identified another ten free blacks who had served as auxiliaries or aides-de-camp in North America, men such as James Walden, who served with the Loyal Irish Volunteers of New York and received a certificate of freedom in 1778.[21]

Astute planters recognized that military service or religious conversions ultimately taught people of color and slaves "that they are men" and undermined white hegemony.[22] The mass conversion of slaves and free colored people to Christianity was "one of the most potent social forces at work" in the late eighteenth-century British West Indies and was related to events of the American Revolutionary War. The movement gained impetus from the arrival of black loyalist preachers leaving the United States, including George Liele, Moses Baker, George Vinyard, Boston King, David George, and William Kitt, who introduced native Baptism. George Liele established the first Baptist church in Kingston, where he had baptized more than 450 people by 1790.

Free blacks and slaves were able to appropriate the revolutionary rhetoric that placed a premium on the value of liberty. The republican ideology of the American Revolution fostered the growth of antislavery sentiment, which gained sudden momentum after the war in both Britain and in the northern states of America. Although it did not initiate the concept of liberty among free colored people and slaves, it "gave the idea greater currency and reality."[23] Some Jamaican planters thought the spread of such ideas was the cause of the slave rebellion in 1776. Within eight years of the American War, the free colored population petitioned for the right to vote in Jamaica, emphasizing their loyalty to the island. Like the North American patriots and those involved in the growing reform movement in England, they argued that taxation and representation were inseparable.[24]

*   *   *

Finally, the division of British America helped the cause of abolitionists in both Britain and the United States. It more than halved the number of slaves in the British Empire and made slavery appear virtually limited to the southern United States. The "peculiar institution" of slavery was not peculiar before 1776. On the contrary, slavery characterized the wealthiest and most populous colonies of British America. There were almost a million slaves in British America before 1776. It is little wonder that antebellum southern expansionists dreamed of incorporating islands in the Caribbean into the United States in order to enlarge their power and to balance the slave-owning states in the Senate against the North.

Abolitionists were well aware of the significance of the division of the British Empire. "As long as America was ours," wrote Clarkson in 1788, "there was no chance that a minister would have attended to the groans of the sons and daughters of Africa, however he might feel for their distress."[25] It prevented the island and southern planters from uniting against the abolitionists. The West India lobby was unable to appeal for support from the colonial lobbies of Virginia and South Carolina after 1776.

*   *   *

The American Revolution was a crucial event in the British West Indies. Edward Brathwaite's *Development of Creole Society in Jamaica, 1770–1820* (1971) found that the war "destroyed the cultural unity of British America" and isolated Jamaica, which gave an "impetus to the creolization of society." The American Revolutionary War made Jamaica more self-reliant and "culturally autonomous." The same was true for the rest of the British West Indies. This was reflected in the threats of secession and the challenges to parliamentary sovereignty, which only occurred after the war. Only after the war did the white colonists develop various strategies of opposition to imperial policies, which they had conspicuously failed to use between 1763 and 1774.[26]

Whereas Edward Long had acknowledged the right of Parliament to legislate for the internal affairs of the islands in 1774, Bryan Edwards challenged the doctrine of parliamentary supremacy after the American War. The

Figure 38. Jamaica mace of 1787, reproduced in Sir Harry Luke, *Caribbean Circuit* (London: Nicholson and Watson, 1950), plate xxv. The mace was ordered by the assembly of Jamaica after the American Revolutionary War. The crown on the mace was crushed which was symbolic of the radical postwar shift in planter politics.

assembly of Jamaica adopted a resolution in 1789 that Parliament was "not competent to destroy, nor partially to mutilate private properties" and claimed that the "violation of property of any subject of the British realm (not under legal forfeiture) without our consent, or without full compensation, would be an unconstitutional assumption of power, subversive of all public faith and confidence." The assembly cautioned that such a policy "must ultimately tend to alienate their affections from the parent state."[27] A West Indian reminded Parliament in 1815 "that by persisting in the question of right we lost America." A memorial of the representatives of Jamaica stated bluntly in 1832 that "we owe no more allegiance to the inhabitants of Great Britain than we owe to our brother colonists in Canada."[28]

This radical shift was a consequence of the postwar conflict of interests between the white colonial elite and the imperial government. They had emerged from the war embittered by its cost and seeming futility and resented the restrictions on their trade with the United States. However, their radicalism was primarily a reaction to the success of the metropolitan antislavery movement and the threat of parliamentary intervention against slavery. In both the British and French West Indies, the planters equated the defense of colonial liberties with the defense of slavery. Bryan Edwards, Edward Long, Moreau de Saint Méry, and d'Auberteuil asserted the right of the colonies alone to decide the issue of slavery.

John Adams believed that in the event of another war with England, the West Indies "would now declare for us if they dared." The governor of Canada warned that it was "not in the Revolted provinces alone that a Republican Spirit is to be found, but the tint has spread to other parts of America, and the West Indies." Horatio Nelson found that West Indians "are as great rebels as ever they were in America, had they the power to show it."[29] During the year of the parliamentary inquiry into the slave trade in 1788, the Jamaican assembly began to use a new mace in which the arches of the royal crown were "flattened, and heavily depressed in the middle where they support the orb and cross" in contrast to the upright position of the crown on the old mace.[30]

Anthony Stokes, the loyalist chief justice of Georgia, did not "question the attachment of the present set of men to their Sovereign and Parent State," but suspected that another generation of West Indians "may be inclined to give the Mother Country as much trouble as the Colonies on the Continent have done" and that they might obtain assistance from the United States. Granville Sharpe warned William Wilberforce that a strong movement might arise in the West Indies to declare independence and to federate themselves with the United States. During the nineteenth century, such threats of secession and federation with the United States became common.[31]

Yet, even in the nineteenth century, West Indian threats of secession were hollow. Self-interest dictated the continued loyalty of the white colonists to Britain. Their reliance on their monopoly of the home market was greater than ever with the rise of competition in Brazil and Cuba. They continued to rely on British naval protection and on the presence of ever larger numbers of British troops to police their slaves. They retained their besieged mentality, fearful of major slave insurrections especially after the great rebellion in St. Domingue. The white elite returned to live in Britain in ever larger numbers, and a higher proportion of the plantations belonged to owners in Britain after the American War.

The white colonial elite wanted autonomy and self-government but within the British Empire. Their constitutional thought consequently remained ambivalent. They were never able to reconcile their claims to being both equal and subordinate to Britain.

Abbreviations

AAS	*Proceedings of the American Antiquarian Society*
Adm.	Admiralty Papers, Public Record Office
AH	*Agricultural History*
AHR	*American Historical Review*
BCL	Boston College Library
BL	British Library
BUL	Bristol University Library
CO	Colonial Office Papers, Public Record Office
CQ	*Caribbean Quarterly*
CS	*Caribbean Studies*
EcHR	*Economic History Review*
EHR	*English Historical Review*
GP	Germain Papers, William L. Clements Library, University of Michigan, Ann Arbor
HJ	*Historical Journal*
JAA	Journal of the Assembly of Antigua
JAB	Journal of the Assembly of Barbados
JAD	Journal of the Assembly of Dominica
JAG	Journal of the Assembly of Grenada
JAH	*Journal of American History*
JAJ	Journal of the Assembly of Jamaica
JAM	Journal of the Assembly of Montserrat
JAN	Journal of the Assembly of Nevis
JAS	*Journal of American Studies*
JAStK	Journal of the Assembly of St. Kitts
JAStV	Journal of the Assembly of St. Vincent
JAT	Journal of the Assembly of Tobago
JBH	*Journal of Business History*
JBMHS	*Journal of the Barbados Museum and Historical Society*
JCH	*Journal of Caribbean History*
JEH	*Journal of Economic History*
JHR	*Jamaican Historical Review*
JIH	*Journal of Interdisciplinary History*

JJ	*Jamaica Journal*
JMH	*Journal of Modern History*
JNH	*Journal of Negro History*
JSH	*Journal of Social History*
LP	Lyttelton Papers, William L. Clements Library, University of Michigan, Ann Arbor
MHSC	*Massachusetts Historical Society Collection*
MM	*Mariner's Mirror*
MP	Macartney Papers, William L. Clements Library, University of Michigan, Ann Arbor
MSWIM	Minutes of the Society of West India Merchants
NCHR	*North Carolina Historical Review*
NEQ	*New England Quarterly*
PRO	Public Record Office, Kew, London
PSQ	*Political Science Quarterly*
RHL	Rhodes House Library, Oxford University
S&A	*Slavery and Abolition*
SCHM	*South Carolina Historical Magazine*
SHP	Shelburne Papers, William L. Clements Library, University of Michigan, Ann Arbor
SP	Sydney Papers, William L. Clements Library, University of Michigan, Ann Arbor
StJC	*St. James's Chronicle*
TRHS	*Transactions of the Royal Historical Society*
VP	Vaughan Papers, William L. Clements Library, University of Michigan, Ann Arbor
WLCL	William L. Clements Library, University of Michigan, Ann Arbor
WMQ	*William and Mary Quarterly*
WO	War Office Papers, Public Record Office
WRO	Worcester Record Office

Notes

Preface

1. There were twenty-six British colonies in America in 1776: Nova Scotia (Halifax), Quebec, and St. John (Prince Edward Island) in Canada; the Bahamas and Bermuda; Massachusetts, Connecticut, Rhode Island, New Hampshire, New York, Pennsylvania, Delaware, New Jersey, Maryland, Virginia, North Carolina, South Carolina, Georgia, East Florida, and West Florida in North America; and Jamaica, Barbados, the Leeward Islands, Grenada, St. Vincent, and Dominica. There were, in addition, unofficial British settlements in the Bay of Honduras (Belize) and on the Mosquito Shore (the east coast of Nicaragua). Lawrence Henry Gipson, *The British Empire Before the American Revolution*, 15 vols. (New York, reprinted 1936–70), 13:206, speaks of thirty-two colonies. His number is based on a definition of colonies as territorial units rather than administrative units, in which the Leeward Islands are counted as four colonies rather than one.

2. Jack Greene, "Preconditions of the American Revolution," in *Essays on the American Revolution*, ed. Stephen G. Kurtz and James H. Hutson (Chapel Hill, N.C., 1973), 40, argues that the islands shared four of five necessary conditions for rebellion; Greene, "Commentary," in *Eighteenth Century Florida and the Caribbean*, ed. Samuel Proctor (Gainesville, Fla., 1976), 4; Joseph Galloway, *Cool Thoughts* (London, 1780), 26, quoted in G. B. Hertz, *The Old Colonial System* (Manchester, 1905), 121.

3. Sir John Fortescue, *A History of the British Army*, 13 vols. (London, 1902), 3:259; Piers Mackesy, *The War for America* (London, 1964), 518; Barbara Tuchman, *The First Salute: A View of the American Revolution* (New York, 1988), 137, and see also 134, 136, 139, 140, 154, 216–217, 223.

4. John Higham, *History: Professional Scholarship in America*, 2nd edn. (Princeton, N.J., 1989), 164.

5. Frank Wesley Pitman, *The Development of the British West Indies, 1700–1763* (New Haven, Conn., 1917), vii, 360; Leonard W. Labaree, *Royal Government in America: A Study of the British Colonial System Before 1783* (New Haven, Conn., 1930), 426; Lowell Joseph Ragatz, *The West Indian Approach to the Study of American Colonial History* (London, 1935), 19.

6. Alison Games, "History Without Borders: Teaching American History in an Atlantic Context," *Indiana Magazine of History* 91 (1995), 159–178.

7. Bernard Bailyn and Philip D. Morgan, eds., *Strangers Within the Realm: Cultural Margins of the First British Empire* (Chapel Hill, N.C., 1991), 3; Richard B. Morris, "The Spacious Empire of Lawrence Henry Gipson," *WMQ* 3rd ser., 24 April (1967), 169–190; Gipson, *The British Empire Before the American Revolution*, 13:206–207. The final three volumes of the series, excluding the bibliography and source volumes, make no reference to the British West Indies.

8. Peter Marshall, "The British Empire and the American Revolution," *Huntington Library Quarterly* 27 (1963–64), 135–145; G. F. Tyson and C. Tyson, *Preliminary Report on Manuscript Materials in British Archives Relating to the American Revolution in the West Indian Islands* (Millwood, N.Y., 1978), i; Roy T. R. Clayton, "Sophistry, Security, and Socio-Political Structures in the American Revolution; Or, Why Jamaica Did Not Rebel," *HJ* 19 (1986), 321. The 1976 bicentenary publications included Charles Toth, ed., *The American Revolution and the West Indies* (Washington, D.C., 1975), which was a useful collection of largely reprinted articles, dating back to the beginning of the twentieth century, which were "scattered, or buried in scholarly journals, across the years" (x). Toth also edited a special edition of the *Revista/Review Interamericana* 5 (1975–76), which contained a new set of essays devoted to the subject of the American Revolution in the Caribbean.

9. Selwyn H. H. Carrington, *The British West Indies During the American Revolution* (Dordrecht, 1988), 3.

10. Eric Williams, *From Columbus to Castro: The History of the Caribbean* (New York, 1970), 226; Robert W. Tucker and David C. Hendrickson, *The Fall of the First British Empire: Origins of the War of American Independence* (Baltimore, 1982), 60; K. G. Davies, *The North Atlantic World in the Seventeenth Century* (Minneapolis, 1974), 330–331; Agnes Whitson, "The Outlook of the Continental American Colonies on the British West Indies, 1760–1775," *PSQ* 45, no. 1 (Mar. 1930), 86.

11. Robert V. Wells, *The Population of the British Colonies in America Before 1776: A Survey of Census Data* (Princeton, N.J., 1975), 286, 261; Cyril Hamshere, *The British in the Caribbean* (Cambridge, Mass., 1972), 136; Gordon K. Lewis, *Main Currents in Caribbean Thought: The Historical Evolution of Caribbean Society in Its Ideological Aspects, 1492–1900* (Baltimore, 1983), 322; Franklin W. Knight, "The American Revolution and the Caribbean," in *Slavery and Freedom in the Age of the American Revolution*, ed. Ira Berlin and Ronald Hoffman (Charlottesville, Va., 1983), 241–242, 253–254 (Knight acknowledges a range of factors); Edward Brathwaite, *The Development of Creole Society in Jamaica, 1770–1820* (Oxford, 1978), 100.

12. Jack Greene, review of *The British West Indies During the American Revolution*, by Selwyn H. H. Carrington, *New West Indies Guide/Nieuwe West-Indische Gids* 63, no. 384 (1989), 253.

13. One exception is Clayton, "Sophistry, Security, and Socio-Political Structures in the American Revolution," 319–344, but the force of the article is weakened by its almost exclusive reliance on the papers of the Taylor family of Jamaica. Carrington, *The British West Indies During the American Revolution*, 159, makes the most sustained case that "If the West Indians were not overtly engaged in the fighting, it was not because they did not sympathise with, or even share in, many of the goals of the American colonies"; Carrington, 73, 105, 123, 130, 135, 151, 157. There are numerous sporadic references suggesting British West Indian support for the American Revolution: H. C. Bell, "The West India Trade Before the American Revolution," *AHR* 22, no. 2 (1917), 287; Arthur P. Watts, *Nevis and St. Christopher, 1782–1784: Unpublished Documents* (Paris, 1925), xvi; R. L. Schuyler, "The Constitutional Claims of the British West Indies," *PSQ* 40, no. 1 (1925), 3, 22–23; W. M. James, *The British Navy in Adversity: A Study of the War of American Independence* (London, 1926), 113; J. W. Herbert, "Constitutional Struggles in Jamaica, 1748–1776" (M.A. thesis, London University, 1927); M. J. Hewitt, "The West Indies and the American Revolution" (D.Phil. thesis, Oxford Uni-

versity, 1937); F. R. Augier, S. C. Gordon, D. G. Hall, and M. Reckford, *The Making of the West Indies*, 5th edn. (London, 1964), 108; D. A. G. Waddell, *The West Indies and the Guianas* (Englewood Cliffs, N.J., 1967), 64–65; Merrill Jensen, *The Founding of a Nation* (Oxford, 1968), 98; C. E. Carrington, *The British Overseas: Exploits of a Nation of Shopkeepers*, 2 vols., 2nd edn. (Cambridge, 1968), 2:124; George Metcalf, *Royal Government and Political Conflict in Jamaica, 1729–1783* (London, 1965), xi, 2, 166, 228, 237; Hamshere, *The British in the Caribbean*, 136, 209; Donna J. Spindel, "The Stamp Act Crisis in the British West Indies," *JAS* 2, no. 2 (Aug. 1977), 203–222; Knight, "The American Revolution and the Caribbean," 237–261.

14. Jack Greene, *Pursuits of Happiness: The Social Development of Early Modern British Colonies and the Formation of American Culture* (Chapel Hill, N.C., 1988); Greene, "Society and Economy in the British Caribbean During the Seventeenth and Eighteenth Centuries," in his *Interpreting Early America: Historiographical Essays* (Charlottesville, Va., 1996), 175: "But neither in their materialistic orientation, their disease environments, their number of African inhabitants, their concern to cultivate British values and institutions, nor perhaps even their commitment to the colony was there a sharp break between the island and mainland societies. Rather, there was a social continuum that ran from the Caribbean through Georgia and South Carolina to the Chesapeake through Pennsylvania and New York to urban and then rural New England."

Part I. Foundations of Loyalty

Note to epigraph: Germain Papers, volume 7, William L. Clements Library.

Chapter 1. British Sojourners

1. Edward D. Seeber, trans., *On the Threshold of Liberty: Journal of a Frenchman's Tour of the American Colonies in 1777* (Bloomington, Ind., 1959), 123–124.

2. Edward Lyttelton, *The Groans of the Plantations* (London, 1689), 34, 37, cited in Carl Bridenbaugh and Roberta Bridenbaugh, *No Peace Beyond the Line: The English in the Caribbean, 1624–1690* (New York, 1972), 401; Charles Townshend, quoted in Sir Lewis Namier, *Crossroads of Power: Essays on Eighteenth-Century England* (London, 1962), 173–174.

3. (William Scott?), *A Discourse Concerning the Special Causes of Irreligion in the West Indies with the Apparent Symptoms of Its Decrease* (London, 1764?), 9; Lord Adam Gordon, "Journal of an Officer in the West Indies, 1764–65," in *Travels in the American Colonies*, ed. Newton D. Mereness (New York, reprinted 1961), 378–380; Bryan Edwards, *Thoughts on the Late Proceedings of Government Respecting the Trade of the West India Islands with the United States of North America*, 2nd edn. (London, 1784), 29 (my emphasis).

4. Edward Brathwaite, *The Development of Creole Society in Jamaica, 1770–1820* (Oxford, 1978), dates the development of a creole culture in Jamaica, the largest and most populous of all the British West Indies, from the American Revolution. However, Brathwaite is careful to qualify the extent of creolization, which "continued to be

limited by the colonial relationship" while the descendants of both Europeans and Africans "rejected or disowned" their creole identity (306, 308). Gordon K. Lewis, *Main Currents in Caribbean Thought: The Historical Evolution of Caribbean Society in Its Ideological Aspects, 1492–1900* (Baltimore, 1983), 322, finds the American Revolution much too early for the development of a creole society. Alan L. Karras, *Sojourners in the Sun: Scottish Migrants in Jamaica and the Chesapeake, 1740–1800* (Ithaca, N.Y., 1992), 47 fn. 4, does not believe that "what could be called a creole society developed in the eighteenth century" British Caribbean. F. W. Pitman, *The Development of the British West Indies, 1700–1763* (Hamden, Conn., reprinted 1967), 1, similarly argued that "Local patriotism was established early in the life of North America, while in the West Indies devotion to one's island was attained slowly and with difficulty." For West Indians' ambivalence about their identity in Britain, see Craton, "Reluctant Creoles: The Planter's World in the British West Indies," in *Strangers Within the Realm: Cultural Margins of the First British Empire*, ed. Bernard Bailyn and Philip D. Morgan (Chapel Hill, N.C., 1991), 348–349.

5. Charles Davenant, writing in 1698, quoted in Namier, *Crossroads of Power*, 173; Michael Craton, "Property and Propriety: Land Tenure and Slave Property in the Creation of a British West Indian Plantocracy, 1612–1740," in *Conceptions of Property*, ed. John Brewer (London, 1996), 520. See Richard Dunn, *Sugar and Slaves: The Rise of the Planter Class in the English West Indies* (New York, reprinted 1973), 102, 177, for the beginnings of absenteeism in the English Caribbean.

6. Rev. Robert Robertson, *A Detection of the State and Situation of the Present Sugar Planters of Barbadoes and the Leeward Islands* (London, 1732), 50, 53; James George Douglas to the Board of Trade, received Mar. 19/6, 1745, CO, 152/25, Y76, 164, quoted in Pitman, *The Development of the British West Indies*, 39 fn.82. List of Purchasers of Land in Tobago, May 1, 1768, CO, 101/12, f. 158. Although most of these were local absentees of whom only six lived in Britain, another thirty-six lived in the other Windward Islands, fourteen in the Leeward Islands, and one in Surinam. For Grenada, see Governor Melvill to Hillsborough, July 31, 1770, CO, 101/14, f. 124; Governor Macartney to Germain, Oct. 18, 1778, CO, 101/22. Douglas Hall, "Absentee-Proprietorship in the British West Indies to About 1850," *JHR* 4 (1964), 15–35, notes that some absenteeism was indeed local.

7. Edward Long, *The History of Jamaica*, 3 vols. (London, 1774), 1:377, 378; Richard B. Sheridan, "The Development of the Plantations to 1750" and "An Era of West Indian Prosperity, 1750–1775," in *Chapters in Caribbean History*, ed. Douglas Hall, Elsa Goveia, and F. Roy Augier (Barbados, 1970), 103: a 1775 "Account Produce" for Jamaica shows that 234 of the 775 sugar plantations were owed by absentees and minors; Evangeline W. Andrews and Charles Andrews, eds., *Journal of a Lady of Quality* . . . (New Haven, Conn., 1921), 62; Craton, "Property and Propriety," 520. See also Governor Burt to Germain, Mar. 30, 1780, CO, 152/60, f. 103; Governor Payne to Dartmouth, Oct. 28, 1779, CO, 152/54.

8. Long, *History*, 2:22; Bryan Edwards, *The History Civil and Commercial of the British West Indies*, 5 vols., 5th edn. (London, 1819), 2:9–10; O. F. Christie, ed., *The Diary of the Revd William Jones, 1777–1821. Curate and Vicar of Broxbourne and the Hamlet of Hoddesdon, 1781–1821* (New York, 1929), 39; James Anthony Froude, *The English in the West Indies or the Bow of Ulysses* (London, reprinted 1888), 256, see also 191. For a discussion of the architectural remains, see A. W. Ackworth, *Treasures in the Caribbean:*

A First Study of Georgian Buildings in the British West Indies (London, 1949), and David Buisseret, *Historic Architecture of the Caribbean* (London, 1980).

9. Jack Greene, "Changing Identity in the British Caribbean: Barbados as a Case Study," in *Colonial Identity in the Atlantic World, 1500–1800*, ed. Nicholas Canny and Anthony Pagden (Princeton, N.J., 1987), 251; A. Caldecott, *The Church in the West Indies* (London, 1898), 38. For examples of West Indian artistic and literary contributions, see David S. Shields, *Oracles of Empire: Poetry, Politics and Commerce in British America, 1690–1750* (Chicago, 1990), 18, 73–77, 82–83; Pamela O'Gorman, "An Eighteenth Century Jamaica Oratorio," *JJ* 22, no. 4 (Nov. 1989–Jan. 1990), 41–45; O'Gorman, "The Music of Samuel Felsted's Jonah," *JJ* 23, no. 1 (Feb.–Apr. 1990), 14–19.

10. Brathwaite, *The Development of Creole Society*, 73–75.

11. Greene, "Changing Identity in the British Caribbean," 213–267. See also Karl Watson, *The Civilised Island Barbados: A Social History, 1750–1816* (Barbados, reprinted 1983), 2, 3, 40–41; Lowell J. Ragatz, *The Fall of the Planter Class in the British Caribbean, 1763–1833* (Washington, D.C., 1928), 4 fn.1; William Dickson, *Letters on Slavery* (London, 1789), 58; P. F. Campbell, *The Anglican Church in Barbados in the Seventeenth Century* (St. Michael, Barbados, 1982). Barbados alone resisted the attempts to disestablish and disendow the Anglican Church in the late nineteenth century by voting a local subsidy. Similarly, the assembly survived the nineteenth century, unlike the other legislatures of the British West Indies. For belief that Barbados was more healthy, see *Remarks on the Evidence delivered on the Petition Presented by the West-India Planters and Merchants . . .* (London, 1777), 7; Sir William Young, *The West-India Common-Place Book* (London, 1807), 222. Jack Greene, "Colonial South Carolina and the Caribbean Connection," in his *Imperatives, Behaviors and Identities: Essays in Early American Cultural History* (Charlottesville, Va., 1992), 78, finds that Barbados was the healthiest English settlement after 1710 "in the West Indies, on the southern North American mainland, or even in continental cities such as Boston and Philadelphia." Philip D. Curtin, *Death by Migration: Europe's Encounter with the Tropical World of the Nineteenth Century* (Cambridge, 1989) did not find significant differences from other islands.

12. Greene, "Changing Identity in the British Caribbean," 232; See also Watson, *The Civilised Island Barbados*, 2.

13. Jean Bullen and Helen Livingston, "Of the State and Advancement of the College for the Whole West Indian World," *Codrington Chronicles: An Experiment in Anglican Altruism on a Barbados Plantation, 1710–1834*, ed. Frank J. Klingberg (Berkeley, 1949), 108, 110; Caldecott, *Church in the West Indies*, 225, 227. For absenteeism in Barbados, see Craton, "Property and Propriety," 520.

14. Pitman, *The Development of the British West Indies*, 1. His argument echoes that of Sir John Seeley, *The Expansion of England*, ed. John Gross (Chicago, reprinted 1971), 123.

15. Trevor Burnard, "European Migration to Jamaica, 1655–1780," *WMQ* 3rd ser., 53, no. 4 (Oct. 1996), 790.

16. Richard B. Sheridan, *Doctors and Slaves: A Medical and Demographic History of Slavery in the British West Indies, 1680–1834* (Cambridge, 1985), 328; Peter Quennell, ed., *The Prodigal Rake: Memoirs of William Hickey* (New York, 1962), 194–195; J. A. Houlding, *Fit for Service: The Training of the British Army, 1715–1795* (Oxford, 1981), 73, 315; J. Hector St. John de Crèvecoeur, *Letters from an American Farmer*, ed. Albert E. Stone (New York, 1986), 167.

17. Quote of William Beckford in Derrick Knight, *Gentlemen of Fortune: The Men Who Made Their Fortunes in Britain's Slave Colonies* (Guildford, Surrey, 1978), 44; Karen Ordahl Kupperman, "Fear of Hot Climates in the Anglo-American Colonial Experience," *WMQ* 3rd ser., 41, no. 2 (Apr. 1984), 213–241; Dunn, *Sugar and Slaves*, 300–335; W. R. Bailey, "The Geography of Fevers in Early Jamaica," *JHR* 10 (1973), 23–31; Francisco Guerra, "The Influence of Disease on Race, Logistics and Colonization in the Antilles," *Journal of Tropical Medicine and Hygiene* 69 (1966), 23–35; Philip Curtin, "Epidemiology of the Slave Trade," *PSQ* 83 (June 1968), 190–216; John McNeil, "The Ecological Basis of Warfare in the Caribbean, 1700–1804," in *Adapting to Conditions: War and Society in the Eighteenth Century*, ed. Maarten Ultee (University, Ala., 1986), 29.

18. Trevor Burnard, "A Failed Settler Society: Marriage and Demographic Failure in Early Jamaica," *JSH* 28 (1994), 65.

19. Creoles composed only 8 percent of the members of the assembly of Grenada in 1770. Long, *History*, 1:510, estimated that 1,800 people emigrated annually to the West Indies. David Galenson, *White Servitude in Colonial America: An Economic Analysis* (Cambridge, 1981), 218, estimates that 368 people emigrated annually to Jamaica in the eighteenth century, which "should be doubled" according to Burnard, "European Migration to Jamaica," 778. *Audi alteram Partem . . .* (London, 1770), 132, lists the ethnic composition of the assembly of Grenada in 1770: 2 creole members, 3 English, 4 French, 5 Irish, 1 North American, and 9 Scots.

20. Christie, *The Diary of the Revd William Jones*, 23. Bernard Bailyn, *Voyagers to the West: A Passage in the Peopling of America on the Eve of the Revolution* (New York, 1986), 92, finds that Jamaica absorbed 69 percent of emigrants to the West Indies (312 of 495) for the years when the best figures are available between 1773 and 1776. Galenson, *White Servitude in Colonial America*, 218, estimates that about one-third of total emigrants to the Caribbean went to Jamaica. This is about proportionate to the relative size of the white populations of the other British islands and the white population of Jamaica. See Burnard, "European Migration to Jamaica," 790, and 772–773 for the proportion of young white immigrant males.

21. Philip D. Morgan, "British Encounters with Africans and African Americans, Circa 1600–1780," in *Strangers Within the Realm: Cultural Margins of the First British Empire*, ed. Bernard Bailyn and Philip D. Morgan (Chapel Hill, N.C., 1991), 174–175. See population tables in David Watts, *The West Indies: Patterns of Development, Culture and Environmental Changes Since 1492* (Cambridge, 1987), 311, 313, 316.

22. Neville A. T. Hall, "Some Aspects of the Deficiency Question in Jamaica in the Eighteenth Century," *JJ* 1–2 (Mar.–June 1973), 36–42. Watts, *The West Indies*, 361, finds no deficiency laws in Barbados, but Barbados had a military tenant system that similarly required plantations to maintain one white for every 30–50 acres. See Watson, *The Civilised Island Barbados*, 57; Jill Sheppard, *The "Redlegs" of Barbados: Their Origins and History* (Millwood, N.Y., 1977), 38–39, 55, 59. Jamaica passed a tax on absentees in 1718. According to F. W. Pitman, "The West Indian Absentee Planter as a British Colonial Type," *AHR* (1927), 118–20, the absentees successfully blocked such efforts. See Neil R. Stout, *The Royal Navy in America, 1760–1775: A Study of Enforcement in the Era of the American Revolution* (Annapolis, Md., 1973), 72, for the exemption of whites from naval impressment.

23. Christie, *The Diary of the Revd. William Jones*, 16; Long, *History*, 2:278; John C.

Fitzpatrick, ed., *The Diaries of George Washington*, 4 vols. (Boston, 1925), 1:28; Wylie Sypher, "The West Indian as a 'Character' in the Eighteenth Century," *Studies in Philology* 36 (1939), 516.

24. Winthrop Jordan, "American Chiaroscuro: The Status and Definition of Mulattoes in the British Colonies," *WMQ* 19 (1962), 196, 198; Jordan, *White over Black: American Attitudes Toward the Negro, 1550–1812* (Baltimore, reprinted 1969), 145. The most revealing account of sexual relations between blacks and whites is contained in the papers of Thomas Thistlewood, an overseer in Jamaica. See Trevor Burnard, "Thomas Thistlewood Becomes a Creole," in *Varieties of Southern History: New Essays on a Region and Its People*, ed. Bruce Clayton and John Salmond (Westport, Conn., 1996), 99–118.

25. William Dickson, *The Mitigation of Slavery* (London, 1814), xxiv. The account is based on Dickson's experiences in Barbados as the secretary of Governor Hay during the American Revolution. John Pinney to Robert Robertson Jones, June 10, 1779, Pinney Letter Book V, f. 28, BUL; Stephen Fuller to ?, March 28, 1763, Fuller MSS 255, f. 21, Nicholas M. Williams Collection, BCL.

26. Long, *History*, 2:254, 276–280; Charles Leslie, *History of Jamaica* (London, 1740), 28, 30, 31, 35–39.

27. Adam Smith, *The Wealth of Nations* (1776), bk. I, ch. 10, pt. 1, ed. Edwin Cannan (Chicago, 1976), 176. According to Peter A. Coclanis, "The Wealth of British America on the Eve of the Revolution," *JIH* 21 (1990), 259, the wealth of the average white Jamaican was ten times greater than that of the average North American. The differences between the wealth of the respective colonial elites was actually greater because of the greater concentration of wealth among elites on the islands than on the mainland.

28. Kenneth Morgan, "Bristol West India Merchants in the Eighteenth Century," *TRHS* 6th ser., 3 (1993), 185–208; Philip C. Yorke, ed., *The Diary of John Baker: Barrister of the Middle Temple and Solicitor General of the Leeward Islands* (London, 1931).

29. William Cobbett, ed., *The Parliamentary History of England from the Earliest Period to 1803*, 36 vols. (London, 1806–22), 19:1316.

30. Peter (Pelham?) to Copley, Barbados, Apr. 28, 1766, "Letters and Papers of John Singleton Copley and Henry Pelham," *MHSC* 71 (1914), 40; Copley to Peter (Pelham), Boston, Sept. 12, 1766, *MHSC* 71 (1914), 47. I am grateful to Deborah Prosser for bringing these letters to my attention. See also Richard H. Saunders and Ellen G. Miles, *American Colonial Portraits, 1760–1776* (Washington, D.C., 1987), 42; Richard B. Sheridan, "William Beckford (1744–1799), Patron of Painters in Jamaica," *Register of the Museum of Art. University of Kansas* 3, nos. 8–9 (Winter 1967), 14–23; David Morris, *Thomas Hearne and His Landscape* (London, 1989).

31. Samuel Foote, *The Patron* (London, 1764), 13; *Public Advertiser*, Nov. 23, 1770 and Nov. 18, 1769. See also *StJC*, June 25–28, 1774.

32. See, for example, "The Peerage &c. in Jamaica," in W. A. Fuertado, *Official and Other Personages of Jamaica from 1655–1790* (Kingston, Jamaica, 1896), 109–30.

33. Lawrence Stone and Jeanne C. Fawtier Stone, *An Open Elite? England, 1540–1880* (Oxford, 1984).

34. *Herald: A Gazette for the Country*, Aug. 23, 1797, cited in Alice B. Keith, "Relaxations in the British Restrictions on the American Trade with the British West Indies, 1783–1802," *JMH* 20, no. 1 (Mar. 1948), 16.

35. Lillian M. Penson, "The London West India Interest in the Eighteenth Century," *EHR* 30 (July 1921), 374; Penson, *The Colonial Agents of the British West Indies: A Study in Colonial Administration Mainly in the Eighteenth Century* (London, reprinted 1971), v; Michael G. Kammen, *A Rope of Sand: The Colonial Agents, British Politics and the American Revolution* (Ithaca, N.Y., 1968), 11. Jack M. Sosin, *Agents and Merchants: British Colonial Policy and the Origins of the American Revolution, 1763–1775* (Lincoln, Neb., 1965), 176–177, lists only three North American agents in late 1774.

36. Long, *History*, 1:122. For a discussion of the specific qualities of Fuller, see Andrew J. O'Shaughnessy, "The Formation of a Commercial Lobby: The West India Interest, British Colonial Policy and the American Revolution," *HJ* 40, no. 1 (1997), 77–78.

37. Penson, "The London West India Interest," 202, 381, 383, 386. The Minutes of the Society of West India Merchants are now in the library of the University of the West Indies at the St. Augustine campus in Trinidad. A microfilm copy was retained by the Royal Commonwealth Society, London.

38. Morgan, "Bristol West India Merchants," 201–202.

39. Long, *History*, 1:377; Richard B. Sheridan, *Sugar and Slavery: An Economic History of the British West Indies, 1623–1775* (London, reprinted 1976), 59; Sheridan, "The British Sugar Planters and the Atlantic World, 1763–1775" in *Eighteenth Century Florida and the Caribbean*, ed. Samuel Proctor (Gainesville, Fla., 1976), 4.

40. Agent for Massachusetts, quoted in Penson, *The Colonial Agents*, 228; *Gentleman's Magazine and Historical Chronicler*, 36 (London, 1766), 229, quoted in Sheridan, *Sugar and Slavery*, 60; "Colony Members of parliament 1781 resident in Great Britain," Fuller MSS 265, f. 305, BCL. The list is printed in O'Shaughnessy, "The Formation of a Commercial Lobby," 73 n.10.

41. Franklin to Collinson, Apr. 30, 1764, quoted in G. L. Beer, *British Colonial Policy, 1754–1765* (New York, 1922), 136. See Jacob M. Price, "Who Cared About the Colonies? The Impact of the Thirteen Colonies on British Society and Politics, 1714–1775," in *Strangers Within the Realm: Cultural Margins of the First British Empire*, eds. Bernard Bailyn and Philip D. Morgan (Chapel Hill, N.C.), 401–5, for the relatively weak political presence of North Americans in London. For conflict within the lobby, see Barry Higman, "The West India Interest in Parliament, 1807–1833," *Historical Studies* 13 (1967), 6; Roger Anstey, *The Atlantic Slave Trade and British Abolition, 1760–1810* (N.J., 1975), 341, notes the divisions within the interest even in opposition to the abolitionists; Michael Kammen, *Empire and Interest: The American Colonies and the Politics of Mercantilism* (Philadelphia, 1970), 13.

42. For the South Carolina–Barbados connection, see Warren Alleyne and Henry Fraser, *The Barbados-Carolina Connection* (London, 1988); Richard S. Dunn, "The English Sugar Islands and the Founding of South Carolina," *SCHM* 72, no. 3 (1971), 81–93; Richard Waterhouse, "England, the Caribbean and the Settlement of Carolina," *JAS* 9 (1975), 259–281. George C. Rodgers, Jr. and George W. Williams, review of *The Barbados-Carolina Connection*, by Warren Alleyne and Henry Fraser, *SCHM* 92, no. 1 (1991), 50–53, questions the extent of the transfer of architectural styles from Barbados to Charleston. For informal ties, see Mary Lumsden, *The Barbados American Connection* (London, reprinted 1988).

43. Douglas McMurtie, *Early Printing on the Island of Antigua* (Evanston, Ill., 1943); Wilberforce Eames, "The Antigua Press and Benjamin Mecom, 1748–1765,"

AAS 38 (1929), 303–48; Lowell J. Ragatz, *The West Indian Approach to the Study of American Colonial History* (London, 1935), 6.

44. Saunders and Miles, *American Colonial Portraits*, 31–2, 33, 37, 42, 43, 177, 207, 260–61, 273, 275, 311, 313, 323; Richardson Wright, *Revels in Jamaica, 1682–1838* (New York, 1937), 51, 45, see also 27–28, 31–32, 34–35, 36, 38, 41, 43; J. I. Cooper, "The West Indies, Bermuda and the Mainland Colleges," *JHR* 2, no. 1 (Dec. 1949), 4. For examples of religious networks, see Harriet Florer Durham, *Caribbean Quakers* (Hollywood, Fla., 1972), 59, 61, 67.

45. Long, *History*, 2:246–50, 510–11.

46. Ibid., 2:246. The decayed state of the schools was the subject of reports by the legislature: JAJ, Dec. 11, 1764, CO, 140/44, Dec. 13, 1770, CO, 140/50; Brathwaite, *The Development of Creole Society*, 269–70 n.144.

47. Pitman, *The Development of the British West Indies*, 10; J. Harry Bennett, Jr., "Sir John Gay Alleyne and the Mansion House School: Codrington College, 1775–1797," *JBMHS* 17, nos. 2–3 (1950), 63, 65, 67. Watson, *The Civilised Island Barbados*, 110, provides a list of 1712 showing that there were forty-six licensed schoolmasters in Barbados; see also pp. 111, 113, 114.

48. Charles Rose to Bishop Gibson, Nov. 6, 1732, Fulham MSS XIX, fos. 214–215, Lambeth Palace Library; *Dictionary of National Biography*, ed. Sir Leslie Stephen and Sir Sidney Lee (London, reprinted 1937–38), 6:530; Answers to Queries, May 7, 1724, Fulham MSS XXXVI, f. 308.

49. Pinney to Coker, Apr. 26, 1781, Letter Book V, f. 112, Pinney MSS; Claire Taylor, "The Journal of an Absentee Proprietor, Nathaniel Phillips of Slebech," *JCH* 18 (1984), 72; Andrews and Andrews, *Journal of a Lady of Quality*, 92.

50. Edward Cochran of Antigua is buried in the college churchyard at Eton, where he was stabbed by another boy in 1730. John Newton Gay Alleyne, the oldest son of the speaker of the assembly of Barbados, died as a pupil from "the effects of overbathing," and his memorial tablet in St. James Church in Barbados contains a relief picturing Eton College. Jonathan Gathorn-Hardy, *The Old School Tie: The Phenomenon of the English Public School* (New York, 1978), 60; John Chandos, *Boys Together: English Public Schools, 1800–1865* (New Haven, Conn., 1985), 137; *Leaving Portraits from Eton College: Dulwich Picture Gallery, 18 July–20 October 1991* (Kent, 1991), 15, 17, 30, 35.

51. Cobbett, *Parliamentary History*, 35:1102: July 5, 1789.

52. Edward Alfred Jones, *A Catalogue of the Plate of Merton College* (Oxford, 1938). The gifts included a salver given by Sir John Williams of St. Kitts, who was a gentleman commoner of the college in 1757; a bowl presented by Thomas Beckford of Jamaica; a pair of salvers donated by Sir Thomas Barnard of Jamaica; and the "Stokso Cup" given by Thomas Stokes of Barbados. I am grateful for the above information to Roger Highfield, Fellow of Merton College, and to Scott Madelbrote, Fellow of All Souls. According to Brathwaite, *The Development of Creole Society*, 41, 229 Jamaicans were educated at Oxford between 1770 and 1820.

53. According to Richard B. Sheridan, "The Role of the Scots in the Economy and Society of the West Indies," in *Comparative Perspectives on Slavery* ed. Vera Rubin and Arthur Tuden (New York, 1977), 96, 84 students from the West Indies went to Glasgow University between 1728 and 1800.

54. Vere Langford Oliver, *Caribbeana*, 6 vols. (London, 1914), 3:291–294; Sheridan, *Sugar and Slavery*, 371.

55. Dr. John Witherspoon, *Address to the Inhabitants of Jamaica and the Other West India Islands, in Behalf of the College of New Jersey* (Philadelphia, 1772), 20.

56. Cooper, "The West Indies, Bermuda and the American Mainland Colleges," 1–7.

57. Quote of Philip Fithian in ibid., 3; James McLachlan, ed. *Princetonians, 1748–1768: A Biographical Dictionary* (Princeton, N.J., 1976).

58. *Candid Remarks on Dr. Witherspoon's Address To the Inhabitants of Jamaica, And the other West India Islands &c. In a Letter to Those Gentlemen* (Philadelphia, 1772), 13–14, 19.

59. Karras, *Sojourners in the Sun*, 88, 162–163, 168, 176. Brathwaite, *The Development of Creole Society*, 18, 61, notes that there were seventy attorneys-at-law and twenty barristers in Jamaica in 1790.

60. Sheridan, *Doctors and Slaves*, 46, 5, 57, 61. Edinburgh emerged as the premier medical college during the eighteenth century; twenty-three of its graduates practiced in the British West Indies before 1780.

61. Robert Barker, "Jamaican Goldsmiths and Assayers, 1665 to 1765," *The Silver Society* 3–5 (Spring 1986), 136–37; Baker, "Jamaican Goldsmiths—Some Early Eighteenth Century Inventories," *The Silver Society* 3, nos. 7–9 (1987), 190.

62. Andrews and Andrews, ed. *Journal of a Lady of Quality*, 92; Long, *History of Jamaica*, 2:249; see also 246–250. See also *Observations from a Gentleman in Town . . .* (London, 1781), 199: The "planters naturally wish to be allied to, and associated with the English gentry with whom they have been educated, and from the early period of youth linked in the endearments of discourse."

63. Fitzpatrick, *The Diaries of George Washington*, 28–29.

64. Dunn, *Sugar and Slaves*, 97, 218–29, 267; Watts, *The West Indies*, 336; Richard B. Sheridan, "The Wealth of Jamaica in the Eighteenth Century," *EcHR* 2nd ser., 18 (1965), 299. See also Sheridan, *The Development of the Plantations*, 31, for an analysis of wealth distribution in Barbados in 1750.

65. The Letterbook of the Rev. James Ramsay, Rhodes House (Oxford), Brit. Emp. MSS S2, fos. 53–54, RHL; *A New and Exact Map of the Islands of St. Christopher* (1753) by Samuel Baker, CO, 700; Rev. James Ramsay, *An Essay on the Treatment and Conversion of African Slaves in the British Sugar Colonies* (London, 1784), 57; Watts, *The West Indies*, 334; Sheridan, *Sugar and Slavery*, 194.

66. Long, *History*, 1:386, 2:511.

67. This was the case for the plantations of Lady Frances Stapleton of St. Kitts in 1746 and Shute Shrimpton Yeamans of Antigua in 1760. See J. R. V. Johnston, "The Sugar Plantations of the Heirs of Lady Frances Stapleton in Nevis and St. Christopher (1746–1810)" (M.A. thesis, University of Wales, 1964), 69; U. B. Phillips, "An Antigua Plantation, 1769–1818," *NCHR* 3 (July 1926), 439; Richard B. Sheridan, "The Rise of a Colonial Gentry: A Case Study of Antigua, 1730–1775," *EcHR* 2nd ser., 13 (1961), 344–345.

68. Long, *History*, 1:456–63; Sheridan, *Sugar and Slavery*, 231; Letter Book of the Rev. James Ramsay, Brit. Emp. MSS S2, f. 87; James Ramsay, *An Essay on the Reduction of Interest* (St. Kitts, 1770), 19–20. In the 1730s, Rev. Robert Robertson, who was "trying to inflame the account," put the cost at £10,000. According to Elsa Goveia, *Slave Society in the British Leeward Islands* (New Haven, Conn., 1965), 107, Sir Patrick Blake estimated in 1790 that the same estate in St. Kitts would cost £80,000 sterling. Sheridan,

Sugar and Slavery, 229, indicates that the median value of 502 sugar estates increased from £3,819 in 1741–45 to £9,361 in 1771–75. Karras, *Sojourners in the Sun*, 175, reports a 259 percent increase in the value of Jamaican estates between 1742 and 1796.

69. Sheridan, *Sugar and Slavery*, 229.

70. Long, *History*, 1:511, 2:288, 289; Dickson, *Letters on Slavery*, 26; Goveia, *Slave Society in the British Leeward Islands*, 147; Watson, *The Civilised Island Barbados*, 74.

71. Dickson, *Mitigation of Slavery*, 174; Dickson, *Letters on Slavery*, 40, 42; Rev. Robert Robertson, *A Letter to the Bishop of London* (London, 1730), 74; Young, *The West-India Common-Place Book*, 18; Watson, *The Civilised Island Barbados*, 56, 58. For origins of white poor, see Hilary Beckles, *White Servitude and Black Slavery in Barbados, 1627–1715* (Knoxville, Tenn., 1989).

72. Memorial of His Majesty's Adopted Subjects in the Island of Grenada, n.d., CO, 101/1, f. 110. See also Edwards, *The History . . . of the British West Indies*, 2:7.

73. Goveia, *Slave Society in the British Leeward Islands*, 161, 163–166, 218, 225; D. B. Gaspar, *Bondmen and Rebels: A Study of Master-Slave Relations in Antigua with Implications for Colonial British America* (Baltimore, 1985), 107 n.189.

74. Lovell Stanhope to the Board of Trade, 1763, CO, 137/33, f. 35, quoted in Hall, "Some Aspects of the Deficiency Question in Jamaica," 37. See also Goveia, *Slave Society in the British Leeward Islands*, 88, 151, 250, 253, 312, and 320 for the racial rigidities of slave societies.

75. Governor Hay of Barbados to Lord George Germain, Apr. 13, 1776, CO, 28/56, f. 36; Long, *History*, 2:20.

76. *Abridged Minutes of the Society of Arts &c in Barbados* (1782), vol. 87, 310, SHP. See also Sheppard, *The "Redlegs" of Barbados*, 71, 74.

77. *A Grenada Planter Or, A Full and Impartial Answer to a Letter in the Gazetteer of October 22, 1768* (London, 1768), 17.

78. William Johnson to S.P.G. Secretary, Barbados, Jan. 14, 1737, S.P.G. MSS, A 26, 385–389, quoted in Klingberg, *Codrington Chronicles*, 86.

79. Petition of the Presbyterian inhabitants of Kingston, Oct. 22, 1788, *Journals of the Assembly of Jamaica* (Jamaica, 1804), 8, 413; James Ramsay, *Reply to Personal Invectives and Objections . . .* (London, 1785), 14; Long, *History*, 2:297; Durham, *Caribbean Quakers*, 31–32, 55; Dunn, *Sugar and Slaves*, 104–105, 249. For persecution of Quakers in the seventeenth century, see Durham, *Caribbean Quakers*, 18–25, 31, 34, 35, 52; [Henry Frere] *A Short History of Barbados, From its First Discovery and Settlement, To the End of the Year 1767* (London, 1768), 34.

80. Donald Harman Akenson, *If the Irish Ran the World: Montserrat, 1630–1730* (Montreal, 1997), 46, 150.

81. Long, *History of Jamaica*, 2:295; Dunn, *Sugar and Slaves*, 108, 178; Pitman, *The Development of the British West Indies*, 29–30; Gordon Merrill, "The Role of Sephardic Jews in the British Caribbean Area During the Seventeenth Century," *CS* 4, no. 3 (1964), 32–49.

82. Quoted in Goveia, *Slave Society in the British Leeward Islands*, 289; see also pp. 271–83, 289–307. Caldecott, *Church in the West Indies*, 75.

83. *A Narrative of the Complaint against Governor Melvill* (London, 1770), 89; Edward L. Cox, *Free Coloreds in the Slave Societies of St. Kitts and Grenada, 1763–1833* (Knoxville, Tenn., 1984), 4.

84. Rev. William Smith of Nevis, quoted in Jordan, *White over Black*, 185. The only

exception was the Society for the Propagation of the Gospel, which aimed to convert slaves in Barbados but ran a slave plantation to finance the mission. James Ramsay, *An Essay on the Treatment and Conversion of African Slaves in the British Sugar Colonies* (London, 1784), 178–79.

85. Linda Colley, *Britons: Forging the Nation, 1707–1837* (New Haven, Conn., 1992), 5.

86. R. John Singh, *French Diplomacy in the Caribbean and the American Revolution* (New York, 1977); Altagracia Ortiz, *Eighteenth Century Reforms in the Caribbean: Miguel de Mesas, Governor of Puerto Rico, 1769–76* (Rutherford, N.J., 1983).

87. Walter Nisbit to Ellis Yonge (?), Oct. 5, 1772, quoted in Johnston, "The Sugar Plantations of the Heirs of Lady Frances Stapleton," 140; John Pinney to Peter Eaton, June 2, 1776, Pinney MSS, Letter Book IV.

88. Samuel Martin to Rev. Mr. Wharton, Feb. 15, 1774, BL Add MSS 41350, f. 157.

89. Michael Zuckerman, "Identity in British America: Unease in Eden," in *Colonial Identity in the Atlantic World, 1500–1800*, ed. Nicholas Canny and Anthony Pagden (Princeton, N.J., 1987), 115.

Chapter 2. Black Majorities

1. Philip Morgan, "British Encounters with Africans and African Americans, Circa 1600–1780," in *Strangers Within the Realm: Cultural Margins of the First British Empire*, ed. Bernard Bailyn and Philip D. Morgan (Chapel Hill, N.C., 1991), 214; Orlando Patterson, "Slavery and Slave Revolts: A Sociohistorical Analysis of the First Maroon War, 1665–1740," in *Maroon Societies*, ed. Richard Price 2nd edn. (Baltimore, 1979), 276; M. J. Steel, "A Philosophy of Fear: The World View of the Jamaican Plantocracy in a Comparative Perspective," *JCH* 27, no. 1 (1993), 2, 4–5, 7, 15–16.

2. Memorial of Stephen Fuller to Lord George Germain, Dec. 23/24, 1778, Fuller MSS 256, f. 103, Nicholas M. Williams Ethnological Collection, BCL.

3. *Journal of the Assembly of Jamaica*, Nov. 28, 1749, quoted in Monica Schuler, "Ethnic Slave Rebellions in the Caribbean and the Guianas," *JSH* 3 (1969–70), 381.

4. For a summary of the causes of high mortality rates among slaves in the British Caribbean, see Richard B. Sheridan, *Doctors and Slaves: A Medical and Demographic History of Slavery in the British West Indies, 1660–1834* (Cambridge, 1985), 98–101, 168, 188–203, 221–227, 243–247, 323, 329; Richard S. Dunn, *Sugar and Slaves: The Rise of the Planter Class in the English West Indies, 1624–1713* (Chapel Hill, N.C., 1972), 319; David Watts, *The West Indies: Patterns of Development, Culture and Environmental Change Since 1492* (Cambridge, 1987), 366, 368.

5. Monica Schuler, "Akan Slave Rebellions in the British Caribbean," in *Caribbean Slave Society and Economy*, ed. Hilary Beckles and Verene Shepherd (Kingston, Jamaica, 1991), 374; John Thornton, "The Coromantees: An African Cultural Group in Colonial America," Paper presented to the National Endowment of the Humanities Summer Seminar at Johns Hopkins University, Summer 1993; Michael Mullin, *Africa in America: Slave Acculturation and Resistance in the American South and the British Caribbean, 1736–1831* (Urbana, Ill., reprinted 1994), 13–14, 27, 30, 235.

6. Mullin, *Africa in America*, 42, 2, 201–2, 268.

7. Edward Long, *The History of Jamaica*, 3 vols. (London, 1774), 2:462; Zachary Bayly to Lyttelton, Nov. 26, 1765, LP 1763–66; JAJ, Aug. 6, 1766, CO, 142/45.

8. *StJC*, May 2–26 and June 12–14, 1768; *Westminster Journal*, June 18, 1768; extract of a letter from Montserrat, to a gentleman in Glasgow, dated June 8, 1768, *Gazetteer and New Daily Advertiser*, Aug. 6, 1768; Petition of the Council and Assembly of Montserrat to King, enclosed in Governor Woodley to Hillsborough, Nov. 16, 1770, CO, 152/50; Admiral Pye to Stephens, May 16, 1768, CO, 152–48. Mullin, *Africa in America*, 221, gives a different explanation of the discovery of the plot from the *StJC*, June 14–16, 1768.

9. *StJC*, Dec. 21–23, 1769; Minutes of the Council of Nevis, Apr. 14, 1768, CO, 186/4; *Middlesex Journal*, June 16–19, 1770; Governor Payne to Dartmouth, Dec. 17, 1773, CO, 152/54.

10. Council Minutes of Barbados, Dec. 20, 1768, quoted in Karl Watson, *The Civilised Island Barbados: A Social History, 1750–1816* (Barbados, reprinted 1983), 89; *StJC*, June 26–29, 1773.

11. JAT, Jan. 23, Aug. 7, 1771, CO, 288/1; *Bingley's Journal*, Apr. 20, 1771.

12. JAT, Aug. 7, 1771, CO, 288/1; Governor Leyborne to Dartmouth, Apr. 1, 1774, CO, 101/17 fos. 249, 250; JAT, Apr. 4, 1774, Oct. 10, 1775, CO, 288/1.

13. Long, *History*, 2:348.

14. Memorial of Stephen Fuller to Germain, Dec. 23/24, 1778, Fuller MSS 256, f. 113, BCL; extract from Bryan Edwards in Price, *Maroon Societies*, 243–244; Long, *History of Jamaica*, 2:344, 350. See also Mavis Campbell, *The Maroons of Jamaica, 1655–1796: A History of Resistance, Collaboration and Betrayal* (Trenton, N.J., 1990), 54, 142, 153, 214, 246.

15. Edwards, quoted in Price, *Maroon Societies*, 234. See also R. C. Dallas, *History of the Maroons*, 2 vols. (London, 1803), 1:128–129.

16. *Audie alterem Partem . . .* (London, 1770), 56–57; JAD, Mar. 12, 1772, CO, 74/3.

17. William L. Leyborne to Thomas Gage, Oct. 11, 1772, Gage Papers, American Series 114, WLCL. The *Boston Gazette* is quoted in Pauline Maier, *From Resistance to Revolution: Colonial Radicals and the Development of American Opposition to Britain, 1765–1776* (New York, reprinted 1974), 188. J. Paul Thomas, "The Caribs of St. Vincent: A Study in Imperial Maladministration, 1763–73," *JCH*, 18, no. 2 (1983), 60–73, reviews the British debate about ethics of the war. Resolution of the Special Council, St. Vincent, Dec. 18, 1772, CO, 101/17, f. 37.

18. Troop distributions in the colonies are usefully summarized in J. A. Houlding, *Fit for Service: The Training of the British Army, 1715–1795* (Oxford, 1981), 412–413: eight regiments in 1764; six in 1765–72; five in 1772–75; three in 1776. The size of regiments varied especially between war and peace. After 1763, there was a total of about 440 men in each regiment when complete.

19. A. P. Thornton, *West-India Policy Under the Restoration* (Oxford, 1955), 251; John Shy, *Toward Lexington: The Role of the British Army in the Coming of the American Revolution* (Princeton, N.J., 1965), 20, 40–43; Dunn, *Sugar and Slaves*, 145; Helen Hill Miller, *Colonel Parke of Virginia: "The Greatest Hector in Town"* (Chapel Hill, N.C., 1989), 194, 199.

20. Jamaica paid additional subsistence allowances to locally recruited provincial

regiments as early as the reign of Charles II and again in the 1730s. Additional subsistence on an ad hoc basis was common during the early French Wars, King William's and Queen Anne's wars with Louis XIV. Examples are given in Shy, *Toward Lexington*, 27, 28; Reginald Hargreaves, *The Bloodybacks: The British Servicemen in North America and the Caribbean, 1655–1783* (London, 1968), 185.

21. Lord Hillsborough to Governor Trelawny, Aug. 11, 1768, CO, 137/63, f. 52; "Some Observations of the Best Methods of Victualling the Troops in Jamaica," P. Hunter Lt. Col. 1st Battl. 60th Regt., Nov. 12, 1783, CO, 137/83, f. 204. Hargreaves, *The Bloodybacks*, 52, 55, lists army salaries in the mid-eighteenth century. The calculations are based on an average for the 1750s and 1760s of £140 local currency in Jamaica per £100 sterling and £170 local currency in Antigua per £100 sterling. Exchange rates are listed in John J. McCusker, *Money and Exchange in Europe and America, 1600–1775: A Handbook* (Chapel Hill, N.C., 1978), 253, 261.

22. In 1774, an officer received an additional allowance of £1 per week, 10s week for a wife, 5s per week for a child; a private soldier received 5s per week, 3s 9d for a wife, and 2s 6d for a child. Lodging allowances of between £20 per year and £50 per year were paid to officers, the amount depending on their rank and seniority. Long, *History*, 2:304.

23. JAA, Dec. 14, 1778, CO, 9/28; David Barry Gaspar, *Bondmen and Rebels: A Study of Master-Slave Relations in Antigua with Implications for Colonial British America* (Baltimore, 1985), 268.

24. JAJ, Committee of Correspondence to Stephen Fuller, Sept. 21, 1768, CO, 140/47; Richard Pares, *War and Trade in the West Indies* (Oxford, 1963), 262; "Return of sick in the three regiments in the ceded islands" (1768), WO, 1/50, f. 25.

25. JAJ, Dec. 13, 1766, CO, 140/44; JAA, Aug. 19, 1762, CO, 9/27.

26. Roger Hope Elletson to Charles Lownes, July 11, 1766, Roger Hope Elletson Letter book, *JHR* 1 (Dec. 1946), 212. According to Campbell, *The Maroons of Jamaica*, 72, 196, troops received bounties from the legislature of Jamaica for slitting the ears and maiming the bodies of maroons, similar to the practice in Surinam. Long, *History*, 2:304, reports that troops in Jamaica saved between 1s and 1s 6d per gallon. The legislature hoped that the incentive would encourage soldiers to purchase better quality rum, which might be less detrimental to their health. See also p. 316.

27. JAA, June 28, 1764, CO 9/27, and Dec. 5, 1772, CO, 9/34; Hargreaves, *The Bloodybacks*, 94.

28. Roger Hope Elletson to Alexr. Brown, July 16, 1766, Roger Hope Elletson Letter Book, *JHR* 1 (Dec. 1946), 213; JAJ, Dec. 11, 1771, CO, 140/50, Nov. 20, 1767, CO, 140/44, Nov. 25, 1767, and Dec. 3, 1766, CO, 140/45; John French Capt. 48th Foot to Lord Barrington, Dominica, Aug. 1, 1776, WO, 1/50, f. 123.

29. Governor Lyttelton to the Board of Trade, Oct. 8, 1765, CO, 137/33. The building of parish barracks was part of a series of measures introduced in response to the 1760 slave revolt in Jamaica. See C. Roy Reynolds, "Tacky and the Great Slave Rebellion of 1760," *JJ* 6 (June 1972), 7, 2–3; Long, *History*, 2:308–309. "Journal of an Officer Travelling in America and the West Indies" (Lord Adam Gordon), in *Travels in the American Colonies, 1690–1783*, ed. Newton D. Mereness (New York, 1961), 376, 379; JAJ, Sept. 30, 1770, CO, 140/50; "An Account of the ordinary and extraordinary expenses of the Government of the Island of Jamaica," 1773, CO, 137/70, f. 102;

Memorial of Parish of St. Dorothy to the Assembly of Jamaica, JAJ, Dec. 6, 1767, CO, 140/44.

30. Pares, *War and Trade*, 262, 258–261; JAJ, Jan. 26, 1775, CO, 9/35, and Dec. 9, 1768, CO, 140/47. Henry Wilmot, agent of Leeward Islands, to the Secretary of State for War, Jan. 22, 1763, WO, 1/981. Wilmot requested an increase to the previous peak of seven hundred troops in Antigua rather than a decrease; for Jamaica, see the Address to the King (1764), in *Acts of Privy Council of England: Colonial Series*, ed. William L. Grant and James Munro, 6 vols. (London, 1908–12), 4:548. "Journal of an Officer," in *Travels in the American Colonies*, 379. Lord Adam Gordon described the disappointment of Jamaicans who expected two thousand troops to remain on the island.

31. JAB, Feb. 23, 1780, CO, 31/39. See also Selwyn H. H. Carrington, "West Indian Opposition to British Policy: Barbadian Politics, 1774–82," *JCH* 17 (1982), 26–48; Neville A. T. Hall, "Governors and Generals: The Relationship of Civil and Military Commands in Barbados, 1783–1815," *CS* 10 (Jan. 1971), 93–112. C. P. Clarke, "Imperial Forces in Barbados," *JBMHS* 32 (1968), 174–180. Troops were periodically stationed on the island during wartime, including the American Revolutionary War when General Vaughan withdrew most of his troops in protest at the defiance of the local assembly, which refused to quarter the army.

32. William Dickson, *Letters on Slavery* (London, 1789), 93; Captain Bruce to Governor Spry, Jan. 1, 1771, CO, 28/54, f. 19; Dickson, *Letters on Slavery*, 107. For exceptional characteristics of Barbados, see Jack Greene, *Pursuits of Happiness: The Social Development of Early Modern British Colonies and the Formation of American Culture* (Chapel Hill, N.C., 1988), 155–157; Karl Watson, *The Civilised Island Barbados: A Social History, 1750–1816* (Bridgetown, Barbados, reprinted 1983); Michael Craton, *Testing the Chains: Resistance to Slavery in the British West Indies* (Ithaca, N.Y., 1982), 49.

33. Hilary Beckles, *A History of Barbados from Amerindian Settlement to Nation State* (Cambridge, 1990), 55–56; John C. Fitzpatrick, ed., *The Diaries of George Washington*, 4 vols. (Boston, 1925), 1:29; Sir John Gay Alleyne in the *Barbados Mercury*, Nov. 24, 1787, quoted by Beckles, *A History of Barbados*, 56. For the effective internal policing of Barbados, see Beckles, *Black Rebellion in Barbados: The Struggle Against Slavery, 1627–1838* (Bridgetown, Barbados, 1984), 27, 30–36, 42, 48–51, 121; Governor Spry to Lord Hillsborough, Nov. 12, 1768, CO, 28/51, f. 62; Hilary Beckles and Karl Watson, "Social Protest and Labour Bargaining: The Changing Nature of Slaves' Responses to Plantation Life in Eighteenth Century Barbados," *S&A* 8 (Dec. 1987), 274; Report of Captain Robert George Bruce (1771), CO, 28/54, fos. 18, 19; Governor Parry to Secretary Sydney, Nov. 12, 1784, CO, 28/60, f. 175.

34. Governor Campbell to Lord Shelburne, Apr. 26, 1782, CO, 137/82. See also Memorial of Stephen Fuller to Germain, Dec. 23, 1778, Fuller MSS, 256, f. 110; JAJ, Nov. 14, 1775, CO, 140/50; Alexander Dirom, *Thoughts on the State of the Militia of Jamaica* (Jamaica, 1783), 12, 16, 19; Long, *History*, 1:123–156.

35. *Public Advertiser*, Aug. 28, 1771. See also *Bingley's Journal*, Aug. 31, 1771.

36. Memorial of Stephen Fuller, Agent for Jamaica, to Lord George Germain, Sept. 20, 1779, CO, 137/75, f. 57; French governor quoted in Pares, *War and Trade*, 264. David Buisseret, "The Elusive Deodand: A Study of Fortified Refuges," *JCH* 6–7 (1973), 70, notes that the British surrendered at Tobago in 1781 when the French commander began to systematically burn the plantations.

37. Sir William Young, *The West-India Common-Place Book* (London, 1807), 210; Petition of the West India Planters and Merchants to the King, Dec. 16, 1779, SHP, vol. 88, f. 32; Christopher Codrington, quoted in W. I. Laws, "The Administration of the Leeward Islands, 1699–1721" (M. Litt. thesis, Edinburgh University, 1969), 41; George F. Tyson, "The Carolina Black Corps: Legacy of Revolution (1782–1798)," *Revista/Review Interamericana* 5 (Winter 1975–76), 655.

38. Pares, *War and Trade*, 159, 259, 262; JAA, Nov. 18, 1773, CO, 9/34; Governor Sir Ralph Payne to Lord Dartmouth, Dec. 17, 1773, CO, 152/54, f. 12; Governor Lyttelton to Lord Townshend, Oct. 29, 1762, WO, 1/49, f. 249; Governor Dalling to Sir Peter Parker, July 13, 1781, CO, 137/80, f. 128.

39. Long, *History*, 2:309 (my emphasis); Nathaniel Phillips to Hibbert, Purrier and Horton, Kingston, Jamaica, Oct. 7, 1776, quoted in Clare Taylor, "Planter Comment on Slave Revolts in Eighteenth Century Jamaica," *S&A* 3, no. 3 (1982), 245–246.

40. Gaspar, *Bondmen and Rebels*, 268; Grant and Munro, *Acts of Privy Council*, 4:548.

41. JAStK, June 7, 1770, CO, 241/11; JAJ, Dec. 31, 1773, CO, 140/52.

42. Memorandum of Brig. Gen. Rooke and Dr. Hunter, June 23, 1783, CO, 137/83, f. 198. For personal experience of a soldier, see A. S. Lewis, ed., *Redcoats in the Caribbean: Recollections by James Aytoun* (Blackburn, Lancashire, UK Lancashire 1984), 16. Private James Aytoun recalled a pathetic instance in Dominica in 1791 in which soldiers had accidentally killed some innocent slaves in mistaking them for runaways.

43. Long, *History*, 2:309, contains a list of the barracks including their situation and their capacity for accommodating troops. Governor Keith to Lord George Germain, Mar. 20, 1777, CO, 137/72, f. 81. Note the criticisms of Governor John Dalling against distributing troops throughout the island in his "Thoughts," CO, 137/82, f. 373. Philip Wright, "War and Peace with the Maroons, 1730–1739," *CQ* 16 (1970), 11, notes that as early as 1731, when two regiments were sent to Jamaica against the maroons, the colonels complained about the dispersion of their regiments.

44. Contemporary planter and historian Bryan Edwards, quoted in Craton, *Testing the Chains*, 130–131; W. Woodley to Barrington, June 6, 1768, WO, 1/50, f. 40. For unconventional methods of maroon warfare, see Campbell, *The Maroons of Jamaica*, 62; Patterson, "Slavery and Slave Revolts," 252, 259. Bryon Farwell, *Mr. Kipling's Army: All the Queen's Men* (New York, 1981), 65, describes the tradition of the Twenty-Ninth Foot.

45. JAT, Aug. 7, 1771, CO, 288/1; Address of legislature of Tobago to the King, JAT, Nov. 5, 1774, CO, 288/1. Campbell, *The Maroons of Jamaica*, 40, notes that troops in Jamaica had begun to wear light green and blue, in addition to carrying lighter baggage and arms, as early as the beginning of the eighteenth century.

46. Robert Stewart, President of Tobago, to Admiral (Pye?), Nov. 25, 1770, Adm., 1/309; JAJ, Dec. 18, 1773, CO, 140/52. For use of warships in suppressing slave rebellions, see Campbell, *The Maroons of Jamaica*, 76, 77: Admiral Pye to Stephens, Apr. 1, May 16, 1768, Adm., 1/308; StJC Jan. 8–1 1774.

47. David Geggus, "The Enigma of Jamaica in the 1790s: New Light on the Causes of Slave Rebellions," *WMQ* 3rd ser., 44 (1987), 295. For the 1760 revolt, see Reynolds, "Tacky and the Great Slave Rebellion of 1760," 5–8; Carl A. Lane, "Concerning Jamaica's 1760 Slave Rebellions," *JJ* 7 (Dec. 1973), 2–4. For Jamaican revolts in 1765 and 1766, see JAJ, Nov. 23, 1765 and Aug. 6, 1766, CO 140/45; Committee of

Correspondence to Stephen Fuller, JAJ, Sept. 21, 1768, CO, 140/47, f. 34. For the Carib War, see JAStV, Mar. 14, 1771, CO, 263/2. For the Honduras rebellion, see O. Nigel Bolland, "The Social Structure and Social Relations of the Settlement in the Bay of Honduras (Belize) in the Eighteenth Century," *JCH* 6–7 (1973), 14, 15. For Tobago, see Memorial of the Legislature of Tobago to the Secretary of State for America, Aug. 12, 1775, CO, 288/1; JAT, Jan. 23, 1771, CO, 288/1; JAT, Apr. 10, 1780, CO, 288/3.

48. Geggus, "The Enigma of Jamaica in the 1790s," 293. The Barbados conspiracy of 1689 and the Jamaican conspiracy of 1776 were both planned in anticipation of the withdrawal of troops. Beckles, *Black Rebellion in Barbados*, 45; Wright, "War and Peace with the Maroons," 13. The governor of Dominica complained in 1797 that the maroons "were perfectly acquainted with our expedition and were prepared for us" and "we have reason to suspect that they have too many friends in every direction along the shore to leave them ignorant of any step taken against them." Quoted in Bernard Marshall, "Marronage in Slave Plantation Societies: A Case Study of Dominica, 1785–1815," *CQ* 22 (1976), 28.

49. Edward Long, "History of Taxation," British Library, Long Papers, Add MS 12403, f. 160. D. J. Murray, *The West Indies and the Development of Colonial Government, 1801–1834* (Oxford, 1965), 39, notes that even in the nineteenth century nonpayment was used as a bargaining strategy with the imperial government. For the use of "tacks," see Shy, *Toward Lexington*, 28, 41; JAJ, Apr. 10, 1770, CO, 140/4.

50. For the introduction of better accountability, see JAJ, Dec. 12, 1769, and Feb. 13, Feb. 18, Dec. 20, 1770, CO, 140/47. For the use of troops in civil proceedings, see JAJ, Oct. 31, 1769, Dec. 12, 1769, CO, 140/47. For the opposition to billeting, see JAJ, Apr. 17, 1780, CO, 140/61; Dalling's "Some thoughts relative to the further improvements to be made in the forts and fortifications and General defence of the Island of Jamaica" (1780), CO, 137/82, f. 373.

51. Governor Sir Ralph Payne of the Leeward Islands to Lord Dartmouth, Jan. 12, 1775, CO, 152/55. Jamaican troops were always answerable ultimately to the governor, who was generally a former soldier. Neville A. T. Hall, "The Relationship of Civil and Military Commands," *CS* 10, no. 4 (1971), 93–112 notes that the situation was more complicated in the Lesser Antilles in the American and French Revolutionary Wars when the military commanders assumed responsibility for the troops, to the annoyance of the civil governors and sometimes the assemblies.

52. Assembly Address to the King, JAJ, Sept. 20, 1768, CO, 140/47. See Pares, *War and Trade*, 257–58, for the changing attitude of British government. See JAB, Feb. 23, 1780, CO, 31/39, for the claim that subsistence allowances were a form of indirect taxation.

53. Shy, *Toward Lexington*, 53. Other historians have put more emphasis on the long-term antipathy toward the army, especially Douglas Leach, *Roots of Conflict: British Armed Forces and Colonial Americans, 1677–1763* (Chapel Hill, N.C., 1986).

54. Bouquet, quoted in Leach, *Roots of Conflict*, 87, 93. Bouquet fulminated that South Carolinians were "extremely pleased to have soldiers to protect their plantations, but will feel no inconveniences from them making no great difference between a soldier and a Negro." Quoted in M. Eugene Sirmans, *South Carolina: A Political History, 1663–1763* (Chapel Hill, N.C., 1966), 322. For the opposition of South Carolina to troops, see Jack P. Greene, "The South Carolina Quartering Dispute, 1757–1758," *SCHM* 60

(1959), 193–204; Greene, *The Quest for Power: The Lower Houses of Assembly of the Southern Royal Colonies, 1689–1776* (New York, 1963), 372; W. Roy Smith, *South Carolina as a Royal Province, 1719–1776* (New York, 1903), 194–195, 358–359; Edward McCrady, *The History of South Carolina Under the Royal Government, 1719–1776* (New York, 1899), 619–620; Sirmans, *South Carolina*, 320–324. For security problems in South Carolina, see Jack Greene, "Colonial South Carolina and the Caribbean Connection," in his *Imperatives, Behaviors and Identities: Essays in Early American Cultural History* (Charlottesville, Va., 1992), 68–87. For an account of colonial slavery in South Carolina, see Peter Wood, *Black Majority: Negroes in Colonial South Carolina from 1670 Through the Stono Rebellion* (New York, 1974); Kurt William Nagel, "Empire and Interest: British Colonial Defense Policy, 1689–1748" (Ph.D. thesis, Johns Hopkins University, 1992), 110, 112, 310, 335, 481–82, 483, 486. James A. Henretta, *The Evolution of American Society, 1700–1815: An Interdisciplinary Analysis* (Lexington, Mass., 1973), 113. The number of blacks living in South Carolina was lower than that of any of the island colonies, never exceeding 60 percent of the population during the colonial period and actually declining in the 1760s.

55. Petitions enclosed in Governor Woodley to Lord Hillsborough, Nov. 16, 1770, CO, 152/50; JAN, May 29, Aug. 10, 1770, CO, 186/5.

56. JAD, Oct. 7, 1771, CO, 74/3; JAT, Jan. 23, 1771, CO, 288/1; JAG, Mar. 14, 1771, CO, 263/2; JAJ, Dec. 17, 1771, CO, 140/50. JAJ, Dec. 31, Nov. 27, 1773, CO, 140/52 show that a widow of an officer received £1 3s 9d per week and her child 5s per week; a private's widow received 5s per week and her child 2s 6d per week. Address of the Assembly of Tobago, Apr. 11, 1774, CO, 288/1.

Chapter 3. The Sugar Islands

1. John J. McCusker and Russell R. Menard, *The Economy of British America, 1607–1789* (Chapel Hill, N.C., 1985), 166; David Watts, *The West Indies: Patterns of Development, Culture and Environmental Change Since 1492* (Cambridge, 1990), 272; Richard Sheridan, "The Development of the Plantations to 1750," in *Chapters in Caribbean History*, ed. Douglas Hall, Elsa Goveia, and F. Roy Augier (Barbados, 1970), 22.

2. Richard S. Dunn, *Sugar and Slaves: The Rise of the Planter Class in the English West Indies, 1624–1713* (New York, reprinted 1973), 224.

3. Sheridan, "The Development of the Plantations to 1750," 32, 47; Sheridan, "An Era of West Indian Prosperity, 1750–1775," in *Chapters in Caribbean History*, ed. Douglas Hall, Elsa Goveia, and F. Roy Augier (Barbados, 1970), 85, 88–89; Yu Wu, "Jamaican Trade, 1688–1769: A Quantitative Study" (Ph.D. thesis, Johns Hopkins University, 1995), 69, 525, 563, finds that sugar accounted for between 75.23 percent and 79.26 percent of the value of total exports, molasses 0.75 percent to 1.01 percent, and rum 9.9 percent in 1769. He gives a figure for rum only as a percentage of cargo, but I have calculated rum as a total value of exports using his table 10.6; Philip R. P. Coelho, "The Profitability of Imperialism: The British Experience in the West Indies, 1768–1772," *Explorations in Economic History* 10 (1973), 259–260, finds that sugar, along with rum and molasses, ranged from a low of 73.6 percent in 1769 to a high of 77.9 percent in 1770 as a proportion of the value (at official estimates) of the total exports of the British Caribbean between 1768 and 1772.

4. *The Evidence Delivered on the Petition Presented by the West-India Merchants . . .* (London, 1775), 11; James Ramsay, *An Essay on the Treatment and Conversion of African Slaves in the British Sugar Colonies* (London, 1784), 80; William Dickson, *The Mitigation of Slavery* (London, 1814), 161; Philip Curtin, *The Rise and Fall of the Plantation Complex: Essays in Atlantic History* (Cambridge, 1990), 83.

5. Wu, "Jamaican Trade," 165. See 164, table 3.15, 565, 161. See also 124–61.

6. Edward Long, *The History of Jamaica*, 3 vols. (London, 1774), 1:380. His view is endorsed by recent studies, including Verene A. Shepherd, "Livestock and Sugar: Aspects of Jamaica's Agricultural Development from the Late Seventeenth to the Early Nineteenth Century," *HJ* 34 (1991), 627–28, 631, 634; B. W. Higman, *Jamaica Surveyed: Plantation Maps and Plans of the Eighteenth and Nineteenth Centuries* (Kingston, Jamaica, 1988), 9; Wu, "Jamaican Trade," 212.

7. Richard B. Sheridan, "The Condition of the Slaves in the Settlement and Economic Development of the British Windward Islands, 1763–1775," *JCH* 24, no. 2 (1990), 125; Macartney to Germain, Oct. 12, 1777, CO, 101/21, f. 24.

8. Richard Pares, *A West India Fortune* (London, 1950), 70, called it a "silver age"; Sheridan, "An Era of West India Prosperity," 74, called it an "era of prosperity"; McCusker and Menard, *The Economy of British America, 1607–1789*, 167, note: "On the eve of the American Revolution, the planters of Barbados and the other British sugar islands were near the peak of their prosperity."

9. John McCusker, *Money and Exchange in Europe and America 1600–1775: A Handbook* (Chapel Hill, N.C., 1978), 258, 262, 271; Lowell J. Ragatz, *The Fall of the Planter Class in the British Caribbean, 1763–1833* (Washington, D.C., 1928), 132; Sheridan, "The Condition of the Slaves."

10. The credit crisis had serious economic implications for the British West Indies in 1773. It was precipitated by the collapse of several major trading houses in Europe and the recall of debts by merchants. Some historians have cited the crisis as the trigger cause of the American Revolution in Virginia, but the debts owed by the planters to Britain exceeded those owed throughout North America. Jamaica alone owed between two million and three million pounds; Grenada owed two million pounds; and St. Kitts over seven hundred pounds. The credit crisis did not provoke a confrontation with the imperial government because the recovery from the crisis of 1772 was rapid. Parliament hastened to the aid of the planters with the 1773 Act, which permitted foreigners to advance loans at 5 percent interest, on the security of their land in the islands, and to recover debts even during wartime. Another 1774 Act removed limits on the interest rates of British loans secured against property in the British Caribbean. For discussion of the credit crisis in the British West Indies, see Richard B. Sheridan, "The British Credit Crisis of 1772 and the American Colonies," *JEH* 20, no. 2 (June 1960), 161–186; Sheridan, "The British Sugar Planters and the Atlantic World, 1763–1775," in *Eighteenth-Century Florida and the Caribbean*, ed. Samuel Proctor (Gainesville, Fla., 1976), 4; Sheridan, *Sugar and Slavery: An Economic History of the British West Indies, 1623–1775* (London, 1974), 464, 466; Ragatz, *The Fall of the Planter Class*, 134.

11. Adam Smith, *An Inquiry into the Nature and Causes of the Wealth of Nations*, ed. R. H. Campbell and A. S. Skinner (Oxford, 1976), 4:vii b. 14; David Patrick Geggus, *Slavery, War, and Revolution: The British Occupation of Saint Dominigue, 1793–1798* (Oxford, 1982), 1, 6, 7; Watts, *The West Indies*, 270, 272–73, 286; Dunn, *Sugar and Slaves*, 205.

12. Watts, *The West Indies*, 277; Ragatz, *The Fall of the Planter Class*, 127; Noel Deer, *History of Sugar*, 2 vols. (London, 1949–50), 2:430; Richard Pares, *Yankees and Creoles: The Trade Between North America and the West Indies Before the American Revolution* (London, 1956), 113; R. B. Sheridan, "The Molasses Act and the Market Strategy of the British Sugar Planters," *JEH* 17 (1957), 62–64; Eric Williams, *Capitalism and Slavery*, 5th edn. (London, 1981), 122.

13. Rev. Robert Robertson, *A Supplement to the Detection of the State and Situation of the Present Sugar Planters of Barbados and the Leeward Islands* (London, 1733), 16; Malachy Postlethwayt, *Great Britain's Commercial Interest Explained* (London, 1757), 1:494; *Proceedings and Debates of the British Parliaments Respecting North America, 1754–1783*, ed. R. C. Simmons and P. D. G. Thomas, 6 vols. (New York, 1982–), 2:384: examination of Thomas Collet by William Beckford, May 6, 1766; John Lord Sheffield, *Observations on the Commerce of the American States* 2nd edn. (London, 1783), 161–64.

14. "Comparison Between the French and British Sugar Colonies," *Morning Post*, July 22, 1775; Ragatz, *The Fall of the Planter Class*, 126–27; Ragatz, "Absentee Landlordism in the British Caribbean, 1750–1833," *AH* 5, no. 1 (1931), 7–24; Douglas Hall, "Absentee-Proprietorship in the British West Indies to About 1850," *JHR* 4 (1964), 15–35; William A. Green, "The Planter Class and the British West Indian Sugar Plantation Before and After Emancipation," *EcHR* 2nd ser. 26 (1973), 448–63.

15. Rev. Robert Robertson, *A Detection of the State and Situation of the Present Sugar Planters of Barbados and the Leeward Islands* . . . (London, 1732), 5; F. W. Pitman, *The Development of the British West Indies, 1700–1763* (New Haven, Conn., 1917), 246, 333; Ragatz, *The Fall of the Planter Class*, 68, 102; Oliver M. Dickerson, *The Navigation Acts and the American Revolution* (Philadelphia, 1951), 173, 175; Sheridan, "The Molasses Act," 65, 68–69; David H. Makinson, *Barbados: A Study of North-American-West-Indian Relations, 1739–1789* (The Hague, 1964), 25, 42–43, 55; Richard Stein, "The French Sugar Business in the Eighteenth Century: A Quantitative Study," *JBH* 22, no. 1 (1980), 4; Wu, "Jamaican Trade," 40–41, notes that some 326.60 thousand cwt of illegal sugar was reexported from Jamaica to Britain in 1769, representing a tenfold increase in comparison to the years 1709–1744; Resolutions of the Assembly of Antigua, Jan. 24, 1764, CO, 152/30, Dd. 36.

16. Sheridan, "The Molasses Act," 67; Smith, *The Wealth of Nations*, 4:vii, v, 31; Ragatz, *The Fall of the Planter Class*, 53, 106–107; Richard Pares, *Merchants and Planters* (Cambridge, 1960), 26; E. B. Schumpeter, *English Overseas Trade Statistics, 1697–1808* (Oxford, 1960), 61–62, 65; Ralph Davis, "English Foreign Trade, 1700–1774," in *The Growth of English Overseas Trade in the Seventeenth and Eighteenth Centuries*, ed. W. E. Minchinton (London, 1969), 112; Sheridan, *Sugar and Slavery*, 22, 23, 45, 433–34.

17. Stein, "The French Sugar Business," 10.

18. Coelho, "The Profitability of Imperialism," 260, 254, 264, table 4.

19. The Providence "State of the Trade" MS, Moses Brown Papers (Miscellaneous Series), I, 13, quoted in F. B. Wiener, "The Rhode Island Merchants and the Sugar Act," *NEQ* 3 (1930), 489; Gilman M. Ostrander, "The Colonial Molasses Trade," *AH* 30 (1956), 79, 83; William D. Houlette, "Rum-Trading in the American Colonies Before 1763," *JAH* 27 (1934), 139; John McCusker, "The Rum Trade and the Balance of Payments of the Thirteen Continental Colonies" (Ph.D. thesis, University of Pittsburgh, 1970), 11.

20. Rev. Robert Robertson, *A Supplement to the Detection of the State and Situation*

of the Present Sugar Planters, 23, 19–55, 86–92; Houlette, "Rum-Trading in the American Colonies," 131; Ostrander, "The Colonial Molasses Trade," 79.

21. Pitman, *The Development of the British West Indies*, 260–61 n.38.

22. Neil R. Stout, *The Royal Navy in America, 1760–1775: A Study of Enforcement in the Era of the American Revolution* (Annapolis, Md., 1973), 11–12.

23. Pitman, *The Development of the British West Indies*, 266 n. 6, 301 n.12, 418, 419, 421, 424; Agnes Whitson, "The Outlook of the Continental American Colonies on the British West Indies, 1760–1775" *PSQ* 45, no. 1 (Mar. 1930), 72; Richard Pares, *War and Trade in the West Indies, 1739–1763* (Oxford, 1936), 454; Carl Bridenbaugh and Roberta Bridenbaugh, *No Peace Beyond the Line: The English in the Caribbean, 1624–1690* (New York, 1972), 345; Wiener, "The Rhode Island Merchants and the Sugar Act," 466–67.

24. Commodore Arthur Forrest to Philip Stephens, Oct. 8, 1769, Adm., 1/238; Rodney to Philip Stephens, May 3, 1773, Adm., 1/239.

25. Wiener, "The Rhode Island Merchants and the Sugar Act," 466; Stout, *The Royal Navy in America*, 15, 21–23, 26.

26. Stout, *The Royal Navy in America*, 40.

27. Ibid., 27, 31, 32, 42.

28. George Grenville, the leading minister, wanted a two-pence tax and so did John Temple, the surveyor-general, who suggested that British molasses was taxed in addition. Wiener, "The Rhode Island Merchants and the Sugar Act," 467.

29. "The Farmer," *Pennsylvania Journal*, Aug. 23, 1764; *Collections of the Connecticut Historical Society* xviii, *Fitch Papers* 2 (1920), 271–272, quoted in Sir Lewis Namier, *England in the Age of the American Revolution*, 2nd edn. (London, 1961), 239; *Providence Gazette and Country Journal*, Oct. 27, 1764; *The Works of John Adams, Second President of the United States with a Life of the Author*, ed. Charles Francis Adams, 10 vols. (Boston, 1856), 2:49.

30. Jack Sosin, *Agents and Merchants: British Colonial Policy and the Origins of the American Revolution, 1763–1775* (Lincoln, Neb., 1965), 45, 46 n.23. The view that the Sugar Act of 1764 marked the culmination of a long-standing antagonism between the North Americans and West Indians is a major theme of Pitman, *The Development of the West Indies*, vii–viii, 333–34, 353; Pares, *War and Trade*, 81; Williams, *Capitalism and Slavery*, 117; John C. Miller, *Origins of the American Revolution* (Stanford, Calif., new impression 1985), 101–2; Edmund S. Morgan and Helen M. Morgan, *The Stamp Act Crisis*, rev. edn. (New York, 1963), 44, 51, 57; John L. Bullion, *A Great and Necessary Measure: George Grenville and the Genesis of the Stamp Act, 1763–1765* (Columbia, Mo., 1982), 38.

31. Edmund Burke, "Speech on American Taxation," Apr. 19, 1774, in *Edmund Burke on Government Politics and Society*, ed. B. W. Hill (London, 1975), 125.

32. Dickerson, *The Navigation Acts and the American Revolution*, 175.

33. Report of Committee Investigating the Jurisdiction of Vice Admiralty Courts, Dec. 18, 1789, *Journals of the Assembly of Jamaica* (Jamaica, 1805), 8:548.

34. Stephen Fuller to Governor Lyttelton, Dec. 24, 1765, LP 1763–66 (my emphasis).

35. Joseph Albert Ernst, "The Currency Act Repeal Movement: A Study of Imperial Politics and Revolutionary Crisis, 1764–1767," *WMQ* 25 (1968), 186–87; P. D. G. Thomas, *British Politics and the Stamp Act Crisis: The First Phase of the American Revolu-*

tion, 1763–1767 (Oxford, 1975), 269; Paul Langford, *The First Rockingham Administration* (Oxford, 1973), 204–5; Francis Armytage, *The Free Port System in the British West Indies: A Study in Commercial Policy, 1766–1822* (London, 1953), 39–40, 41.

36. Langford, *The First Rockingham Administration*, 204, 206–7; Thomas, *British Politics and the Stamp Act Crisis*, 271. The terms of the Free Port Act are described in Sheridan, *Sugar and Slavery*, 356, 459–62.

37. Long, *History*, 1:539, 541, 548–55. For newspaper adverts, see *Boston Newsletter*, Feb. 28, 1771; *New York Mercury*, Feb. 25, 1771. Governor William Trelawny to Hillsborough, Nov. 24, 1770, CO, 137/66, f. 7; George Metcalf, *Royal Government and Political Conflict in Jamaica, 1729–1783* (London, 1965), 180.

38. Langford, *The First Rockingham Administration*, 207; Sosin, *Agents and Merchants*, 98; Thomas, *British Politics and the Stamp Act Crisis*, 299–300.

39. See M. Jensen, eds., *Tracts of the American Revolution, 1763–1767* (Indianapolis, Ind., 1967), 313 for John Adams, "Novanglus," Feb. 13, 1775; Sidney Mintz, *Sweetness and Power: The Place of Sugar in Modern History* (New York, reprinted 1986), 256; Ernst, "The Currency Act Repeal Movement," 39.

40. In contrast, the navy, customs, and vice-admiralty courts became objects of vilification in North America owing to their role in enforcing trade laws that were also tax measures. The officials targeted by North Americans did not meet a hostile receptions when they went to the British West Indies, individuals such as Dr. William Spry, the judge of the notorious vice-admiralty court at Halifax; John Robinson, the collector of customs at Rhode Island and then commissioner of the infamous Board of Customs at Boston; and Thomas Oliver, the deputy judge of the vice-admiralty court in Massachusetts. Spry became governor of Barbados (1768–72). For details of Spry's career in Halifax, see Carl Ubbelohde, *The Vice-Admiralty Courts and the American Revolution* (Chapel Hill, N.C., 1960), 128–129. Spry initially continued to receive his salary of £800 in addition to his salary of £2,000 as governor. He tried to keep the position at Halifax as governor but failed. After fighting a duel with James Otis and leaving Boston, Robinson never "sailed for England with his bride and drifted out of the stream of history" but became a plantation attorney in St. Kitts. Morgan and Morgan, *The Stamp Act Crisis*, 376; William Legge, 2nd earl of Dartmouth to Governor Payne, Mar. 2, 1774, CO, 152/54; J. R. V. Johnston, "The Sugar Plantations of the Heirs of Lady Frances Stapleton in Nevis and St. Christopher (1746–1810)" (M.A. thesis, University of Wales, 1964), 144.

41. Samuel Martin, Sr., to Samuel Martin, Jr., Oct. 18, 1768, Add MSS 41348, BL; same to same, Dec. 31, 1768, Add MSS 41348, BL, f. 34; Samuel Martin to Henry Hulton, Feb. 10, 1770, Add MSS 41350, fos. 105–6; same to same, n.d., c. 1770, Add MSS 41350, f. 156; Martin to Ashton Warner Byam, May 8, 1776, Add MSS 41351, f. 80.

42. T. R. Clayton, "Sophistry, Security, and Socio-Political Structures in the American Revolution; Or, Why Jamaica Did Not Rebel," *HJ* 29 (1986), 329; "Reflections on the Situation, Trade, and Connection of Great Britain and the American Colonies," *Middlesex Journal*, Dec. 17, 1775.

43. Wiener, "The Rhode Island Merchants and the Sugar Act," 489.

44. Adam Smith to William Eden, Dec. 15, 1783, *Correspondence of Adam Smith*, ed. E. C. Mossner and Ian Simpson (Oxford, 1977), 271.

45. *Remarks On the Evidence delivered on the Petition Presented by The West-India Planters and Merchants* ... (London, 1777), 11; Dunn, *Sugar and Slaves*, 336; Sheridan,

"The Development of the Plantations," 28, 34, 43; JAB, Jan. 21, 1766, CO, 31/33; *The Evidence Delivered*, 14; "Answers to Queries," enclosed in Sir Ralph Payne to William Legge, 2nd earl of Dartmouth, June 20, 1774, CO 152/54; Robertson, *A Detection of the State and Situation of the Present Sugar Planters*, 49; James Rymer, *A Description of the Island of Nevis* (London, 1775), 3.

46. Michael Mullin, *Africa in America: Slave Acculturation and Resistance in the American South and the British Caribbean, 1736–1831* (Urbana, Ill., reprinted 1994), 129; Wu, "Jamaican Trade," 303, 551, 556.

47. Sheridan, "The Condition of the Slaves," 139; Sheridan, "The Development of the Plantations," 43; Mullin, *Africa in America*, 53, 125–26, 129, 140, 147, 152, 155; Shepherd, "Livestock and Sugar," 631.

48. Wu, "Jamaican Trade," 93.

49. Coelho, "Profitability of Imperialism," 266–268; Sheridan, "The Development of the Plantations," 47; Wu, "Jamaican Trade," 84, 93, finds that 95.33 percent of sugar and 85.40 percent of rum was shipped to Europe, mainly Britain. "North American ports . . . provided relatively small outlets for Jamaica products" (239).

50. Evidence of William Kelly, a New York merchant, Feb. 12, 1766, in *Proceedings and Debates of the British Parliament Respecting North America, 1754–1783*, ed. Simmons and Thomas, 2:212; John Temple to Thomas Whatley, Sept. 10, 1764, in "The Bowdoin and Temple Papers," *MHSC*, 6th ser., 9 (Boston, 1897), 24, quoted in Sosin, *Agents and Merchants*, 87.

51. Wu, "Jamaican Trade," 239, 88–89, 92–93; Karl Watson, *The Civilised Island Barbados: A Social History, 1750–1816* (Barbados, reprinted 1983), 14.

52. Robertson, *A Supplement*, 17; Rymer, *A Description of the Island of Nevis*, 4; Smith, *The Wealth of Nations*, 1:xi b. 32.

53. Robertson, *A Detection of the State and Situation of the Present Sugar Planters*, 43; Johnston, "The Sugar Plantations," 132.

54. Robertson, *A Supplement*, 17, 19; H. C. Bell, "The West Indies Trade Before the American Revolution," *AHR* 22, no. 2 (1917), 275 n.10; John Stevenson, *An Address to Bryan Edwards* (London, 1784), 38.

55. List of Exports from Jamaica, Jan. 1–Dec. 31, 1774, CO, 137/70, f. 94; Sheridan, "An Era of West Indian Prosperity," 95; McCusker, "The Rum Trade," 162, 166, 176, 184, 191, 232.

56. Lawrence A. Harper, "The Effects of the English Navigation Laws," in *The Era of the American Revolution*, ed. Richard B. Morris (New York, reprinted 1965), 12, estimates that the imperial preference cost the consumer in Britain £446,125 sterling per annum; R. P. Thomas, "The Sugar Colonies of the Old Empire: Profit or Loss for Great Britain?" *EcHR* 2nd ser., 21 (1968), 38; Coelho, "The Profitability of Imperialism," 260, 264–65.

57. Sheridan, *Sugar and Slaves*, 299; Kenneth Morgan, "Bristol West India Merchants in the Eighteenth Century," *TRHS* 6th ser., 3 (1993), 187.

58. Malachy Postlethwayt, *The African Trade: The Great Pillar and Support of the British Plantation Trade in America* (London, 1745), 13–14. See also Pares, *Merchants and Planters*, 39–40, 83–83; Philip D. Curtin, *The Atlantic Trade: A Census* (Madison, Wis., 1969), 137, 212, 213, 216; Dunn, *Sugar and Slaves*, 237; S. L. Engerman, "Some Economic and Demographic Comparisons of Slavery in the United States and the British West Indies," *EcHR*, 2nd ser., 29 (1976), 258–275; Engerman, "Quantitative

and Economic Analysis of West Indian Slave Societies," in *Comparative Perspectives on Slavery in the New World Plantation Societies*, ed. N. Rubin and A. Tuden (New York, 1977), 597; Seymour Drescher, *Econocide: British Slavery in the Era of Abolition* (Pittsburgh, 1977), 35; James A. Rawley, *The Transatlantic Slave Trade: A History* (New York, 1981), 14, 324, 330; Sheridan, "An Era of West Indian Prosperity," 81.

59. Coelho, "The Profitability of Imperialism," 270 n.29.

60. Marc Egnal, *A Mighty Empire: The Origins of the American Revolution* (Ithaca, N.Y., 1988), 6–7; Pares, *War and Trade*, 216–226; Namier, *England in the Age of the American Revolution*, 273–82.

61. Evidence of John Sharpe, Apr. 3, 1753, CO, 301/60, quoted in Pitman, *The Development of the British West Indies*, 343 n.23; the letter book of Rev. James Ramsay, Oxford, MSS Brit. Emp. S2 f. 12, RHL; Ramsay, *Objections to the Abolition of the Slave Trade, with Answers* (London, 1788), 9; Edward Long, "History of Jamaica" (draft of 2nd edn., c. 1799), Add MS 12407, fos. 14–15, verso, BL, quoted in Edward Brathwaite, *The Development of Creole Society in Jamaica, 1770–1820* (Oxford, 1978), 76–77; Sheffield, *Observations on the Commerce of the American States*, 86.

Chapter 4. Sons of Liberty?

1. Historians have traditionally focused their discussions on the compliance of Jamaica and Barbados rather than the opposition of the Leeward Islands. For example, Donna J. Spindel, "The Stamp Act Crisis in the British West Indies," *JAS* 11, no. 2 (Aug. 1977), 211, 213, cites the high proportion of slaves, the military and naval presence, and the economic and military dependence on Britain to explain the passivity of Jamaica and Barbados. However, these conditions also existed in the Leeward Islands. Spindel, 216–17, cites the low proportion of slaves in the towns of the Leeward Islands, which again was also true of the towns of Barbados and Jamaica, although the proportion was higher in all the islands than in the towns of the Chesapeake. She also argues (217) that the slaves of the Leeward Islands were more passive, but the 1736 conspiracy in Antigua was unequaled in Barbados in the eighteenth century. Spindel makes no reference to the friction with North America and the impact of the North American boycott.

2. Adolph Koeppel, *The Stamps That Caused the American Revolution: The Stamps of the 1765 British Stamp Act for America* (New York, 1976), 14. The Windward Islands also paid stamp duties, but the tax was unevenly enforced because of logistical problems in the collection after their recent acquisition from France. See Koeppel, 11. Outside the British West Indies, only Quebec and Montreal, together with West Florida, paid stamp duties.

3. Robert W. Tucker and David C. Hendrickson, *The Fall of the First British Empire: Origins of the American War of Independence* (Baltimore, 1982), 215.

4. Spindel, "The Stamp Act Crisis," 203; Merrill Jensen, *The Founding of a Nation* (Oxford, 1968), 98; Jack P. Greene, *Peripheries and Center: Constitutional Development in the Extended Polities of the British Empire and the United States, 1607–1788* (Athens, Ga., 1990), 139.

5. Oliver M. Dickerson, *The Navigation Acts and the American Revolution* (Philadelphia, 1951), 192; Dora May Clark, *The Rise of the British Treasury: Colonial Admin-*

istration of the Eighteenth Century (New Haven, Conn., 1960), 275; Lawrence Henry Gipson, *The British Empire Before the American Revolution*, 15 vols. (New York, reprinted 1936–70), 10:275.

6. Koeppel, *The Stamps That Caused the American Revolution*, 48, 51, 52, 63, 66; Edmund S. Morgan, *Prologue to Revolution: Sources and Documents on the Stamp Act Crisis, 1764–1766* (Chapel Hill, N.C., 1959), 38–40.

7. Report of J. Lloyd on the Stamp Act, Oct. 18, 1772, in Dickerson, *The Navigation Acts*, 192; Koeppel, *The Stamps That Caused the American Revolution*, 34–35; David H. Makinson, *Barbados: A Study of North-American-West-Indian Relations, 1739–1789* (The Hague, 1964), 71. Samuel Martin of Antigua told correspondents that twice as much revenue was likely to be raised in the Caribbean than North America: Samuel Martin, Sr., to Samuel Martin, Jr., Aug. 5, 1765, Add MSS 41347, f. 205, BL; See also same to same, July 1, 1765, Add MSS 41350, f. 19, BL; Martin, Sr., to James Gordon, July 28, 1765, Add MSS 41350, BL.

8. Edward Long, *The History of Jamaica*, 3 vols. (London, 1774), 1:535; Samuel Estwick, *A Letter to the Revd. Josiah Tucker* . . . (London, 1776), 62.

9. *Gentleman's Magazine*, July 1764, 337, and October 1765, 487; Paul Langford, *The First Rockingham Administration, 1765–1766* (Oxford, 1973), 113–114; Add. MS 3303, f. 190, BL, for evidence of Beeston Long in Commons Committee on American Papers, Feb. 17, 1766; Long, *History*, 1:536; A. Christelow, "Contraband Trade Between Jamaica and the Spanish Main, and the Free Port Act of 1766," *Hispanic American Historical Review* 22 (1942), 309–343; F. Armytage, *The Free Port System in the British West Indies* (London, 1953); F. W. Pitman, *The Development of the British West Indies, 1700–1763* (New Haven, Conn., 1917), 150–55; Jensen, *The Founding of a Nation*, 175.

10. William L. Grant and James Munro, eds., *Acts of Privy Council of England: Colonial Series*, 6 vols. (London, 1908–1912), 4:548; "Journal of an Officer," in *Travels in the American Colonies, 1690–1783*, ed. Newton Mereness (New York, reprinted 1961), 379 notes that Lord Adam Gordon described the disappointment of Jamaicans who expected two thousand troops to remain on the island; Henry Wilmot, agent to the Leeward Islands, to the Secretary of State for War, Jan. 22, 1763, WO, 1/981, PRO, requested an increase to the previous peak of seven hundred troops in Antigua.

11. Estwick, *A Letter to the Revd. Josiah Tucker*, 58–59; Charles Price et al. to Stephen Fuller, Dec. 1764, LP 12 (iii), 926, f. 2, WRO. I am grateful to Jack Greene for alerting me to this letter and sending me a photocopy.

12. Elsa Goveia, *A Study on the Historiography of the British West Indies* (Washington, D.C., 1980), 56; T. R. Clayton, "Sophistry, Security, and Socio-Political Structures in the American Revolution; Or, Why Jamaica Did Not Rebel," *HJ* 29 (1986), 319. [Sir John Gay Alleyne], *A Letter to the North American, on Occasion of His Address to the Committee of Correspondence in Barbadoes* (Bridgetown, Barbados, 1766), 16; Charles Price et al. to Stephen Fuller, Dec. 1764, LP 12 (iii), 926, f. 2, WRO; Samuel Martin, Sr., to Samuel Martin, Jr., May 30, 1766, Aug. 5, 1765, Add. MSS 41347, BL; speech of Henry Duke JAB, Sept. 10, 1771, CO, 31/36; [Alleyne], *A Letter to the North American*, 25: Barbadians later regretted their appeal to the charter but felt that "they were led into the Error by their fellow subjects on the continent."

13. Charles Price et al. to Stephen Fuller, Dec. 1764, LP 12 (iii), 926, f. 2, WRO. Makinson, *Barbados*, 71–72. JAB, Nov. 25, 1765, CO, 31/32; Michael Craton, "The Planter's World in the British West Indies," in *Strangers Within the Realm: Cultural*

Margins of the First British Empire, ed. Bernard Bailyn and Philip D. Morgan (Chapel Hill, N.C., 1991), 316; George Walker to the Committee of Correspondence of Barbados, Nov. 26, 1765, CO, 31/33.

14. *Barbados Mercury*, Apr. 19, 1766, Library Company of Philadelphia; Charles Price et al. to Stephen Fuller, Dec. 1764, LP 12 (iii), 926, f. 2, WRO; Samuel Martin, Sr., to Samuel Martin, Jr., May 30, 1766, Aug. 5, 1765, Add. MSS 41347; P. D. G. Thomas, *British Politics and the Stamp Act Crisis: The First Phase of the American Revolution, 1763–1767* (Oxford, 1975), 91, 93, 98; Sir Lewis Namier and John Brooke, *British House of Commons 1754–1790*, 3 vols. (London, 1964), 2:75–78.

15. [Alleyne], *A Letter to a North American*, 10; *Candid Observations on Two Pamphlets Lately Published . . .* (Barbados, 1766), 25; Samuel Martin, Sr., to Samuel Martin, Jr., May 30, 1766, Aug. 5, 1765, Add. MSS 41347.

16. Pauline Maier, "John Wilkes and American Disillusionment with Britain," *WMQ* 3rd ser., 20 (1963), 373–395. This was ironic because Wilkes had little interest in colonial affairs at the time and even aspired to become governor of Jamaica where he hoped "to extinguish party in that island, and to give real strength to government." See John Sainsbury, *Disaffected Patriots: London Supporters of Revolutionary America, 1769–1782* (Montreal, 1987), 32. His famous duel was fought against the son of Samuel Martin of Antigua.

17. Rev. John Lindsay to Robertson, Aug. 6, 1776, Robertson-McDonald Papers, National Library of Scotland, Edinburgh, MS 3942, fos. 259–264, quoted in Clayton, "Sophistry, Security, and Socio-Political Structures in the American Revolution," 335; John Gardiner to John Wilkes, Basseterre, St. Christopher, Mar. 26, 1769, Wilkes Correspondence, Add MSS 30, 870, BL; John de Ponthieu to Wilkes, Grenada, n.d., Add MSS 30, f. 204, BL. *StJC*, Sept. 26–28, 1769; *StJC*, Jan. 7–10, 1769, claimed that the Assembly of St. Kitts voted money for John Wilkes. The names of West Indians do not appear in anti-Wilkes petitions of the same period. See George Rudé, "The Anti-Wilkite Merchants of 1769," *The Guildhall Miscellany* 2 (1965), 283–304.

18. Agnes M. Whitson, "The Outlook of the Continental American Colonies on the British West Indies, 1760–1775," *PSQ* 45, no. 1 (Mar. 1930), 66 n. 1; [Alleyne], *A Letter to the North American*, 16; Thomas, *British Politics and the Stamp Act Crisis*, 55–60, 74, 94–95; Stephen Fuller to the Jamaican Committee of Correspondence, Feb. 7, Feb. 10, Feb. 16, 1765, Fuller Letter Book 1762–1773, Nicholas M. Williams Ethnological Collection, BCL; R. C. Simmons and P. D. G. Thomas, eds., *Proceedings and Debates of the British Parliaments Respecting North America, 1754–1783*, 6 vols. (New York, 1982–), 2:25, 184.

19. Michael Kammen, *A Rope of Sand: The Colonial Agents, British Politics and the American Revolution* (Ithaca, N.Y., 1968), 29; Langford, *The First Rockingham Administration*, 127; Thomas, *British Politics and the Stamp Act Crisis*, 144; John L. Bullion, "British Ministers and American Resistance to the Stamp Act, October–December 1765," *WMQ* 3rd ser., 49, no. 1 (1992), 100, 103; George Walker to the Barbados Committee of Correspondence, Nov. 19, 1765, Minutes of the Council of Barbados, CO, 31/33.

20. Jack M. Sosin, *Agents and Merchants: British Colonial Policy and the Origins of the American Revolution, 1765–1775* (Lincoln, Neb., 1965), 6, 77, 79; Kammen, *A Rope of Sand*, 29, 76; Langford, *The First Rockingham Administration*, 113, 127; Thomas, *British Politics and the Stamp Act Crisis*, 226; Paul Langford, "The First Rockingham Ministry and the Repeal of the Stamp Act: The Role of the Commercial Lobby and

Economic Pressures," in *Resistance, Politics, and the American Struggle for Independence, 1765–1775*, ed. Walter H. Conser Jr. et al. (Boulder, Colo., 1986), 93–94, 97–100, 103–5; Stephen Fuller to the Committee of Correspondence, Feb. 22, 1766, LP 1763–1766; Jensen, *The Founding of a Nation*, 173; Spindel, "Stamp Act Crisis in the British West Indies," 206, states that six West Indians voted against the repeal; *StJC*, Mar. 6–8, 1766.

21. William Tuckett to George Thomas, Dec. 5, 1765, CO, 152/47.

22. Ibid., *Massachusetts Gazette*, Dec. 6, 1765; *Boston Post-Boy*, Dec. 9, 1765.

23. *London Chronicle*, Jan. 25–28, 1766; Tuckett to Thomas, Dec. 5, 1765, CO, 152/47.

24. *Massachusetts Gazette*, Dec. 6, 1765; *Boston Post-Boy*, Dec. 9, 1765; *Maryland Gazette*, Dec. 10, 1765; Council Minutes of St. Kitts, Nov. 5, 1765, CO, 241/9. Koeppel, *The Stamps That Caused the American Revolution*, 14, 40.

25. *Supplement to the Massachusetts Gazette*, Feb. 27, 1766; *An Apparition of the Late Maryland Gazette*, Dec. 10, 1765; *Boston Gazette*, Dec. 13, 1765.

26. *Boston Gazette*, Dec. 13, 1765; *Massachusetts Gazette*, Dec. 12, 1765; Tuckett to Thomas, Dec. 5, 1765, CO, 152/47; *Supplement to the Massachusetts Gazette*, Feb. 27, 1766, Dec. 6, 1765; *Maryland Gazette*, Nov. 14, 1765; *Boston Post-Boy*, Dec. 30, 1765; Tuckett to Thomas, Dec. 5, 1765 Council Minutes of St. Kitts, CO, 152/47; Thomas to Conway, Dec. 21, 1765, CO, 152/47; *Boston Evening Post*, June 30, 1766. The riots on November 5 were evidently planned and not spontaneous, according to a Philadelphian correspondent in the *Halifax Gazette*, Dec. 19–26, 1765. For later unflattering references to Tuckett, see *The Caribbean and General Gazette*, Nov. 24, 1770, in the Fulham MSS XX, f. 34, Lambeth Palace, London.

27. John Batho to his father, Nov. 10, 1766, Historical Society of Pennsylvania, AM 9067, John Batho Letter Book, quoted in Spindel, "The Stamp Act Crisis," 217; *Halifax Gazette*, Dec. 18–26, 1765, American Antiquarian Society, Worcester, Mass. Thomas to Conway, Dec. 21, 1765, CO, 152/47; *Maryland Gazette*, Mar. 13, 1766; *Virginia Gazette* (Purdie and Dixon), Apr. 4, 1766; extract from Antigua, Dec. 24, 1765, in *The Boston Gazette and Country Journal*, Feb. 3, 1766.

28. *Pennsylvania Journal and Weekly Advertiser*, Dec. 26, 1765; Thomas to Conway, Dec. 21, 1765, CO, 152/47. Thomas to Conway, Dec. 21, 1765, CO, 152/47; Vernon O. Stumpf, "Josiah Martin and His Search for Success: The Road to North Carolina," *NCHR* 53 (Winter 1976), 64–65; Harper and Hartshorn to Clifford, Nov. 25, 1765, Clifford Correspondence, Historical Society of Pennsylvania, quoted in Spindel, "The Stamp Act Crisis," 217; John Batho to his father, Nov. 10, 1765, Batho Letterbook 1765–67, quoted in Spindel, "The Stamp Act Crisis," 217.

29. *Virginia Gazette* (Purdie and Dixon), Mar. 21, 1766; *Massachusetts Gazette*, Feb. 6, 1766; *Boston Gazette and Country Journal*, Feb. 3, 1766; *Virginia Gazette* (Purdie and Dixon), Mar. 7, Apr. 4, 1766; Harper and Hartshorn to Clifford, Jan. 21, 1766, quoted in Spindel "The Stamp Act Crisis," 219.

30. Koeppel, *The Stamps That caused the American Revolution*, 13, 23; *Maryland Gazette*, Apr. 17, 1766; Report of J. Lloyd on the Stamp Act, Oct. 18, 1772, AO 3 1086, in Dickerson, *The Navigation Acts*, 206; *Pennsylvania Gazette*, June 19, 1766.

31. *New York Mercury*, Dec. 16, 1765. Address of the Assembly of Barbados to Governor Pinfold, Nov. 26, 1765, CO, 31/32; JAB, Dec. 17, 1765, Jan. 21, 1766, CO, 31/32; George Walker to the Barbados Committee of Correspondence, Nov. 19, 1765, CO, 31/33;

32. *StJC*, Feb. 1–4, 1766; *Massachusetts Gazette*, Mar. 27, 1766; Pinfold to Walker,

Pinfold Manuscripts, Library of Congress, quoted in Spindel, "The Stamp Act Crisis," 213; [Alleyne], *A Letter to the North American*, 31, 32; JAB, July 7, 1766, CO, 31/32.

33. Extract of a letter from Barbados, Jan. 23, 1766, *Massachusetts Gazette*, Mar. 27, 1766; Dickerson, *The Navigation Acts*, 193; Pinfold to Halifax, Dec. 17, 1765, CO, 28/50, 68; [Henry Frere], *A Short History of Barbados: From Its First Discovery and Settlement, to the End of the Year 1767* (London, 1768), 79; Koeppel, *The Stamps That Caused the American Revolution*, 14, 84; Makinson, *Barbados*, 75 n. 17; Isaiah Thomas, *The History of Printing in America*, ed. M. A. McCorison (Mass., 1970), 607; *Halifax Gazette*, Jan. 16–23, 1766; *Massachusetts Gazette*, Mar. 20, Mar. 27, 1766. There are four extant examples of stamped Barbadian newspapers deposited at the Public Record Office at Kew (London), the Library Company in Philadelphia, and the American Antiquarian Society at Worcester (Massachusetts).

34. JAB, Jan. 21, 1766; [John Dickinson], *An Address to the Committee of Correspondence in Barbados* . . . (Philadelphia, 1766), iv; JAB, Mar. 18, 1766, CO 31/32; [Kenneth Morrison], *An Essay Toward the Vindication of the Committee of Correspondence in Barbadoes* . . . (Bridgetown, Barbados, 1766), 5; [Alleyne], *A Letter to the North American*, 5, 8; *Candid Observations on Two Pamphlets Lately Published*, 7.

35. *New York Mercury*, Dec. 16, 1765; *The Barbados Mercury*, Feb. 1, 1766; Pinfold to the Board of Trade, Feb. 21, 1766, CO, 28/32, 197; Pinfold to Secretary of State, Aug. 26, 1765, CO, 28/50, 99, and Feb. 21, 1766, CO, 28/50, 105; *Gazetteer and New Daily Advertiser* Sept. 21, 1766; JAB, Jan. 13, 1767, Dec. 3, 1766, CO, 31/32.

36. Charles Price et. al. to Stephen Fuller, Dec. 1764, LP 12 (iii), 926. Grenville warned the colony agents of the Stamp Act in May 1764: John Howell to the secretary of state, May 31, 1766, CO, 137/62, 208; Howell to ?, Feb. 7, 1766, Wentworth Woodhouse Muniments, Sheffield Central Library, England; Thomas, *British Politics and the Stamp Act Crisis*, 93. Neither petition was from Jamaica but rather the work of the agent on behalf of the assembly. For opposition in Jamaica, see also *Halifax Gazette*, Jan. 9–16, 1766, American Antiquarian Society; *StJC*, Jan. 16–18, 1766.

37. Carl Anthony Lane, "The Roots of Jamaican Loyalism, 1760–1766" (Ph.D. thesis, City University of New York, 1978), 364–394; Thomas, *British Politics and the Stamp Act Crisis*, 217; *Georgia Gazette*, Aug. 20, 1766.

38. Dickerson, *The Navigation Acts*, 193; Koeppel, *The Stamps That Caused the American Revolution*, 14. The distributor claimed that the duties raised almost £4,000 sterling in Jamaica: Howell to the secretary of state, May 31, 1766, CO, 137/62, f. 208; *Maryland Gazette*, Feb. 20, 1766; *Halifax Gazette*, Feb. 13–20, 1766; Conway to Lyttelton, Apr. 10, 1766, CO, 137/62.

39. George Metcalf, *Royal Government and Political Conflict in Jamaica, 1729–1783* (London, 1965), 164; Spindel, "The Stamp Act Crisis," 206; Clayton, "Sophistry, Security, and Socio-Political Structures in the American Revolution", 325; Jack Greene, "The Jamaica Privilege Controversy, 1764–66," in his *Negotiated Authorities: Essays in Colonial Political and Constitutional History* (Charlottesville, Va., 1994), 350–94; Lane, "The Roots of Jamaican Loyalism," 367–368; Michael Mullin, *Africa in America: Slave Acculturation and Resistance in the American South and the British Caribbean, 1736–1831* (Urbana, Ill., reprinted 1994), 42.

40. Charles Price et. al. to Stephen Fuller, Dec. 1764, LP 12 (iii), 926.

41. Ibid; Petition of Persons interested in and trading to the Island of Jamaica, Fuller MSS 255, f. 87; Newcastle Papers CCCXLV, Add MS 33030, fos. 186–188. The

difference between the local stamp duties and the Stamp Act was explained before the American Committee in February 1766 by James Irwin. Lane, "The Roots of Jamaican Loyalism," 307–312, makes a much more comprehensive comparison of the different duties. Long, *History*, 2:465–71; Orlando Patterson, *Sociology of Slavery: An Analysis of the Origins, Development and Structure of Negro Slave Society in Jamaica* (Teaneck, N.J., 1969), 271–272.

42. Jack Greene, *Pursuits of Happiness: The Social Development of Early Modern British Colonies and the Formation of American Culture* (Chapel Hill, N.C., 1988), 157–159, 173–174.

43. Richard Glover, *The Evidence Delivered on the Petition Presented by the West-India Planters and Merchants to the Hon. House of Commons* (London, 1775), 14; Richard B. Sheridan, "The Development of the Plantations to 1750," in *Chapters in Caribbean History*, ed. Douglas Hall, Elsa Goveia, and F. Roy Augier (1970), 34, 43; "Answers to Queries," Payne to Dartmouth, June 20, 1774, CO, 152/54; Robert Robertson, *A Detection of the State and Situation of the Present Sugar Planters . . .* (London, 1732), 49; James Rymer, *A Description of the Island of Nevis* (London, 1775), 3; Richard B. Sheridan, "The Crisis of Slave Subsistence in the British West Indies During and After the American Revolution," *WMQ* 3rd ser., 33 (1976), 615–641.

44. John C. Miller, *Origins of the American Revolution*, 2nd edn. (Stanford, Calif., 1959), 180; Whitson, "The Outlook of the Continental American Colonies," 70, 76; Morgan, *The Stamp Act Crisis*, 43–45.

45. *Maryland Gazette*, Jan. 30, 1766; *Georgia Gazette*, June 11, 1766; F. W. Pitman, "Slavery on the British West India Plantations in the Eighteenth Century," *JNH* 11 (1926), 588; Whitson, "The Outlook of the Continental American Colonies," 78, 79, 81; Morgan, *The Stamp Act Crisis*, 215; Makinson, *Barbados*, 72–73; David Brion Davis, *The Problem of Slavery in Western Culture* (Ithaca, N.Y., 1966), 442; F. W. Knight, "The American Revolution and the British Caribbean," in *Slavery and Freedom in the Age of the American Revolution*, ed. Ira Berlin and Ronald Hoffman (Charlottesville, Va., 1983), 242.

46. Lyman H. Butterfield, ed., *The Diary and Autobiography of John Adams*, 4 vols. (Cambridge, Mass., 1961), 1:261; Charles Francis Adams, ed., *The Works of John Adams*, 10 vols. (Boston, 1856), 2:173–174; *Massachusetts Gazette*, Jan. 2, 1766.

47. *Massachusetts Gazette*, Mar. 27, 1766; *Maryland Gazette*, Jan. 30, 1766.

48. Morgan, *The Stamp Act Crisis*, 215; Pinfold to the Board of Trade, Feb. 21, 1766, CO, 28/32; *Massachusetts Gazette*, Jan. 2, 1766.

49. Samuel Martin, Sr., to Samuel Martin, Jr., Dec. 20, 1765, Add MSS 41347, 211, BL; copy of a letter from Antigua, Dec. 20, 1765, in Historical Manuscripts Commission, ed., 3 vols. *Dartmouth Papers of William Legge, 2d Earl of Dartmouth* (London, 1895), 2:495.

50. Kender Mason to Charles Lowndes, July 15, 1766, R. 32, 4.1, Wentworth Woodhouse Muniments; evidence of Beeston Long in the House of Commons, Feb. 17, 1766, Add MSS 330 30, 190, BL.

51. Sir William Young, *The West-India Common-Place Book* (London, 1807), 161.

52. *Massachusetts Gazette*, Feb. 6, 1766; *Halifax Gazette*, Feb. 27–Mar. 6, 1766; *Maryland Gazette*, Mar. 13, 1766; extract of a letter from St. Kitts, *New York Mercury*, Dec. 23, 1765.

53. Ralph Payne, Lord Lavington, to John Sargent, secretary to the treasury,

Aug. 14, 1803, West Indies Misc. Box 1, New York Public Library; see Elsa Goveia, *Slave Society in the British Leeward Islands* (New Haven, Conn., 1965), 51–102, for an excellent discussion of the administration and political system of the Leeward Islands; C. S. S. Higham, *The Development of the Leeward Islands Under the Restoration* (Cambridge, 1920); W. I. Laws, "The Administration of the Leeward Islands, 1699–1721" (M. Litt. thesis, Edinburgh University, 1969); J. H. Parry, "The Patent Offices in the British West Indies," *EHR* 69 (Apr. 1954), 220–25.

54. Thomas to Halifax, Apr. 11, 1765, CO, 152/47, 6; Thomas to Conway, Dec. 21, 1765, CO, 152/47, fos. 116–118; Treasury Minutes, Aug. 19, 1765, Wentworth Woodhouse Muniments; *Massachusetts Gazette*, Dec. 6, Jan. 23, 1766. The distance between islands also encouraged insularity—Tuckett was probably particularly unpopular in St. Kitts because he was a native of Nevis.

55. Thomas to Conway, Dec. 21, 1765, CO, 152/47, fos. 116–118; Minutes of the Council of St. Kitts, Dec. 5, 1765, CO, 241/9; *Virginia Gazette* (Purdie and Dixon), Apr. 4, 1766.

56. Samuel Martin, Sr., to Samuel Martin, Jr., Jan. 13, 1766, Add MSS 41347, 214, BL; Same to Same, Mar. 5, 1766, Add MSS 41347, 218; Thomas to the Board of Trade, Jan. 29, 1766, CO, 152/30, 50–51; Anthony Stokes, *A View of the Constitution of the British Colonies* . . . (London, 1783), 240; Bryan Edwards, *The History Civil and Commercial of the British West Indies*, 5 vols., 5th edn. (London, 1819), 2:395.

57. Extracts relating to the Stamp Act, President Verchild, June 14, 1766, SHP, vol. 49.

58. Rev. Robert Robertson, *A Detection of the State and Situation of the Present Sugar Planters* . . . (London, 1732), 50, 52; James George Douglas to the Board of Trade, received Mar. 19, 1745, in Pitman, *The Development of the British West Indies*, 39; Evangeline W. Andrews and Charles M. Andrews, eds., *Journal of a Lady of Quality* . . . (New Haven, Conn., 1921), 92; Burt to Germain, Mar. 30, 1780, CO, 152/60, 103.

59. Isaiah Thomas, *The History of Printing in America*, ed. Marcus A. McCorison (Worcester Mass., 1970), 601–10; Waldo Lincoln, "List of Newspapers of the West Indies and Bermuda in the Library of the A.A.S.," in *AAS* 36 (1926), 130–55; Bradford F. Swan, *The Spread of Printing, Western Hemisphere: The Caribbean Area* (Amsterdam, 1970); Swan, "A Checklist of Early Printing on the Island of Antigua, 1745–1800," in *Papers of the Bibliographical Society of America* (3rd qtr. 1956), 1:285–92; Frank Cundall, "The Press and Printers of Jamaica Prior to 1820," *AAS* 26 (1916), 290–412; Cundall, *A History of Printing in Jamaica from 1717 to 1834* (Kingston, Jamaica, 1935); Douglas McMurtrie, *The First Printing in Dominica* (London, 1932); McMurtrie, *Early Printing in Barbados* (London, 1933); McMurtrie, *The First Printing in Jamaica* (Evanston, Ill., 1942); McMurtrie, *Early Printing on the Island of Antigua* (Evanston, Ill., 1943); Glory Robertson, "Early Jamaican Printing," *JJ* 3, no. 4 (Dec. 1969); Robert Cave, "Printing Comes to Jamaica," *JJ* 9, no. 283 (1975), 11–18; Wilberforce Eames, "The Antigua Press and Benjamin Mecom, 1748–1765," *AAS* 38 (Oct. 1928), 303–48; E. M. Shiltstone, "Some Notes on Early Printing Presses and Newspapers in Barbados," *JBMHS* 26 (1958), 119–33. In 1718 *The Weekly Jamaica Courant* became the first newspaper in Jamaica and the second regular newspaper to "appear anywhere in the Americas." *The Barbados Mercury* was the first newspaper "to have been published twice a week, for any considerable time, in any part of America," although it reverted to a weekly edition. About 1746, Thomas Howe "probably was the first printer" at St.

Kitts where he published the *St. Christopher Gazette*. In 1748, Benjamin Franklin founded the *Antiguan Gazette* in Antigua through Thomas Smith who had worked for him in Philadelphia and New York. When Smith died in 1752, Franklin sent his own nephew to win the business of all the Leeward Islands "there being no other Printer." In 1765, William Smith founded *The Freeport Gazette, or the Dominica Chronicle* in Dominica and William Weyland founded *The Royal Grenada Gazette* in Grenada.

60. Cave, "Printing Comes to Jamaica," 12; Thomas, *History of Printing*, 604, 607; Eames, "The Antigua Press and Benjamin Mecom," 304, 308.

61. Koeppel, *The Stamps That Caused the American Revolution*, 83–84. Thomas printed criticisms of the British West Indies in the *Halifax Gazette* during the Stamp Act crisis and later denounced the island printers in his *History of Printing*. Ironically, Thomas "nearly completed a contract to go and settle in the West Indies" in 1770 (163).

62. Namier and Brooke, *The Commons, 1754–1790*, 2:479; Stephen Fuller to the Jamaican Committee of Correspondence, Feb. 16, 1765, Fuller Letter Book 1762–1773, 70, BCL.

63. Stumpf, "Josiah Martin and His Search for Success," 64–65; *Barbados Mercury*, Apr. 19, 1766; speech of James Maycock, JAB, Sept. 10, 1771, CO, 31/36; [Dickinson], *An Address to the Committee of Correspondence in Barbados*, iv, v, 3–4, 15.

64. Minutes of the Council of St. Kitts, Dec. 17, 1765, CO, 241/9; JAN, Feb. 8, 1766, CO, 186/5; *Virginia Gazette* (Purdie and Dixon), Apr. 4, 1766; *Massachusetts Gazette*, Mar. 20, 1766; Stumpf, "Josiah Martin and His Search for Success," 64–65; JAA, Dec. 19, 1765, CO, 9/28; Josiah Martin to Samuel Martin, Jr., Apr. 15, 1767, Martin Papers, Add MSS XVI, 41361, fos. 99–100; JAN, June 24, 1766; Address of the Council and Assembly of St. Kitts, SHP vol. 49.

65. [Morrison], *An Essay*, [John Gay Alleyne], *A Letter to the North American on Occasion of His Address to the Committee of Correspondence in Barbadoes* (Bridgetown, Barbados, 1766); *Candid Observations on Two Pamphlets*; Whitson, "The Outlook of the Continental American Colonies, 77–81; Jerome S. Handler, *A Guide to the Source Materials for the Study of Barbados, 1627–1834* (Carbondale, Ill., 1971), 38–41; Jack P. Greene, "Changing Identity in the British Caribbean: Barbados as a Case Study," in *Colonial Identity in the Atlantic World, 1500–1800*, ed. Nicholas Canny and Anthony Pagden (Princeton, N.J., 1987), 260–62.

66. [Morrison], *An Essay*, 14.

67. [Alleyne], *A Letter to the North American*, 8; *Candid Observations on two pamphlets*, 4.

68. [Morrison], *An Essay*, 9, 12; [Alleyne], *A Letter to the North American*, 27; *Candid Observations on Two Pamphlets*, 13.

69. [Alleyne], *A Letter to the North American*, 27.

70. [Morrison], *An Essay*, 13; [Alleyne], *A Letter to the North American*, 30.

71. [Morrison], *An Essay*, 4; [Alleyne], *A Letter to the North American*, 10–12; *Candid Observations on Two Pamphlets*, 4.

72. [Morrison], *An Essay*, 15–16; [Alleyne], *A Letter to the North American*, 27.

73. [Morrison], *An Essay*, 10; [Alleyne], *A Letter to the North American*, 42.

74. Bullion, "British Ministers and American Resistance to the Stamp Act," 92.

75. Josiah Martin to Samuel Martin, Jr., Aug. 7, 1767, Add MSS XVI 41361, fos. 110–13.

76. P. D. G. Thomas, *The Townshend Duties Crisis: The Second Phase of the American Revolution, 1767–1773* (Oxford, 1987); John Sainsbury, *Disaffected Patriots: London Supporters of Revolutionary America, 1769–1782* (Montreal, 1987), 37–39, 42, 113, 176, 178; Kammen, *A Rope of Sand*, 232.

77. Samuel Martin, Sr., to Samuel Martin, Jr., Oct. 18, 1768, Add. MSS 41348, f. 28, BL; Same to Same, Dec. 31, 1768, ibid., f. 34; Same to Henry Hulton, June 14, 1768, Add. MSS 41350, f. 71; Same to Samuel Martin, Jr., Sept. 29, 1769, Add. MSS 42347, f. 285.

78. JAB, Feb. 14, 1769, CO, 31/36; *Public Advertiser*, Sept. 14, 1770.

79. [Frere], *A Short History of Barbados*, iv-vi; *Proceedings and Debates*, 2:465, 471, 476, 479; Thomas, *The Townshend Duties Crisis*, 128; *Proceedings and Debates*, 3:226.

80. Franklin B. Wickwire, *British Subministers and Colonial America, 1763–1783* (Princeton, N.J., 1966), 120–30; Dickerson, *The Navigation Acts*, 199; Dora May Clark, *The Rise of the British Treasury: Colonial Administration of the Eighteenth Century* (New Haven, Conn., 1960), 185; Sosin, *Agents and Merchants*, 105 n.29; Lillian M. Penson, *The Colonial Agents of the British West Indies: A Study in Colonial Administration Mainly in the Eighteenth Century* (London, reprinted 1971), 276.

81. Metcalf, *Royal Government and Political Conflict in Jamaica*, 174, notes that Hillsborough, Dartmouth, and Lord George Germain who were all rigid on the questions of British rights in North America but "Nevertheless, regarding Jamaica, all three showed a more tactful consideration and a greater appreciation of the governor of the spot than had most of their predecessors." In other words, they allowed the governors to negotiate with the legislature. The same was true of the other islands. *Essex Gazette*, Oct. 2–9, 1770: "It is said, as an encouragement to the West-India planters for not entering into the views of the American refractory Colonies, that an additional duty will be laid next sessions on foreign Brandies, in order to increase the value and consumption of rum."

82. John Derry, *English Politics and the American Revolution* (New York, 1976), 72, 83; Thomas, *The Townshend Duties Crisis*, 175.

Chapter 5. Winning the Initiative

1. Bernard Bailyn, *The Origins of American Politics* (New York, 1968), 9–10.

2. Details of the rise of the assemblies in the British Caribbean appear in Agnes M. Whitson, *The Constitutional Development of Jamaica, 1620–1729* (Manchester, 1929); Frederick F. Spurdle, *Early West Indian Government: Showing the Progress of Government in Barbados, Jamaica and the Leeward Islands, 1660–1783* (Palmerston, New Zealand, 1963); J. Williamson, *The Caribbee Islands Under Proprietary Patent* (Oxford, 1926); Mary Patterson Clarke, *Parliamentary Privilege in the American Colonies* (New Haven, Conn., 1943); A. P. Thornton, *West-India Policy Under the Restoration* (Oxford, 1956); C. S. S. Higham, *The Development of the Leeward Islands Under the Restoration, 1660–1688: A Study of the Foundations of the Old Colonial System* (Cambridge, 1921); Vincent T. Harlow, *A History of Barbados, 1625–1685* (Oxford, 1926); J. W. Herbert, "Constitutional Struggles in Jamaica, 1748–1776" (M.A. thesis, London University, 1927); George Metcalf, *Royal Government and Political Conflict in Jamaica, 1729–1783* (London, 1965); Warren Alleyne, *The Houses of the Barbados Assembly* (Barbados,

1989); Michael Watson, "The British West Indian Legislatures in the Seventeenth and Eighteenth Centuries: An Historiographical Introduction," in *Parliament and the Atlantic Empire*, ed. Philip Lawson (Edinburgh, 1995), 89–99. Hume Wrong, *Government of the West Indies* (Oxford, 1923), is superficial and often inaccurate.

3. Robert Livingston Schuyler, *Parliament and the British Empire: Some Constitutional Controversies Concerning the Imperial Legislative Jurisdiction* (New York, 1929), 110; Harlow, *A History of Barbados*, 65.

4. Jack P. Greene, *Peripheries and Center: Constitutional Development in the Extended Polities of the British Empire and the United States, 1607–1788* (Athens, Ga., reprinted 1986), 48; Leonard Labaree, *Royal Government in America: A Study of the British Colonial System Before 1783* (New Haven, Conn., 1930), 260.

5. Bailyn, *The Origins of American Politics*, 9–10; John M. Murrin, "Political Developments," in *Colonial British America: Essays in the New History of the Early Modern Era*, ed. Jack Greene and J. R. Pole (Baltimore, 1984), 436.

6. *StJC*, Jan. 12–14, 1769; *Middlesex Journal*, Apr. 19–21, 1770.

7. *Middlesex Journal*, May 26–29, 1770; *Letters to the Earl of Hillsborough . . .* (London, 1770), 33.

8. *Maryland Gazette*, June 1, 1769; JAStK, Oct. 26, 1768; Hillsborough to Woodley, July 31, 1770, CO, 151/50; Aretas Akers to the Rev. James Ramsay, Oct. 29, (1770?), Correspondence of Aretas Akers.

9. Mary Patterson Clarke, "Parliamentary Privilege in the American Colonies," in *Essays in Colonial History Presented to Charles McLean Andrews by His Students* (New York, reprinted 1966), 131, 262. The best account of the privilege dispute, a model of such studies, is Jack Greene, "The Jamaica Privilege Controversy, 1764–66," in his *Negotiated Authorities: Essays in Colonial Political and Constitutional History* (Charlottesville, Va., 1994), 350–394. See also Metcalf, *Royal Government and Political Conflict in Jamaica 1729–1783*, 152–166.

10. JAJ, Mar. 26, 1766, CO, 140/42; [Nicholas Bourke], *The Privileges of the Island of Jamaica Vindicated* (London, 1766), 66.

11. JAJ, Aug. 12, 1766, CO, 140/50, f. 215.

12. Hillsborough to Lt. Gov. Elletston, Feb. 29, 1768, CO, 137/63, f. 11; Hillsborough to Governor Trelawny, June 12, 1770, CO, 137/65, f. 151; JAJ, Nov. 15, 1770, CO, 140/50; JAJ, Sept. 20–21, 1768, CO, 140/47, f. 20; JAJ, Sept. 20, 1768, CO, 140/47; *StJC*, Jan. 21–24, 1769; JAJ, Nov. 20, 1771, CO, 140/50; Governor Trelawny to Hillsborough, May 28, 1770, CO, 137/65, f. 173.

13. JAJ, Nov. 21, 1770, CO, 140/50; Greene, "The Jamaica Privilege Controversy," 393.

14. Edward Long, *The History of Jamaica*, 3 vols. (London, 1774), 1:561; [Bourke], *The Privileges of the Island of Jamaica Vindicated*, 27–28, 44, 45.

15. Long, *History*, 1:4; see *Gazetteer and New Daily Advertiser*, Jan. 11, 1765; for "A discourse from an Old Gentleman to two young members of promising parts, of the Assembly at Jamaica spoken Oct. 5, 1745"; *A Narrative of the Complaint Against Governor Melvill* (London, 1770), 84.

16. Jack Greene, "Political Mimesis: A Consideration of the Historical and Cultural Roots of Legislative Behavior in the British Colonies in the Eighteenth Century," *AHR* 75, no. 2 (1969), 350, 354.

17. Long, *History*, 1:162.

18. Jonathan Blenman, *Remarks on Several Acts of Parliament Relating More Especially to the Colonies Abroad* (London, 1742), 17; Sir John Gay Alleyne, *Remarks upon a Book, Intitled, A Short History of Barbados* (Bridgetown, Barbados, 1768), 70; Long, *History*, 1:56; Governor Melville to the Board of Trade, May 28, 1766, CO, 101/1, f. 132. See also Melville to Shelburne, Dec. 27, 1767, CO, 101/12, f. 54.

19. Anthony Stokes, *A View of the Constitution of the British Colonies* . . . (London, 1783), 243–44; JAB, June 3, 1767, CO, 31/32; Long, *History*, 1:56, 177, 185–186; Greene, "Political Mimesis," 347. See also (Alleyne), *Remarks upon a Book*, 56–57, in which he argues that the differences from the English model only make an independent assembly all the more necessary.

20. Sir Harry Luke, *Caribbean Circuit* (London, 1950), 170–174; A. Caldecott, *The Church in the West Indies* (London, 1898), 33.

21. JAB, June 3, 1767, CO, 31/32; John Poyer, *History of Barbados* (London, 1808), 358–359, misrepresents Alleyne by claiming that he gave himself the right to vote on all occasions. The reverse was in fact the case.

22. JAB, Jan. 21, 1768, CO, 31/32; (Alleyne), *Remarks upon a Book*, 59, 7.

23. JAM, July 4, 1767, CO, 177/10; Losack, acting governor, to Hillsborough, Apr. 27, 1771, CO, 152/51, f. 31; Losack to Michael White, Oct. 7, 1770, CO, 152/51, f. 71; Enclosure of Journal of the Assembly of Montserrat, Sept. 29, Oct. 17, Oct. 24, 1770, CO, 152/51, fos. 75–78; Losack to Hillsborough, Aug. 6, 1771, CO, 152/51, f. 105; Address and Remonstrance of the Assembly of Montserrat with the reply of the acting governor, Richard Hawkshaw Losack, Nov. 3, 1770, CO, 152/51, f. 79.

24. Losack to Hillsborough, Apr. 27, 1771, CO, 152/52, f. 31.

25. JAD, Jan. 6, Jan. 18, Feb. 8, 1768; Governor Melville to Walter Pringle, president of the Council of Dominica, Jan. 28, 1768, CO, 101/12, fos. 61–68; JAD, Mar. 23, Mar. 24, 1774, CO, 74/2.

26. JAStV, Feb. 17, 1772, CO, 263/3; JAStV, in correspondence of the governor, CO, 101/16, f. 191; JAStV, July 1774, CO, 101/17, f. 227.

27. Greene, "Legislative Turnover in British Colonial America," 217. Antigua had three elections between 1766 to 1775 with a 24 percent turnover; Barbados had nine elections in the same time period with a 13.2 percent turnover; Jamaica had six elections with a 35.7 percent turnover; Montserrat had three elections with 25.3 percent turnover; Nevis had ten elections with 29.2 percent turnover; and St. Kitts had nine elections with 43.2 percent turnover. Greene does not give figures for the Windward Islands. My calculations, based on elections from the incomplete minutes in the Public Record Office, are based on his formula. Dominica, in five elections between 1776 and 1775, had a 58.7 percent turnover; Grenada, seven elections with a 57.4 percent turnover; Tobago, three elections with a 51.8 percent turnover; and St. Vincent, two elections with a 44.4 percent turnover.

28. For a full account of the dispute in St. Kitts, cf. A. J. O'Shaughnessy, "The Politics of the Leeward Islands, 1763–1783" (D.Phil. thesis, Oxford University, 1988), 100–135.

29. *New Hampshire Gazette*, Sept. 18, 1772.

30. James Ramsay, *A Reply to the Personal Invectives and Objections* . . . (London, 1785), 26; O'Shaughnessy, "The Politics of the Leeward Islands," 107–111, 120–121; Hillsborough to Losack, Feb. 11, 1771, CO, 152/51. See also Hillsborough to Woodley, Apr. 23, July 31, 1770, CO, 152/50.

31. O'Shaughnessy, "The Politics of the Leeward Islands," 111–115.

32. See William L. Grant and James Munro, eds., *Acts of Privy Council of England: Colonial Series*, 6 vols. (London, 1908–12), 5:278–279, 280, for instructions ordered Apr. 22, 1772 and confirmed June 19, 1772; Ramsay, *A Reply to the Personal Invectives and Objections*, 26.

33. Extract of a letter, dated Grenada, Dec. 23, 1771, *Westminster Journal*, Apr. 4, 1772.

34. *Audi alteram Partem* . . . (London, 1770), 119.

35. Governor Melville to Hillsborough, Oct. 31, 1770, CO, 101/15, fos. 30, 33; "A short state of a few facts and consequences that have happened in the island of Grenada since its submission to the British Arms in 1762," vol. 4; *Bingley's Journal*, July 27, 1771.

36. "Strictures on the Conduct of two successive Administrations with Respects to the civil and religious Establishments in Canada and the Grenadines," *Middlesex Journal*, May 25–27, 1769. See also *Letters to the Earl of Hillsborough* . . . iii–vii. The author of this last pamphlet is identified as Governor Robert Melville in a pamphlet titled *Audi alteram Partem*, 41.

37. "Strictures on the Conduct . . . [concluded]," *Middlesex Journal*, June 8–10, 1769. An unfavorable contrast between British policy in Grenada and North America is also made in *Letters to the Earl of Hillsborough*, 30.

38. "Strictures on the Conduct . . . [concluded]," *Middlesex Journal*, June 8–10, 1769.; extract of a letter, dated Grenada, Dec. 23, 1771, *Westminster Journal*, Apr. 4, 1772.; *Letters to the Earl of Hillsborough*, 28.

39. David H. Makinson, *Barbados: A Study of North-American-West-Indian Relations, 1739–1789* (The Hague, 1964), 85; Michael Craton and James Walvin, *A Jamaica Plantation: The History of Worthy Park, 1670–1970* (London, 1970), 76; T. R. Clayton, "Sophistry, Security, and Socio-Political Structures in the American Revolution; Or, Why Jamaica Did Not Rebel," *HJ* 29 (1986), 327, 343, 344; Governor Leyborne to Dartmouth, Mar. 24, 1773, CO, 101/17, f. 112; same to same, Mar. 12, 1774, CO, 101/17, f. 240.

40. *Virginia Gazette* (Purdie and Dixon), July, 30, 1772, Dec. 23, 1775; JAA, Feb. 13, 1772, CO, 9/31; JAA, Apr. 6, 1775, CO, 9/35.

41. *Virginia Gazette* (Purdie and Dixon), July 30, 1772, Dec. 23, 1775; JAA, Apr. 6, 1775, CO, 9/31; JAA, Apr. 6, 1775, CO, 9/35. CO 152/57 contains the printed addresses of the assemblies of the Leeward Islands to Sir Ralph Payne.

42. Jack Greene, *The Quest for Power: The Lower Houses of Assembly of the Southern Royal Colonies, 1689–1776* (New York, 1963), 416.

43. [John Dickinson], *An Address to the Committee of Correspondence in Barbados* . . . (Philadelphia, 1766).

44. Letter from an eminent Planter in Jamaica to a Gentleman of great consequence in England, July 25, 1765, *Public Ledger*, Oct. 21, 1765. For instructions to the agent relative to the Stamp Act, see Charles Price et. al. to Stephen Fuller, Dec. 1764, LP 12 (iii), 962, f. 2.

45. JAB, June 3, 1772, CO, 31/36.

46. Ibid.; Governor Hay to Dartmouth, Aug. 31, 1774, CO, 28/55.

47. Samuel Martin, Sr., to Henry Hulton, Feb. 10, 1770, Add MSS 41350, fos. 105–106, BL; Same to Samuel Martin, Jr., July 6, 1774, Add MSS 41348, f. 189; Same

to Same, June 13, 1775, ibid., fos. 197–198, 221; Same to Josiah Martin, n.d., Add MSS 41351.

48. Governor Payne to Dartmouth, July 3, 1774, CO, 152/54; Taylor to Arcedeckne, Nov. 19, 1774, Vanneck MSS, 2/7, quoted in Clayton, "Sophistry, Security, and Socio-Political Structures in the American Revolution," 328.

49. MSWIM, Mar. 3, Mar. 16, 1774; Public Ledger Jan. 18 1773 quoted in Lillian M. Penson, *The Colonial Agents of the British West Indies: A Study in Colonial Administration Mainly in the Eighteenth Century* (London, reprinted 1971), fn. 3 203–4.

50. "Debate of 23 March 1774," *StJC*, Jan. 29, 1774; Michael G. Kammen, *A Rope of Sand: The Colonial Agents, British Politics and the American Revolution* (Ithaca, N.Y., 1968), 246; Sir Lewis Namier and John Brooke, *The House of Commons, 1754–1790*, 3 vols. (London, 1964), 2:480; Bollan to John Erving et al., Apr. 1, 1774, Misc. Bound MSS, Massachusetts Historical Society, quoted in Kammen, *A Rope of Sand*, 294; Arthur Lee to Samuel Adams, May 16, 1774, Adams MSS, New York Public Library.

51. Fuller to the Committee of Correspondence, June 25, 1774, Fuller MSS, 265, f. 267, Stephen Fuller Letter Books, Nicholas M. Williams Collection no. 6001, BCL; Fuller to Price, June 25, 1774, ibid., fos. 266–267; Paul Langford, "The British Business Community and the Later Nonimportation Movements, 1768–1776," in *Resistance, Politics, and the American Struggle for Independence, 1765–1775*, ed. Walter H. Conser, Jr., et al. (Boulder, Colo., 1986), 281; Michael G. Kammen, *Empire and Interest: The American Colonies and The Politics of Mercantilism* (Philadelphia, 1970), 134–135.

52. *To the King's Most Excellent Majesty in Council The Humble Petition and Memorial of the Assembly of Jamaica [Voted in the Assembly, on the 28th of December, 1774.]* (Philadelphia, 1775), 6.

53. J. W. Fortescue, *A History of the British Army*, 13 vols. (London, 1902), 3:259, 263.

54. [Bourke], *The Privileges of the Island of Jamaica Vindicated*, 46–47; quoted in Greene, "The Jamaica Privilege Controversy," 377.

55. JAB, Aug. 31, 1773, CO, 31/36; Long, *History*, 1:56.

56. JAB, Feb. 14, 1776, CO, 31/39; *To the King's Most Excellent Majesty in Council*, 6; Philip Curtin, *Two Jamaicas: The Role of Ideas in a Tropical Colony, 1830–1865* (New York, reprinted 1970), 75.

57. Quote of Sir John Dalrymple in Greene, *Peripheries and Center*, 134–135; Robert W. Tucker and David C. Hendrickson, *The Fall of the First British Empire: Origins of the War of American Independence* (Baltimore, 1982), 173, 137, 303, 342.

58. For a *Campbell v. Hall* case, see *Documents Relating to the Constitutional History of Canada, 1759–1791*, 2 vols., ed. A. Short and A. G. Doughty (Ottawa, 1918) 1:522–531; a summary is printed in *British Colonial Documents, 1774–1834*, ed. Vincent Harlow and Frederick Madden (Oxford, 1953), 78–79; Vincent Harlow, "The New Imperial System, 1783–1815," in *The Cambridge History of the British Empire: The Growth of the New Empire, 1783–1870*, ed. J. H. Rose et al. (Cambridge, 1940), 2:153–154; *StJC*, June 14–16, Nov. 26–27, 1774.

59. JAA, Oct. 3, 1776, CO, 9/38; JAG, Mar. 16, 1768, CO, 104/3; JAB, Nov. 27, 1770, CO, 31/36; JAB, Oct. 1, 1777, CO, 31/39; Poyer, *History of Barbados*, 352–354.

60. Jack P. Greene, "Legislative Turnover," 234, for ratio of members to adult white males in British America, 1700–1770; Steele to Shelburne, Apr. 6, 1782, Shelburne Papers, f.307, WLCL; Richard S. Dunn, *Sugar and Slaves: The Rise of the Planter*

Class in the English West Indies, 1624–1713 (New York, reprinted 1973), 93. For Barbados, see also Karl Watson, *The Civilised Island Barbados: A Social History, 1750–1816* (Bridge-town, Barbados, reprinted 1983), 43–45, for examples of the concentration of political power among a few families in Barbados. For franchise requirements see ibid., 7; Elsa Goveia, *Slave Society in the British Leeward Islands at the End of the Eighteenth Century* (New Haven, Conn., 1965), 90. Edward Brathwaite, *The Development of Creole Society in Jamaica, 1770–1820* (Oxford, 1978), 44, notes that the franchise in Jamaica, Barbados, and St. Kitts was limited to twenty-one-year-old white Christian males who were British subjects with a minimum of ten acres of land or a house with an annual taxable value of £10 in local currency. Antigua required possession of a twenty-acre freehold or an annual rent of £20 by an electoral act of 1776. Candidates for elections in St. Kitts had to be free, white, male British subjects over twenty years of age with a freehold of forty acres of land or a rental of at least £40 per annum.

61. Long, *History*, 1:57–58, 59; Curtin, *Two Jamaicas*, 74–75; Governor Trelawny to Hillsborough, Jan. 4, 1771, CO, 137/66, f. 36.

62. Opinion of Henry Brouncker, Craister Greatheed, and Samuel Crooke, Jan. 10, 1768, Council Minutes of St. Kitts, CO, 152/12; *An Answer to the Reverend James Ramsay's Essay . . .* (Basseterre, St. Kitts, 1784), 15, notes that the quality of sugar in Cayon "was near £20 better than in Saint Johns"; JAStK, Feb. 4, Oct. 19, 1772, Mar. 26, 1773, CO, 241/15; Clarke, *Parliamentary Privilege in the American Colonies*, 159.

63. JAG contained in the correspondence of the governor, Dec. 15, 1767, CO, 101/12, f.141, gives a breakdown of British and French freeholders by parish; John de Ponthieu to John Wilkes, n.d., Correspondence of John Wilkes, Add MSS 30 870, f. 204, BL; Steele to Shelburne, Apr. 6, 1782, SHP, f. 307; Bryan Edwards, "Notes on Edward Long," vol. 1, p. 33, Codex Eng 87, F1865 C8, John Carter Brown Library, Providence, Rhode Island.

64. Dunn, *Sugar and Slaves*, 338.

Chapter 6. The Crisis of American Independence

1. *Danish American Gazette*, Nov. 20, 1776.

2. Address of the Assembly of Jamaica to the King, JAJ, Dec. 22, 1774, CO, 140/53. In July 1774, the assembly of Barbados had petitioned the governor in "fearful expectation" of events in North America. However, it did not attempt to suggest a remedy nor did it express any sympathy for the mainland patriots. See JAB, July 19, 1774, CO, 31/36.

3. Address of the Assembly of Jamaica, JAJ, Dec. 22, 1774, CO, 140/53.

4. Peter Force, ed., *American Archives*, 4th ser., 6 vols. (Washington, D.C., 1837–53), 2:108, 1890–1891.

5. Ibid.

6. *To the King's Most Excellent MAJESTY IN COUNCIL The Humble PETITION AND MEMORIAL OF THE ASSEMBLY OF JAMAICA [voted in ASSEMBLY, on the 28th December, 1774]* (Philadelphia, 1775); Arthur Lee to Sam Adams, Mar. 4, 1775, Adams MSS, New York Public Library; Lowell J. Ragatz, *The Fall of the Planter Class in the British Carib-bean, 1763–1833* (Washington, D.C., 1928), 143; George Metcalf, *Royal Government and Political Conflict in Jamaica, 1729–1783* (London, 1965), 189; James E. Bradley, *Popular*

Politics and the American Revolution in England: Petitions, the Crown and Public Opinion (Macon, Ga., 1986), 42.

7. MSWIM, Jan. 3, 1775; Douglas Hall, *A Brief History of the West India Committee* (London, 1971), 3. It is unclear whether these planters were derived from the old Planters' Club or whether they were simply an ad hoc society. Alison Olson, "The London Mercantile Lobby and the Coming of the American Revolution," *JAH* 69, no. 1 (1982), 35, suggests that the January meetings of the merchants represented a victory for the moderates. The radicals wanted to hold crisis meetings in late December when the conservative merchants were out of town.

8. *The London Chronicle*, Jan. 17–19, 1775.

9. Ibid.

10. Ibid.; MSWIM, Feb. 7, 1775.

11. Paul Langford, "The British Business Community and Later Nonimportation Movements, 1768–1776," in *Resistance, Politics and the American Struggle for Independence*, ed. Walter H. Conser, Jr., Ronald M. McCarthy, David J. Toscano, and Gene Sharp (Boulder, Colo., 1986), 97; Jack M. Sosin, *Agents and Merchants: British Colonial Policy and the Origins of the American Revolution, 1763–1775* (Lincoln, Neb., 1965), 220.

12. *Gazetteer and New Daily Advertiser*, Feb. 16, 1775; Burke, quoted in Bradley, *Popular Politics and the American Revolution in England*, 24; Jacob Price, "Who Cared About the Colonies?" in *Strangers Within the Realm: Cultural Margins of the First British Empire*, ed. Bernard Bailyn and Philip D. Morgan (Chapel Hill, N.C., 1991), 414–415; *Proceedings and Debates of the British Parliaments Respecting North America, 1754–1783*, ed. R. C. Simmons and P. D. G. Thomas, 6 vols., (New York, 1982–), 4:342–43; William Cobbett and Thomas Hansard, eds., *The Parliamentary History of England from the Earliest Period to 1803*, 36 vols. (London, 1806–22), 18:219.

13. *Morning Chronicle and London Advertiser*, Feb. 8, 1775; Sosin, *Agents and Merchants*, 220, claims that the West Indians wanted Lord Dartmouth to present the petition to the House of Lords; John Sainsbury, *Disaffected Patriots: London Supporters of Revolutionary America, 1769–1782* (Montreal, 1987), 77.

14. Michael G. Kammen, *A Rope of Sand: The Colonial Agents, British Politics, and the American Revolution* (Ithaca, N.Y., 1968), 74–75; Sir Lewis Namier and John Brooke, *The House of Commons, 1754–1790*, 3 vols. (London, 1964), 2:81, 504–505; *Gazetteer and New Daily Advertiser*, Jan. 5, 1775.

15. *The Evidence Delivered on the Petition Presented by the West-India Planters and Merchants . . .* (London, 1775); MSWIM, Apr. 4, May 2, 1775; *The West India Merchant . . .* (London, 1778), 79. The printer of the latter, J. Almon, published numerous tracts sympathetic to the American cause.

16. Sainsbury, *Disaffected Patriots*, 194, notes that West Indians made up 2 percent of the pro-American petition of October 11, 1775 and 1 percent of the progovernment petitioners of the October 14 and 20, 1775; Address of the Assembly of Grenada to the King, June 1775, CO, 101/18, part 1, f. 180; JAG, June 25, 1775, CO, 104/4; Governor Young to Dartmouth, June 26, 1775, CO, 101/18, part 1, f. 176.

17. John Brown to Samuel William Vernon, Mather Bray [Jamaica], June 24, 1775, Newport Historical Society Special Collections, Box 656, Newport, Rhode Island; *London Evening Post*, June 30, 1775; Governor Morris to Dartmouth, Apr. 25, 1775, CO, 101/18, f. 121.

18. *StJC*, Apr. 6–8, 1775, also reports dues in Jamaica; *Barbados Mercury*, Sept. 2,

1775, American Antiquarian Society, Worcester, Mass.; Sainsbury, *Disaffected Patriots*, 194.

19. Simmons and Thomas, *Proceedings and Debates of the British Parliament*, 4:284, Nov. 22, 1775, and 6:325, 330, 343, Dec. 7, 1775; *Adams Weekly Courant*, Dec. 19, 1775; Namier and Brooke, *The House of Commons*, 2:68.

20. JAB, Feb. 13, Feb. 14, 1776, CO, 31/39; Gayton to Stephens, Mar. 28, 1776, Adm. 1/240, part 1, fos. 179, 181; "Epitaph, On General Montgomery, 1776," in Bryan Edwards, *Poems Written Chiefly in the West-Indies* (Kingston, Jamaica, 1792), 61; Governor Hay to Germain, Oct. 12, 1776, CO, 28/56, f. 76.

21. *Royal Danish American Gazette*, May 18, 1776; *Virginia Gazette* (Purdie, Williamsburg), Aug. 16, 1776; Governor Keith to Germain, Mar. 27, 1776, CO, 137/71, f. 98; *StJC*, Aug. 22–29, 1776; Lord Dunmore to Lord George Germain, July 31, 1776, William Bell Clark and William James Morgan, eds., *Naval Documents of the American Revolution*, 10 vols. (Washington, D.C., 1970), 5:1313–1314.

22. Samuel Estwick, *A Letter to the Revd. Josiah Tucker . . .* (London, 1776), 99, 101–5, 117, 119, 121, 124. The association of the Scots and ministerial corruption was fueled by the premiership of Lord Bute (1762–63), a Stuart, whom many blamed for the excesses of George III. Estwick listed the senior officeholders in Jamaica to show that they were all Scots (105).

23. *The West India Merchant*, 3–4, 9, 86, 119, 121–124, 146.

24. Agnes Whitson, "The Outlook of the Continental American Colonies on the British West Indies, 1760–1775," *PSQ* 45, no. 1 (Mar. 1930), 83, 86.

25. *London Chronicle*, Jan. 17–19, 1775; *Gazetteer and New Daily Advertiser*, Feb. 16, 1775; *The Evidence Delivered . . .* 2.

26. S. H. H. Carrington, "Economic and Political Developments in the British West Indies During the period of the American Revolution" (Ph.D. thesis, University of London, 1975), 245–247; Jack Greene, *Peripheries and Center: Constitutional Development in the Extended Polities of the British Empire and the United States, 1607–1788* (Athens, Ga., 1986), 139. See also H. C. Bell, "The West Indies Trade Before the American Revolution," *AHR* 22, no. 2 (1917), 287; F. R. Augier, S. C. Gordon, D. G. Hall, and M. Reckford, *The Making of the West Indies*, 5th edn. (London, 1964), 108.

27. Lawrence Henry Gipson, *The British Empire Before the American Revolution*, 15 vols. (New York, 1967), 13:75–76; Selwyn H. H. Carrington, *The British West Indies During the American Revolution* (Dordrecht, Holland, 1988), 129.

28. *General Evening Post*, Oct. 7, 1775; Governor Keith to Dartmouth, Jan. 4, June 12, 1775, CO, 137/70.

29. JAJ, Dec. 9, 1774, CO, 150/53; JAJ, Dec. 22, 1774, CO, 140/52; John Knowles to Samuel and William Vernon, Montego Bay, April 27, [1775], Special Collections, Box 656, Newport Historical Society, Newport, Rhode Island.

30. *General Evening Post*, Oct. 7, 1775; *Gazetteer and New Daily Advertiser*, Jan. 12, 1775; *Royal Danish American Gazette*, Mar. 22, 1775; Governor Keith to Dartmouth, May 16, 1775, CO, 137/70.

31. Macartney to Germain, June 30, 1776, CO, 101/20, f. 29. Whitson, "The Outlook of the Continental American Colonies," 86: "Perhaps it might be said that in 1774–75, there was a greater measure of sympathy between West Indians and Americans than ever before. But, while one does not wish to minimize unduly the sincerity of West Indian Whiggism, it is impossible not to feel that the expression of Whiggism at

this juncture was, quite naturally, as much the result of prospective privation as of principle."

32. *The Evidence Delivered*, 13, 15, 52; StJC, Mar. 12–23, 1776.

33. Governor Leyborne to Dartmouth, Apr. 1, Mar. 10, 1774, CO, 101/17, fos. 249–250; JAT, Apr. 4, Apr. 11, 1774; Oct. 10, 1775, Nov. 5, 1774, CO, 288/1.

34. JAJ, Nov. 3, 1774, CO, 140/53; *Lloyd's Evening Post*, Feb. 20, 1775; *Gazetteer and New Daily Advertiser*, Aug. 3, 1775.

35. *Gazetteer and New Daily Advertiser*, May 12, 1775; Governor Morris to Dartmouth, Mar. 24, 1775, CO, 101/18, fos. 46, 50–53; Address of the Assembly of St. Vincent to Governor Morris, Mar. 22, 1775, ibid., f. 56; Governor Leyborne to Dartmouth, Mar. 31, 1775, ibid., f. 75; Wm. Scott to Governor Morris, Mar. 23, 1775, ibid., f. 97; JAStV, Mar. 22, Mar. 23, 1775, CO, 263/2.

36. JAN, Mar. 30, 1775, Sept. 14, 1774, CO, 186/5.

37. Rodney to Stephens, Apr. 24, 1774, Adm. 1/239; Same to Same, Sept. 24, 1774, Adm. 1/239; Same to Same, Oct. 8, 1774, Adm. 1/240.

38. R. C. Dallas, *History of the Maroons*, 2 vols. (London, 1803), 1:129; StJC, July 7–9, 1774.

39. StJC, July 7–9, 1774; Dallas, *History of the Maroons*, 1:129; extract from a letter from Kingston, Jamaica, Apr. 23, 1774, *Gazetteer and New Daily Advertiser*, June 27, 1774, gives terms of truce. Extract of a letter from the Hon. Bryan Edwards to Mr Mark Davis of Bristol, Apr. 18, 1774, StJC, July 7–9, 1774; Edwards dismissed the episode as a misunderstanding and was even critical of the "imprudent white People of that Place." On the other hand, Dallas, *History of the Maroons*, 1:129, regarded the actions of the maroons as quite deliberate and argued that Grant was acquitted because he was too high ranking to be executed without terrible reprisals against the whites.

40. Bradley, *Popular Politics and the American Revolution in England*, 204; Address of the Assembly of Grenada to the King, JAG, Apr. 10, 1776, CO, 104/4; *Remarks on the Evidence Delivered on the Petition Presented by the West-India Planters and Merchants . . .* (London, 1777).

41. Silas Deane to Robert Morris, Apr. 26, 1776, in *Naval Documents of the American Revolution*, ed. Clark and Morgan, 4:1275; *Royal Danish American Gazette*, June 1, 1776. The merchant may be the same man accused of being an agent of Congress and an officer in the Continental Army in Dominica described in *London Chronicle*, Apr. 16–18, 1776.

42. *Providence Gazette*, Aug. 17, 1776; *Chester Chronicle*, Feb. 29, 1776, CO, 152/55, contains a large quantity of documents relating to the arrest of Hubbard; StJC, Sept. 24–26, 1776.

43. *London Chronicle*, July 25–27, 1776; *New York Journal*, July 18, 1776.

44. *New York Journal*, July 18, 1776; "St. John's (in Antigua), Oct. 12," *Royal Danish American Gazette*, Nov. 12, 1776; *Virginia Gazette* (Rind), Aug. 28, 1774.

45. Campbell to Germain, Jan. 16, 1776, GP, vol. 4; *Pennsylvania Journal and Weekly Advertiser*, June 12, 1776: John Ellis and Peter Ingram who were both former members of the assembly of Jamaica; Peter Ingram to Germain, July 26, 1776, Oct. 22, 1777, CO, 137/71, f. 327. See also Same to Same, Dec. 4, 1777, CO, 137/73, f. 51.

46. Campbell to Germain, Jan. 16, 1776, GP, vol. 4; StJC, Nov. 5–7, 1776.

47. Address of Assembly of Jamaica to the King, Dec. 14, 1775, CO, 140/52; JAJ, Dec. 22, 1775, CO, 140–52; Address and Petition of the Assembly of Jamaica to the

King, Dec. 21, 1776, CO, 140/56; Metcalf, *Royal Government in Jamaica*, 190, notes that the poor attendance in the assembly in this period weakened the Kingston party by making their "majority uncertain from day to day" while Philip Pinnock, the speaker of the house, "was now a tired and sick man, deeply in debt and suffering from paralytic strokes."

48. Assembly of Tobago to Lieut. Governor William Young, 1776, CO, 101/19, f. 121; JAG, Apr. 10, 1776, CO, 104/4. See also debate of Mar. 15, 1776, CO, 104/4.

49. JAG, Apr. 10, 1776, CO, 104/4; Address of the Assembly of the Virgin Islands to the King, Apr. 6, 1776, CO, 152/55; James Dawson, the speaker of the Virgin Islands to Admiral Barrington, Aug. 14, 1778, in D. Bonner-Smith, ed., *The Barrington Papers*, 2 vols. (London, 1981), vol. 81, 50–51; Macartney to Germain, June 30, 1776, CO, 101/20, f. 28.

50. *Lloyd's Evening Post*, Oct. 4–6, 1775; Richardson Wright, *Revels in Jamaica, 1682–1838* (New York, 1937), 28, 59, 62; Judith Layng, "The American Company of Comedians and the Disruption of Empire," *Revista/Review Interamericana* 5 (1975–76), 665–75; Wilbur H. Siebert, *The Legacy of the American Revolution to the British West Indies and the Bahamas: A Chapter Out of the History of the American Loyalists* (Columbus, Mo., 1913), 14.

51. Governor Keith to Lord George Germain, Aug. 6, 1776, CO, 137/71, fos. 228–229; "A List of Negroes Tried in the Parish of Hanover for intending to raise in Rebellion conspiracies &c being concerned in Rebellious Conspiracies &c from the 20th July to the 18th of September 1776," CO, 137/71, fos. 71, 397; Gayton to Stephens, Aug. 5, 1776, Adm. 1/240, f. 267; *StJC*, Oct. 24–26, 1776.

52. Geo. Scott to John Allen, July 21, 1776, CO, 137/71, f. 254; Edward Long, *The History of Jamaica*, 3 vols. (London, 1774), 2:212. Governor Keith to Germain, Aug. 6, 1776, CO, 137/71, f. 229; Sir Simon Clark to Benj. Lyon, July 23, 1776, CO, 137/71, f. 256; Governor Keith to Germain, Aug. 6, 1776, CO, 137/71, f. 230.

53. JAJ, Dec. 17, 1776, CO, 140–56: Richard B. Sheridan, *JNH* 61, no. 3 (1976), 297–298, 305; Governor Keith to Admiral Gayton, Aug. 28, 1776, Adm. 1/240, f. 260; A List of Negroes . . . , CO, 137/71, fos. 71, 397.

54. Examination of Pontack, July 28, 1776, CO, 137/71, fos. 276–278; *StJC*, Oct. 24–26, 1776; Deane to Jay, Paris, Dec. 3, 1776, in Force, *American Archives*, 3:1051.

55. Rev. J. Lindsay to the Principal Dr. Wm. Robertson in Edinburgh, Aug. 6, 1776, National Library of Scotland, MS 3942, Robertson-Macdonald Letters, fos. 259–263, quoted in Sheridan, "The Jamaican Slave Revolt of 1776," 300–301; John Purrier to Nathaniel Phillips, Oct. 27, 1776, Phillips to Purrier, Mar. 25, 1777, Slebech Papers, National Library of Wales, Letter Book 11485, quoted in Clare Taylor, "Planter Comment on Slave Revolts in Eighteenth Century Jamaica," *S&A* 3, no. 3 (1982), 246.

56. Phillips to Purrier, Mar. 25, 1777.

57. Governor Keith to Lord George Germain, June 2, 1776, CO, 137/71, f. 152.

58. Governor Keith to Lord George Germain, Aug. 6, 1776, CO, 137/71, f. 227; Germain to Governor Keith, July 1, 1776, CO, 137/71, fos. 201, 229.

59. See Governor Keith to Germain, Aug. 6, 1776, CO, 137/71, f. 229; Same to Same, July 1, 1776, ibid., f. 201; Examination of Adam, July 17, 1776, ibid., f. 234; Magistrates to Governor Keith, July 20, 1776, ibid., f. 250; Geo. Scott to John Allen, July 21, 1776, ibid., f. 254; John Dalling to Germain, July 14, 1776, ibid., f. 318.

60. JAJ, Dec. 17, 1776, CO, 140/56.

61. *StJC*, Sept. 17–19, 1776; Acting Governor Greatheed to Vice Admiral Young, Sept. 21, 1776, Adm., 1/309, f. 552; *StJC*, Nov. 9, Nov. 12, 1776, for suspicious circumstances of Basseterre fire of Sept. 5, 1776, and possible implication of slaves; JAM, Sept. 17, 1776, CO, 177/15; *StJC*, Sept. 17–19, 1776; JAM, Dec. 21, 1776, CO, 177/15; *StJC*, Jan. 16–18, 1777; a letter from a gentleman in Grenada, June 14, 1776, in *New York Gazette*, Jan. 13, 1777.

62. Extract of a Letter from Antigua, June 12, *Public Advertiser*, Aug. 15, 1777.

63. *London Chronicle*, Sept. 5–7, 1776; Washington C. Ford, ed., *Journals of Continental Congress*, 35 vols. (Washington, D.C., 1976–85), 5:572, 591, 606; Whitson, "The Outlook of the Continental American Colonies," 83, 86.

64. Robert C. Alberts, *The Golden Voyage: The Life and Times of William Bingham, 1752–1804* (Boston, 1969), 10, 28; Margaret L. Brown, "William Bingham, Agent of the Continental Congress in Martinique," *Pennsylvania Magazine of History and Biography* 61 (1937), 56.

65. Byron to Stephens, Apr. 2, 1779, Adm. 1/312, f. 39.

66. Petition of the Assembly of Jamaica to the King, Nov. 21, 1777, CO, 140/57; John J. McCusker, Jr., "The American Invasion of Nassau in the Bahamas," *The American Neptune* 25, no. 3 (July 1965), 189–217; JAJ, Nov. 21, 1777, CO, 140/57; JAB, July 8, 1777, CO, 31/39; John Pinney to Simon Pretor, June 12, 1777, Pinney MSS, Letter Book IV, f. 114, BUL.

67. Young to Stephens, Mar. 9, 1777, Adm. 1/309 (part 3), f. 656; Alberts, *The Golden Voyage*, 456, appendix, 454–463, reproduces "A Clear and Succinct Account of My Agency" by William Bingham for Congress, written before his departure from Martinique, June 29, 1779; Brown, "William Bingham," 71. The activities of Bingham are described at some length in Macartney to Germain, Oct. 23, 1777, CO, 101/21.

68. *Morning Post*, Sept. 29, 1779.

69. Warner to Greatheed, Jan. 14, 1777, CO, 152/56, f. 50; Young to Greatheed, Jan. 16, 1777, ibid., f. 52; Greatheed to Warner, Jan. 19, 1777, ibid., f. 5; Petition of the owners of the *Reprisal* to the King, ibid., f. 58.

70. Fahie to Greatheed, Mar. 4, 1777, CO, 152/56; Burt to Germain, July 30, 1777, ibid., f. 422; Thomas Burch & Co. to Thomas Munford, Feb. 17, Mar. 29, 1777, quoted in Asa E. Martin, "American Privateers and the West Indies Trade, 1776–1777," *AHR* 39 (1934), 706; Cruger to Cox, Mar. 15, 1777, in *Powder, Profits and Privateers: A Documentary History of the Virgin Islands During the Era of the American Revolution*, ed. George F. Tyson (St. Thomas, 1977), 37.

71. H. K. to Lord George Macartney, Apr. 11, 1777, CO, 101/20; extract of a letter from St. Eustatius, Apr. 12, 1776, in the *Virginia Gazette* (Purdie), May 24, 1776; Robert Morris to Silas Deane, Mar. 10, 1778, in Paul H. Smith, ed., *Letters of Delegates to Congress, 1774–1789*, 12 vols. (Washington, D.C., 1976–1985), 3:366; *Naval Documents of the American Revolution*, 5:1339; *Pennsylvania Evening Post*, Oct. 20, 1776; *Naval Documents*, 8:333–35; *Pennsylvania Journal*, May 28, Apr. 13, 1777. Tyson, *Powder, Profits and Privateers*, 89–98; William Bell Clark, "That Mischievous Hoker: The Story of a Privateer," *Pennsylvania Magazine of History and Biography* 71 (1955), 54–58.

72. Thomas Shirley to Lord Barrington, Oct. 28, 1776, WO 1/50 f. 127, notes that the son and nephew of Governor Thomas Shirley of Dominica were taken prisoners;

see *StJC*, Feb. 5–7, 1778, for debate in the House of Lords; JAB, Nov. 6, 1776, CO, 31/39; Alberts, *The Golden Voyage*, 50; *Royal Danish American Gazette*, Apr. 23, 1777.

73. Extract of a letter from a gentleman in Barbados to his friend in England, dated June 15, 1776, *New York Gazette*, Sept. 2, 1776.

74. William Payne Georges to the Assembly of St. Kitts, Apr. 25, 1776, CO, 241/11; J. R. V. Johnston, "The Sugar Plantations of the Heirs of Lady Frances Stapleton in Nevis and St. Christopher (1746–1810)" (M.A. thesis, University of Wales, 1964), 120; John Pinney to Thompson Hicks, Mar. 12, 1776, Pinney MSS, Letter Book IV; extract of a letter from a gentleman in Barbados to his friend in England, dated June 15, 1776, *New York Gazette*, Sept. 2, 1776.

75. "To the West India Planters and Merchants," *The Antigua Gazette*, Sept. 16, 1778, CO, 101/22, f. 128; MSWIM, Mar. 3, 1778, implies that the idea of West Indian neutrality was rejected without reference to the government, but the *StJC*, Apr. 2–4, 1778, reported that the merchants petitioned Lord North in favor of neutrality; *London Chronicle*, Apr. 12–18, 1778.

76. *Dictionary of National Biography*, ed. Sir Leslie Stephen and Sir Sidney Lee (London, 1937–38), 18:1310; Namier and Brooke, *The House of Commons, 1754–1790*, 3:486; Philip C. Yorke, ed., *The Diary of John Baker Barrister of the Middle Temple and Solicitor General of the Leeward Islands* (London, 1931), 17, 447–48.

Chapter 7. The Groans of the Plantations

1. Macartney to Germain, Apr. 10, 1778, CO, 101/21, f. 178; Mrs. Abigail Redwood to Mr. Brindley, Antigua, June 11, 1779, Newport Historical Society, Newport, Rhode Island; *Antigua Gazette*, Sept. 16, 1778; To the West India Planters and Merchants, CO, 101/22, f. 128.

2. Copy of a petition of the West India Planters and Merchants presented to the King, Dec. 16, 1778, SHP MSS, vol. 88, f. 32.

3. Richard B. Sheridan, *Doctors and Slaves: A Medical and Demographic History of Slavery in the British West Indies, 1680–1834* (Cambridge, 1985), 156; JAM, Aug. 28, 1777, CO, 177/15; The Council and Assembly of Montserrat to Governor Burt, Sept. 4, 1777, CO, 152/56, f. 205; Governor Burt to Germain, Oct. 7, 1777, GP, vol. 6; Same to Same, Dec. 1, 1777, CO, 152/57.

4. Burt to Germain, Mar. 17, 1778, CO, 152/57.

5. "Extract of a Letter from Barbadoes, by the Little Will, arrived at Liverpoole, dated the 15th of February, 1776," *General Evening Post*, Apr. 20–22, 1776; Captain B. L. Payne to Admiral Young, Jan. 30, 1776, Adm. 1/309, part 3, fos. 415, 419; Governor Hay to Germain, Feb. 13, 1776, CO, 28/56, f. 23; JAB, Feb. 14, Mar. 19, Oct. 1, 1776, CO, 31/39; Payne to Howe, Feb. 15, 1776, CO, 5/93, part 1, fos. 126–27d.

6. Governor Hay to Vice Admiral Young, Mar. 24, 1776, CO, 28/56, f. 48; Same to Germain, Apr. 13, 1776, CO, 28/56, f. 36; Memorial of George Walker, Agent for Barbados, 1776, CO, 28/56, f. 69; *Boston Gazette*, Sept. 8, 1776; *Royal Danish American Gazette*, Sept. 28, 1776; extract of a Letter from Jamaica, by the Grenville Packet, May 2, *StJC*, July 3–5, 1777; Hazel Morse Hartley, "Of the Produce of the Plantations," in *Codrington Chronicles: An Experiment in Anglican Altruism on a Barbados Plantation, 1710–1834*, ed. Frank J. Klingberg (Berkeley, 1949), 79; extract of a Letter from Bar-

bados, March 1, *London Chronicle*, Apr. 30–May 2; Burt to Germain, May 3, 1779, CO, 152/59, f. 111; Selwyn H. H. Carrington, *The British West Indies During the American Revolution* (Dordrecht, Holland, 1988); 105–8, for contradictions of Governor Hay.

7. J. R. Ward, *British West Indian Slavery, 1750–1834: The Process of Amelioration* (Oxford, reprinted 1991), 66; "The Antigua Planter; or War and Famine," in *Poems, On Subjects Arising in England, And the West Indies. By a Native of the West Indies* (London, 1783), 23–24, 34; Evidence of Dr. Adair, *Report of the Lords of the Committee of Council . . .* (London, 1789), part 3, Antigua No. 2; Thomas Southey, *Chronological History of the West Indies* (London, 1827), 2:459, 479. Ward, *British West Indian Slavery*, 122–23, has challenged the argument of Richard Sheridan that the American War caused a general subsistence crisis in the British West Indies. In the most detailed survey of plantation accounts of this period, Ward finds that "the records of individual estates show that, apart from Antigua, slave mortality was on average no higher during the war and its aftermath than in the preceding period" (283). He argues that planters were relatively successful in becoming more self-sufficient in planting provisions and in finding alternative sources of supply. Unlike Sheridan, Ward confines his estimate of mortality rates to war-related conditions and he does not include deaths caused by hurricanes.

8. J. R. Ward, "The Profitability of Sugar Planting in the British West Indies, 1650–1834," *EcHR*, 2nd ser., 31 (1978), 207–209; William Dickson, *The Mitigation of Slavery* (London, 1814), 113; John A. Schutz and Maud E. O'Neill, "Of the Plantations Intire: Concerning the Conduct of Affairs," in *Codrington Chronicles: An Experiment in Anglican Altruism on a Barbados Plantation, 1710–1834*, ed. Frank J. Klingberg (Berkeley, 1949), 57; Richard Pares, *A West India Fortune* (London, 1950), 91, notes that the rate of profit is based on the assumption that the estate had a prewar value of about £30,000; [Samuel Estwick], *Considerations on the Present Decline of the Sugar-Trade* (London, 1782), 54.

9. Mathew Powell to Germain, Sept. 2, 1780, CO, 137/78, f. 319; Lowell J. Ragatz, *The Fall of the Planter Class in the British Caribbean, 1763–1833* (Washington, D.C., 1928), 151; Selwyn Carrington, "The American Revolution and the British West Indies' Economy," *JIH* 17, no. 4 (1987), 827; Pares, *A West India Fortune*, 91; Edward Brathwaite, *The Development of Creole Society in Jamaica, 1770–1820* (Oxford, 1978), 141.

10. Extract of a letter from Antigua, Oct. 26, *Morning Chronicle*, Jan. 3, 1778; *StJC*, Apr. 28–30, 1778; David H. Makinson, *Barbados: A Study of North-American West-Indian-Trade Relations, 1739–1789* (The Hague, 1964), 107. For general price increases in Barbados see Makinson, 108, table 5; Macartney to Lord Viscount Howe and Sir William Howe, Nov. 26, 1778, CO, 101/21, f. 198; Morris to Cunningham, June 2, 1781, CO, 28/58, f. 164; Selwyn H. H. Carrington, "British West Indian Economic Decline and Abolition, 1775–1807: Revisiting Econocide," *Canadian Journal of Latin American and Caribbean Studies* 14 (1989), 45; *StJC*, July 3–5, 1777.

11. Memorial and Petition of the Assembly of Jamaica to the King, Dec. 4, 1784, *Journals of the Assembly of Jamaica* (Jamaica, 1804), 8:40–41; General Grant to Germain, Nov. 3, 1779, CO, 318/5, f. 413.

12. Governor Lord Dunmore to Admiral Young, Apr. 9, 1776, Adm. 1/309, part 3, fos. 463, 468; Young to Dunmore, May 13, 1776, Adm. 1/309, part 3, f. 470; Capt. B. L. Payne to Young, Jan. 30, 1776, Adm. 1/309, part 3, f. 415; Grant to Germain, Jan. 4, 1779, CO, 318/5, f. 36; Governor Hay to Germain, Sept. 25, 1779, CO, 28/57,

f. 109; Admiral Hood to Stephens, Dec. 10, 1781, Adm. 1/313, f. 125; Cunningham to Germain, Mar. 9, 1782, GP, vol. 15.

13. Macartney to Germain, Apr. 2, 1777, CO, 101/20, f. 142; Address of Assembly of Jamaica to the King, Nov. 21, 1777, CO, 140/57; Carrington, *The British West Indies During the American Revolution*, 93.

14. Ragatz, *The Fall of the Planter Class*, 165–66; Smith, *Letters of Delegates*, 4:584: Richard Henry Lee to Patrick Henry, Apr. 15, 1777; Franklin, Deane, and Lee to the Committee of Secret Correspondence, Feb. 6, 1777, in *The Revolutionary Diplomatic Correspondence of the United States*, ed. Francis Wharton, 6 vols. (Washington, D.C., 1889), 2:262–263; Franklin and Deane to Committee of Foreign Affairs, May 26, 1777, in *Revolutionary Diplomatic Correspondence*, 325; Hints for the Management of the War, Mar. 2, 1778, GP, vol. 7.

15. Extract of a Letter from Jamaica, *London Chronicle*, Aug. 22–24, 1780; Ragatz, *The Fall of the Planter Class*, 146; *Report of the Lords of the Committee of Council*, part 5, St. Kitts, C. No. 7; Patrick Crowhurst, *The Defence of British Trade, 1689–1815* (London, 1977), 200.

16. Fuller to the Committee of Correspondence, Mar. 1781, CO, 137/81, f. 173; Fuller to Germain, Nov. 20, 1781, CO, 137/81, f. 173.

17. Memorial and Petition of the Assembly of Jamaica to the King, Dec. 4, 1784, *Journals of the Assembly of Jamaica*, 8:40–41; Carrington, "The American Revolution and the British West Indies' Economy," 835; JAJ, July 1, 1779, CO, 140/61.

18. A True State of the Explanation given to the Lords on Monday, by Mr. Chrichton of the Causes of the Rise of Price of Sugars, which had been mentioned loosely by another witness on Friday last, *Public Advertiser*, Feb. 11, 1778; [Estwick], *Considerations on the Present Decline of the Sugar-Trade*, 5; Ragatz, *The Fall of the Planter Class*, 145, 59, tables 37, 38; Carrington, "The American Revolution and the British West Indies' Economy," 835; Sir William Young, *The West-India Common-Place Book* (London, 1807), 19; Carrington, *The British West Indies During the American Revolution*, 59, table 37, 118–120, table 57.

19. Carrington, *The British West Indies During the American Revolution*, 55–56; Aretas Akers to Rev. James Ramsay, Feb. 20, 1775, Papers of Aretas Akers (private collection); [Estwick], *Considerations on the Present Decline of the Sugar-Trade*, 30.

20. D. H. Murdoch, "Land Policy in the Eighteenth-Century British Empire: The Sale of Crown Lands in the Ceded Islands, 1763–1783," *HJ* 27, no. 3 (Sept. 1984), 571; Macartney to Germain, Oct. 25, 1778, CO, 101/22, fols. 157–58.

21. [Estwick], *Considerations on the Present Decline of the Sugar-Trade*, 30, 54, table 9.

22. O. F. Christie, ed., *The Diary of the Revd William Jones, 1777–1821* (New York, 1929), 42 (Oct. 22, 1778); *StJC*, Oct. 15–17, 1776; Hay to Germain, July 12, 1777, CO, 28/56, f. 115; Cunningham to Germain, Nov. 26, 1780, Germain Papers, vol. 13; JAB, Nov. 7, 1780, CO, 31/41; Hay to Germain, June 4, 1778, CO, 28/57, fos. 35–36; Stephen Fuller to Hon. Gentlemen, Dec. 4, 1777, Fuller MSS 256, fos. 46–47, BCL; Memorial of same to Lord Le Despencer, Postmaster General, n.d., Fuller MSS 256, fos. 51–52, BCL.

23. *Observations from a Gentleman* . . . (London, 1781), 10–11, 4; JAB, July 11, 1780, CO, 31/41.

24. *Observations from a Gentleman*, 6; "The Abridged Minutes of the Society of Arts &c in Barbados" (1782), Shelburne Papers, vol. 87, f. 314; WLCL; Ward, *British*

West Indian Slavery, 1750–1834, 283; Carrington, *The British West Indies During the American Revolution*, 66; Carrington, "The American Revolution and the British West Indies' Economy," 839–840, 840, table 7.

25. Shickle to Pennant, Sept. 30, 1776, Penrhyn MSS 1224, quoted in Carrington, "The American Revolution, British Policy and the West Indian Economy, 1775–1808," 80; Carrington, "British West Indian Economic Decline and Abolition," 53; *StJC*, Feb. 5–7, 1777; David Watts, *The West Indies: Patterns of Development, Culture and Environmental Change Since 1492* (Cambridge, 1982), 277.

26. John Pinney to Mills and Swanston, May 3, Nov. 3, 1777, Pinney Papers, Letter Book IV, f. 106, BUL; JAB, July 11, May 27, 1783, CO, 31/41; Chas. Winstone to David Chollet, Oct. 26, 1778, Letter Book of Charles Winstone, vol. 1, WLCL; John Poyer, *The History of Barbados* (London, 1808), 422, 461.

27. Michael Craton and James Walvin, *A Jamaican Plantation: The History of Worthy Park, 1670–1970* (London, 1970), 157.

28. Chas. Winstone to Messrs. Langston and Dixon, July 6, 1779, Winstone Letter Book; *StJC*, July 12–15, 1777; Karl Watson, *The Civilised Island Barbados: A Social History, 1750–1816* (Barbados, reprinted 1983), 46. This was the theme of the final letters of the "West India Merchant," which appeared in the *London Evening Post* in 1778.

29. T. R. Clayton, "Sophistry, Security, and Socio-Political Structures in the American Revolution; Or, Why Jamaica Did Not Rebel," *HJ* 29 (1986), 332–333.

30. Timothy Mowl, *William Beckford: Composing for Mozart* (London, 1998), 79, 105–108, 119.

31. *Antigua Gazette*, Sept. 16, 1778: "To the West India Planters and Merchants," CO, 101/22, f. 128; [Estwick], *Considerations*, 6; Christie, *Diary of the Revd William Jones*, 39.

32. Piers Mackesy, *The War for America, 1775–1783* (London, 1964), 182, 227. There were between 1,500 and 1,600 troops including the sickly according to the *Public Advertiser*, Aug. 29, 1778.

33. *Public Advertiser*, Nov. 11, 1778; An Account of the Capture of the Island of Dominica published by authority at Paris, WO, 1/51, f. 72, *London Chronicle*, Nov. 5–7, 1778; *StJC*, Nov. 28–Dec. 1, Dec. 1–3, 1778; *Morning Post*, Nov. 3, 1778; "Statement of Facts Relative to Dominica Addressed to the Gentlemen of the West-Indies," *General Advertiser and Morning Intelligence*, May 20, 1779.

34. Valentine Morris, *A Narrative of the Official Conduct of Valentine Morris . . .* (London, 1787), 43, 68–69, 72; Extract from an Officer in the Island of St. Vincent, Oct. 22, 1778, *General Advertiser*, Dec. 29, 1778; Letter to Lord North from I. B., *Morning Chronicle*, July 10, 1783.

35. *StJC*, Sept. 21–23, 1779; Richard B. Sheridan, "Planters and Merchants: The Oliver Family of Antigua and London, 1716–1784," *BH* 13 (1971), 107; Germain to Stephen Fuller, Oct. 14, 1779, Shelburne MSS, vol. 78.

36. Extract of a Letter . . . dated St. Kitt's, Aug. 28, 1779, *Public Advertiser*, Oct. 21, 1779.

37. Samuel Jones to Shelburne, Sept. 10, 1779, Shelburne MSS, vol. 78; Christie, *Diary of the Revd. William Jones*, 61, Sept. 1, 1779; Morris, *A Narrative of the Official Conduct of Valentine Morris*, 73; Abigail Redwood to Mr. Brindley?, Antigua, July 26, 1779, Anderson Family MSS, Newport Historical Society, Rhode Island; *A Speech Which was Spoken in the House of Assembly of St. Christopher . . .* (London, 1782), 41; See

Watson, *The Civilised Island Barbados*, 22, for the terror inflicted by D'Estaing in Barbados in August 1779.

38. Extract of a letter of Mr. White, Montserrat, July 26, 1779, CO, 152/59, f. 282; extract of a letter from Montserrat, dated July 27, *Public Advertiser*, Sept. 9, 1779; *StJC*, Sept. 1–9, 1779; extract of a Letter . . . dated St. Kitt's, Aug. 28, 1779, *The Public Advertiser*, Oct. 21, 1779; Burt to Germain, July 25, 1779, CO, 152/59, f. 239; John Pinney to Simon Pretor, Nevis, July 28, 1779, Letter Book 5, f. 48; Byron to the Admiralty, Aug. 3, 1779, Adm., 1/312; D. Bonner-Smith, "Byron in the Leeward Islands," *MM* 30–31 (1944), 91.

39. *Public Advertiser*, Nov. 23, 1778; Macartney to Germain, Sept. 22, 1778, CO, 101/22, f. 122, makes explicit connection between British reversals and the rise of opposition; *The West India Merchant* . . . (London, 1778), 203: "The little regard shewn to *West India property*, on this side of the Atlantic, gives him reason to suppose our great men don't care whether those islands are preserved to this state, or pass to some other." This is one of the major themes of the letters.

40. Philip Gibbes to Germain, Nov. 20, 1778, GP, vol. 8; Namier and Brooke, *The House of Commons*, 2:140.

41. Extract from the MSWIM, Sept. 30, 1779, GP, vol. 10; extract of Minutes of Merchants and Planters of Jamaica, Nov. 22, 1779, GP, vol. 11.

42. Speech in the House of Lords, Feb. 21, 1780, *StJC*, Feb. 19–22, 1780.

43. Burt to Germain, Apr. 18, 1778, CO, 152/58, f. 32.

44. Vaughan to Germain, Oct. 30, 1780, CO, 318/6, f. 266; extract of a Letter from an Officer of rank, dated Barbados, Feb. 24, 1781, *London Courant*, May 2, 1781; "Cape François, Oct. 29, 1780," *Maryland Gazette*, Dec. 22, 1780. The same article appears in the *Boston Gazette and Country Journal*, Jan. 1, 1781.

45. Extract of a letter from Port Royal, in Jamaica, Sept. 26, *Lloyd's Evening Post*, Jan. 4–6, 1779 (the account also appears in the *British Mercury and Evening Advertiser* Jan. 7, 1779); Silas Deane to Bingham, Oct. 1776, State Department Territorial Papers, Florida Series, 1777–1824, National Archives, vol. 1, roll 1, no. 116, cited in R. John Singh, *French Diplomacy in the Caribbean and the American Revolution* (New York, 1977), 181; Deane to John Jay from Paris, Dec. 3, 1776, in Peter Force, ed., *American Archives . . . A Documentary History of . . . the America Colonies*, 3 vols. (Washington, D.C., 1837–53), 5th ser., 3:col. 1051.

46. *StJC*, Sept. 21–23, 1779.

47. Memorial of Proprietors and Merchants of Tobago to Germain n.d., CO, 101/20, f. 242; JAT, Apr. 10, 1780, in CO, 288/3; Geo. Ferguson to Vaughan, Mar. 24, 1780, VP, vol. 1, f. 150.

48. A. St. Leger to Maj. Ferguson, Depty. Adj. General, St. Lucia, June 19, 1780, VP, vol. 1, f. 102; State of the Island of St. Vincent, July 11, 1774, CO, 101/17, f. 284.

49. Valentine Morris to Burt, Oct. 4, 1777, WO, 1/51, f. 4; Morris, *A Narrative of the Official Conduct of Valentine Morris*, ix, x, 15, 20–21; Valentine Morris to Burt, June 2, 1777, WO, 1/51, f. 19; St. Leger to Vaughan, Dec. 17, 1780, VP, vol. 2, f. 87.

50. *StJC*, Oct. 12–14, 1780; *Lloyd's Evening Post*, Oct. 11–13, 1780; JAJ, Dec. 8, Dec. 28, 1780, Jan. 10, 1781, Dec. 5, 1783, CO, 140/59; *StJC*, Oct. 12–14, 1780; Richardson Wright, *Revels in Jamaica, 1682–1832* (New York, 1937), 192, 352; Dorothy Minchin-Comm, "The Changing Concepts of the West Indian Plantocracy in English Poetry and Drama, 1740–1850" (Ph.D. thesis, University of Alberta, 1971), 83–91.

51. Orlando Patterson, *Slavery and Social Death: A Comparative Study* (Cambridge, Mass., 1982).

52. Governor Valentine Morris of St. Vincent to Dartmouth, June 14, 1775, CO, 101/18, f. 151.

53. Sylvia R. Frey, *The British Soldier in America* (Austin, Tex., 1981), 37; David Patrick Geggus, *Slavery, War and Revolution: The British Occupation of Saint Domingue, 1793–1798* (Oxford, 1982), 363; Brathwaite, *The Development of Creole Society*, 278–279; John Hunger, *Observations on the Diseases of the Army in Jamaica and on the Best Means of Preserving the Health of Europeans in That Climate* (London, 1788).

54. *London Chronicle*, Nov. 24–26, 1778; Burt to Germain, Sept. 30, 1778, CO, 152/58, f. 263.

55. Governor Macartney to Germain, Aug. 2, 1778, CO, 101/22, f. 102.

56. Petition of William Henry Ricketts to the Assembly of Jamaica, Oct. 30, 1778, CO, 140/60; Memorial of William Henry Ricketts, William Lewis, Thomas Barker, Richard Bucknor James, Samuel Jones, John Bertrand, Thomas Simcocks, and John Morrant Morris, enclosed in Dalling to Germain, Feb. 7, 1780, CO, 137/77, f. 28. The same arguments are repeated in the Memorial of William Henry Ricketts, Richard Bucknor James, Philip Vanhorne, and Thomas Barker, in Campbell to Germain, Mar. 25, 1782, CO, 137/82, f. 204.

57. Christie, *Diary of the Revd. William Jones*, 40, Sept. 5, 1778; Memorial of Stephen Fuller to Lord George Germain, Dec. 23/24, 1778, Fuller MSS 256, f. 133.

58. Dalling to Germain, May 25, 1779, CO, 137/75. His portrayal was very different from the Jamaica agent, Fuller to Germain, Dec. 23–24, 1778, Fuller MSS 256, f. 113. Fuller describes them as "the most idle, debauched, distemper'd, profligate wretches upon earth."

59. Meeting of the principal merchants and planters, Sept. 29, 1779, Fuller MSS 256, f. 142; John Dalling to Germain, May 25, 1779, CO, 137/75, f. 16; Fuller to Germain, Sept. 30, 1779, CO, 137/75, f. 86; Memorial of Stephen Fuller to Germain, Sept. 29, 1779, CO, 137/75, f. 88; Germain to Dalling, Oct. 8, 1779, CO, 137/75, f. 102; Memorial of William Henry Ricketts, Richard Bucknor James, Philip Vanhorne, and Thomas Barker of the County of Cornwall, enclosed in Campbell to Germain, Mar. 25, 1782, CO, 137/82, f. 204.

60. JAJ, Apr. 12, 1782; Campbell to Shelburne, May 3, 1782, CO, 137/82; Shelburne to Campbell, June 6, 1782, CO, 137/82; Campbell to Thomas Townshend, Nov. 4, 1782, CO, 137/82, f. 320; Sylvia Frey, *Water from the Rock: Black Resistance in a Revolutionary Age* (Princeton, N.J., 1991), 71–77; Christie, *The Diary of the Revd. William Jones*, 40.

61. Campbell to Germain, Jan. 16, 1776, GP, vol. 4; Frey, *Water from the Rock*, 69, 89; Fuller to Shelburne, Apr. 2, 1782, Fuller MSS 256, f. 281.

62. Edward Long, *The History of Jamaica*, 3 vols. (London, 1774), 1:130–131; Minutes of A General Council of War, held at the King's-House in the Town of Saint Jago de la Vega on the 2d and 3d Days of March 1782, CO, 137/82, f. 160; Alexander Dirom, *Thoughts on the State of the Militia of Jamaica* (Jamaica, 1783), 15.

63. JAB, July 22, 1779, CO, 31/39; JAStK, Aug. 2, 1779, CO, 241/11; Governor Burt to Germain, July 4, 1780, CO, 152/60, f. 171; Extract of a Letter from St. Kitts, Mar. 29, *London Chronicle*, May 9–11, 1780; Robert Prescott to General Vaughan,

May 25, 1780, VP, vol. 1, f. 71; Same to Lt. Col. Ferguson, Feb. 22, 1781, CO, 318/8, f. 307; JAA, May 8, 1783, CO, 9/41.

64. William Dickson, *Letters on Slavery* (London, 1789), 94; Dickson, *Mitigation of Slavery*, 362; Estwick, *The Present Decline of the Sugar-Trade*, 52.

65. Admiral Hyde Parker to Stephens, Aug. 26, 1779, Adm. 1/312, fos. 138–139, 143; Young to Stephens, June 12, 1777, Adm. 1/310, f. 112.

66. Admiral Young's orders to the King's ships in the Leeward Island Squadron, Nov. 21, 1775, Adm. 1/309 (part 3); *Supplement to the Barbados Mercury*, Dec. 15, 1781, CO, 28/59, f. 154; Petition of the Legislature of Antigua to the Admiralty Lords Commissioners, JAA, Sept. 24, July 31, 1783, CO, 9/41.

67. Petition of the Legislature of Antigua to the Admiralty Lords Commissioners, JAA, Sept. 24, 1783, CO, 9/41.

68. Petition of John Perkins of Kingston, Journal of the Assembly of Jamaica, Nov. 2, 1790; *Journals of the Assembly of Jamaica*, 8:581. See also ibid., Dec. 10, 1790, 620; Nicholas A. M. Rodgers, *The Wooden World: Anatomy of the Georgian Navy* (London, 1986), 272.

69. *Journals of the Assembly of Jamaica*, 8: 581–82.

70. Frey, *Water from the Rock*, 150–151, 178, 190; General Mathew to Henry White, July 2, 1782, CO, 318/9, f. 435; Same to Welbore Ellis, Apr. 22, 1782, CO, 318/9, f. 291; Secretary of State to General Mathew (with enclosed memorial), Nov. 28, 1781, CO, 318/9, fos. 579, 593.

71. Fuller to Germain, Dec. 23/24, 1778, Fuller MSS 256, fos. 110, 113.

72. Frey, *Water from the Rock*, 71–77.

73. Tom Pocock, *The Young Nelson in the Americas* (London, 1980), 98; Burt to Germain, Nov. 25, 1778, CO, 152/59, f. 21; extract of a letter from St. Christopher's, May 20, *London Evening Post*, Aug. 19, 1779; Cunningham to Welbore Ellis, Apr. 23, 1782, CO, 28/59, f. 305. See also Same to Germain, Mar. 9, 1782, GP, vol. 15; Dickson, *Mitigation of Slavery*, xxii.

74. Burt to Germain, Sept. 30, 1778, CO, 152/58, f. 277; Sir Gillies Payne versus Wm. Matthew Burt, Mar. 1775, Court of King's Bench and Common Pleas, 1770–1775, f. 483, St. Kitts' Record Office; Burt versus Payne, June 13, 1775, ibid., f. 501; John Doe, on the Demise of Payne, versus Burt, July 12, 1775, ibid., fos. 551–52; Payne vs Burt, Aug. 21, 1775, ibid., 1775–79, fos. 46–47; Roe (Burt) against Doe (Payne), May 12, 1775, Court of Errors 1772–1819, fos. 64–71; Burt against Payne, Apr. 16, 1777, William L. Grant and James Munro, eds., *Acts of Privy Council of England: Colonial Series*, 6 vols. (London, 1908–12), 8, no. 350, 453.

75. Burt to Germain, July 5, 1779, CO, 152/59, f. 226; Burt to Germain, July 5, 1779, CO, 152/59, f. 226; Wilkes to Curson and Governour, Jan. 23, 1781, CO, 239/1, f. 211.

76. Burt to Germain, July 5, 1779, CO, 152/61, f. 226; Johnson to Germain, May 13, 1781, CO, 152/61, f. 82.

77. Campbell to Shelburne, Apr. 26, 1782, CO, 137/82, f. 221; Alexander Cumine to Germain, Oct. 8, 1778, CO, 137/74, f. 11; Campbell to Germain, Sept. 27, 1781, CO, 137/81, f. 100; Walter Pollard to Lord Harwicke, n.d., Pollard Letters, Harwick Papers, Add. MS. 35655, f. 338, quoted in Watson, *The Civilised Island Barbados*, 24; Pollard to Harwicke, May 1781, Pollard Letters, Harwick Papers, Add. MS 35655,

f. 143. Watson says that Walter Pollard, the author of the letter, left North America because he disagreed with the republican sentiment in 1776. G. W. Gignilliat, *A Life of Thomas Day* (New York, 1932), 208–12, says that Pollard particularly appealed to Thomas Day because of his enthusiasm for the American cause and his antipathy to slavery. He was a friend of Benjamin Franklin and William Pitt.

78. To the West India Planters and Merchants, CO, 101/22, f. 128, *Antigua Gazette*, Sept. 16, 1778; Morris, *A Narrative of the Official Conduct of Valentine Morris*, 40–42.

79. Morris, *A Narrative of the Official Conduct of Valentine Morris*, 22, 30, 42–43; Burt to Germain, June 17, 1778, CO, 152/58, f. 115, and Sept. 30, 1778, CO, 152/58, f. 277; Deposition of James Joshua Reynold, Mar. 7, 1780, CO, 152/60, f. 93; *An Answer to the Reverend James Ramsay's Essay* . . . (Basseterre, St. Kitts, 1784), 9; Vere Langford Oliver, 6 vols. *Caribbeana* (London, 1912–17), 3:104.

80. Campbell to North, Nov. 28, 1783, CO, 137/83, f. 23; Macartney to Germain, Apr. 10, 1778, CO, 101/21, f. 178; Campbell to North, Jan. 18, 1784, CO, 137/84, f. 86; Makinson, *Barbados*, 107.

81. Campbell to North, Nov. 28, 1783, CO, 137/83, f. 23; Admiral Hyde Parker to Stephens, Sept. 13, 1779, Adm. 1/312, f. 142; *StJC*, Sept. 24–26, 1776; Burt to Germain, Oct. 9, 1778, CO, 152/58, f. 58, and July 30, 1778, CO, 152/58, f. 226.

82. Extract of a Letter from Antigua, June 12, *Public Advertiser*, Aug. 15, 1777; Pares, *A West India Fortune*, 92.

83. Fuller to the Committee of Correspondence, Dec. 15, 1779, Fuller MSS 256, f. 167. See Andrew J. O'Shaughnessy, "The West India Interest and the Crisis of American Independence," in *West Indies Accounts: Essays on the History of the British Caribbean and the Atlantic Economy in Honour of Richard Sheridan*, ed. Roderick McDonald (Kingston, Jamaica, 1996), 129–49, for a fuller discussion of divisions within the West India lobby during the American War.

84. Petition presented to Chaloner Archdeckne, Feb. 7, 1780, Fuller MSS 256, f. 183; *StJC*, Feb. 10–12, 1780. Lord Onslow is listed as a member of the West India interest in Fuller's list of 1781, Fuller MSS 265, f. 305.

Chapter 8. Rule Britannia

1. Selwyn H. H. Carrington, *The British West Indies During the American Revolution* (Dordrecht, 1988), 130; Carrington, "The American Revolution and the Sugar Colonies," in *The Blackwell Encyclopedia of the American Revolution*, ed. Jack Greene and J. R. Pole (Oxford, 1991), 514.

2. Christie to Vaughan, Jan. 29, 1781, VP, vol. 3, f. 40; [Mrs. Flannigan], *Antigua and the Antiguans*, 2 vols. (London, 1844), 1:115–116.

3. Burt to the Board of Trade, Jan. 14, 1778, CO, 152/34, Hh 18; Selwyn Carrington, "Eighteenth Century Political Conflict in the British Empire: A Case Study of St. Vincent, 1775–1779," *JCH* 20, no. 2 (1985–86), 151, 153; [George Macartney], "Essay supporting the right of Parliament to tax American colonies," [1765?], MP; Cunningham to Germain, Sept. 14, 1780, CO, 28/58, f. 307.

4. Burt to the Board of Trade, Jan. 14, 1778, CO, 152/34, Hh 14. Governors Sir Ralph Payne and Thomas Shirley in the Leeward Islands both suggested modest re-

forms like those submitted by Governor Burt. See Payne to Dartmouth, June 23, 1771, July 23, Sept. 18, 1772, CO, 152/32; J. H. Parry, "The Patent Offices in the British West Indies," *EHR* 69 (Apr. 1954), 204–205.

5. George Metcalf, *Royal Government and Political Conflict in Jamaica, 1729–1783* (London, 1965), 200–201; Elsa Goveia, *Slave Society in the British Leeward Islands at the End of the Eighteenth Century* (New Haven, Conn., 1965), 62, 76. See attitudes toward Burt among army officers in Christie to Vaughan, Mar. 28, 1780, VP, vol. 1; Same to Maj. Ferguson, Apr. 24, 1780, ibid.

6. JAStK, Oct. 20, 1778, CO, 241/11; Burt to Germain, Nov. 25, 1778, CO, 152/59, f. 21; Germain to Burt, Aug. 4, 1779, CO, 152/58, f. 193; Same to Same, Aug. 5, 1779, CO, 152/58, f. 195; Same to Same, Sept. 27, 1779, CO, 152/58, f. 318.

7. Burt to the Board of Trade, July 28, 1780, CO, 152/34, f. 54; Same to the President of the Council of St. Kitts, Sept. 11, 1780, CO, 152/34, f. 77; Same to the Board of Trade, Oct. 11, 1780, CO, 152/34, f. 75; Anthony Johnson, acting governor of the Leeward Islands, to the Board of Trade, May 13, 1781, CO, 152/35, f. 5; JAStK, May 23, 1780, CO, 241/11; Minutes of the Council of St. Kitts, Oct. 26, 1780, CO, 241/12; Frederick G. Spurdle, *Early West Indian Government* (Palmerston, New Zealand, 1963), 188–189.

8. Germain to Cunningham, Mar. 7, 1781, CO, 28/58, f. 66; JAB, July 10, 1781, CO, 31/41.

9. Harrison to Dalling, Jan. 22, 1780, enclosed in Dalling to Germain, June 25, 1780, CO, 137/78; Metcalf, *Royal Government and Political Conflict in Jamaica*, 211–212.

10. The correspondence between Burt and the inspector general of customs is voluminous: CO, 152/56, f. 221; CO, 152/57; CO, 152/58, fos. 9–11, 13, 15, 19, 21, 23, 25, 57, 62, 64, 66, 70, 75, 88–103, 105, 108–109, 152, 154–77. For dispute about patent officeholders, see Burt to Germain, Sept. 17, 1777, CO, 152/56; Same to Same, Sept. 30, 1778, CO, 152/58, f. 262; Germain to Burt, Feb. 3, 1779, CO, 152/59, f. 1; Burt to Germain, May 6, 1779, CO, 152/59, f. 176; Same to Same, Aug. 5, 1779, CO, 152/59, f. 276; Pownall to Germain, Sept. 6, 1779, CO, 152/59, fos. 201–204. See also John Pinney to Wm. Leslie Hamilton, Mar. 23, 1779, Pinney Letter Book V, f. 20, BUL; Same to John Henry Clarke, Apr. 6, 1779, Pinney Letter Book V, f. 21.

11. Burt to Germain, Aug. 14, 1779, CO, 152/59, f. 267; Same to Prescott, Jan. 29, 1779; Burt to Musgrave, Dec. 8, 1779, CO, 152/60, f. 51; Vaughan to Germain, Mar. 8, 1780, CO, 318/6; Burt to Germain, Nov. 2, 1777, GP, vol. 6. For Burt's character, see Robert McLarty, "The Expedition of Major-General John Vaughan to the Lesser Antilles, 1779–81" (Ph.D. thesis, University of Michigan, 1951), 101–124; Goveia, *Slave Society in the British Leeward Islands*, 67.

12. *London Evening Post*, June 21, 1779; Samuel Jones to Shelburne, Sept. 10, 1779, SP, vol. 78.

13. Dalling to Germain, Feb. 4, 1780, CO, 137/76, f. 194.

14. Germain to Campbell, Sept. 7, 1781, GP, vol. 19, f. 290; quoted in Tom Pocock, *The Young Nelson in the Americas* (London, 1980), 157. The expedition is described in Thomas Dancer, *A Brief History of the late Expedition against Fort San Juan, so far as it relates to the Diseases of the troops* (Kingston, Jamaica, 1781).

15. Parker to Stephens, Feb. 20, 1780, Adm. 1/312, f. 181; Burt to Knox, May 25, 1779, CO, 152/59, f. 187; General Grant to Germain, Jan. 4, 1779, CO, 318/5, f. 36; Vaughan to Same, July 6, 1780, CO, 318/6, f. 176.

16. Germain to Burt, Feb. 3, 1779, CO, 152/59, f. 1; Same to Same, Jan. 3, 1781, CO, 152/61, fos. 3–4; Same to Same, Sept. 3, 1779, CO, 152/59, f. 198; Same to Same, Dec. 7, 1780, CO, 152/60, f. 247.

17. Valentine Morris, *A Narrative of the Official Conduct of Valentine Morris . . .* (London, 1787), xi–xii; JAB, Apr. 18, 1781, CO, 31/41; Germain to Cunningham, Feb. 7, 1781, CO, 28/58, f. 46; Same to Same, Oct. 12, 1781, CO, 28/58, f. 288; John Poyer, *The History of Barbados* (London, 1808), 476.

18. Germain to Cunningham, Nov. 16, 1780, CO, 28/57; Same to Dalling, Oct. 8, 1779, CO, 137/75, f. 103.

19. Germain to Cunningham, Nov. 16, 1780, CO, 28/57, f. 198.

20. Morris, *A Narrative of the Official Conduct of Valentine Morris*, v, notes the government repaid Governor Melville, the government reimbursed both Lord Macartney and John Dalling. See also p. 60.

21. Germain to Macartney, June 25, 1779, MP WLCL; Germain to Dalling, Feb. 2, 1780, GP, vol. 11; Same to Same, Oct. 30, 1780, GP, vol. 19, f. 235; Same to Prescott, Dec. 4, 1779, GP, vol. 18; Same to Vaughan, Dec. 7, 1779, GP. See Piers Mackesy, *The War for America, 1775–1783* (London, 1964), 187, for an alternative view which argues that Germain pursued the best and cheapest strategy.

22. Memorial of Stephen Fuller to Lord George Germain, Dec. 8, 1779, Fuller MSS 256, f. 155; Samuel Estwick, *Considerations on the Present Decline of the Sugar-Trade* (London, 1782), 52.

23. JAJ, Oct. 21, 31, 1778, CO, 140/60; Carrington, *The British West Indies During the American Revolution*, 132–134, 148; Burt to Germain, Sept. 30, 1778, CO, 152/58, f. 262.

24. Hay to Germain, June 4, 1778, CO, 28/57, f. 36.

25. See chapter 7, nn. 22, 26.

26. "The case of the Island of Barbados submitted to the public; or a short estimate of the losses sustained in that island by the late dreadful hurricane, upon the following incontestible data"; by Samuel Estwick, Esq., Agent for the island, in *London Courant and Westminster Chronicle*, Feb. 1, 1781. For a slightly lower estimate, see *StJC*, Jan. 23–25, 1781.

27. *StJC*, Dec. 26–28, 1780; *Barbados Mercury*, Oct. 28, 1780, ibid., f. 214. The article on the hurricane is reprinted in the *London Chronicle*, Dec. 26–28, 1780.

28. Rodney to Stephens, Dec. 10, 1780, Adm. 1/311, f. 423. See also accounts in Cunningham to Germain, Oct. 20, 1780, CO, 28/57, fos. 202, 203, 205; Journal of the Hurricane, CO, 28/57, f. 207; *Barbados Mercury*, Oct. 28, 1780, CO, 28/57, f. 214; Cunningham to Germain, Sept. 22, 1780, CO, 28/58, f. 14; A List of the Inhabitants, Slaves, Cattle, and Horse Killed, and estimated Damage, occasioned by the late Hurricane, CO, 28/58, f. 33; Vaughan to Germain, Oct. 30, 1780, CO, 318/6, f. 266; St. Leger to Vaughan, Oct. 30, 1780, CO, 318/6, f. 270; Vaughan to Germain, Nov. 2, 1780, CO, 318/6, f. 274.

29. JAB, July 11, 1780, CO, 31/41; Germain to Cunningham, Oct. 4, 1780, CO, 28/57, f. 153; *London Chronicle*, Nov. 25–27, 1784.

30. JAB, Nov. 28, 1781, CO, 31/41; Rodney to Philip Stephens, Mar. 15, 1782, *Letter-Books and Order-Book of George Lord Rodney . . . 1780–82*, ed. Dorothy C. Barck, 2 vols. (New York, 1932–33), 1:294.

31. Macartney to Germain, Jan. 10, 1779, CO, 101/23, f. 95; E. M. Johnston,

"Grenada, 1775–79," in *Public Service and Private Fortune: The Life of Lord Macartney, 1737–1806*, ed. Peter Roebuck (Belfast, 1983), 97, 125; Macartney to Germain, Dec. 7, 1777, CO, 101/21, f. 144; Germain to Macartney, June 24, 1779, CO, 101/23, f. 99; *Public Advertiser*, Sept. 29, 1779; *Morning Post*, June 5, 1770. Macartney and Staunton were later painted in a portrait together by Lemuel F. Abbot.

32. Address of the Assembly of Jamaica, Dec. 1778, CO, 137/74, f. 139; Metcalf, *Royal Government and Political Conflict in Jamaica*, 208; Estwick, *Considerations on the Present Decline of the Sugar-Trade*, 53; JAJ, Jan. 12, 1781, CO, 140–59.

33. JAA, May 8, 1783, CO, 9/41; Address and Petition of the Council and Assembly of Antigua to the King, enclosed in Burt to Germain, June 11, 1780, CO, 152/60, f. 161; Burt to Germain, May 3, 1779, CO, 152/59, f. 111d; Same to Same, May 4, 1780, CO, 152/60, f. 115; Evidence of Dr. Adair, *Report of the Lords of the Committee of Council . . . Concerning the Present State of the Trade to Africa* (London, 1789), part 3, Antigua, no. 2; Thomas Southey, *Chronological History of the West Indies*, 2 vols. (London, 1827), 459, 479; Burt to Germain, Sept. 17, 1777, CO, 152/56, f. 190; Same to Same, Feb. 22, CO, 152/59, f. 88; Same to Same, June 11, 1780, CO, 152/60, f. 161; Same to Same, Mar. 17, 1780, CO, 152/60, f. 85; Colonel Christie to Germain, Feb. 3, 1781, GP, vol. 14.

34. JAStK, Aug. 3, 1779, Jan. 20, 1780, CO, 241/11; JAStK, Dec. 17, 1778, Apr. 27, 1779, CO, 241/17; Burt to Germain, May 3, 1779, CO, 152/59, f. 115; JAStK, ibid., May 14, June 2, 1779, CO, 241/11; Governor Burt to the Board of Trade, Sept. 26, 1779, CO, 152/34.

35. Poyer, *The History of Barbados*, 500–501; Rodney to Stephens, June 29, 1781, in Godfrey Basil Mundy, *The Life and Correspondence of the Late Admiral Lord Rodney*, 2 vols. (London, 1830), 2:135.

36. JAStK, Apr. 13, 1779, CO, 241/11; Burt to Germain, July 25, 1779, CO, 152/59, f. 239; JAStK, July 16, 1779, CO, 241/11; Christie to Vaughan, Apr. 17, 1780, VP, vol. 1, f. 36.

37. Extract of a letter from Barbados, Feb. 2, *Lloyd's Evening Post*, May 21–24, 1779; Christie to Vaughan, Apr. 28, 1780, VP, vol. 1, f. 43.

38. The Rev. Robert Robertson, *A Detection of the State and Situation of the Present Sugar Planters . . .* (London, 1732), 67–68; Trelawny to Hillsborough, May 28, 1770, CO, 137/65, f. 176; Speech of Sir John Gay Alleyne (Speaker), JAB, July 11, 1780, CO, 31/41; Richard Pares, *War and Trade in the West Indies* (London, reprinted 1963), 241, 257, 259; Spurdle, *Early West Indian Government*, 61, 170, 188; Margaret Deane Rouse-Jones, "St. Kitts, 1713–1763: A Study of the Development of a Plantation Colony" (Ph.D. thesis, Johns Hopkins University, 1978), 190.

39. Sir William Young, *The West-India Common-Place Book* (London, 1807), 208; Ferguson to Vaughan, Aug. 13, 1780, VP, vol. 1, f. 162; Governor Burt to Germain, Oct. 9, 1778, CO, 152/58, f. 58; Robert Prescott to Vaughan, July 7, 1780, VP, vol. 1, f. 76.

40. Memorial of Stephen Fuller to Germain, Dec. 24, 1778, Fuller MSS 256, f. 113; *Lloyd's Evening Post*, July 16–18, 1764; Burt to Germain, Sept. 7, 1778, CO, 152/58, f. 248; Governor Shirley to Germain, Nov. 26, 1781, CO, 152/62, f. 11; Same to Sydney, May 1784, CO, 152/63; *London Chronicle*, July 20–22, 1784.

41. Memorial of Samuel Estwick to the King, n.d. (1781), CO, 28/58, f. 278.

42. Dalling to Germain, Feb. 22, 1779, CO, 137/74, f. 182; Dalling, "Some

thoughts relative to the further improvements to be made in the forts and fortifications and general defence of the island of Jamaica," CO, 137/82, f. 373; Campbell to Germain, Sept. 26, 1781, CO, 137/81, fos. 97–98; Same to Ellis, July 10, 1782, CO, 137/82, f. 268. Governor Thomas Shirley in Antigua thought the fortresses too spread out and he anticipated future British strategy by suggesting that the inhabitants concentrate their defenses. See JAA, July 31, Sept. 24, 1783, CO, 9/41; Germain to Shirley, Feb. 6, 1782, CO, 152/62, f. 23.

43. JAStK, Mar. 31, 1784, Archives of St. Kitts; Shirley to Sydney, May 1784, CO, 152/63; Sir Robert Schomburgk, *The History of Barbados* (London, 1847), 193, 348.

44. Address of the Assembly of St. Kitts to Governor Burt, Sept. 25, 1778, JAStK, CO, 241/17.

45. Address to the King of the Gentlemen, Freeholders, Merchants and Inhabitants of the Town of Savannah la Mar, and the Parish of Westmoreland in the County of Cornwall, CO, 137/72, f. 85; Address to the Governor of the Gentlemen, Freeholders, Merchants and Inhabitants of the Town of Savannah la Mar and the Parish of Westmoreland, Feb. 21, 1777, CO, 137/72, f. 86; Keith to Germain, Mar. 20, 1777, CO, 137/72, f. 82.

46. Shirley to Young, Feb. 11, 1777, Adm. 1/309, f. 647; JAA, May 1, 1777, CO, 9/38. JAM, May 24, 1777, CO, 177/15; JAB, Oct. 1, 1777, CO, 31/39; Germain to Dalling, Aug. 5, 1778, CO, 137/73, f. 151; JAJ, Nov. 12, Dec. 8, 1777, CO, 140/57.

47. Address of the Council of St. Kitts to Governor Burt, CO, 152/57, f. 252; Address of the Council and Assembly of Nevis to the King, 1778, CO, 152/59, f. 73; JAM, July 25, 1778, CO, 1777/15; JAA, Sept. 17, Dec. 14, 1778, CO, 9/38. The offending article in Antigua was reprinted in the *Royal Danish American Gazette*, July 8, 1778.

48. Extract of a letter from a gentleman in Kingston, to his friend in this town, dated March 16, 1778, *Royal Danish American Gazette*, July 8, 1778; *Morning Chronicle*, Sept. 28, 1778; Address of Council and Assembly of Barbados to the King, Jan. 20, 1778, CO, 31/39; Reply to Governor, JAB, Dec. 22, 1778, CO, 31/39; William Hewitt to the Lords of the Treasury, Barbados, Sept. 10, 1779, Hewitt Papers, 522/142, f. 15, quoted in Karl Watson, *The Civilised Island Barbados: A Social History, 1750–1816* (Bridgetown, Barbados, reprinted 1983), 24.

49. StJC, Aug. 26–29, 1780; *Whitehall Evening Post*, Aug. 29, 1780; Council of Nevis to Admiral Rodney, n.d. [July 1780], Adm. 1/310, f. 277; Burt to Vaughan, Apr. 3, 1780, VP, vol. 1, f. 6; JAB, Nov. 7, Mar. 20, 1780, CO, 31/41; JAJ, July 13, 1781, CO, 140/59. Parker to Stephens, Feb. 15, 1778, Adm. 1/241, f. 11; Richardson Wright, *Revels in Jamaica, 1682–1838* (New York, 1937), 159, 176.

50. Isaiah Thomas, *The History of Printing in America*, ed. Marcus McCorison (Worcester, Mass., 1970), 602; Wright, *Revels in Jamaica*, 342 n. 5; *Royal Charibbean Gazette*, vol. 1, no. 1, Feb. 20, 1781, CO, 152/61, f. 85; Howe to Germain, Apr. 30, 1781, CO, 152/61, fos. 82, 84–85.

51. Samuel Martin to Christopher Baldwin, Apr. 16, 1776, Add. MSS 41351, f. 76, BL; John Pinney to Messrs. Mills and Swanston, Oct. 31, 1778, Pinney MSS, Letter Book V, f. 16; Address of Assembly of St. Kitts, Sept. 25, 1778, CO, 241/17; Bryan Edwards, *History Civil and Commercial of the British Colonies in the West Indies*, 5 vols., 5th edn. (London, 1819), 1, book 3, 376, 438; Joseph Boromé, "Dominica During the French Occupation, 1778–1784," *EHR* 330 (1969), 36–58; *London Chronicle*, Jan. 16–18, 1783.

52. Speech of Governor Burt, July 16, 1779, CO, 241/17; Paul H. Smith, ed., *Letters of Delegates to Congress, 1774–1789*, 35 vols. (Washington, D.C., 1976–85), 9:768, x, 602; Francis Wharton, ed., *The Revolutionary Diplomatic Correspondence of the United States*, 6 vols. (Washington, D.C., 1889), 2:304; William Bell Clark and William James Morgan, eds., *Naval Documents of the American Revolution*, 10 vols. (Washington, D.C., 1964–), 8:750; *An Answer to the Revd James Ramsay's Essay . . .* (Basseterre, St. Kitts, 1784), 31.

53. Campbell to Knox, Sept. 15, 1782, William Knox MSS, Box 6, f. 54, WLCL; Metcalf, *Royal Government and Political Conflict in Jamaica*, 220.

54. Boswell, *Private Papers*, x, 24, 29, cited in Sir Lewis Namier and John Brooke, *The House of Commons, 1754–1790*, 3 vols. (London, 1964), 2:180; Campbell, quoted in Sidney Kaplan and Emma Nogrady Kaplan, *The Black Presence in the Era of the American Revolution*, rev. edn. (Amherst, Mass., 1989), 68; Sylvia Frey, *Water from the Rock: Black Resistance in a Revolutionary Age* (Princeton, N.J., 1991), 84; Shelburne to Fuller, in *Journals of the Assembly of Jamaica* (Jamaica, 1805), 7:568, quoted in Metcalf, *Royal Government and Political Conflict in Jamaica*, 222; Shelburne to Campbell, July 9, 1782, CO, 137/82.

55. An act for establishing and declaring rules and articles of war in Jamaica, CO, 137/82, f. 162; Shelburne to Campbell, Apr. 30, 1782, CO, 137/82, f. 173; Campbell to Knox, May 3, 1782, Knox MSS, Box 6, f. 46; "A Memoir of Jamaica," vol. 214, King's MS in the British Museum of which there is a summary in Metcalf, *Royal Government and Political Conflict in Jamaica*, 223–225.

56. Minutes of the Principal Planters and Merchants, Oct. 15, 1779, Fuller MSS 256, fos. 146–147, BCL; Fuller to Dalling, Nov. 13, 1779, Fuller MSS 256, f. 163; Fuller to the Committee of Correspondence, Dec. 15, 1779, Fuller MSS 256, f. 1661; Extracts of the minutes of a general meeting of the subscribers for giving bounties to soldiers rais'd for service in Jamaica, Apr. 19, 1780, GP, vol. 12; Extract of Minutes of Jamaica Planters and Merchants, Oct. 15, 1779, GP, vol. 10.

57. David Syrett, "The West India Merchants and the Conveyance of the King's Troops to the Caribbean, 1779–1782," *Journal of the Society for Army Historical Research* 14 (1967), 169, 170, 176; Syrett, *Shipping and the American War, 1775–1783* (London, 1970), 67, 69; Fuller to the Committee of Correspondence, Apr. 26, 1782, JAJ, Nov. 19, 1782, CO, 140/64.

58. JAD, Aug. 25, 1777, CO, 74/5, indicates that Cumberland was elected by an 11:5 majority and was opposed by a minority who wanted a knowledgeable local candidate; Piers Mackesy, *The Coward of Minden: The Affair of Lord George Sackville* (London, 1979), 254–255; Michael Kammen, *A Rope of Sand: The Colonial Agents, British Politics, and the American Revolution* (Ithaca, N.Y., 1968), 260; Germain to William Burt, Feb. 3, 1779, CO, 152/59, f. 1; Pownall to Germain, Sept. 6, 1779, CO, 152/59, fos. 201–204.

59. Fuller to Committee of Correspondence, Feb. 3, 1779, Fuller MSS 256, f. 122; JAJ, Nov. 10, 1780, CO, 140–59; Same to Dalling, June 19, 1779, Fuller MSS 256, f. 134; Same to Committee of Correspondence, June 22, 1780, Fuller MSS 256, f. 216. Germain had a personal interest in Jamaica, having appointed his six-year-old son receiver general of the island with an estimated wartime income of some £70,000 sterling or the equivalent of 5 percent of the public revenue.

60. Samuel Estwick, *A Letter to the Revd Josiah Tucker . . .* (London, 1776); R. R. Palmer, *The Age of Democratic Revolution: A Political History of Europe and America, 1760–*

1800. The Challenge, 2 vols. (Princeton, N.J., 1989), 1:180; Brathwaite to the Hon. Robert Brathwaite, Feb. 20, 1778, in JAB, Mar. 17, 1778, CO, 31/39; JAB, May 1, 1781, CO, 31/41; Germain to Cunningham, Feb. 6, 1782, CO, 31/42.

61. Fuller to the Committee of Correspondence, May 3, 1780, Fuller MSS 256, f. 197; Same to Dalling, Jan. 30, 1778, Fuller MSS 256, f. 59; Same to the Committee of Correspondence, Feb. 3, 1779, Fuller MSS 256, f. 122; MSWIM, May 2, 1775.

62. MSWIM, June 3, 1777; extract of the Minutes of the Treasury, Oct. 21, 1777, JAB, Jan. 20, 1778, CO, 31/39; Fuller to the Committee of Correspondence, Mar. 3, 1778, Fuller MSS 256, fos. 75–76; Lowell J. Ragatz, *The Fall of the Planter Class in the British Caribbean, 1763–1783* (Washington, D.C., 1928), 149, 164; Carrington, "The American Revolution and the Sugar Colonies, 1775–1783," 511; Carrington, "The American Revolution and the British West Indies' Economy," *JIH* 17, no. 4 (1987), 831; Carrington, *The British West Indies During the American Revolution*, 125; Burt to Vaughan, Apr. 3, 1780, VP, vol. 1, f. 6; *London Chronicle*, May 13–16, 1780; Fuller to the Committee of Correspondence, Apr. 2, 1781, Fuller MSS 256, f. 237.

63. Petition of the Planters and Merchants, May 28, 1781, *StJC*, June 5–8, 1781; Fuller to the Committee of Correspondence, May 29, 1781, Fuller MSS 256, f. 246; Ragatz, *The Fall of the Planter Class*, 170.

64. Piers Mackesy, *The War for America, 1775–1783* (London, 1964), 183–84; Robert W. Tucker and David C. Hendrickson, *The Fall of the First British Empire: Origins of the War of American Independence* (Baltimore, 1982), 112, 113; W. B. Willcox, ed., *The American Rebellion: The British Commander-in-Chief's Narrative of His Campaigns, 1775–1782* (New Haven, Conn., 1954), 10.

65. *StJC*, Dec. 10–12, 1778; George III to Sandwich, Sept. 13, 1779, in *The Private Papers of John, Earl of Sandwich, 1771–1782*, ed. G. R. Barnes and J. H. Owen, 4 vols. (London, 1932–38), 3:163–164; Mackesy, *The War for America*, 183, 184; William B. Willcox, "British Strategy in America, 1778," *JMH* 19, no. 2 (1947), 101; David Syrett, *The Royal Navy in American Waters, 1775–1783* (Aldershot, Eng., 1989), 121.

66. Willcox, *The American Rebellion*, 86, 107, 397, 401, 416; Mackesy, "British Strategy in the War of American Independence," 177; Gerald S. Brown, "The Anglo-French Naval Crisis, 1778: A Study of Conflict in the North Cabinet," *WMQ* 3rd ser., 13 (1956), 5; Willcox, "British Strategy in America, 1778," 102, 104–10, 113, 119–20.

67. The Letter Book of the Rev. James Ramsay, Brit. Emp. MSS. S2 f. 17, RHL.

68. *StJC*, Feb. 10–12, 1780; Admiral Arbuthnot to Admiral Parker, Sept. 17, 1779, Adm. 1/241, f. 338; Willcox, *The American Rebellion*, 143–144, 421, 422; Robert Neil McLarty, "Jamaica Prepares for Invasion 1779," *CQ* 4, no. 1 (1955), 62–67; John A. Tilley, *The British Navy and the American Revolution* (Columbia, Mo., 1987), 170; O. F. Christie, ed., *Diary of the Revd William Jones* (New York, 1929), 58–61.

69. Germain to Dalling, Mar. 1, 1780, GP, vol. 12; Fuller to the Committee of Correspondence, Dec. 22, 1781, Fuller MSS 256, f. 262.

70. Pocock, *The Young Nelson in the Americas*, 17, 180; *Maryland Gazette*, Aug. 20, 1779. For French interest in the Caribbean, see Pierre H. Boulle, "The Caribbean in French Policy on the Eve of the American Revolution," *Revista/Review Interamericana* 5 (1975–76), 564–582; Claude Van Tyne, "French Aid Before the Alliance of 1778," *AHR* 31 (1925), 39. Edward Corwin tends to downplay the importance of the Caribbean in French strategy, although he concedes that the defense of the French West Indies was a pretext for war given by Vergennes, in *French Policy and the American*

Alliance of 1778 (Princeton, N.J., 1916); Corwin, "French Objectives in the American Revolution," *AHR* 21 (1915–16), 34–35, 42–43.

Chapter 9. The Other Road to Yorktown

1. Orlando W. Stephenson, "The Supply of Gunpowder in 1776," *AHR* 30, no. 2 (1924–25), 271, 274, 277, 279, 281.

2. Macartney to Germain, Oct. 22, 1777, CO, 101/21.

3. Young to Stephens, Apr. 7, 1776, Adm. 1/309, f. 458; Same to Same, Mar. 9, 1777, Adm. 1/309, f. 657; Macartney to Germain, Oct. 22, 1777, CO, 101/21, f. 63; Robert C. Alberts, *The Golden Voyage: The Life and Times of William Bingham, 1752–1804* (Boston, 1969), 44.

4. Franklin Jameson, "St. Eustatius and the American Revolution," *AHR* 8 (1902–3), 703; Governor Burt to Germain, June 13, 1777, CO, 152/56; Same to Governor Peter Clausen of St. Eustatius, July 9, 1777, CO, 152/56; Same to Germain, July 30, Sept. 17, 1777, CO, 152/56; Alberts, *The Golden Voyage*, 31.

5. Jn. Colpoys to Admiral Young, Nov. 27, 1776, Adm. 1/309 (part 3), f. 589; Barbara W. Tuchman, *The First Salute: A View of the American Revolution* (New York, 1988), 5–6, 16, 43, 54–55, 57. For salute of the flag in St. Croix, see H. Kelly to Vice Admiral Young, Antigua, Oct. 27, 1776, enclosed in Germain to Suffolk, Mar. 14, 1777, Adm. 1/309, parts 3 and 4.

6. The article from St. Kitts was reproduced in the *Danish American Gazette*, Apr. 16, 1777; quoted by Jameson, "St. Eustatius and the American Revolution," 691.

7. Evangeline W. Andrews and Charles M. Andrews, eds. *Journal of a Lady of Quality* . . . (New Haven, Conn., 1921), 136.

8. Ibid., 136–137.

9. Young to Heylinger, May 20, 1776, Adm. 1/309, f. 488; John Colpoys to Young, Nov. 27, 1776, Adm. 1/309, f. 589; F. C. Van Oosten, "Some Notes Concerning the Dutch West Indies During the American Revolutionary War," *The American Neptune* 36 (1976), 165; Letters of van Bibber, Nov. 1776, Maryland Archives, 12:423, 436, quoted by Jameson, "St. Eustatius and the American Revolution," 690–691; Florence Lewisohn, "St. Eustatius: Depot for Revolution," *Revista/Review Interamericana* 5 (1975–76), 625.

10. Lewisohn, "St. Eustatius," 625, 626; "Extract of a private letter from a gentleman in St. Kitt's, to his friend in Stirling, date June 14," *Morning Post*, Aug. 17, 1779; [James Ramsay], "Observations on the Caribbean Station," Jan. 1780, vol. 11, GP; [James Ramsay], "Thoughts on the Charibbean Station," Dec. 5, 1778, vol. 8, GP.

11. Christie to Germain, Feb. 8, 1781, GP, vol. 14; James Ramsay to Germain, Mar. 1, 1781, ibid.; [James Ramsay], "Of St. Eustatius," Mar. 1781, ibid.; Speech of Lord George Germain in the House of Commons, May 14, 1781, *StJC*, May 12–14, 1781.

12. William Cobbett and Thomas Hansard, eds., *The Parliamentary History of England from the Earliest Period to 1803*, 36 vols. (London, 1806–22), 22, 220–221.

13. Extract of a letter from St. Eustatia, Mar. 6, *London Chronicle*, Apr. 12–14, 1781; Richard Downing Jennings, "Case of an English Subject at the Capture of St. Eustatius by Lord Rodney and General Vaughan in the year 1781" (1784), SP, vol. 12, f. 14; Speech of Edmund Burke, Dec. 4, 1782, *StJC*, Feb. 2–5, 1782, May 12–14, 1781.

14. *StJC*, 12–14, May 1781; Rodney to Stephens, Feb. 12, 1781, Adm. 1/314, f. 50; *Royal Gazette*, Apr. 14, 1781; Ramsay to Germain, Mar. 31, 1781, GP, vol. 14.

15. Ramsay to Germain, March 31, 1781, GP, vol. 14.

16. General Howe to Admiral James Young, Jan. 30, 1776, Adm. 1/309, f. 415; Sir Henry Calder to Germain, St. Lucia, Sept. 19, 1779, CO, 318/7, f. 55; Petition of the West India Merchants and Planters to the King, Apr. 6, 1781, SHP, vol. 79, f. 173; *A Speech Which was Spoken in the House of the Assembly of St. Christopher* . . . (London, 1782), 28; Jennings, "Case of an English Subject at the Capture of Saint Eustatius," SP, vol. 12, f. 5.

17. Vaughan and Rodney to Germain, July 3, 1781, CO, 318/7; David Spinney, *Rodney* (London, 1969), 375, 377; Orders given by Sir George Bridges Rodney to his Agents, July 31, 1781, SP, vol. 9; *A Speech Which was Spoken in the House of the Assembly of St. Christopher*, 25.

18. Ronald Hurst, *The Golden Rock: An Episode in the American War of Independence, 1775–1783* (London, 1996), 7; Norman F. Barka, "Citizens of St. Eustatius, 1781: A Historical and Archaeological Study," in *The Lesser Antilles in the Age of European Expansion*, ed. Robert L. Paquette and Stanley L. Engerman (Gainesville, Fla., 1996), 228.

19. Andrews and Andrews, *Journal of a Lady of Quality*, 136–137.

20. Jennings, "The Case of an English Subject"; Speech of Edmund Burke, May 14, 1781, *StJC*, May 12–14, 1781; Ramsay to Germain, Mar. 31, 1781, GP, vol. 14.

21. Jennings, "Case of an English Subject"; SP, vol. 11, f. 14; Speech of Edmund Burke, May 14, 1781, *StJC*, May 12–14, 1781. David Spinney's biography of Rodney is wary of the partisan accounts of critics like Sir Samuel Hood. However, collectively, their testimony is a damning indictment in the context of our knowledge of Rodney's financial state and his failure to provide an adequate explanation.

22. Speech of Edmund Burke, May 14, 1781, *StJC*, May 12–14, 1781; *A Speech Which was Spoken in the House of the Assembly of St. Christopher*, 16; Richard Neave to Germain, Apr. 26, 1781, GP, vol. 14; Germain to Vaughan, Mar. 30, 1781, CO, 318/8, f. 89.

23. Ramsay to Germain, Mar. 1, 1781, GP, vol. 14.

24. Spinney, *Rodney*, 369; Hurst, *The Golden Rock*, 26; Rodney to Stephens, Feb. 12, 1781, Adm. 1/314, fos. 48–49; copy of a letter from Admiral Rodney to the Marquis de Bouillé, *Maryland Gazette*, May 31, 1781.

25. Rodney to Stephens, Mar. 9, 1781, quoted in *General Advertiser*, July 4, 1786, of which there is a copy in SP, vol. 13; Same and Vaughan to Germain, June 25, 1781, CO, 28/58, f. 224; Same to Lady Rodney, Apr. 23, 1781, in Godfrey Basil Mundy, *The Life and Correspondence of the Late Admiral Lord Rodney*, 2 vols. (London, 1830), 2:97; Same to Stephens, June 29, 1781, Adm. 1/314, f. 214.

26. Ibid.; Rodney to Stephens, Mar. 6, 1781, Adm. 1/314; Same to Same, Mar. 17, 1781, Adm. 1/314, f. 61.

27. Hood to Jackson, May 21, 1781, quoted in W. M. James, *The British Navy in Adversity: A Study of the War of American Independence* (London, 1926), 257; Hood to Jackson, June 24, 1781, *Letters Written by Sir Samuel Hood . . . 1781–1783*, ed. David Hannay (London, 1895), 18; N. A. M. Rodgers, *The Wooden World: Anatomy of the Georgian Navy* (London, 1986), 323; David Syrett, *The Royal Navy in American Waters, 1775–1783* (Aldershot, Eng., 1989), 154; John A. Tilley, *The British Navy and the American Revolution* (Columbia, Mass., 1987), 201.

28. Spinney, *Rodney*, 367.

29. Rodney to Lady Rodney, Apr. 23, 1781, in Mundy, *Life and Correspondence of the Late Admiral Lord Rodney*, 2:100; Rodney to Lady Rodney, Mar. 18, 1781, Greenwich 35 MS. 0292, quoted in Spinney, *Rodney*, 367; Rodney to George Rodney, Feb. 6, 1781, Rodney Papers (Belsize Park), quoted in Spinney, *Rodney*, 380; Donald MacIntyre, *Admiral Rodney* (London, 1962), 16; Hood to Jackson, June 24, 1781, in *Letters Written by Sir Samuel Hood*, 18.

30. Tilley, *The British Navy and the American Revolution*, 201; Syrett, *The Royal Navy in American Waters*, 154–55.

31. Jennings, "Case of an English Subject," SP, vol. 12, fos. 15, 20, 17; Speech of Edmund Burke, Dec. 4, 1781, *StJC*, Dec. 4–6, 1781; Spinney, *Rodney*, 368.

32. Hurst, *The Golden Rock*, 143; Ramsay to Germain, March 1, 1781, GP, vol. 14; Jennings, "Case of an English Subject," SP, vol. 12, f. 14; Rodney to Vaughan, Feb. 6, 1781, VP, vol. 3, f. 21; Ramsay to Germain, Mar. 1, 1781, GP, vol. 14; The Most Humble Address of the Wardens and Elders of the Hebrew Congregation to His Excellency the Hon. John Vaughan, Major General and Commander in Chief of His Majesty's Army in the Leeward Islands, CO, 28/58, f. 246.

33. Rodney to Stephens, Feb. 8, 1772, Adm. 1/238; Same to Same, Mar. 12, 1774, Adm. 1/239; *Westminster Journal*, Apr. 18, 1772.

34. Ramsay to Germain, Mar. 15, 1781, GP, vol. 14; *Pennsylvania Journal*, Aug. 4, 1781.

35. Petition of the West India Merchants and Planters to the King, Apr. 6, 1781, SHP, vol. 79, f. 173; Richard Neave, chairman of the society, to Germain, Apr. 26, 1781, GP, vol. 14; *Pennsylvania Journal*, Dec. 22, 1781. The petition does not appear in the minutes of the West India Merchants. It is printed in the *London Chronicle*, Apr. 12–14, 1781, and *Lloyd's Evening Post*, Apr. 13–15, 1781.

36. Spinney, *Rodney*, 420–421, 423, 426; Hurst, *The Golden Rock*, 139; Jennings, "Case of an English Subject," SP, vol. 12, f. 22.

37. Spinney, *Rodney*, 420; Jennings, "Case of an English Subject," SP, vol. 12, fos. 15, 19.

38. Affidavit of Major Nichols, Mar. 24, 1786, quoted in the *General Advertiser*, July 4, 1786; Spinney, *Rodney*, 383; "Account of the controversy over Rodney's actions in the St. Eustatius Affair," *General Advertiser*, July 4, 1786, of which there is a copy in the Sydney Papers, vol. 13. There was testimony accusing Arthur Savage, an American loyalist employed in the colonial office, of selling the papers to one of the British merchants in St. Eustatius, Richard Downing Jennings. However, Rodney made no use of this document in his possession. Indeed, Savage admitted returning the papers of Jennings because they contained nothing that incriminated their owner. See Hurst, *Golden Rock*, 229; Declaration of Arthur Savage concerning St. Eustatius, July 1786, SP, vol. 13.

39. *General Advertiser*, July 4, 1786, copy in SP, vol. 13. The fall of St. Eustatius was in reality due to a classic coup de main which became the example of military manuals: Robert Selig, "The French Capture of St. Eustatius, 26 November, 1781," *JCH* 27, no. 2 (1993), 129–143.

40. From the *Martinico Gazette*, June 14, 1781, *Pennsylvania Journal*, Aug. 4, 1781; David Wedderburn to Alexander Wedderburn, Jan. 1765, Wedderburn Papers, vol. 2, f. 4, WLCL; Barka, "Citizens of St. Eustatius," 235; An Alphabetical List of Burghers Resident in St. Eustatius, CO, 318/8, fos. 117–119.

41. Ibid., CO, 318/8, fos. 117–19. Richard Downing Jennings, "Account of the Proceedings of Lord Rodney and General Vaughan at St. Eustatius," Apr. 9, 1789, SP, vol. 15.

42. Macartney to Germain, Jan. 10, 1779, CO, 101/23, f. 96; Col. Christie to Germain, Antigua, Feb. 3, 1781, GP, vol. 14; Christie to Germain, Feb. 17, 1782, CO, 318/9, f. 109.

43. Germain to Keith, Dec. 23, 1775, CO, 137/70, f. 167; *StJC*, Aug. 10–13, 1776; *New York Gazette*, Nov. 25, 1776; Printed Resolution of Congress, July 15, 1776, Adm. 1/309, f. 368; Admiral Young to the Governor of Martinique, Oct. 7, 1775, Adm. 1/309, f. 368.

44. Young to Governors of the Leeward and Windward Islands, and Barbados, Aug. 22, 1775, Adm. 1/309, f. 344; Craister Greatheed to James Young, Aug. 30, 1775, Adm. 1/309, f. 360; Syrett, *The Royal Navy in American Waters, 1775–1783*, 20; Keith to Germain, Aug. 31, 1775, CO, 137/70, f. 157; Greatheed to Young, Aug. 30, 1776, Adm. 1/309, f. 360; Hay to Young, Sept. 25, 1775, Adm. 1/309, f. 361; Same to Germain, Feb. 13, 1776, CO, 28/56, fos. 22–23; Keith to Germain, Mar. 27, 1776, CO, 137/71, f. 98.

45. Admiral Sir Peter Parker to Stephens, Apr. 10, 1778, Adm. 1/241, f. 11.

46. J. H. Parry, "American Independence: A View from the West Indies," *Massachusetts Historical Society Proceedings* 87 (1975), 16–21; the case of Fitch appears in numerous letters in CO, 137/73 and 137/84. It was also discussed in JAJ, 1783.

47. V. S. Naipaul, *A Way in the World: A Sequence* (London, 1994), 246.

48. Paragraph from a correspondent at St. Kitts, *Connecticut Courant*, Feb. 10, 1777; Richard Downing Jennings, "Account of the proceedings of Lord Rodney and General Vaughan at St. Eustatius," Apr. 9, 1789, SP, vol. 15; Hood to Young, Apr. 9, 1781, Greenwich 50 MS0096; Hood to Rodney, Feb. 7, 1783, PRO, 30/20/22.

49. Byron to Stephens, Aug. 3, 1779, Adm. 1/312, f. 111; Aretas Akers to Charles Lyell, July 27, 1779, Adm. 1/312, f. 115; Richard Downing Jennings, "Account of the proceedings of Lord Rodney and General Vaughan at St. Eustatius," Apr. 9, 1789, SP, vol. 15; James Ramsay to Vaughan, June 26, 1780, CO, 318/6, f. 169, acknowledges help of Akers in procuring information; Akers to Rodney, Dec. 28, 1780, PRO, 30/20/261, f. 9; Same to Same, Jan. 19, 1781, PRO, 30/20/261, fos. 14–15; Same to Same, Jan. 31, 1781, PRO, 30/20/261, f. 17; Capt. W. Young to Sir Charles Middleton, Dec. 26, 1780, Sir J. K. Laughton, ed., *Letters and Papers of Charles, Lord Barham, Admiral of the Red Squadron, 1758–1813*, 3 vols. (London, 1906–10), 1:86.

50. Burt to Germain, Dec. 17, 1778, no. 25, CO, 152/59; John Luffman, *Brief Account of Antigua* (London, 1789), Letter LXXVII, June 30, reprinted in Vere Langford Oliver, ed., *History of Antigua*, 3 vols. (London, 1895), 2:cxxxvi; Lord Macartney to Germain, Jan. 10, 1779, CO, 101/23, f. 96; James Ramsay, "Thoughts on the Charibbean Station," Dec. 5, 1778, GP, vol. 8; Ramsay to Germain, Jan. 18, 1780, GP, vol. 11.

51. *A Speech Which was Spoken in the House of the Assembly of St. Christopher*, 11; Spinney, *Rodney*, 362–63.

52. Hood to George Jackson, May 21, 1781, in Hannay, *Letters Written by Sir Samuel Hood*, 13–15.

53. Rodney, quoted in Tuchman, *The First Salute*, 235; Germain to Vaughan, Apr. 4, 1781, CO, 318/8, f. 103; and July 4, 1781, CO, 318/8, f. 127.

54. Rodney to Philip Stephens, June 29, 1781, *Letters from Sir George Brydges now*

Lord Rodney, To His Majesty's Ministers, &c. &c. Relative to the Capture of St. Eustatius, And Its Dependencies; And Shewing the State of the War in the West-Indies, at that Period (London, 1789), 81–82.

55. Spinney, *Rodney*, 381–82.

56. *StJC*, Jan. 3–5, 1782; extract of a letter from a clergyman in the Island of Jamaica, dated May 13, 1782, *London Chronicle*, Aug. 6–8, 1782; *Morning Herald*, Aug. 7, 1782.

57. A. J. Jamieson, "War Among the Islands: The Naval and Military Campaigns in the Leeward Islands, 1775–83" (D.Phil. thesis, Oxford University, 1982), 282; see A. J. O'Shaughnessy, "The Politics of the Leeward Islands, 1763–1783" (D.Phil. thesis, Oxford University, 1988), 230–54, for a detailed discussion of the fall of St. Kitts.

58. Debate on the Resolution moved by General Conway against the further prosecution of offensive warfare on the continent of North America, Feb. 27, 1782, William Cobbett and Thomas Hansard, eds., *The Parliamentary History of England from the Earliest Period to 1803*, 36 vols. (London, 1806–22), 22:1096, 1110.

59. *Catalogue of Political and Personal Satires Preserved in the Department of Prints and Drawings in the British Museum, 1771–1783*, ed. M. Dorothy George (London, 1935), 5, nos. 5961 and 5986. The political impact of the loss of St. Kitts can be gauged in George III to Lord North, Mar. 4, 1782, in *Correspondence of George III*, ed. Sir John Fortescue, 6 vols. (London, 1928), 5, no. 3540; George Selwyn to Lord Carlisle, Mar. 6, 1782, *Carlisle Manuscripts*, ed. Historical Manuscripts Commission (London, 1891–94), no. 42, 586; Same to Same, Mar. 26, 1782, ibid., 606; Richard Neave to Ellis Yonge, London, Mar. 7, 1782, in "West Indian Planter Attitudes to the American and French Revolutions As Seen in MSS in the National Library of Wales," ed. C. Taylor (Aberwystwyth, Wales, 1977; typescript at the Institute of Historical Research in London), 368; Lord Sandwich to George III, Mar. 12, 1782, in *Correspondence of George III*, 5, no. 3540; George III to Lord Sandwich, Mar. 12, 1782, in *The Private Papers of John, Earl of Sandwich*, ed. G. R. Barnes and J. H. Owen, 4 vols. (London, 1932–38), 4:78, 243; Edmund Malone to Charlemont, July 5, 1780, in *Charlemont Manuscripts*, ed. Historical Manuscripts Committee, 2 vols. (London, 1891–94), 1:374; I. R. Christie, *The End of North's Ministry* (London, 1958), 344–345.

60. Edmund Burke to Lord Rodney, July 1782, PRO, 30/21/6, f. 73; *The Parliamentary Register* (London, 1782), v, 92, quoted in Christopher Lloyd, "Sir George Rodney: Lucky Admiral," in *George Washington's Opponents: British Generals and Admirals of the American Revolution*, ed. George Billias (New York, 1969), 343; *Morning Herald and Daily Advertiser*, Nov. 6, 1783.

61. *Journals of the Assembly of Jamaica*, 8:565, 567.

Conclusion. Revolutionary Legacy

1. Franklin Knight, "The American Revolution and the Caribbean," in *Slavery and Freedom in the Age of the American Revolution*, ed. Ira Berlin and Ron Hoffman (Charlottesville, Va., 1983), 237; Eric Williams, *Capitalism and Slavery*, 121, 120.

2. John McCusker, "The Economy of the British West Indies, 1763–1790," in his *Essays in the Economic History of the Atlantic World* (London, 1997), 324, 328. See also Jamaica figures in Seymour Drescher, *Econocide: British Slavery in the Era of Abolition*

(Pittsburgh, 1977), 50. My forthcoming article, "Eric Williams as Economic Historian," in *Capitalism and Slavery Fifty Years Later*, ed. Heather Cateau (Peter Lang Publishing), reconciles the evidence of mounting planter debt with the continued profitability of the plantations. It argues that the profits increasingly went to merchants in Britain rather than planters in the West Indies. However, it is irrelevant to this discussion who profited. The real issue is that the plantations continued to be profitable after the war and they continued to be valued by Britain.

3. J. R. Ward, "The Profitability of Sugar Planting in the British West Indies, 1650–1834," *EcHR*, 2nd ser., 31 (1978), 207; Michael Craton, *Search for the Invisible Man: Slaves and Plantation Life in Jamaica* (Cambridge, Mass., 1978), 138–139, was a revision of his earlier view in his coauthored work with James Walvin, *A Jamaican Plantation: The History of Worthy Park, 1670–1970* (London, 1970), 118; Clare Taylor, "The Journal of an Absentee Proprietor, Nathaniel Phillips of Slebech," *JCH* 18 (1984), 68–69; Drescher, *Econocide*, 44; Frank J. Klingberg, ed., *Codrington Chronicles: An Experiment in Anglican Altruism on a Barbados Plantation, 1710–1834* (Berkeley, 1949), 57–58; William Beckford, quoted in Derrick Knight, *Gentlemen of Fortune: The Men Who Made Their Fortunes in Britain's Slave Colonies* (Guildford, Surrey, 1978), 121; Brian Fothergill, *Beckford of Fonthill* (London, 1979), 251.

4. Ward, "The Profitability of Sugar Planting," 207, 208–209. However, the immediate economic impact of the war on the planters was not integral to the validity of Williams's thesis, which also incorporated the economic effects of the French Revolutionary Wars and Napoleonic Wars. William A. Darity, Jr., "A General Equilibrium Model of the Eighteenth Century Atlantic Slave Trade: A Least Likely Test for the Caribbean School," *Research in Economic History* 7 (1982), 291, even goes so far as to say that "the Anstey-Drescher observation that abolition occurred during a peak period of West Indian prosperity is in no way inconsistent with Williams's thesis." Williams placed emphasis on economic changes within Britain. He saw the period of the American Revolution as crucial because it coincided with the birth of free trade ideas and the beginnings of industrial capitalism which were ultimately hostile to the sugar monopoly of the West Indians.

5. S. G. Checkland, "Finance for the West Indies, 1780–1815," *EcHR* 10 (1957–58), 462; Edward Sargent, "The Planning and Early Buildings of the West India Docks," *MM* 77, no. 2 (1991), 119–41. For the impact of the St. Domingue revolt, see Drescher, *Econocide*, 78, 88.

6. R. Thompson to C. Stapleton, July 28, 1783, Stapleton-Cotton MS 23 (vi), quoted in J. R. V. Johnston, "The Sugar Plantations of the Heirs of Lady Frances Stapleton in Nevis and St. Christopher (1746–1810)" (M.A. thesis, University of Wales, 1964), 230; Simon Taylor to Sir John Taylor, Nov. 2, 1783, Simon Taylor Letter Books, vol. 1A, Institute of Commonwealth Studies (ICS), University of London, quoted by Selwyn H. H. Carrington, "The United States and the British West Indian Trade, 1783–1807," in *West Indies Accounts: Essays on the History of the British Caribbean and the Atlantic Economy in Honour of Richard Sheridan*, ed. Roderick McDonald (Kingston, Jamaica, 1996), 150.

7. Petition of freeholders, planters and inhabitants of parish of St. Andrew to the Assembly of Jamaica, Dec. 4, 1784, in *Journals of the Assembly of Jamaica* (Jamaica, 1804), 8:40–41; Petitions of the Councils and Assemblies of St. Kitts and Antigua to the King, enclosed in Shirley to Townshend, Apr. 15, 1783, CO, 152/63; Francis Armytage, *The*

Free Port System in the British West Indies: A Study in Commercial Policy, 1766–1822 (London, 1953), 53–56; JAB, May 27, 1783, CO, 31/4; William Knox, *Extra Official State Papers*, vol. 2 (London, 1789), appendix 13, 54–59 and appendix 16; H. C. Bell, "British Commercial Policy in the West Indies, 1783–1793," *EHR*, 31 (1916), 429–441; Charles R. Ritcheson, *Aftermath of Revolution: British Policy Toward the United States, 1783–1795* (Dallas, 1969), 9. The disappointment in the United States and the diplomacy pursued to revive the trade are discussed in Charles W. Toth, "The British West Indies in American Diplomacy: The Growing Debate, 1789–1901," *CS* 15, no. 3 (1975), 16–30.

8. Selwyn Carrington, *The British West Indies During the American Revolution* (Dordrecht, Holland, 1988), 164; *Maryland Gazette* (Annapolis), Dec. 18, 1783, quoted item from the *Bahama Gazette*, Oct. 6, 1783; Shirley to North, Nov. 17, 1783, CO, 152/63; JAStK, 1782–85, f. 466, Record Office of St. Kitts; Tom Pocock, *The Young Nelson in the Americas* (London, 1980), 189; Sydney to Shirley, Mar. 2, 1785, CO, 152/64.

9. Elsa Goveia, *Slave Society in the British Leeward Islands at the End of the Eighteenth Century* (New Haven, Conn., 1965), 77; Geoffrey Rawson, ed., *Nelson's Letters from the Leeward Islands* (London, 1953); Pocock, *The Young Nelson in the Americas*, 189–192; Brian S. Kirby, "Nelson and American Merchantmen in the West Indies, 1784–1787," *MM* 75, no. 2 (1989), 137–147.

10. Memorial and Petition of the Assembly of Jamaica to the King, Dec. 4, 1784, *Journals of the Assembly of Jamaica*, 8:40–41; Address of the Assembly of Barbados to George III, enclosed in Parry to Sydney, Sept. 7, 1784, CO, 28/60, f. 163.

11. Resolutions of the Committee of West India Planters and Merchants, Feb. 6, 1784, *British Colonial Documents, 1774–1834*, ed. Vincent Harlow and Frederick Madden (Oxford, 1953), 256; MSWIM, Feb. 27, 1784, quoted in *British Colonial Documents*, 257.

12. *Reflections on the Proclamation of the Second of July, 1783, Relative to the Trade Between the United States of America and the West India Islands; Addressed to the Right Honourable William Pitt, First Lord of the Treasury and Chancellor of the Exchequer* (London, 1783); James Allen, *Considerations on the Present State of the Intercourse between His Majesty's Sugar Colonies and the Dominions of the United States of America* (London, 1784); Bryan Edwards, *Thoughts on the Late Proceedings Of Government . . .* , 2nd edn. (London, 1784); Edward Long, *A Free and Candid Review of a Tract Entitled "Observations on the Commerce of the American States . . ."* (London, 1784); Edwards, *History Civil and Commercial, of the British Colonies in the West Indies*, 5 vols., 5th edn. (London, 1819), 2:392–425, also makes a case for the establishment of free trade with America; Stephen Fuller, *The Representation of the Agent for Jamaica, to His Majesty's Ministers* (London, 1785); Fuller, *The communication of the substance of eleven petitions from as many different parishes of Jamaica to the island House of Assembly, recommending the taking of such measures as would bring about a renewal of free intercourse with the United States, and the Memorial of the Council and Assembly of Jamaica to the Crown on that subject, December 1784, to both houses of parliament* (no imprint); "A West India Planter," *Morning Chronicle*, Nov. 11, 1783; *Morning Herald*, Dec. 27, 1783; "A West Indian," *Morning Chronicle*, Jan. 23, 1784.

13. Williams, *Capitalism and Slavery*, 154.

14. Lowell J. Ragatz, *The Fall of the Planter Class in the British Caribbean, 1763–1833* (Washington, D.C., 1928), 206, 212.

15. The Society of West India Merchants eventually became a shadow of itself and

was amalgamated with the combined Society of West India Merchants and Planters to form the West India Committee in 1843.

16. Checkland, "West Indian Finance," 463.

17. "Colony Members of Parliament 1781 Resident in Great Britain," Fuller MSS 265, f. 305, BCL.

18. Knight, "The American Revolution and Caribbean," 251.

19. *Journals of the Assembly of Jamaica*, 8:581, 620; Nicholas A. M. Rodger, *The Wooden World: Anatomy of the Georgian Navy* (London, 1986), 582, notes Perkins went on to command the *Arab* and *Tartar* frigates in the French Revolutionary Wars. He retired from ill health in 1805 and died in Kingston in 1812.

20. Petition of the free people of colour in Hanover, Mar. 2, 1782, JAJ, CO, 140/59; Petition of brown infantry and other people of colour in the parish of Westmoreland to the lieutenant governor, Minutes of the Assembly of Jamaica, Apr. 16, 1782, JAJ, CO, 140/59.

21. Edward L. Cox, *Free Coloreds in the Slave Societies of St. Kitts and Grenada, 1763–1833* (Knoxville, Tenn., 1984), 15, notes that the free black and mulatto population of St. Kitts rose from 391 in 1770 to 908 in 1788 and in Grenada from 455 in 1763 to 1,688 in 1812; John W. Pulis, "Bridging Troubled Waters: Moses Baker, George Liele, and the North-American Diaspora to Jamaica," First Annual Conference of the Institute of Early American History and Culture, June 4–6, 1995, University of Michigan, Ann Arbor, 6.

22. Goveia, *Slave Society in the British Leeward Islands*, 307; Benjamin Quarles, *The Negro in the American Revolution* (New York, reprinted 1973), 177; Sylvia Frey, *Water from the Rock: Black Resistance in a Revolutionary Age* (Princeton, N.J., 1991), 38, 201–202; Sydney Kaplan and Emma Nogrady Kaplan, *The Black Presence in the Era of the American Revolution*, rev. edn. (Amherst, Mass., 1989), 92; Pulis, "Bridging Troubled Waters," 8–16; Roger Norman Buckley, *Slaves in Red Coats: The British West India Regiments, 1795–1815* (New Haven, Conn., 1979), 33.

23. Knight, "The American Revolution and the Caribbean," 257.

24. Mavis C. Campbell, *The Dynamics of Change in a Slave Society: A Sociopolitical History of the Free Coloreds of Jamaica, 1800–1865* (Cranbury, N.J., 1976), 64.

25. Clarkson, "Essay on Impolicy," 34, quoted in Williams, *Capitalism and Slavery*, 122. This argument is also made by David Brion Davis, *The Problem of Slavery in the Age of Revolution, 1770–1823* (Ithaca, N.Y., 1975), 119. However, Drescher, *Econocide*, is unimpressed by this argument because "before 1776, the Americans were far more active against the [slave] trade, if only for political reasons, than were their metropolitan counterparts" (33). Davis, "American Slavery and the American Revolution," in *Slavery and Freedom in the Age of the American Revolution*, ed. Ira Berlin and Ronald Hoffman (Charlottesville, Va., 1983), 265–267, reversed his earlier argument on grounds similar to those of Drescher. Davis also noted that the slaveholders themselves were divided over the slave trade.

26. Edward Brathwaite, *The Development of Creole Society in Jamaica, 1770–1820* (Oxford, 1981), xiv–xv, 80, 94, 151, 244–245, 302; Robert L. Schuyler, "The Constitutional Claims of the British West Indies," *PSQ* 40, no. 1 (1925), 23; Williams, *Capitalism and Slavery*, 199–200; Elsa V. Goveia, *A Study on the Historiography of the British West Indies to the End of the Nineteenth Century* (Washington, D.C., 1980), 56; Gordon K.

Lewis, *Main Currents in Caribbean Thought: The Historical Evolution of Caribbean Society in Its Ideological Aspects, 1492–1900* (Baltimore, 1983), 246–247.

27. *Journal of the Assembly of Jamaica*, 8:536. In 1792, a committee of the Jamaican assembly denied the right of Parliament to legislate for the colonies or to lay a proposed tax against slaves imported onto the islands, declaring that the colonists "have the indefeasible right of giving and granting their own money, and of legislating for themselves . . . it is the indispensable duty of the assembly of Jamaica to maintain . . . the just privileges of the colonials; and . . . they will oppose, in every constitutional manner, any attempt to deprive them of such rights and privileges," in *Proceedings of the Hon. House of Assembly of Jamaica . . . in a Session which Began the 23rd of October, 1792*, cited in Ragatz, *The Fall of the Planter Class*, 266.

28. Speech of Bryan Edwards, reprinted in *Supplement to the Cornwall Chronicle*, Nov. 7, 1789; Edwards, *History Civil and Commercial, of the British Colonies in the West Indies*, 2:341–43, 414–16; William Cobbett and Thomas Hansard, eds., *The Parliamentary History of England from the Earliest Period to 1803*, 36 vols. (London, 1806–22), 31:781–782, cited by Williams, *Capitalism and Slavery*, 200; Memorial of the Jamaica deputies to Britain, Nov. 29, 1832, CO, 137/186, cited in *Capitalism and Slavery*, 200.

29. Francis Wharton, ed., *The Revolutionary and Diplomatic Correspondence of the United States*, 6 vols. (Washington, D.C., 1889), 6:533; Minutes of the Committee of the Privy Council for Trade, Mar. 15, 1784, B.T. 5/1, f. 14d; *Despatches and Letters of Lord Nelson*, 1:114, quoted in R. Southey, *Life of Nelson* (London, 1905), 42.

30. Sir Harry Luke, *Caribbean Circuit* (London, 1950), 173. The mace is dated 1787. *Journal of the Assembly of Jamaica*, 8:405: the journals of the assembly do not contain any reference to the order or description of the desired mace. They simply refer to the arrival of the new mace and new robes.

31. Anthony Stokes, *A View of the Constitution of the British Colonies . . .* (London, 1783), 144; Sharpe to Wilberforce, Dec. 11, 1796, Bodleian Library, Oxford University, c.3.22, quoted in John Pollock, *Wilberforce* (London, 1982), 88; Campbell, *The Dynamics of Change in a Slave Society*, 142–143; Philip Curtin, *Two Jamaicas: The Role of Ideas in a Tropical Colony, 1830–1865* (New York, reprinted 1970), 78; Lewis, *Main Currents in Caribbean Thought*, 103–123; Williams, *Capitalism and Slavery*, 200; Brathwaite, *The Development of Creole Society*, 70–71.

Select Bibliography

BIBLIOGRAPHIES

Adams, Thomas R. *The American Controversy: A Bibliographical Study of the British Pamphlets About the American Disputes, 1764–1783*. New York, 1980.

Andrews, C. M. *A Guide to the Materials for American History to 1783 in the Public Record Office of Great Britain*. 2 vols. Washington, D.C., 1912–14.

Andrews, C. M., and Frances G. Davenport. *Guide to Manuscript Materials for a History of the United States to 1783 in the British Museum, in Minor London Archives, and in the Libraries of Oxford and Cambridge*. Washington, D.C., 1908.

Baker, E. C. *A Guide to the Records in the Leeward Islands*. Oxford, 1965.

Bell, Herbert C., David W. Parker, et al. *Guide to British West Indian Archives Materials in London and in the Islands, for the History of the United States*. Washington, D.C., 1926.

Handler, Jerome S. *A Guide to the Source Materials for the Study of Barbados History, 1627–1834*. Carbondale, Ill., 1971.

———. *Supplement to A Guide to Source Materials for the Study of Barbados History, 1627–1834*. Providence, R.I., 1991.

Hough, Samuel J., and Penelope R. O. Hough. *The Beinecke Lesser Antilles Collection at Hamilton College: A Catalogue of Books, Manuscripts, Prints, Maps and Drawings, 1521–1860*. Gainesville, Fla., 1994.

Ingram, K. E. *Manuscript Relating to Commonwealth Caribbean Countries in United States and Canadian Repositories*. Bridgetown, Barbados, 1975.

———. *Sources of Jamaican History, 1655–1838*. 2 vols. Zug, Switzerland, 1976.

———. *Sources for West Indian Studies: A Supplementary Listing, With Particular Reference to Manuscript Sources*. Zug, Switzerland, 1983.

Manross, W. M. *The Fulham Palace Papers in Lambeth Palace Library, American Colonial Section: Calendar and Indexes*. Oxford, 1965.

Pares, Richard. "Public Records in the British West Indies Islands." *Bulletin of the Institute of Historical Research* 7 (1929–30).

Paulin, C. O., and F. L. Paxton. *Guide to the Materials in London Archives for the History of the United States Since 1783*. Washington, D.C., 1914.

Penfold, P. A., ed. *Maps and Plans in the Public Record Office: America and the West Indies*. London, 1974.

Ragatz, L. J. *Guide to the Study of the British Caribbean, 1763–1834*. Washington, D.C., 1932.

Tyson, G. F. *A Guide to Manuscript Sources in United States and West Indian Depositories Relating to the British West Indies During the Era of the American Revolution*. Wilmington, Del., 1978.

Tyson, G. F., and C. Tyson. *Preliminary Report on Manuscript Materials Relating to the American Revolution in the West Indian Islands*. Millwood, N.Y., 1978.

Walne, Peter, ed. *A Guide to Manuscript Sources for the History of Latin America and the Caribbean in the British Isles*. London, 1973.

MANUSCRIPT SOURCES

Britain

BEDFORD

Bedford County Record Office

B.S. 1429–1505: Payne MSS. Payne family estates in Tempsford in Bedfordshire
B.S. 1509–37: Payne MSS. Title deeds and other papers relating to properties in St. Kitts, Nevis, and the Virgin Islands, 1743–1875
D.D.W. 10–39: Payne MSS. Legal papers relating to the West Indies

BRISTOL

Bristol University Library

Pinney Letter Books III–VII: Pinney Family Correspondence, 1761–87

LONDON

British Library

Add. MSS 12402–40: Long Papers, Jamaica, 1655–1800
Add. MSS 18959–63: Collections relating to Jamaica presented by Edward Long
Add. MSS 22676–77: Papers relating to the Island of Jamaica, Long family
Add. MSS 33030: Newcastle Papers
Add. MSS 41347–48: Martin MSS. Samuel Martin of Antigua to Samuel Martin Jr.
Add. MSS 41350–51: Martin MSS. Letter book of Samuel Martin Sr., 1765–78
Add. MSS 41353: Martin MSS. Family Correspondence, 1695–1795
Add. MSS 42354: Martin MSS. Correspondence of Samuel Martin Jr., 1734–84

Lambeth Palace

Fulham Palace Ms. xix–xx: General Correspondence, Leeward Islands, 1681–1818
Fulham Palace Ms xxx–xxxl: Ordination Papers, Leeward Islands, 1749–1819

Public Record Office, Kew

CO, 1 Colonial Office Papers, Class 1
CO, 5 America and West Indies, Original Documents
CO, 7 Antigua: Original Correspondence with Secretary of State
CO, 8, Antigua: Acts of Assembly
CO, 9 Antigua: Council and Assembly Minutes
CO, 28 Barbados: Original Correspondence with Secretary of State
CO, 30 Barbados: Acts of Assembly
CO, 31 Barbados: Council and Assembly Minutes
CO, 71 Dominica: Original Correspondence to Secretary of State
CO, 74 Dominica: Council and Assembly Minutes
CO, 101 Grenada: Original Correspondence to Secretary of State
CO, 104 Grenada: Council and Assembly Minutes
CO, 137 Jamaica: Original Correspondence with the Board of Trade
CO, 140 Jamaica: Council and Assembly Minutes
CO, 152/19–26 Leeward Islands: Entry Books, Commissions, and Instructions, 1763–
     1783
CO, 152/30–35 Leeward Islands: Original Correspondence with Board of Trade,
     1763–83
CO, 153/19–25 Leeward Islands: Entry Books, 1761–82
CO, 155 Leeward Islands: Miscellaneous Minutes of Council and Assembly
CO, 175 Montserrat: Original Correspondence with Secretary of State
CO, 176 Montserrat: Acts of Assembly
CO, 177 Montserrat: Minutes of Council and Assembly
CO, 184 Nevis: Original Correspondence with Secretary of State
CO, 186 Nevis: Council and Assembly Minutes
CO, 185 Nevis: Acts of Assembly
CO, 239 St. Kitts: Original Correspondence to Secretary of State
CO, 240 St. Kitts: Acts of Assembly
CO, 241 St. Kitts: Council and Assembly Minutes
CO, 246 St. Eustatius: Original Correspondence to the Secretary of State
CO, 260 St. Vincent: Original Correspondence to Secretary of State
CO, 263 St. Vincent: Council and Assembly Minutes
CO, 288 Tobago: Council and Assembly Minutes
CO, 316 Virgin Islands: Council and Assembly Minutes
CO, 318 Military Despatches
Adm. 1/238–243 Despatches from Admirals on the Jamaica Station, 1763–83
Adm. 1/308–314 Despatches from Admirals on the Leeward Island Station, 1763–83
PRO, 30/20 Admiral Rodney Papers, West Indies, 1772–84
WO, 1/49–57 Military Papers

Institute of Commonwealth Studies, University of London

Microfilm Minutes of the Society of West India Merchants and the Society of West
     India Merchants and Planters. The originals are now deposited at the University
     of the West Indies, at St. Augustine, Republic of Trinidad and Tobago.

OXFORD

Rhodes House, Oxford University

MSS Brit Emp S2: An MS volume of the Rev. James Ramsay
Macartney MSS Papers of Lord Macartney as governor of Grenada
Senhouse Diary (Barbados)
Pares MSS (Transcripts by Richard Pares)

SHEFFIELD

Department of Local History, Central Library, Sheffield

Wentworth Woodhouse Muniments (by permission of Olive, Countess Fitzwilliam's
    Wentworth Settlement Trustees)

DENMARK

COPENHAGEN

Statsbiblioteket, State and University Library

Royal Danish American Gazette, 1770–75, 1776–79

UNITED STATES

MICHIGAN

William L. Clements Library, University of Michigan, Ann Arbor

Papers relating to Antigua, 1719–1837
Thomas Gage Papers, 1754–83
Lord George Germain Papers
William H. Lyttelton Papers, 1755–66
William Knox Papers, 1757–1809
George, First Earl of Macartney Papers, 1776–1800
Lord Shelburne Papers, 1663–1797
Sydney Family Papers, 1685–1829
Sir John Vaughan Papers, 1779–81
Alexander Wedderburn Papers, 1764–73
Charles Winstone Letter book (Dominica), 1777–86

NEW YORK

New York Historical Society

Barbados Mercury, October 1772–September 1773

New York Public Library

Adams MSS
Great Britain, Navy Case 35/D West Indies Misc. (Box 1)

MASSACHUSETTS

Boston College Library

Fuller MSS 255–256 Stephen Fuller Letterbooks, 1762–83
Nicholas M. Williams Ethnological Collection

American Antiquarian Society, Worcester

Halifax Gazette

RHODE ISLAND

John Carter Brown Library, Providence

Anthony Stokes, "A View of the Constitution of the British Colonies in North America
     and the West Indies." 2 vols. (1783), annotated copy for a second edition
[Daniel Patterson], Distribution of British Troops, 1766–70
John Dovaston, "Agricultura Americana, or improvements in West India Husbandry"
     (1774)
Autobiographical Memoir of Henry Hulton, 1751–83
Bryan Edwards, Notes on Edward Long's *History of Jamaica*, c. 1790
Journal of a Jamaican Slave Overseer, Somerset Vale, 1776–80

Newport Historical Society Library

Letterbooks of Peleg Clarke, vols. 75–76
NHS Library Special Collection, Box 656
Redwood Ms. Letterbook IV (1756–73)
Transcript of letters of the Anderson family

WEST INDIES

ST. KITTS

Government Buildings, Church Street, Basseterre

Council and Assembly Minutes
King's Bench and Common Pleas
Court of Errors
Grand Sessions
Court of Chancery
Ordinary Deeds
Deed Books

PRIMARY PRINTED SOURCES

PAMPHLETS AND CONTEMPORARY MATERIALS

Allen, James. *Considerations on the Present State of the Intercourse between His Majesty's Sugar Colonies and the Dominions of the United States of America*. London, 1784.

[Alleyne, Sir John Gay]. *A Letter to the North American, on Occasion of His Address to the Committee of Correspondence in Barbadoes*. Bridgetown, Barbados, 1766

An Answer to the Reverend James Ramsay's Essay on the Treatment and Conversion of Slaves in the British Sugar Colonies by Some Gentlemen of St. Christopher. Basseterre, St. Kitts, 1784.

[Anon.] *Report of the Lords of the Committee of Council . . . Concerning the Present State of the Trade to Africa, and Particularly the Trade in Slaves; and Concerning the Effects and Consequences of this Trade, as well in Africa and the West Indies, as then to the General Commerce of the Kingdom*. London, 1788.

Atwood, Thomas. *The History of the Island of Dominica*. London, 1791.

Audi alteram Partem, or A Counter-Letter to the Right Hon. E——l of H——ll——bh, His M——'s P——l S——y for the C——s. London, 1770.

Blenman, Jonathan. *Remarks on Several Acts of Parliament Relating More Especially to the Colonies Abroad*. London, 1742.

[Bourke, Nicholas]. *The Privileges of the Island of Jamaica Vindicated*. London, 1766.

Candid Observations on Two Pamphlets Lately Published, Viz. An Address to the Committee of Correspondence in Barbadoes by a North-American. A Letter to the North American 1766. Barbados, 1766.

Candid Remarks on Dr. Witherspoon's Address To the Inhabitants of Jamaica, &c In a Letter to Those Gentlemen. Philadelphia, 1772.

Considerations on the Present State of Intercourse Between His Majesty's Sugar Colonies and the Dominions of the United States of America. London, 1784.

Cumberland, Richard. *The West Indian*. London, 1771.

Dallas, R. C. *History of the Maroons*. 2 vols. London, 1803.

[Dickinson, John]. *An Address to the Committee of Correspondence in Barbados Occasioned by a Late Letter from Them to Their Agent in London, By a North American.* Philadelphia, 1766.

Dickson, William. *Letters on Slavery.* London, 1789.

——. *The Mitigation of Slavery.* London, 1814.

Dirom, Alexander. *Thoughts on the State of the Militia of Jamaica.* Kingston, Jamaica, 1783.

Edwards, Bryan. *Thoughts on the Late Proceedings of Government Respecting the Trade of the West India Islands with the United States of North America.* 2nd edn. London, 1784.

——. *Poems Written Chiefly in the West-Indies.* Kingston, Jamaica, 1792.

——. *The History Civil and Commercial of the British West Indies.* 5 vols. 5th edn. London, 1819.

The Election, A Poem: With Corrections and Additions by the Author. Written Immediately After the General Election in 1787, and First Published in Numbers in the Kingston Journal; New Re-Published at the Request of Several Gentlemen. Kingston, Jamaica, 1793.

The Evidence Delivered on the Petition Presented by the West India Planters and Merchants to the Hon. House of Commons, As it was Introduc'd at the Bar, and Summ'd up by Mr Glover. London, 1775.

Estwick, Samuel. *A Letter to the Revd. Josiah Tucker, D.D. Dean of Gloucester, in Answer to his Humble Address And Earnest Appeal, etc. With a Postscript in which the Present War against America is Shewn to the Effect, Not of the Causes Assigned by him and Others, But of a Fixed Plan of Administration.* London, 1776.

——. *Considerations on the Present Decline of the Sugar-Trade.* London, 1782.

Foote, Samuel. *The Patron.* London, 1764.

[Frere, Henry]. *A Short History of Barbados, From Its First Discovery and Settlement, to the End of the Year 1767.* London, 1768.

Gardiner, John. *The Argument or Speech of John Gardiner, Esq., Barrister at Law who Stood Committed by the Pretended Assembly of this Island for a Pretended Contempt.* Basseterre, St. Kitts, 1770.

——. *The Memorial and Petition of John Gardiner.* Boston, 1783.

A Grenada Planter Or, A Full and Impartial Answer to a Letter in the Gazetteer of October 22, 1768. London, 1968.

The Humble Petition and Remonstrance of William Wharton, Joseph King, William Feuilleteau, Aretas Akers, Christopher Mardenbrough Sr., Anthony Bryan, and Henry Seaton, Esqs., Present to His Excellency William Woodley, Esq., on Wednesday the 22nd of November, 1769. Basseterre, 1769.

Journals of the Assembly of Jamaica. Jamaica, 1805

Letters to the Earl of Hillsborough, Secretary of State for the Colonies, the Marquis of Rockingham, and the Archbishops and Bishops; On the late Subversion of the Political System of the Glorious Revolution . . . in the Government of His Majesty's Islands of Grenada and the Grenadines, which are Part of the Empire of Great Britain. By Pliny, Junior. London, 1770.

Long, Edward. *The History of Jamaica.* 3 vols. London, 1774.

Mathews, Samuel Augustus. *The Lying Hero Or an Answer to J. B. Moreton's Manners and Customs in the West Indies.* St. Eustatius, 1793.

Morris, Valentine. *A Narrative of the Official Conduct of Valentine Morris, Esq., Late Captain General, Governor in Chief, & etc. & etc. Of the Island of St. Vincent and its Dependencies.* London, 1787.

[Morrison, Kenneth]. *An Essay Toward the Vindication of the Committee of Correspondence in Barbadoes, From the Aspersions and Calumnies Thrown upon them, In an Anonymous Piece Printed in Philadelphia, Under the Title of an Address to them, Occasion by their Letter to their Agent in London*. Bridgetown, Barbados, 1766.

A Narrative of the Complaint against Governor Melvill. London, 1770.

Observations from a Gentleman in Town to his Friend in the Country Relative to the Sugar Colonies Proving their Importance to England. London, 1781.

Poems, On Subjects Arising in England, And the West Indies. By a Native of the West Indies. London, 1783.

Ramsay, James. *An Essay on the Reduction of Interest*. St. Kitts, 1770.

——. *An Essay on the Treatment and Conversion of African Slaves in the British Sugar Colonies*. London, 1784.

——. *A Reply to the Personal Invectives and Objections Contained in Two Answers Published by Certain Anonymous Persons, To An Essay on the Treatment and Conversion of African Slaves in the British Sugar Colonies*. London, 1785.

——. *Objections to the Abolition of the Slave Trade, with Answers, to Which are Prefixed, Strictures on a Late Publication, intitled, "Considerations on the Emancipation of Negroes, and the Abolition of the Slave Trade, by a West Indian Planter."* London, 1788.

Remarks on the Evidence delivered on the Petition Presented By the West-India Planters and Merchants, To The Hon. House of Commons, On the 16th March 1775, As it was introduced at the Bar and summed up by Mr. Glover, So far as the same respects Barbadoes and the Leeward Islands. In a Letter to a Member of Parliament By a West India Planter. London, 1777.

——. *Remarks upon a Book, Intitled, A Short History of Barbados*. Bridgetown, Barbados, 1768.

Report of the Lords of the Committee of Council . . . Concerning the Present State of the Trade to Africa. London, 1789.

Robertson, Rev. Robert. *A Letter to the Bishop of London*. London, 1730.

——. *A Detection of the State and Situation of the Present Sugar Planters of Barbadoes and the Leeward Islands*. London, 1732.

——. *A Supplement to the Detection of the State and Situation of the Present Sugar Planters of Barbados and the Leeward Islands*. London, 1733.

Rodney, Lord. *Letters from Sir George Brydges now Lord Rodney, to His Majesty's Ministers, &c &c Relative to The Capture of St. Eustatius, and its Dependencies, and Shewing the State of the War in the West Indies, at that Period. Together with A Continuation of His Lordships's Correspondence With the Governors and Admirals in the West Indies and America, During the Year 1781, and Until the Time of his Leaving the Command and Sailing for England*. London, 1789.

Rymer, James. *A Description of the Island of Nevis; With an Account of its Principal Diseases*. London, 1775.

[William Scott?]. *A Discourse Concerning the Special Causes of Irreligion in the West Indies with the Apparent Symptoms of Its Decrease*. London, 1764?.

Sheffield, John Lord. *Observations on the Commerce of the American States*. 2nd edn. London, 1783.

Smith, Rev. William. *A Natural History of Nevis, and the Rest of the English Charibee Islands in America*. Cambridge, Eng., 1745.

Stevenson, John. *An Address to Bryan Edwards*. London, 1784.

Stokes, Anthony. *A View of the Constitution of the British Colonies in North America and the West Indies, at the Time the Civil War Broke Out On the Continent of North America*. London, 1783.

The West India Merchant. A Series of Papers Originally Under That Signature in the London Evening Post. London, 1778.

Witherspoon, Dr. John. *Address to the Inhabitants of Jamaica and the Other West India Islands, In Behalf of the College of New Jersey*. Philadelphia, 1772.

Young, Sir William, *The West-India Common-Place Book*. London, 1807.

CONTEMPORARY PERIODICALS AND NEWSPAPERS

Adams Weekly Courant
Annual Register
Antigua Gazette
Antigua Weekly or St. Johns Weekly Advertiser
Barbados Mercury
Bingley's Journal
Boston Gazette
Boston Newsletter
Boston Post-Boy
British Mercury and Evening Advertiser
Charibbean and General Gazette or Saint Christopher Chronicle
Chester Chronicle
Cornwall Chronicle
Craftsman
Essex Gazette
Freeport Gazette or the Dominica Chronicle
Gazetteer and New Daily Advertiser
General Evening Post
Gentleman's Magazine and Historical Chronicler
Georgia Gazette
Lloyd's Evening Post
Kingston Gazette
Kingston Journal
London Chronicle
London Courant
London Courant and Westminster Chronicle
London Evening Post
London Packet and New Lloyd's Evening Post
Maryland Gazette
Middlesex Journal
Morning Chronicle and London Advertiser
Morning Post
New Hampshire Gazette
New York Gazette

New York Mercury
Pennsylvania Evening Post
Pennsylvania Journal and Weekly Advertiser
Providence Gazette
Public Advertiser
Public Advisor
Public Ledger
Royal Danish American Gazette
Royal Gazette (New York)
The St. Christopher Gazette
Saint Christopher Journal
St. James' Chronicle
Virginia Gazette (Purdie and Dixon)
Virginia Gazette (Rind)
Westminster Journal

EDITED DOCUMENTS

Andrews, Evangeline W., and Charles M. Andrews. *Journal of a Lady of Quality; Being the Narrative of a Journey from Scotland to the West Indies, North Carolina and Portugal, in the Years 1774–1776.* New Haven, Conn., 1921.

Barck, Dorothy C. *Letter-Books and Order-Book of George, Lord Rodney . . . 1780–82.* 2 vols. New York, 1932–33.

Burnett, Edmund C. *Letters of Members of the Continental Congress.* 8 vols. Washington, D.C., 1921–36.

Christie, O. F. *The Diary of the Revd William Jones, 1777–1821. Curate and Vicar of the Broxbourne and the Hamlet of Hoddesdon, 1781–1821.* New York, 1929.

Clark, William Bell, and William James Morgan. *Naval Documents of the American Revolution.* 10 vols. Washington, D.C., 1964–.

Cobbett, William, and Thomas Hansard. *The Parliamentary History of England from the Earliest Period to 1803.* 36 vols. London, 1806–22.

Crossley, David, and Richard Saville. *The Fuller Letters: Guns, Slaves and Finance, 1728–1775.* Southampton, Eng., 1991.

Crèvecoeur, J. Hector St. John de. *Letters from an American Farmer*, ed. Albert E. Stone. New York, 1986.

Davis, Kenneth Gordon. *Documents of the American Revolution.* 21 vols. Shannon, Ire., 1972–81.

Fitzpatrick, John C. *The Diaries of George Washington.* 4 vols. Boston, 1925.

Force, Peter. *American Archives . . . A Documentary History of . . . the American Colonies.* 4th ser., I–VI; 5th ser., I–III. Washington, D.C., 1837–53.

Ford, Washington C. *Journals of the Continental Congress, 1774–1789.* 12 vols. Washington, D.C., 1904–76.

Grant, William L., and James Munro. *Acts of Privy Council of England: Colonial Series.* 6 vols. London, 1908–12.

Historical Manuscripts Commission. *Dartmouth Manuscripts.* No. 20. 3 vols. London, 1887–96.

——. *Rutland Manuscripts*. No. 24. 4 vols. London, 1888–1905.

——. *Charlemont Manuscripts*. No. 28. 2 vols. London, 1891–94.

——. *Carlisle Manuscripts*. No. 42. London, 1897.

——. *Stopford Sackville Manuscripts*. No. 49. 2 vols. London, 1904–10.

——. *Various Collections*. No. 55. 8 vols. London, 1901–14.

Jensen, Merrill. *Tracts of the American Revolution*. Indianapolis, 1967.

Journal of the Board of Trade and Plantations, 1704–82. 14 vols. London, 1920–38.

Lewis, A. S. *Redcoats in the Caribbean: Recollections by James Aytoun*. Blackburn, Lancashire. 1984.

Mereness, Newton D. *Travels in the American Colonies, 1640–1783*. New York, reprinted 1961.

Mundy, Godfrey Basil. *The Life and Correspondence of the Late Admiral Lord Rodney*. 2 vols. London, 1830.

Naval Historical Records Society. No. 3. David Hannay. *Letters written by Sir Samuel Hood . . . 1781–83*. London, 1895.

——. nos. 32, 38, 39. Sir J. K. Laughton. *Letters and Papers of Charles, Lord Barham, Admiral of the Red Squadron, 1758–1813*. 3 vols. London, 1906–10.

——. nos. 69, 71, 75, 78. G. R. Barnes and J. H. Owen. *The Private Papers of John, Earl of Sandwich, 1771–1782*. 4 vols. London, 1932–38.

——. nos. 77, 81. D. Bonner-Smith. *The Barrington Papers*. 2 vols. London, 1937–41.

Oliver, Vere Langford. *History of Antigua*. 3 vols. London, 1890–99.

——. *Caribbeana*. 6 vols. London, 1912–19.

Rawson, Geoffrey. *Nelson's Letters from the Leeward Islands*. London, 1953.

"Roger Hope Elletson Letter Book." *Jamaican Historical Review* 1, no. 2 (1946): 187–220; 1, no. 3 (1948): 310–366; 2, no. 1 (1949): 77–119; 2, no. 2 (1951): 65–109; 2, no. 3 (1953): 44–90.

Seeber, Edward D., trans. *On the Threshold of Liberty: Journal of a Frenchman's Tour of the American Colonies in 1777*. Bloomington, Ind., 1959.

Shaw, W. A. *Calender of State Papers: Colonial Series. America and the West Indies*. 44 vols. London, 1862–1953.

Sheridan, R. B. "Letters from a Sugar Plantation in Antigua, 1739–1758." *Agricultural History* 31 (1957): 3–24.

Simmons, R. C., and P. D. G. Thomas. *Proceedings and Debates of the British Parliaments Respecting North America, 1754–1783*. 6 vols. New York, 1982–.

Smith, Paul H. *Letters of Delegates to Congress, 1774–1789*. 35 vols. Washington, D.C., 1976–85.

Taylor, Clare. "The Journal of an Absentee Proprietor, Nathaniel Phillips of Slebech." *Journal of Caribbean History* 18 (1984): 67–82.

Thomas, Isaiah. *The History of Printing in America*, ed. Marcus McCorison. Mass., 1970.

Tyson, George, Jr. *Powder, Profits and Privateers: A Documentary History of the Virgin Islands During the Era of the American Revolution*. St. Thomas, 1977.

Watts, Arthur P. *Nevis and St Christopher, 1782–1784: Unpublished Documents*. Paris, 1925.

Wharton, Francis. *The Revolutionary Diplomatic Correspondence of the United States*. 6 vols. Washington, D.C., 1889.

Willcox, W. B. *The American Rebellion: The British Commander-in-Chief's Narrative of His Campaigns, 1775–1782*. New Haven, Conn., 1954.

Yorke, Philip C. *The Diary of John Baker: Barrister of the Middle Temple and Solicitor General of the Leeward Islands*. London, 1931.

SECONDARY SOURCES

Ackworth, A. W. *Treasures in the Caribbean: A First Study of Georgian Buildings in the British West Indies*. London, 1949.

Alberts, Robert C. *The Golden Voyage: The Life and Times of William Bingham, 1752–1804*. Boston, 1969.

Alleyne, Warren, and Henry Fraser. *The Barbados-Carolina Connection*. London, 1988.

Anstey, Roger. *The Atlantic Slave Trade and British Abolition, 1760–1810*. Atlantic Highlands, N.J., 1975.

Armytage, Francis. *The Free Port System in the British West Indies: A Study in Commercial Policy, 1766–1822*. London, 1953.

Bailey, W. R. "The Geography of Fevers in Early Jamaica." *Jamaican Historical Review* 10 (1973): 23–31.

Bailyn, Bernard. *The Origins of American Politics*. repr. New York, 1968.

———. *Voyagers to the West: A Passage in the Peopling of America on the Eve of the Revolution*. New York, 1986.

Bailyn, Bernard, and Philip D. Morgan, eds. *Strangers Within the Realm: Cultural Margins of the First British Empire*. Chapel Hill, N.C., 1991.

Barker, Robert. "Jamaican Goldsmiths and Assayers, 1665 to 1765." *The Silver Society* 3, no. 5 (Spring 1986): 133–37.

———. "Jamaican Goldsmiths — Some Early Eighteenth Century Inventories." *The Silver Society* 3, nos. 7–9 (1987): 190–93.

Beckles, Hilary. *White Servitude and Black Slavery in Barbados, 1627–1715*. Knoxville, Tenn., 1989.

Beckles, Hilary, and Verene Shepherd, eds. *Caribbean Slave Society and Economy*. Kingston, Jamaica, 1991.

Beckles, Hilary, and Karl Watson. "Social Protest and Labour Bargaining: The Changing Nature of Slaves' Responses to Plantation Life in Eighteenth Century Barbados." *Slavery and Abolition* 8 (Dec. 1987): 272–293.

Begnaud, Allen Eustasis, "British Operations in the Caribbean and the American Revolution." Ph.D. thesis, Tulane University, 1966.

Bell, H. C. "British Commercial Policy in the West Indies, 1783–1793." *English Historical Review* 31 (1916): 429–41.

———. "The West Indies Trade Before the American Revolution." *American Historical Review* 22, no. 2 (1917): 272–87.

Bennett, Harry, Jr. "Sir John Gay Alleyne and the Mansion House School: Codrington College, 1775–1797." *Journal of the Barbados Museum and Historical Society* 17, nos. 2–3 (1950): 63–78.

Berlin, Ira, and Ronald Hoffman, eds. *Slavery and Freedom in the Age of the American Revolution*. Charlottesville, Va., 1983.

Bolland, O. Nigel. "The Social Structure and Social Relations of the Settlement in the Bay of Honduras (Belize) in the Eighteenth Century." *Journal of Caribbean History* 6–7 (1973): 1–42.

Bonner-Smith, D. "Byron in the Leeward Islands." *Mariner's Mirror* 30–31 (1944): 38–48, 81–92.

Boromé, Joseph. "Dominica During the French Occupation, 1778–1784." *English Historical Review* 330 (1969): 36–58.

Boulle, Pierre H. "The Caribbean in French Policy on the Eve of the American Revolution." *Revista/Review Interamericana* 5 (1975–76): 564–82.

Bradley, James E. *Popular Politics and the American Revolution in England: Petitions, the Crown and Public Opinion.* Macon, Ga., 1986.

Brathwaite, Edward. *The Development of Creole Society in Jamaica, 1770–1820.* Oxford, 1978.

Breen, Kenneth. "Divided Command: The West Indies and North America, 1780–81." In *The British Navy and the Use of Naval Power in the Eighteenth Century*, ed. Jeremy Black and Philip Woodfine. Leicester, 1988. 191–206.

Breen, T. H. *Tobacco Culture: The Mentality of the Great Tidewater Planters on the Eve of the Revolution.* Princeton, N.J., 1985.

Brewer, John. *The Sinews of Power: War, Money and the English State, 1688–1783.* New York, 1989.

Bridenbaugh, Carl, and Roberta Bridenbaugh. *No Peace Beyond the Line: The English in the Caribbean, 1624–1690.* New York, 1972.

Brown, Gerald S. "The Anglo-French Naval Crisis, 1778: A Study of Conflict in the North Cabinet." *William and Mary Quarterly* 3rd ser., 13 (1956): 3–26.

———. *The American Secretary: The Colonial Policy of Lord George Germain, 1775–1778.* Ann Arbor, Mich., 1963.

Brown, Margaret L. "William Bingham, Agent of the Continental Congress in Martinique." *Pennsylvania Magazine of History and Biography* 61 (1937): 54–87.

Brown, Wallace. "The Loyalists of the American Revolution in the Bahamas and the British West Indies." *Revista/Review Interamericana* 5 (1975–76): 638–647.

———. "The Loyalists in the West Indies." In *Red, White and Blue: The Loyalists in the American Revolution*, ed. Esmond Wright. New York, 1976.

———. "The Governorship of John Orde, 1783–1793: The Loyalist Period in Dominica." *Journal of Caribbean History* 24, no. 2 (1990): 146–77.

———. "The American Loyalists in Jamaica." *Journal of Caribbean History* 26, no. 2 (1992): 121–47.

Buckley, Roger Norman. *Slaves in Redcoats: The British West India Regiments, 1795–1815.* New Haven, Conn., 1979.

Buisseret, David. "The Elusive Deodand: A Study of Fortified Refuges." *Journal of Caribbean History* 6–7 (1973): 43–80.

Bullion, John L. *A Great and Necessary Measure: George Grenville and the Genesis of the Stamp Act, 1763–1765.* Columbia, Mo., 1982.

———. "British Ministers and American Resistance to the Stamp Act, October–December 1965." *William and Mary Quarterly* 3rd ser., 46, no. 1 (1992): 89–107.

Burnard, Trevor. "A Failed Settler Society: Marriage and Demographic Failure in Early Jamaica." *Journal of Social History* 28 (1994): 63–82.

———. "Thomas Thistlewood Becomes a Creole." In *Varieties of Southern History: New Essays on a Region and Its People*, ed. Bruce Clayton and John Salmond. Westport, Conn., 1996. 99–118.

——. "European Migration to Jamaica, 1655–1780." *William and Mary Quarterly* 3rd ser., 53, no. 4 (Oct. 1996): 769–94.

Campbell, Mavis C. *The Dynamics of Change in a Slave Society: A Sociopolitical History of the Free Coloreds of Jamaica, 1800–1865.* Cranbury, N.J., 1976.

——. *The Maroons of Jamaica, 1655–1796: A History of Resistance, Collaboration and Betrayal.* Trenton, N.J., 1990.

Canny, Nicholas, and Anthony Pagden, eds. *Colonial Identity in the Atlantic World, 1500–1800.* Princeton, N.J., 1987.

Carrington, Selwyn H. H. "West Indian Opposition to British Policy: Barbadian Politics, 1774–82." *The Journal of Caribbean History* 17 (1982): 26–49.

——. "Econocide — Myth or Reality?" *Rolet in de estudios latinoamericanos y del Caribe* 36 (1984): 13–48.

——. "Eighteenth Century Political Conflict in the British Empire: A Case Study of St. Vincent, 1775–1779." *Journal of Caribbean History* 20, no. 2 (1985–86): 147–67.

——. "The American Revolution and the British West Indies' Economy." *Journal of Interdisciplinary History* 17, no. 4 (1987): 823–50.

——. *The British West Indies During the American Revolution.* Dordrecht, Holland, 1988.

——. "The State of the Debate on the Role of Capitalism in the Ending of the Slave System." *Journal of Caribbean History* 22 (1988): 20–41.

——. "British West Indian Economic Decline and Abolition, 1775–1807: Revisiting Econocide." *Canadian Journal of Latin American and Caribbean Studies* 14 (1989): 33–59.

——. "The American Revolution, British Policy and the West Indian Economy, 1775–1808." *Revista/Review Interamericana* 22 (1992): 72–108.

Checkland, S. G. "Finance for the West Indies, 1780–1815." *Economic History Review* 10 (1957–58): 461–69.

Christelow, A. "Contraband Trade Between Jamaica and the Spanish Main, and the Free Port Act of 1766." *Hispanic American Historical Review* 22 (1942): 309–43.

Clark, Dora May. *The Rise of the British Treasury: Colonial Administration of the Eighteenth Century.* New Haven, Conn., 1960.

Clarke, C. P. "Imperial Forces in Barbados." *Journal of the Barbados Museum and Historical Society* 32 (1968): 174–80.

Clarke, Mary Patterson. *Parliamentary Privilege in the American Colonies.* New Haven, Conn., 1943.

Clayton, T. R. "Sophistry, Security, and Socio-Political Structures in the American Revolution; Or, Why Jamaica Did Not Rebel." *Historical Journal* 29 (1986): 319–44.

Coelho, Philip R. P. "The Profitability of Imperialism: The British Experience in the West Indies, 1768–1772." *Explorations in Economic History* 10 (1973): 253–80.

Colley, Linda. *Britons: Forging the Nation, 1707–1837.* New Haven, Conn., 1992.

Conser, Walter H., Jr., et al. *Resistance, Politics, and the American Struggle for Independence, 1765–1775.* Boulder, Colo., 1986.

Cooper, J. I. "The West Indies, Bermuda and the Mainland Colleges." *Jamaican Historical Review* 2, no. 1 (Dec. 1949): 1–6.

Corwin, Edward S. "French Objectives in the American Revolution." *American Historical Review* 21 (1915–16): 33–61.

——. *French Policy and the American Alliance of 1778*. Princeton, N.J., 1916.

Cox, Edward L. *Free Coloreds in the Slave Societies of St. Kitts and Grenada, 1763–1833*. Knoxville, Tenn., 1984.

Craton, Michael. *Search for the Invisible Man: Slaves and Plantation Life in Jamaica*. Cambridge, Mass., 1978.

——. "The Passion to Exist: Slave Rebellions in the British West Indies, 1650–1832." *Journal of Caribbean History* 13 (1980): 1–20.

——. *Testing the Chains: Resistance to Slavery in the British West Indies*. Ithaca, N.Y., 1982.

——. "Property and Propriety: Land Tenure and Slave Property in the Creation of a British West Indian Plantocracy, 1612–1740." In *Conceptions of Property*, ed. John Brewer. London, 1996. 497–529.

Craton, Michael, and James Walvin. *A Jamaican Plantation: The History of Worthy Park, 1670–1970*. London, 1970.

Crowhurst, Patrick. *The Defence of the British Trade, 1689–1815*. London, 1977.

Cundall, Frank. *Catalogue of the Portraits in the Jamaica History Gallery of the Institute of Jamaica*. Kingston, Jamaica, 1914.

Curtin, Philip. "Epidemiology of the Slave Trade." *Political Science Quarterly* 83 (June 1968): 190–216.

——. *Two Jamaicas: The Role of Ideas in a Tropical Colony, 1830–1865*. New York, reprinted 1970.

——. *The Atlantic Slave Trade: A Census*. Madison, Wis., 1964.

——. *The Rise and Fall of the Plantation Complex: Essays in Atlantic History*. Cambridge, 1990.

Davies, K. G. "The Origins of the Commission System in the West India Trade." *Transactions of the Royal Historical Society* 5th ser., 1–2 (1952), 89–107.

——. *The Rise of Atlantic Economies*. London, 1973.

——. *The North Atlantic World in the Seventeenth Century*. Minneapolis, 1974.

Davis, David Brion. *The Problem of Slavery in Western Culture*. Ithaca, N.Y., 1966.

——. *The Problem of Slavery in the Age of Revolution, 1770–1823*. Ithaca, N.Y., 1975.

Deer, Noel. *The History of Sugar*. 2 vols. London, 1949–50.

Dickerson, Oliver M. *The Navigation Acts and the American Revolution*. Philadelphia, 1951.

Dookhan, Isaac. *A History of the British Virgin Islands, 1672–1970*. Essex, Eng., 1975.

Drescher, Seymour. *Econocide: British Slavery in the Era of Abolition*. Pittsburgh, 1977.

Duffy, Michael. *Soldiers, Sugar and Seapower: The British Expeditions to the West Indies and the War Against Revolutionary France*. Oxford, 1987.

Dunn, Richard S. *Sugar and Slaves: The Rise of the Planter Class in the English West Indies, 1624–1713*. New York, reprinted 1973.

Durham, Harriet Florer. *Caribbean Quakers*. Hollywood, Fla., 1972.

Eames, Wilberforce. "The Antigua Press and Benjamin Mecom, 1748–1765." *Proceedings of the American Antiquarian Society* 38 (Oct. 1928): 303–348.

Egnal, Marc. *A Mighty Empire: The Origins of the American Revolution*. Ithaca, N.Y., 1988.

Engerman, S. L. "Some Economic and Demographic Comparisons of Slavery in the United States and the British West Indies." *Economic History Review* 2nd ser., 29 (1976): 258–75.

Ernst, Joseph Albert. "The Currency Act Repeal Movement: A Study of Imperial Politics and Revolutionary Crisis, 1764–1767." *William and Mary Quarterly* 25 (1968): 177–211.

Fortescue, Sir John. *A History of the British Army*. 13 vols. London, 1902.

Frey, Sylvia. *The British Soldier in America*. Austin, Tex., 1981.

——. *Water from the Rock: Black Resistance in a Revolutionary Age*. Princeton, N.J., 1991.

Froude, James Anthony. *The English in the West Indies or the Bow of Ulysses*. London, reprinted 1888.

Fuertado, W. A. *Official and Other Personages of Jamaica from 1655–1790*. Kingston, Jamaica, 1896.

Galenson, David. *White Servitude in Colonial America: An Economic Analysis*. Cambridge, 1981.

Gaspar, D. B. *Bondmen and Rebels: A Study of Master-Slave Relations in Antigua with Implications for Colonial British America*. Baltimore, 1985.

Geggus, David Patrick. *Slavery, War, and Revolution: The British Occupation of Saint Domingue, 1793–1798*. Oxford, 1982.

——. "The Enigma of Jamaica in the 1790s: New Light on the Causes of Slave Rebellions." *William and Mary Quarterly* 3rd ser., 44 (1987): 274–385.

Gipson, Lawrence Henry. *The British Empire Before the American Revolution*. 15 vols. New York, reprinted 1936–70.

Goebel, Dorothy B. "The 'New England Trade' and the French West Indies, 1763–1774: A Study in Trade Policies." *William and Mary Quarterly* 3rd ser., 20, no. 2 (July 1963): 331–72.

Goveia, Elsa V. *Slave Society in the British Leeward Islands at the End of the Eighteenth Century*. New Haven, Conn., 1965.

——. *A Study on the Historiography of the British West Indies to the End of the Nineteenth Century*. Washington, D.C., 1980.

Green, William A. "The Planter Class and British West Indian Sugar Production Before and After Emancipation." *Economic History Review* 2nd ser., 26 (1973): 448–63.

Greene, Jack P. *The Quest for Power: The Lower Houses of Assembly of the Southern Royal Colonies, 1689–1776*. New York, 1963.

——. *Pursuits of Happiness: The Social Development of Early Modern British Colonies and the Formation of American Culture*. Chapel Hill, N.C., 1988.

——. *Peripheries and Center: Constitutional Development in the Extended Polities of the British Empire and the United States, 1607–1788*. Athens, Ga., 1990.

——. *Imperatives, Behaviors and Identities: Essays in Early American Cultural History*. Charlottesville, Va., 1992.

——. *Negotiated Authorities: Essays in Colonial Political and Constitutional History*. Charlottesville, Va., 1994.

——. *Interpreting Early America: Historiographical Essays*. Charlottesville, Va., 1996.

Greene, Jack, and Jack Pole. *Colonial British America: Essays in the New History of Early Modern Era*. Baltimore, 1984.

——. *The Blackwell Encyclopedia of the American Revolution*. Oxford, 1991.

Guerra, Francisco. "The Influence of Disease on Race, Logistics and Colonization in the Antilles." *Journal of Tropical Medicine and Hygiene* 69 (1966): 23–35.

Hall, Douglas. "Absentee-Proprietorship in the British West Indies to About 1850." *Jamaican Historical Review* 4 (1964): 15–35.

Hall, Neville A. T. "Governors and Generals: The Relationship of Civil and Military Commands in Barbados, 1783–1815." *Caribbean Studies* 10 (Jan. 1971): 93–112.

——. "Some Aspects of the Deficiency Question in Jamaica in the Eighteenth Century." *Jamaica Journal* 1–2 (Mar.–June 1973): 36–42.

Hamshere, Cyril. *The British in the Caribbean*. Cambridge, Mass. 1972.

Hancock, David. *Citizens of the World: London Merchants and the Integration of the British Atlantic Community, 1735–1785*. Cambridge, 1995.

Handler, Jerome. "Slave Revolts and Conspiracies in Seventeenth-Century Barbados." *New West Indian Guide/Nieuw West-Indische Gids* 56 (1982): 5–43.

Hargreaves, Reginald. *The Bloodybacks: The British Servicemen in North America and the Caribbean, 1655–1783*. London, 1968.

Harlow, Vincent. *A History of Barbados, 1625–1685*. Oxford, 1926.

Harper, Lawrence A. "The Effects of the English Navigation Laws." In *The Era of the American Revolution*, ed. Richard B. Morris. New York, 1939. 3–40.

Herbert, J. W. "Constitutional Struggles in Jamaica, 1748–1776." M.A. thesis, London University, 1927.

Hewitt, M. J. "The West Indies and the American Revolution." D.Phil. thesis, Oxford University, 1937.

Higham, C. S. S. *The Development of the Leeward Islands Under the Restoration, 1660–1688: A Study of the Foundations of the Old Colonial System*. Cambridge, 1921.

Higman, Barry. "The West India Interest in Parliament, 1807– 1833." *Historical Studies* 13 (1967): 1–19.

——. *Jamaica Surveyed: Plantation Maps and Plans of the Eighteenth and Nineteenth Centuries*. Kingston, Jamaica, 1988.

——. "British West Indies Economic and Social Development." In *Cambridge Economic History and the United States*, ed. Stanley Engerman and Robert E. Gallman. Cambridge, 1996.

Houlding, J. A. *Fit for Service: The Training of the British Army, 1715–1795*. Oxford, 1981.

Houlette, William D. "Rum-Trading in the American Colonies Before 1763." *Journal of American History* 27 (1934): 129–152.

Hurst, Ronald. *The Golden Rock: An Episode in the American War of Independence, 1775–1783*. London, 1996.

James, W. M. *The British Navy in Adversity: A Study of the War of American Independence*. London, 1926.

Jameson, A. J. "War Among the Islands: The Naval and Military Campaigns in the Leeward Islands, 1775–83." D.Phil. thesis, Oxford University, 1982.

Jameson, Franklin. "St. Eustatius and the American Revolution." *American Historical Review* 8 (1902–3): 683–708.

Jamieson, A. G. "Admiral James Young and the 'Pirateers,' 1777." *Mariner's Mirror* 65 (1979): 69–75.

Jensen, Merrill. *The Founding of a Nation*. Oxford, 1968.

Johnston, J. R. V. "The Sugar Plantations of the Heirs of Lady Frances Stapleton in Nevis and St. Christopher (1746–1810)." M.A. thesis, University of Wales, 1964.

Jordan, Winthrop. "American Chiaroscuro: The Status and Definition of Mulattoes in the British Colonies." *William and Mary Quarterly* 19 (1962): 183–200.

——. *Black over White: American Attitudes Towards the Negro, 1550–1812*. Baltimore, reprinted 1969.

Judd, Gerrit P. *Members of Parliament, 1734–1832*. New Haven, Conn., 1955.

Kammen, Michael G. *A Rope of Sand: The Colonial Agents, British Politics, and the American Revolution*. Ithaca, N.Y., 1968.

——. *Empire and Interest: The American Colonies and the Politics of Mercantilism*. Philadelphia, 1970.

Karras, Alan L. *Sojourners in the Sun: Scottish Migrants in Jamaica and the Chesapeake, 1740–1800*. Ithaca, N.Y., 1992.

Keith, Alice B. "Relaxations in the British Restrictions on the American Trade with the British West Indies, 1783–1802." *Journal of Modern History* 20, no. 1 (Mar. 1948): 1–18.

Kirby, Brian S. "Nelson and American Merchantmen in the West Indies, 1784–1787." *Mariner's Mirror* 75, no. 2 (1989): 137–147.

Klingberg, Frank J., ed. *Codrington Chronicles: An Experiment in Anglican Altruism on a Barbados Plantation, 1710–1834*. Berkeley, 1949.

Klooster, W. M. *Dutch Trade in the Caribbean, 1648–1795*. Leiden, Netherlands, 1998.

Knight, Derrick. *Gentlemen of Fortune: The Men Who Made Their Fortunes in Britain's Slave Colonies*. Guildford, Surrey, 1978.

Koeppel, Adolph. *The Stamps That Caused the American Revolution: The Stamps of the 1765 British Stamp Act for America*. New York, 1976.

Kozy, Charlene Johnson. "Tories Transplanted: The Caribbean Exile and Plantation of the Southern Loyalists." *Georgia Historical Quarterly* 75 (1991): 18–42.

Kupperman, Karen Ordahl. "Fear of Hot Climates in the Anglo-American Colonial Experience." *William and Mary Quarterly* 3rd ser., 41, no. 2 (Apr. 1984): 213–241.

——. *Providence Island, 1630–1641: The Other Puritan Colony*. Cambridge, 1993.

Kurtz, Stephen G., and James H. Hutson. *Essays on the American Revolution*. Chapel Hill, N.C., 1973.

Labaree, Leonard W. *Royal Government in America: A Study of the British Colonial System Before 1783*. New Haven, Conn., 1930.

Lane, Carl Anthony. "The Roots of Jamaican Loyalism, 1760–1766." Ph.D. thesis, City University of New York, 1978.

Langford, Paul. *The First Rockingham Administration, 1765–1766*. Oxford, 1973.

——. "The Rockingham Whigs and America, 1763–1773." In *Statesmen, Scholars and Merchants: Essays in Eighteenth Century History Presented to Dame Lucy Sutherland*, ed. Anne Whiteman, John S. Bromley, and Peter G. M. Dickson. Oxford, 1973.

Laws, W. I. "The Administration of the Leeward Islands, 1699–1721." M.Litt. thesis, Edinburgh University, 1969.

Layng, Judith. "The American Company of Comedians and the Disruption of the Empire." *Revista/Review Interamericana* 5 (1975–76): 665–675.

Lewis, Gordon K. *Main Currents in Caribbean Thought: The Historical Evolution of Caribbean Society in Its Ideological Aspects, 1492–1900*. Baltimore, 1983.

Lewisohn, Florence. "St. Eustatius: Depot for Revolution." *Revista/Review Interamericana* 5 (1975–76): 623–637.

Luke, Sir Harry. *Caribbean Circuit*. London, 1950.

Lumsden, Mary. *The Barbados American Connection*. London, reprinted 1988.

Mackesy, Piers. *The War for America, 1775–1783*. London, 1964.

Maier, Pauline. *From Resistance to Revolution: Colonial Radicals and the Development of American Opposition to Britain, 1765–1776*. New York, reprinted 1974.

Makinson, David H. *Barbados: A Study of North-American-West-Indian Relations, 1739–1789*. The Hague, 1964.

Manning, Helen Taft. *British Colonial Government After the American Revolution, 1782–1820*. New Haven, Conn., 1933.

Marshall, Bernard. "The Black Caribs — Native Resistance to British Penetration in the Windward Side of St. Vincent, 1763–1773." *Caribbean Quarterly* 19, no. 4 (1973): 4–20.

———. "Marronage in Slave Plantation Societies: A Case Study of Dominica, 1785–1815." *Caribbean Quarterly* 22 (1976): 26–32.

———. "Slave Resistance and White Reaction in the British Windward Islands, 1763–1833." *Caribbean Quarterly* 28, no. 3 (1982): 33–47.

Marshall, Peter. "Empire and Authority in the Later Eighteenth Century." *Journal of Imperial and Commonwealth History* 15, no. 2 (1987): 105–22.

Marshall, Peter, and Glyndwr Williams. *The British Atlantic Empire Before the American Revolution*. London, 1980.

Martin, Asa E. "American Privateers and the West Indies Trade, 1776–1777." *American Historical Review* 39 (1934): 700–706.

McCusker, John. "The American Invasion of Nassau in the Bahamas." *The American Neptune* 25, no. 3 (July 1965): 189–217.

———. "The Rum Trade and the Balance of Payments of the Thirteen Colonies, 1650–1775." Ph.D. thesis, University of Pittsburgh, 1970.

———. *Money and Exchange in Europe and America, 1600–1775: A Handbook*. Chapel Hill, N.C., 1978.

———. *Essays in the Economic History of the Atlantic World*. London, 1997.

McCusker, John J., and Russell R. Menard. *The Economy of British America, 1607–1789*. Chapel Hill, N.C., 1985.

McDonald, Roderick, ed. *West Indies Accounts: Essays on the History of the British Caribbean and the Atlantic Economy in Honour of Richard Sheridan*. Kingston, Jamaica, 1996.

McLarty, Robert Neil. "The Expedition of Major-General John Vaughan to the Lesser Antilles, 1779–81." Ph.D. thesis, University of Michigan, 1951.

———. "Jamaica Prepares for Invasion 1779." *Caribbean Quarterly* 4, no. 1 (1955): 62–67.

McMurtrie, Douglas. *Early Printing on the Island of Antigua*. Evanston, Ill., 1943.

McNeil, John. "The Ecological Basis of Warfare in the Caribbean, 1700–1804." In *Adapting to Conditions: War and Society in the Eighteenth Century*, ed. Martin Utlee. University, Alabama, 1986.

Metcalf, George. *Royal Government and Political Conflict in Jamaica, 1729–1783*. London, 1965.

Miller, Helen Hill. *Colonel Parke of Virginia: "The Greatest Hector in Town."* Chapel Hill, N.C., 1989.

Miller, John C. *Origins of the American Revolution*. London, reprinted 1959.

Minchinton, W. E., ed. *The Growth of English Overseas Trade in the Seventeenth and Eighteenth Centuries*. London, 1969.

Mintz, Sidney. *Sweetness and Power: The Place of Sugar in Modern History*. New York, reprinted 1986.

Morgan, Edmund S., and Helen M. Morgan. *The Stamp Act Crisis*. Rev. edn. New York, 1963.

Morgan, Kenneth. "Bristol West India Merchants in the Eighteenth Century." *Transactions of the Royal Historical Society* 6th ser., 3 (1993): 185–208.

Morris, David. *Thomas Hearne and His Landscape*. London, 1989.

Mullin, Michael. *Africa in America: Slave Acculturation and Resistance in the American South and the British Caribbean, 1736–1831*. Urbana, Ill., reprinted 1994.

Murdoch, D. H. "Land Policy in the Eighteenth-Century British Empire: The Sale of Crown Lands in the Ceded Islands, 1763–1783." *Historical Journal* 27, no. 3 (Sept. 1984): 549–75.

Nagel, Kurt William. "Empire and Interest: British Colonial Defense Policy, 1689–1714." Ph.D. thesis, Johns Hopkins University, 1992.

Namier, Sir Lewis. *England in the Age of the American Revolution*. 2nd edn. London, 1961.

——. *Crossroads of Power: Essays on Eighteenth-Century England*. London, 1962.

Namier, Sir Lewis, and John Brooke. *The House of Commons, 1754–1790*. 3 vols. London, 1964.

O'Gorman, Pamela. "An Eighteenth Century Jamaica Oratorio." *Jamaica Journal* 22, no. 4 (Nov. 1989–Jan. 1990): 41–45.

——. "The Music of Samuel Felsted's Jonah." *Jamaica Journal* 23, no. 1 (Feb.–Apr. 1990): 14–19.

Oosten, F. C. Van. "Some Notes Concerning the Dutch West Indies During the American Revolutionary War." *American Neptune* 36 (1976): 155–169.

Ortiz, Altagracia. *Eighteenth Century Reforms in the Caribbean: Miguel de Mesas, Governor of Puerto Rico, 1769–76*. Rutherford, N.J., 1983.

O'Shaughnessy, Andrew J. "The Politics of the Leeward Islands, 1763–1783." D.Phil. thesis, Oxford University, 1988.

——. "The Formation of a Commercial Lobby: The West India Interest, British Colonial Policy and the American Revolution." *Historical Journal* 40, no. 1 (1997): 71–95.

Ostrander, Gilman M. "The Colonial Molasses Trade." *Agricultural History* 30 (1956): 77–84.

Palmer, R. R. *The Age of Democratic Revolution: A Political History of Europe and America, 1760–1800. The Challenge*. 2 vols. Princeton, N.J., 1989.

Paquette, Robert L., and Stanley L. Engerman. *The Lesser Antilles in the Age of European Expansion*. Gainesville, Fla., 1996.

Pares, Richard. *A West India Fortune*. London, 1950.

——. "The London Sugar Market, 1740–1769." *Economic History Review* 2nd ser., 9, no. 2 (1956): 254–270.

——. *Yankees and Creoles: The Trade Between North America and the West Indies Before the American Revolution*. London, 1956.

——. *Merchants and Planters*. Cambridge, 1960.

——. *The Historian's Business and Other Essays*. Oxford, 1961.

——. *War and Trade in the West Indies, 1739–1763*. London, 1963.

Parry, J. H. "The Patent Offices in the British West Indies." *English Historical Review* 69 (Apr. 1954): 200–225.

——. "Eliphalet Fitch: A Yankee Trader in Jamaica During the American War of Independence." *History* 40 (1955): 84–98.

——. "American Independence: A View from the West Indies." *Massachusetts Historical Society Proceedings* 87 (1975): 14–32.

Patterson, Orlando. *Sociology of Slavery: An Analysis of the Origins, Development and Structure of Negro Slave Society in Jamaica*. Cranbury, N.J., 1969.

Penson, Lillian M. "The London West India Interest in the Eighteenth Century." *English Historical Review* 30 (July 1921): 373–392.

——. *The Colonial Agents of the British West Indies: A Study in Colonial Administration Mainly in the Eighteenth Century*. London, reprinted 1971.

Philips, U. B. "An Antigua Plantation, 1769–1818." *North Carolina Historical Review* 3 (July 1926): 439–445.

Pitman, F. W. *The Development of the British West Indies, 1700–1763*. New Haven, Conn., 1917.

——. "Slavery on the British West India Plantations in the Eighteenth Century." *Journal of Negro History* 11 (1926): 584–668.

——. "The West Indian Absentee Planter as a British Colonial Type." *American Historical Review* (1927): 113–27.

Pocock, Tom. *The Young Nelson in the Americas*. London, 1980.

Poyer, John. *The History of Barbados*. London, 1808

Price, Richard, ed. *Maroon Societies*. 2nd edn. Baltimore, 1979.

Puckrein, Gary A. *Little England: Plantation Society and Anglo-Barbadian Politics, 1627–1700*. New York, 1984.

Ragatz, Lowell J. *The Fall of the Planter Class in the British Caribbean, 1763–1833*. Washington, D.C., 1928.

——. "Absentee Landlordism in the British Caribbean, 1750–1833." *Agricultural History* 5, no. 1 (1931): 7–26.

——. *The West Indian Approach to the Study of American Colonial History*. London, 1935.

Rawley, James A. *The Transatlantic Slave Trade: A History*. New York, 1981.

Reynolds, C. Roy. "Tacky and the Great Slave Rebellion of 1760." *Jamaica Journal* 6 (June 1972): 5–8.

Ritcheson, Charles R. *Aftermath of Revolution: British Policy Toward the United States, 1783–1795*. Dallas, Tex., 1969.

Robertson, Eileen A. *The Spanish Town Papers*. London, 1959.

Robinson, St. John. "Southern Loyalists in the Caribbean and Central America." *South Carolina Historical Magazine* 93 (1992): 204–220.

Rodger, Nicholas A. M. *The Wooden World: Anatomy of the Georgian Navy*. London, 1986.

Roebuck, Peter, ed. *Public Service and Private Fortune: The Life of Lord Macartney, 1737–1806*. Belfast, 1983.

Rouse-Jones, Margaret Deane. "St. Kitts, 1713–1763: A Study of the Development of a Plantation Colony." Ph.D. thesis, Johns Hopkins University, 1978.

Sainsbury, John. *Disaffected Patriots: London Supporters of Revolutionary America, 1769–1782.* Montreal, 1987.

Saunders, Richard H., and Ellen G. Miles. *American Colonial Portraits, 1700–1776.* Washington, D.C., 1987.

Schuler, Monica. "Ethnic Slave Rebellions in the Caribbean and the Guianas." *Journal of Society History* 3 (1969–70): 374–385.

Schumpeter, E. B. *English Overseas Trade Statistics, 1697–1808.* Oxford, 1960.

Schuyler, Robert L. "The Constitutional Claims of the British West Indies." *Political Science Quarterly* 40, no. 1 (1925): 1–36.

Seeley, Sir John. *The Expansion of England,* ed. John Gross. Chicago, reprinted 1971.

Selig, Robert. "The French Capture of St. Eustatius, 26 November, 1781." *Journal of the Caribbean History* 27, no. 2 (1993): 129–143.

Shepherd, Verene A. "Livestock and Sugar: Aspects of Jamaica's Agricultural Development from the Late Seventeenth to the Early Nineteenth Century." *Historical Journal* 34 (1991): 627–643.

Sheppard, Jill. *The "Redlegs" of Barbados: Their Origins and History.* Millwood, N.Y., 1977.

Sheridan, Richard B., "The Molasses Act and the Market Strategy of the British Sugar Planters." *Journal of Economic History* 17 (1957): 62–83.

——. "Samuel Martin, Innovating Sugar Planter of Antigua, 1750–1776." *Agricultural History* 34 (1960): 126–39.

——. "The British Credit Crisis of 1772 and the American Colonies." *Journal of Economic History* 20, no. 2 (1960): 161–86.

——. "The Rise of a Colonial Gentry: A Case Study of Antigua, 1730–1775." *Economic History Review* 2nd ser., 13 (1961): 342–57.

——. "Planter and Historian: The Career of William Beckford of Jamaica and England, 1744–1799." *Jamaican Historical Review* 4 (1964): 36–58.

——. "The Wealth of Jamaica in the Eighteenth Century." *Economic History Review* 2nd ser., 18 (1965): 292–311.

——. "William Beckford (1744–1799), Patron of Painters in Jamaica." *Register of the Museum of Art, University of Kansas* 3, nos. 8–9 (1967): 14–23.

——. "The Wealth of Jamaica in the Eighteenth Century: A Rejoinder." *Economic History Review* 2nd ser., 21 (1968): 46–61.

——. "The Development of the Plantations to 1750" and "An Era of West Indian Prosperity, 1750–1775." In *Chapters in Caribbean History,* ed. Douglas Hall, Elsa Goveia, and F. Roy Augier. Bridgetown, Barbados, 1970.

——. "Simon Taylor, Sugar Tycoon of Jamaica, 1740–1813." *Agricultural History* 45 (1971): 285–96.

——. "Planters and Merchants: The Oliver Family of Antigua and London, 1716–1784." *Business History* 13 (1971): 103–13.

——. *Sugar and Slavery: An Economic History of the British West Indies, 1623–1775.* London, 1974.

——. "The British Sugar Planters and the Atlantic World, 1763–1775." In *Eighteenth-Century Florida and the Caribbean,* ed. Samuel Proctor. Gainesville, Fla., 1976. 1–14.

——. "The Jamaican Slave Insurrection Scare of 1776 and the American Revolution." *Journal of Negro History* 61, no. 3 (1976): 290–308.

———. "The Crisis of Slave Subsistence in the British West Indies During and After the American Revolution." *William and Mary Quarterly* 3rd ser., 33 (1976): 615–41.

———. "The Role of the Scots in the Economy and Society of the West Indies." In *Comparative Perspectives on Slavery*, ed. Vera Rubin and Arthur Tuden. New York, 1977. 94–106.

———. "The West Indian Antecedents of Josiah Martin, Last Royal Governor of North Carolina." *North Carolina Historical Review* 54 (1977): 252–70.

———. *Doctors and Slaves: A Medical and Demographic History of Slavery in the British West Indies, 1680–1834*. Cambridge, 1985.

———. "The Condition of the Slaves in the Settlement and Economic Development of the British Windward Islands, 1763–1775." *Journal of Caribbean History* 24, no. 2 (1990): 121–45.

Shields, David S. *Oracles of Empire: Poetry, Politics and Commerce in British America, 1690–1750*. Chicago, 1990.

Shy, John. *Toward Lexington: The Role of the British Army in the Coming of the American Revolution*. Princeton, N.J., 1965.

Shyllon, Folarin. *James Ramsay: The Unknown Abolitionist*. London, 1977.

Siebert, Wilbur H. *The Legacy of the American Revolution to the British West Indies and the Bahamas: A Chapter Out of the History of the American Loyalists*. Columbus, Mo., 1913.

Singh, R. John. *French Diplomacy in the Caribbean and the American Revolution*. New York, 1977.

Sosin, Jack M. *Agents and Merchants: British Colonial Policy and the Origins of the American Revolution, 1763–1775*. Lincoln, Neb., 1965.

Spindel, Donna J. "The Stamp Act Crisis in the British West Indies." *Journal of American Studies* 11, no. 2 (Aug. 1977): 203–22.

Spinney, David. *Rodney*. London, 1969.

———. "Sir Samuel Hood at St. Kitts: A Re-Assessment." *Mariner's Mirror* 58 (1972): 179–82.

Spurdle, Frederick G. *Early West Indian Government: Showing the Progress of Government in Barbados, Jamaica and the Leeward Islands, 1660–1783*. Palmerston, New Zealand, 1963.

Steel, M. J. "A Philosophy of Fear: The World View of the Jamaican Plantocracy in a Comparative Perspective." *Journal of Caribbean History* 27, no. 1 (1993): 1–20.

Stein, Richard. "The French Sugar Business in the Eighteenth Century: A Quantitative Study." *Journal of Business History* 22, no. 1 (1980): 3–17.

Stephen, Sir Leslie, and Sir Sidney Lee, eds. *Dictionary of National Biography*. Oxford, 1937–38.

Stephenson, Orlando W. "The Supply of Gunpowder in 1776." *American Historical Review* 30, no. 2 (1924–25): 271–81.

Stone, Lawrence, and Jeanne C. Fawtier Stone. *An Open Elite? England, 1540–1880*. Oxford, 1984.

Stout, Neil R. *The Royal Navy in America, 1760–1775: A Study of Enforcement in the Era of the American Revolution*. Annapolis, Md., 1973.

Stumpf, Vernon O. "Josiah Martin and His Search for Success: The Road to North Carolina." *North Carolina Historical Review* 53 (1976): 55–79.

Sypher, Wylie. "The West Indians as a 'Character' in the Eighteenth Century." *Studies in Philology* 36 (1939): 503–20.

Syrett, David. "The West India Merchants and the Conveyance of the King's Troops to the Caribbean, 1779–1782." *Journal of the Society for Army Historical Research* 14 (1967): 169–76.

——. *Shipping and the American War, 1775–1783* (London, 1970).

——. "D'Estaing's Decision to Steer for Antigua, 28 November 1778." *Mariner's Mirror* 61, no. 2 (May 1975): 155–162.

——. *The Royal Navy in American Waters, 1775–1783*. Aldershot, Eng., 1989.

Taylor, Clare. "Aspects of Planter Society in the British West Indies Before Emancipation." *National Library of Wales Journal* 20 (1977–78): 361–72.

——. "Planter Attitudes to the American and French Revolutions." *National Library of Wales Journal* 21 (1979–80): 113–30.

——. "Planter Comment on Slave Revolts in Eighteenth Century Jamaica." *Slavery and Abolition* 3, no. 3 (1982): 243–53.

Thomas, J. Paul. "The Caribs of St. Vincent: A Study in Imperial Maladministration, 1763–73." *Journal of Caribbean History* 18, no. 2 (1983): 60–73.

Thomas, P. D. G. *British Politics and the Stamp Act Crisis: The First Phase of the American Revolution, 1763–1767*. Oxford, 1975.

——. *The Townshend Duties Crisis: The Second Phase of the American Revolution, 1767–1773*. Oxford, 1987.

——. *Tea Party to Independence: The Third Phase of the American Revolution, 1773–1776*. Oxford, 1991.

Thomas, R. P. "The Sugar Colonies of the Old Empire: Profit or Loss for Great Britain?" *Economic History Review* 2nd ser., 21 (1968): 30–45.

Thomas, R. P., and D. N. McCloskey. "Overseas Trade and Empire 1700–1860." In *The Economic History of Britain Since 1700*, ed. Roderick Floud and Donald McCloskey. Cambridge, 1981. 87–102.

Thoms, D. W. "West India Merchants and Planters in the Mid-Eighteenth Century With Special Reference to St. Kitts." M.A. thesis, University of Kent, 1957.

——. "The Mills Family: London Sugar Merchants of the Eighteenth Century." *Business History* 11, no. 1 (1969): 3–10.

Thornton, A. P. *West-India Policy Under the Restoration*. Oxford, 1955.

Tilley, John A. *The British Navy and the American Revolution*. Columbia, Mo., 1987.

Toth, Charles W., ed. *The American Revolution and the West Indies*. Washington, D.C., 1975.

——. "The British West Indies in American Diplomacy: The Growing Debate, 1789–1801." *Caribbean Studies* 15, no. 3 (1975): 16–30.

Tuchman, Barbara W. *The First Salute: A View of the American Revolution*. New York, 1988.

Tucker, Robert W., and David C. Hendrickson. *The Fall of the First British Empire: Origins of the War of American Independence*. Baltimore, 1982.

Tweedy, Margaret T. "A History of Barbuda Under the Codringtons, 1738–1833." M.Litt. thesis, Birmingham University, 1980.

Tyne, Claude Van. "French Aid Before the Alliance of 1778." *American Historical Review* 31 (1925): 20–40.

Tyson, George F. "The Carolina Black Corps: Legacy of Revolution (1782–1798)." *Revista/Review Interamericana* 5 (Winter 1975–76): 648–663.

Ubbelohde, Carl. *The Vice-Admiralty Courts and the American Revolution*. Chapel Hill, N.C., 1960.

Valentine, Alan. *Lord George Germain*. Oxford, 1962.

Ward, J. R. "The Profitability of Sugar Planting in the British West Indies, 1650–1834." *Economic History Review* 2nd ser., 31 (1978): 197–209.

———. *British West Indian Slavery, 1750–1834: The Process of Amelioration*. Oxford, reprinted 1991.

Waters, Ivor. *The Unfortunate Valentine Morris*. Chepstow, Monmouth, Eng., 1964.

Watson, Karl. *The Civilised Island Barbados: A Social History, 1750–1816*. Bridgetown, Barbados, reprinted 1983.

Watson, Michael. "The British West Indian Legislatures in the Seventeenth and Eighteenth Centuries: An Historiographical Introduction." In *Parliament and the Atlantic Empire*, ed. Philip Lawson. Edinburgh, 1995.

Watts, David. *The West Indies: Patterns of Development, Culture and Environmental Change Since 1492*. Cambridge, 1987.

Webb, Stephen Saunders. "Army and Empire: English Garrison Government in Britain and America 1569 to 1763." *William and Mary Quarterly* 3rd ser., 34, no. 1 (Jan. 1977): 1–31.

Wells, Robert V. *The Population of the British Colonies in America Before 1776: A Survey of Census Data*. Princeton, N.J., 1975.

Whitson, Agnes. *The Constitutional Development of Jamaica, 1620–1729*. Manchester, Eng., 1929.

———. "The Outlook of the Continental American Colonies on the British West Indies, 1760–1775." *Political Science Quarterly* 45, no. 1 (Mar. 1930): 56–86.

Wickwire, Franklin B. *British Subministers and Colonial America, 1763–1783*. Princeton, N.J., 1966.

Wiener, F. B. "The Rhode Island Merchants and the Sugar Act." *New England Quarterly* 3 (1930): 464–500.

Willcox, William B. "British Strategy in America, 1778." *Journal of Modern History* 19, no. 2 (1947): 97–121.

Williams, Eric. *From Columbus to Castro: The History of the Caribbean*. New York, 1970.

———. *Capitalism and Slavery*. 5th edn. London, 1981.

Wright, Philip. "War and Peace with the Maroons, 1730–1739." *Caribbean Quarterly* 16 (1970): 5–27.

Wright, Richardson. *Revels in Jamaica, 1682–1838*. New York, 1937.

Wu, Yu. "Jamaican Trade, 1688–1769: A Quantitative Study." Ph.D. thesis, Johns Hopkins University, 1996.

Acknowledgments

It is a pleasure to record my special thanks to the many individuals who have helped me along the way. Trevor Burnard, Stanley Engerman, and Roderick McDonald read early drafts of the manuscript. Robert Barker, Trevor Burnard, Tom Cole, Joan Coutu, John Gilmore, Douglas Hamilton, Scott Mandelbrote, Kenneth Morgan, Matt Mulcahy, Deborah Prosser, John Pulis, James Robertson, Robert Selig, Linda Stourtz, John Thornton, and Karl Watson allowed me to read work in progress and provided additional references. David Armitage, Robert Beddard, Patricia Bell, Jeremy Catto, Edgar Challenger, Virginia Crane, Philip Curtin, Alison Games, John Garrigus, David Hancock, Joanna Innes, John Kaminski, Janet Keck, Paul Langford, Richard Leffler, Duncan Macleod, Philip Morgan, Colin Palmer, Robert Paquette, Gilbert Pleugar, Jack Pole, Cynthia Ragland, David Ryden, Richard Sheridan, and Jyotsna Singh informed this work at various stages.

Onno Brouwer and the Cartographic Laboratory at the University of Wisconsin prepared the maps. Material in chapters 2 and 4 appeared respectively in the *William and Mary Quarterly* and *Parts Beyond the Seas: The Lesser Antilles in the Age of European Expansion*, edited by Robert Paquette and Stanley Engerman (University Press of Florida, 1997). They are reproduced by permission of the editors and publishers. The Providence Rhode Island Historical Society permitted me to quote from documents in their Special Collections (Box 656). Jack Greene debated some of my conclusions but was very supportive of this endeavor and most helpful. Selwyn Carrington was similarly encouraging and gave me additional manuscript references. Richard Dunn was an important influence in the development of this project and it was my considerable good fortune to benefit once again from his guidance as series editor of Early American Studies.

I taught the subject of this book as a seminar at the University of Wisconsin, Oshkosh, in 1996 and 1997. The students expanded my research by identifying and photocopying relevant newspaper articles covering the period of the American Revolution. Aaron Palmer won a collaborative research scholarship in which he gave invaluable assistance in preparing the prosopographical data presented in the first chapter. Erin Czech at interlibrary loan negotiated the task of obtaining microfilms for my seminar classes and was most expeditious in the acquisition of books. Robert Chaffin gave me his specialist library of journals, books, and microfilms on the American Revolution. Werner Braatz and Lane Earns, my predecessors as chair of the history department, were indulgent in their support and friendship.

The Kate B. and Hall J. Peterson Fellowship funded the preparation of this project at the American Antiquarian Society. John Hench, Keith Arbour, Joanne Chaison, Nancy Burkett, Marie Lamoureux, and Mary Callahan offered guidance and generous hospitality. The University of Wisconsin System Fellowship enabled me to spend a year at the Institute of the Humanities in the University of Wisconsin, Madison, during 1993–94. It was a pleasure to hear papers outside the confines of my own subject at the vigorous institute seminar directed by Paul Boyer. A Copeland Colloquium Fellowship allowed me to spend a semester at Amherst College in 1995. Mavis Campbell offered thoughtful commentary and many lively lunchtime exchanges. The Jacob M. Price Research Fellowship provided an opportunity to use the rich collection of the William L. Clements Library at the University of Michigan. My work was greatly facilitated by John C. Dann, Arlene Shy, Robert Cox, John Harriman, and Rachel Onuf. The Helen Watson Buckner Memorial Fellowship supported my work at the John Carter Brown Library at Brown University. Norman Fiering, Susan Danforth and the staff ensured that my visit was productive.

The University of Wisconsin, Oshkosh, Faculty Development Board gave continuous support, including grants to travel to archives in the United States, the Caribbean, and Europe. Alissandra Cummins of the Barbados Museum and Historical Society, Valerie Francis of the National Library of Jamaica, Margaret Rouse-Jones of the library at St. Augustine of the University of the West Indies in Trinidad and Tobago, Marie Weekes at the Archives of St. Kitts, Lloyd Mattheson of the Society for the Restoration of Brimstone Hill, Richard Lupinacci of the Nevis Historical and Conservation Society, Desmond Nicholson of the Antigua Archaeological and Historical Society, and Bert and Marion Wheeler of the Montserrat National Trust aided my research in the Caribbean. The Provost and Fellows of Oriel College, Oxford University, extended senior common room privileges to me to do manuscript revisions during the Trinity Term of 1999.

Index